Modern Judgements

HENRY JAMES

MODERN JUDGEMENTS

General Editor: P. N. FURBANK

Dickens   A. E. Dyson
Henry James   Tony Tanner
Milton   Alan Rudrum
Sean O'Casey   Ronald Ayling
Pasternak   Donald Davie and Angela Livingstone
Walter Scott   D. D. Devlin
Racine   R. C. Knight
Shelley   R. B. Woodings
Swift   A. Norman Jeffares
Marvell   M. Wilding
Ford Madox Ford   Richard A. Cassell

IN PREPARATION

Matthew Arnold   P. A. W. Collins
Freud   F. Cioffi
Pope   Graham Martin

Henry James

MODERN JUDGEMENTS

edited by
TONY TANNER

Aurora Publishers Incorporated
NASHVILLE/LONDON

FIRST PUBLISHED 1969 BY
MACMILLAN AND COMPANY LIMITED
LONDON, ENGLAND

COPYRIGHT © 1970 BY
AURORA PUBLISHERS INCORPORATED
NASHVILLE, TENNESSEE 37219
LIBRARY OF CONGRESS CATALOG CARD NUMBER: 79-125579
STANDARD BOOK NUMBER: 87695-099-3
MANUFACTURED IN THE UNITED STATES OF AMERICA

Contents

Acknowledgements

William Troy, 'The Altar of Henry James', from *The New Republic*, 15 (© Harrison-Blaine of New Jersey Inc 1943); John Henry Raleigh, 'Henry James: The Poetics of Empiricism', from *Publications of the Modern Language Association of America*, lxvi (1951) (The Modern Language Association of America); Maurice Beebe, 'The Turned Back of Henry James', from *South Atlantic Quarterly*, 1954 (Duke University Press); Viola Hopkins, 'Visual Art Devices and Parallels in the Fiction of Henry James', from *Publications of the Modern Language Association of America*, lxxvi (1961) (The Modern Language Association of America); William J. Maseychik, 'Points of Departure from *The American*'; 'James's *The Europeans* and the Structure of Comedy', from *Nineteenth-century Fiction*, pp. 1–16 (Dr J. A. Ward and The Regents of the University of California; © The Regents 1964); Tony Tanner, 'The Fearful Self: Henry James's *The Portrait of a Lady*', from *Critical Quarterly*, 1965; 'Pragmatic Realism in *The Bostonians*', from *Nineteenth-century Fiction*, pp. 339–44 (Dr William McMurray and The Regents of the University of California; © The Regents 1962); Daniel Lerner and Oscar Cargill, 'Henry James at the Grecian Urn', from *Publications of the Modern Language Association of America*, lxvi (1951) (The Modern Language Association of America); Sister Jane Marie Luecke, 'The Princess Casamassima: Hyacinth's Fallible Consciousness', from *Modern Philology*, pp. 274–80 (The University of Chicago Press); Lyall H. Powers, 'James's *The Tragic Muse* – Ave Atque Vale', from *Publications of the Modern Language Association of America*, lxxiii (1958) (The Modern Language Association of America); Robert C. MacLean, 'The Subjective Adventure of Fleda Vetch', from *American Literature*, 1964 (Duke University Press); '*What Maisie Knew*: The Evolution of a "Moral Sense"', from *Nineteenth-century Fiction*, pp. 33–46 (Dr James Gargano and The Regents of the University of California; © The Regents 1961); H. K. Girling, ' "Wonder" and "Beauty" in *The Awkward Age*', from

Essays in Criticism, 1958 (The Editor); Walter Isle, 'The Sacred Fount', from *Experiments in Form: Henry James's Novels, 1896–1901* (Harvard University Press; © The President and Fellows of Harvard College 1968); 'The Abyss and *The Wings of the Dove*: The Image as a Revelation', from *Nineteenth-century Fiction*, pp. 281–300 (Mrs Jack F. Kimball and The Regents of the University of California; © The Regents 1956); Ian Watt, 'The First Paragraph of *The Ambassadors*: An Explication', from *Essays in Criticism*, 1960 (The Editor); William M. Gibson, 'Metaphor in the Plot of *The Ambassadors*', from *The New England Quarterly* (Sept. 1951); 'Maggie Verver: Neither Saint nor Witch', from *Nineteenth-century Fiction*, pp. 59–71 (Dr Walter Wright and The Regents of the University of California; © The Regents 1957); 'Magic and Metamorphosis in *The Golden Bowl*', from *The Sewanee Review*, lxxiii 1 (Winter 1956) (Mrs Naomi Lebowitz and The University of the South).

General Editor's Preface

LITERARY criticism has only recently come of age as an academic discipline, and the intellectual activity that, a hundred years ago, went into theological discussion, now finds its most natural outlet in the critical essay. Amid a good deal that is dull or silly or pretentious, every year now produces a crop of critical essays which are brilliant and profound not only as contributions to the understanding of a particular author, but also as statements of an original way of looking at literature and the world. Hence it often seems that the most useful undertaking for an academic publisher might be, not so much to commission new books of literary criticism or scholarship, as to make the best of what exists easily available. This at least is the purpose of the present series of anthologies, each of which is devoted to a single major writer.

The guiding principle of selection is to assemble the best *modern* criticism – broadly speaking, that of the last twenty or thirty years – and to include historic and classic essays, however famous, only when they are still influential and represent the best statements of their particular point of view. It will, however, be one of the functions of each editor's Introduction to sketch in the earlier history of criticism in regard to the author concerned.

Each volume will attempt to strike a balance between general essays and ones on specialised aspects, or particular works, of the writer in question. And though in many instances the bulk of the articles will come from British and American sources, certain of the volumes will draw heavily on material in other European languages – most of it being translated for the first time.

P. N. FURBANK

Introduction

WHEN Henry James was composing his prefaces for the New York Edition of his works (published 1907–9), he wrote about them to William Dean Howells (17 August 1908): 'They are, in general, a sort of plea for Criticism, for Discrimination, for Appreciation on other than infantile lines – as against the so almost universal Anglo-Saxon absence of these things which tends so, in our general trade, it seems to me, to break the heart.' These prefaces not only remain one of the richest sources of insight into James's intentions in his novels; they elevated discussion of the whole genre of the novel to a height of aesthetic and moral seriousness which had never previously been attained, and which established the point of departure for all subsequent exploration and criticism of 'the novel'. R. P. Blackmur called them 'the most eloquent and original piece of literary criticism in existence': certainly if 'Discrimination' and 'Appreciation' are no longer so entirely absent from the English-speaking world one of the reasons must be the attention which has been paid to the profound critical explications James wrote about his own creations. 'To criticise', he wrote in one of the prefaces, 'is to appreciate, to appropriate, to take intellectual possession, to establish in fine a relation with the criticised thing and make it one's own.' My intention here is to give a brief account of how James's novels have been appreciated and appropriated – or not been so – from the time when he was lamenting the 'infantile' critical faculties of his contemporaries to the present day, when every year brings forth around forty articles, three or four books, and an unknown number of dissertations on his work, much of this critical writing being of a high degree of sophistication.

How was James's work received by his contemporaries? In general we can say that while his books were not received with sufficient popular enthusiasm to ensure him substantial financial success (not a trivial matter for James, contrary to some popular notions of his unearned affluence), and while very few of his defenders showed any very deep understanding of what he was doing, nevertheless he was never really neglected, indeed he was almost immediately recognised as a major writer of some sort, and within his own lifetime he received the genuinely appreciative acclaim of three very different but very important fellow novelists – William Dean Howells, Joseph Conrad, and Ford Madox Ford. One thing is indisputable, however: a reading of the reviews of the time, even the most enthusiastic, reveals a current critical vocabulary of disabling vagueness and crude imprecision. And, inevitably, right from the start, James's attitude towards America and his apparent preference for Europe continually diverted attention from his achievements as a novelist.

An example of the most balanced sort of reaction to the young Henry James may be found in an essay by Thomas Wentworth Higginson, written in 1879.[1] He praises James, not very helpfully, for his 'delicacy, epigram, quickness of touch, penetration', but continually strays back to the question of James's attitude to America.

> Mr James's life has been so far transatlantic that one hardly knows whether he would wish to be counted as an American writer, after all. . . . When he says, for instance, that a monarchical society is 'more available for the novelists than any other', he shows that he does not quite appreciate the strong point of republicanism, in that it develops real individuals in proportion as it diminishes conventional distinction.

He approves of those stories which, like *Daisy Miller* (1878), 'have been written with distinct purpose and convey lessons', and he admits to the power of some of James's work. He faults him for his handling of America, but 'when he draws Americans in Europe he is at home'.

There is no real hostility there, and indeed there was at the time a readiness to admire James as Hawthorne's successor.

It is fair to remember that *The Portrait of a Lady* (1881) was greeted as an important literary event and gave rise to much serious discussion. But even discounting the more parochial and irrelevant reviews (such as those which fastened on the absence of religious sentiments in the characters), one is bound to remark on the ineptness of much of the critical discussion of the novel. 'There is no heart in it; there is plenty of brightness, acuteness, wit and good writing; but not enough to

---

[1] In *Literary World*, x (22 Nov. 1879).

redeem it from the effect of literary Pyrrhonism.' Thus one reviewer dealt with the novel; while the more enthusiastic asserted their liking without offering any very concrete grounds for it. It is worth noting that at this time James was identified by one critic as a product of the 'modern or scientific methods of novel-writing', that he was a realist and a materialist who discounted whatever was spiritual and transcendental. From the start James had been singled out as an unusually deft 'analyst' of human thoughts and feelings, but that word has a very ambiguous status in nineteenth-century discussion of literature. 'Analysis' was felt to be potentially hostile to all that was fine and spiritual in man; it denied the soul and might well destroy the heart. In general, analytical writing was unfeeling and 'cold' – an epithet that was attached to James's work again and again. The majority of late-nineteenth-century readers still preferred 'warm' novelists, such as Dickens, Scott and Thackeray, who seemed so reassuringly simple, so full of heart, so happily above meddling with the devious and problematical motions of the inner world. Before James could gain proper recognition for his work there had to be a change in the prevailing attitude towards the scope and technique of the novel itself. William Dean Howells, acutely aware as ever of what was happening in the literature of his own day, could see that James was really developing a new kind of novel, and he said as much in a forthright article[1] which earned him some angry attacks from English critics. For Howells maintained that James was the 'chief exemplar of the new art of fiction', a fiction which, Howells maintained, was both more refined and more artistic than that of writers such as Dickens and Thackeray. Howells praised James for his scrupulous analysis of motive and intelligently invoked George Eliot as an important contemporary who was also developing a more analytical type of fiction. It was also in this article that Howells praised James for inventing the 'international novel', a felicitous phrase which is still in currency, though it sometimes obscures those matters in James's work which transcend the fruitful fascination of national differences.

For a few years James remained fairly consistently popular, but the publication of *The Bostonians* (1886) provoked a barrage of crude hostility. One typical example: 'Mr James may nowadays be looked upon as the head of a certain college of savants, a man delighting in writing what to the majority of flesh-and-blood men and women

[1] 'Mr Henry James, Jr, and His Critics', in *Literary World*, XIII (14 Jan. 1882).

has no excuse for being so praised, and books that grow more and more arid and dull. This long, prosy, carefully written novel was not worth writing and is unreadable.' Thus a novel which many readers today enjoy as being remarkably free of the idiosyncrasies and complexities which make James's later work unappealing to some, paradoxically all but ruined James's reputation as a novelist in his own time. However *The Princess Casamassima* (1886) was met with more approval and appreciation, with Howells as usual writing the most sympathetic and enlightened review and calling it 'incomparably the greatest novel of the year in our language'. Even more gratifying was the reception accorded to *The Tragic Muse* (1890): it was reviewed extensively and favourably and was one of James's most successful novels. One review, for example, said the novel was 'by far the most brilliant and faithful representation of the successful actress' ever achieved in English fiction. Here we meet a second paradox, because today this fine novel receives less critical attention than any of James's novels (going through the critical journals of the last fifteen years – indeed even further back – I found only one serious article devoted to the novel).

After *The Spoils of Poynton* (1897), which was also fairly successful, James's reputation began to decline again. Reviewers often paid lip-service to his 'brilliance' and 'subtlety', but as often they revealed their bewilderment and boredom. If they applauded the virtuosity of giving us the story of *What Maisie Knew* (1897) from the point of view of the child, they would at the same time condemn the style of the book as tortuous, incoherent and vague. Although the keen social observations in *The Awkward Age* (1899) were praised, the characters were attacked as being bloodless or over-analysed to the point of tedium. (One critic, rather wittily, expressed relief that James 'had arrived at the point of intellectual remoteness from the flesh' because to think of Mrs Brookenham and her crowd, 'those frankly inquiring minds and untrammelled spirits' united with bodies, would be to picture a rotten bunch.) Only one critic noticed that James was trying a radically new technique here – i.e. reducing the privileges of the omniscient author to a minimum and allowing his characters to reveal themselves through conversation. Since this was the first time James had deliberately tried to adapt the technique of drama to the novel, the perceptiveness of this lone critic (in the *Nation*) is much to be praised.

The reception of *The Sacred Fount* (1901) marks the second really low point in James's reputation during his own lifetime: 'morbid analysis', 'brilliantly stupid', 'Mr James was intent on making nothing out of nothing' – these are representative comments. Quite a number of modern readers would not consider these to be so very unfair, but here I want to point out a third paradox in the history of James's reputation. This strange little novel (excluded from the New York Edition by James) has received an increasing amount of attention in recent years – perhaps partly as a result of Edmund Wilson's suggestion that if we could get at the hidden secret of this book we might have a major key to all of James's work. Certainly it is open to a diversity of interpretation, which has made it peculiarly congenial to modern critics. *The Wings of the Dove* (1902) did not do much to restore James's reputation. Many critics were now referring to James's 'latest manner', with the usual implication that it was a manner for the delectation of the very few. Complaints that his late work is too remote from real life, that he cannot make any direct moral judgements on his characters, were common then as they still are now. Some put it crudely: James 'has now successfully lost himself in the ultimate azure of himself'; others more gently: James 'frequently retires so deeply within himself that the more he labors to express his meaning, the more involved and incommunicable he becomes'. In a good-humoured but derisive article[1] Frank Moore Colby made a comment on the book which became quite well known. 'Through page after page he surveys a mind as a sick man looks at his counterpane, busy with little ridges and grooves and undulations. There are chapters like wonderful games of solitaire, broken by no human sound save his own chuckle when he takes some mysterious trick or makes a move that he says is "beautiful".' (It was also Colby who made the dry – yet inaccurate – comment that in James's books 'nobody sins because nobody has anything to sin with'.)

Once again it was Howells who insisted that James's recent books were 'incomparable'.[2] 'It does not matter . . . how the people talk – or in what labyrinthine parentheses they let their unarriving language wander. They strongly and vividly exist, and they construct not a drama, perhaps, but a world, floating indeed in an obscure where it seems to have its solitary orbit, but to be as solidly palpable as any of the planets of the more familiar systems.' At a time when people were

1 'In Darkest James', in *Bookman*, Nov. 1902.
2 'Mr Henry James's Later Work', in *North American*, CLXXVI (Jan. 1903).

starting to ignore James, Howells addressed them firmly: 'here you
have the work of a great psychologist, who has the imagination of a
poet, the wit of a keen humorist, the conscience of an impeccable
moralist, the temperament of a philosopher, and the wisdom of a
rarely experienced witness of the world'. This important article was
one of two main defences of James written around this time: the
other was by Cornelia Pratt,[1] who discerned in James's whole work
'the spectacle of a cumulative artistic life'. She admires and defends
his later style, but once again the sheer inadequacies of her vocabulary
prevent her from saying anything really very helpful about the deeper
meanings and intentions of the books.

Oddly enough, since modern readers still tend to find it quite as
difficult as *The Wings of the Dove*, it was *The Ambassadors* (1903) which
restored James's reputation, and restored it rather sensationally at that.
'The real thing once more!' said the *Literary World*; others greeted
it as a masterpiece, 'a work of noble literature', and so on. The style
was not now criticised, and the plot was praised. Some critics manifested a general grasp of James's subject. 'He has been the sensitive
register of the results of the influence of the older society on the
crudities, the rawness, or, at its best, the inexperience of a new society.
. . . He has recorded the modification or surrender of the provincial
to the Old World spirit. No other report of this phase of recent life
has been at once so searching and so subtle as *The Ambassadors*.' But
here again we see how very little even the admiring critics were able
to say. 'He makes a plot out of so very little, and behold it is so much.'
It must certainly have been preferable for James to see his book referred
to as 'enchanting' than to have it dismissed as incomprehensible, but he
must have wondered at times just what even his most ardent admirers
were getting out of his books. And by this time his admirers were
becoming aware of themselves as a select few, sadly (or perhaps
smugly) recognising that James could not be universal in his appeal.
'A man too great to be ignored', said the American critic Claude
Bragdon of James, but he went on, '[and] too ignored to be great,
for his appeal is, and must ever be . . . to a "parlor audience".' It
was this same critic who praised James as the most modern of modern
novelists because he depicted human nature as it failed or flourished
in highly organised society, distorted, refined or sublimated by forms
of civilisation. James's subjects, 'the voiceless little tragedies of the

[1] 'The Evolution of Henry James', in *Critic*, XXIV (April 1899).

soul: the dilemmas of the super-refined, the intellectual enthusiasms of young men, the abortive love of spinsters', were, he said, more relevant to modern life than the situations to be found in conventional romances. But such comparatively enlightened attitudes to James's work were still counterbalanced by complaints that it was the product of 'the analytic, not the inspired'. Nevertheless it is true to say that *The Ambassadors* was greeted with more respect than almost any other of James's novels. Interestingly, this is the one marked coincidence between modern taste and that of James's contemporaries. For in recent years I would say that *The Ambassadors* has been more written about than any other of James's works.

After *The Ambassadors* James's reputation remained high for some time, and interest and enthusiasm among American critics was aroused by his proposed return visit to his homeland in 1904. An extremely fair essay by Herbert Croly published in that year is worth singling out: 'Henry James and His Countrymen'.[1] He appreciates James's reasons for finding Europe a more fruitful ground for his art and denies the trivial objections that he has been unpatriotic: 'one can easily understand that an artist who places such a high value upon a large and disinterested intellectual outlook may find it desirable to exalt his art at the expense of his patriotism'. He notes – without outrage – James's preoccupation with a class of people who are for the most part 'economic parasites' and describes the sort of situation which James likes to work on. 'It is a subtle, exciting, and finished social situation, which he isolates, analyzes, interprets, and composes, with his eyes fastened exclusively upon the psychological aesthetics of the people and the social aesthetics of their attitudes toward one another.' He is clearly aware of James's imaginative skill – for instance, he makes the perceptive observation that James uses 'houses and rooms which illuminate and intensify' the characters. 'He has given, indeed, a new value in the art of novel writing to domestic properties and scenery.' But he leaves it at that, whereas a modern critic would make that his point of departure and try to show exactly how James makes architectural setting contribute to the overall meaning of his work. But he also puts James in a class outside the mainstream of the American novel. 'Whatever else this novel possesses, it must possess energy, excitement, momentum, and purpose.' That is, he equates the true American novel with the novel of external action. 'While [James] has

[1] In *Lamp*, XXVIII (Feb. 1904).

renounced any attempt to deal with action, achievement, it is just such action and achievement by which [his contemporary fellow country-men] are fascinated and engrossed.' We can see here signs of that division of American writers into 'palefaces' and 'redskins' which Philip Rahv later discussed in a celebrated essay.[1] But the most impor-tant aspect of Croly's essay is that he sees James as representing a type of artistic integrity which American writers will have to emulate. 'The penalty which Mr James pays for his expatriation, for his exclusive and consistent loyalty to his personal faith and vision, is just the penalty of being wholly separated from this main stream of American literary fulfillment.' But, he goes on, if the 'consummation' of American literature is to be reached, 'it will be reached only by the acquisition on the part of his literary fellow countrymen of an artistic and intel-lectual integrity analogous to that of Henry James'.

The Golden Bowl (1904) sold unusually well, but it received mainly adverse criticism, couched in the by now customary, imprecise emotive phrases. 'It is thin and bloodless . . . it is art without the dimmest adumbration of a soul.' Some comments were more specific: 'we find, standing for subtlety, a kind of restless, finicking inquisitive-ness, a flutter of aimless conjecture'. As against this general relapse into the old impatience with James, Claude Bragdon's review is genuinely sympathetic and understanding.

> Those who lament the forsaking by Mr James of his earlier themes and abandonment of his more direct and objective manner, perhaps betray the limit of their own interests and perceptions. Like all men of original genius arrived at maturity, the outward aspects of the world no longer interest him. Little by little he has come to look for and present the reality behind the seeming.

But such isolated sensitive reviews could do little to stop the general trend towards a state of general indifference towards James's work. People became apathetic about him. The American Scene (1907) was counted disappointing, and the New York Edition was neglected, even ignored.

The autobiographical volumes, A Small Boy and Others (1913) and Notes of a Son and Brother (1914), revived interest in James to some degree, but 'although at the time of his death in 1916 his reputation was secure, he was a somewhat neglected and not fully appreciated

---

[1] 'Paleface and Redskin', in Image and Idea (New York, 1949).

writer'. I take that last comment from a published dissertation by Richard Foley entitled *Criticism in American Periodicals of the Works of Henry James from 1866 to 1916* (Washington, 1944). Mr Foley's research has been copious, and I am indebted to it for some of the information contained in the preceding pages. One of his conclusions emphasises the general point I have been wanting to make about the impressionistically vague, non-analytic tenor of most of the contemporary criticism.

> Surprisingly few intelligent observations were made upon James's own explanation of technical problems such as foreshortening, choice of narrator, revealing center, use of dialogue, and the like in the Prefaces. Granted the fact that no major fiction appeared after the publication of the New York Edition, it is still difficult to account for the dearth of incisive reviews of his last stories or any significant appraisals of his work in general after he had set forth his theory of fiction.

In the years between the turn of the century and the First World War people were not much interested in what James was trying to do with the novel; it was worth remembering that it was during this period that Conrad's works sold so poorly and Proust had his great work turned down by a leading French publishing house. A new vision of man, a shift in focus on his inner and outer world, necessitates the development of new techniques, in fiction as in any other art. The general public and, indeed, most of the critics prior to 1914 were unprepared for a shift in vision, and so, for the most part, were mainly bewildered by the innovations in technique which confronted them.

But there was some other criticism of James's work written during his lifetime which should be noted. In 1905 Joseph Conrad wrote a short appreciation[1] which included at least one phrase which all subsequent criticism of James has scarcely bettered when it comes to summing up James's particular province. 'Mr Henry James is the historian of fine consciences' is Conrad's memorable sentence; and he develops his meaning.

> The range of a fine conscience covers more good and evil than the range of a conscience which may be called, roughly, not fine; a conscience less troubled by the nice discriminations of conduct. A fine conscience is more concerned with essentials; its triumphs are more perfect, if less profitable,

[1] 'Henry James: an appreciation', in *North American Review*, CLXXX (Jan. 1905) 102–8; reprinted in *Notes on Life and Letters* (London and New York, 1921).

in a worldly sense. There is, in short, more truth in its working for a historian to detect and to show. It is a thing of infinite complication and suggestion. None of these escapes the art of Mr Henry James.

Also in 1905 Elisabeth Luther Cary published what is to the best of
my knowledge the first book-length study of James's work.[1] It is
not a deeply probing book, but it contains many felicities of general
appreciation. She says that James combines 'tactile values with the
greatest possible amount of spiritual truth. In other words, his technical
curiosity, his ability to represent life pictorially by a multiplicity of
fine observations, runs hand in hand with a curiosity far more unusual
and far more difficult to satisfy, a curiosity as to moral states and
responsible affections.' She makes lucid comments on his characters
and ideas, and on such aspects of his work as the use he makes of
juxtaposing the present with the past which she describes as his habit
'of using the vanished scene as a touchstone for the one before us, of
holding up his brilliant picture against the soft, thick background of
accumulated associations to try the value of its modern tone'. But
repeatedly she returns to her one basic general perception about his
work: 'his strength was chiefly to lie in combining close observation
of the surface of life with indefatigable exploration of the recondite
truths of the spirit'.

Another short encomium which is certainly worth mentioning
occurs in one of Max Beerbohm's theatre-pieces, written in 1909.[2] He
describes James as having an outlook 'full of reverence for noble
things and horror of things ignoble' and says that his characters are
distinguished by 'the passion of conscience, a sort of lyrical conscience,
conscience raised to the pitch of ecstasy'. And although he later wrote
a parody of James's late style – 'The Mote in the Middle Distance'
(1912)[3] – which failed to amuse James (a parody, incidentally, a good
deal subtler and gentler than H. G. Wells's crude satire of James in
Boon in 1915), he here reveals a genuine sensitivity to 'the later
James' – 'the James who has patiently evolved a method of fiction
entirely new, entirely his own, a method that will probably perish
with him, since none but he, one thinks, could handle it; that amazing
method by which a novel competes not with other novels, but with

---

[1] The Novels of Henry James (New York, 1905).
[2] 'Mr Henry James's Play'; reprinted in Around Theatres (London and New York,
1953).
[3] In A Christmas Garland (1912, new ed., 1950).

life itself; making people known to us as we grow to know them in real life, by hints, by glimpses, here a little and there a little, leaving us always guessing and wondering, till, in the fullness of time, all these scraps of revelation gradually resolve themselves into one large and luminous whole, just as in real life'.

I think *Henry James: A Critical Study* (1913) by Ford Madox Hueffer (later Ford) must be counted as the first really important book on James. It is marked by the mannerisms which many people associate with Ford's writing – the exaggerated statement, the expansive gesture, the half-reliable anecdote – but, despite the idiosyncratic informality of his style, Ford was able to show exactly how James's work differed from the conventional English novel; how it should be seen in conjunction with certain aspects of continental fiction; and just exactly what was important about James's formal and technical innovations. Ford must be one of the first critics to quote extensively from James's critical prefaces, and that fact alone suggests that he really understood what James was doing. He starts his book by declaring emphatically that 'I regard the works of Mr Henry James as those most worthy of attention by the critics' and quickly went on to single out James as greater than all his contemporaries 'for analysis'. The word is now wholly approbative – a fact which reminds us that Ford was one of the earliest and most tireless champions of the whole modern movement in literature. In dealing with James's 'Subjects' Ford applauds him as 'the historian of one, of two, and possibly of three or more, civilisations' and insists that 'he, more than anybody, has observed human society as it now is, and more than anybody has faithfully rendered his observations for us'. As a general proposition he says that the modern novel (this is 1913) was notable for making 'an attempt at shadowing the real problems of the contact of individual with individual', and he praises James for being 'earliest in the field'. The last section of his book is called 'Methods', and while it contains nothing so rigorously analytical as more recent criticism can offer, it reveals a firm grasp of just what was new and important in James's method, just why his books give us the impression of 'vibrating reality'. 'I think the word "vibrating" exactly expresses it; the sensation is due to the fact that the mind passes, as it does in real life, perpetually backwards and forwards between the apparent aspect of things and the essentials of life.' Ford, who made it his life-work to try to inculcate some sense of 'form', some consciousness of artistic technique into the English, deserves high praise for holding up Henry James as an example of a major *artist* at a time when most people were dismissing him as a long-winded bore.

> Looking upon the immense range of the books written by this author, upon the immensity of the scrupulous labours, upon the fineness of the mind, the nobility of the character, the highness of the hope, the greatness of the quest, the felicity of the genius and the truth that is at once beauty and more than beauty – of this I am certain, that such immortality as mankind has to bestow . . . will rest upon the author of *Daisy Miller*. It will rest also with the author of *The Golden Bowl*.

Ford was right, of course, as were Conrad and Howells and one or two more rare intelligences. One can only hope that this minimum of true recognition and appreciation was some consolation for Henry James while he was alive. All the same, it would not be much of an exaggeration to say that at the time of his death all the serious detailed critical work on his novels remained yet to be done.

II

It would be misleading to pretend that the situation changed with dramatic suddenness after James's death. Indeed, five years elapsed before Percy Lubbock published his crucial book *The Craft of Fiction* (1921), but during that period there was some important criticism worth mentioning. In 1917, for instance, Stuart Sherman published an important article called 'The Aesthetic Idealism of Henry James',[1] in which he made a retrospective survey of James criticism and tried to sum up 'what Henry James was "trying for" '.

> Criticism's favorite epithets for him hitherto have been 'cold', 'analytical', 'scientific', 'passionless', 'pitiless' historian of the manners of a futile society. That view of him is doomed to disappear before the closer scrutiny which he demanded and which he deserves. He is not an historian of manners; he is a trenchant idealistic critic of life from the aesthetic point of view.

Sherman willingly admits that 'he has insulted all the popular gods of democratic society' in order to insist that James owed his allegiance to something more important. 'The thing which he, as the high priest solemnly ministering before the high altar, implored someone to

---

[1] In *Nation*, CIV (5 April 1917) 393–9; reprinted in *On Contemporary Literature* (New York, 1917; London, 1923).

observe and to declare is that he adored beauty and absolutely nothing
else in the world.' This stress on 'the exclusiveness of his consecration
to beauty', this insistence that James judged everything on the level
'of the aesthetic consciousness' tends to put James in a rather decadent,
fin-de-siècle light. Nonetheless Sherman is clearly quite a sensitive
critic, and he says some things well. 'What he offers us, as he repeatedly
suggests, is a thousand-fold better than life; it is an escape from life.
It is an escape from the undesigned into the designed, from chaos into
order, from the undiscriminated into the finely assorted, from the
languor of the irrelevant to the intensity of the pertinent.' And clearly
Sherman is an enthusiastic reader of James's prefaces, 'which more
illuminate the fine art of fiction than anything else – one is tempted to
say, than everything else – on the subject'. But remarks like the following could later be damaging to James: 'James is like Pater in his
aversion from the world, his dedication to art, his celibacy, his personal
decorum and dignity, his high aesthetic seriousness, his Epicurean
relish in receiving and reporting the multiplicity and intensity of his
impressions, and in the exacting closeness of his style.' Walter Pater!
It is a surprising, but not wholly foolish, comparison – though very
misleading as a way of getting at the particular greatness of James's
achievement. But the time was not so very far off when the impinging
pressure of economic and political problems would make any artist
who ignored these ugly realities appear at best irrelevant, at worst
suspect or contemptible. Sherman's picture of James as an exquisite
devotee of 'the beautiful' was one which could only do him harm in
the 1930s, when it seemed all but inhuman to lack a social conscience.

But the death of Henry James prompted brief appreciations, in 1918,
from two young American expatriate writers who were to be major
influences in the modern literary movement – Ezra Pound and
T. S. Eliot. Pound used the occasion to scorn the Americans for not
even realising what they had lost[1] – part of his running battle with
the philistinism of America. But at the same time he made some
penetrating remarks about the essential achievement of James. He sees
him as a man who devoted all his energy 'to bring in America on the
side of civilisation' and dismisses all hostile criticisms of James's style
as petty.

What I have not heard is any word of the major James, of the hater of

---

[1] 'A Brief Note', in *Little Review: Henry James Number*, v (Aug. 1918).

tyranny; book after early book against oppression, against all the sordid
petty personal crushing oppression, the domination of modern life. . . .
What he fights is 'influence', the impinging of family pressure, the
impinging of one personality on another; all of them in highest degree
damn'd, loathsome, and detestable.

Pound sees James as one of the first great American writers whose
genius was on the side of 'human liberty, personal liberty, the rights
of the individual against all sorts of intangible bondage! The passion
of it, the continual passion of it in this man who, fools said, didn't
"feel".' And he claims for James the sort of seriousness which the
attitude of people like Sherman tended to overlook. 'His art was great
art as opposed to over-elaborate or over-refined art by virtue of the
major conflicts which he portrays.' Pound's piece was short, but it
was more cogent and penetrating than most of the work written on
James up to that date.

T. S. Eliot adopted a more aloof oracular tone in praising James,
permitting himself, however, the bitter irony of remarking that both
England and America should have been more relieved than they were
at the news of James's death: he was such a brilliant critic of both.[1] It
was in this essay that Eliot made the famous statement: 'James's
critical genius comes out most tellingly in his mastery over, his baffling
escape from, Ideas; a mastery and an escape which are perhaps the
last resort of a superior intelligence. He had a mind so fine that no
idea could violate it.' Eliot's words here are chosen with great care
and the exactness of this short statement points to an aspect of James's
genius which had never been so clearly defined before. Eliot extended
his praise by saying of James: 'He is the most intelligent man of his
generation.'

In the same year, 1918, Joseph Warren Beach published a notable
book on The Method of Henry James, which was full of considered
insights and balanced appraisals. Beach stressed that James was less
concerned to tell a simple 'story' than 'to give us instead the subjective
accompaniment of the story. His "exquisite scheme" was to confine
himself as nearly as possible to the "inward life" of his characters, and
yet to make it as "exciting" for his readers as it was for the author,
as exciting – were that possible – as it was for the characters themselves.' He insists that although the overriding preoccupation in his
books seems to be with 'good taste' and 'refinement', in fact they are

---

[1] 'The Hawthorne Aspect', in *Little Review: Henry James Number*, v (Aug. 1918).

profoundly moral. James's 'exclusive concern with the inward life' explains 'the dominance of ethical considerations'. And Beach makes some attempts to show how this preoccupation with the inner life affected James's techniques and the kind of characters he chose to scrutinise. 'For the characters of James the faculty of supreme importance is the intelligence, or insight, the faculty of perceiving "values" beyond those utilities upon which everyone agrees.'

The year 1918 was certainly an important one for James criticism, and one can see that for a period after the terrible international convulsions of the war James came to represent for some people the supremely civilised intelligence: they saw his work as being opposed to barbarism, tyranny and the crassness of merely utilitarian values. In another brief note on James, written in 1924, Eliot stressed, in his own way, James's dedication to an ideal of peaceful, reasonable civilisation.[1]

> He was possessed by the vision of an ideal society. . . . James did not provide us with 'ideas', but with another world of thought and feeling. For such a world some have gone to Dostoievsky, some to James; and I am inclined to think that the spirit of James, so much less violent, with so much more reasonableness and so much more resignation than that of the Russian, is no less profound, and is more useful, more applicable, for our future.

At the same time essays were appearing from other writers, praising James's fictional techniques – Edith Wharton and Virginia Woolf both wrote respectful articles in the early 1920s.

Percy Lubbock's famous book *The Craft of Fiction* (1921) is not only remarkable for the masterly criticism and appreciation of James contained in it; it was, as Mark Schorer once wrote, 'probably the first that tried to treat fiction as an art'. Other writers of the period made respectful general comments on James's fine technique, but Lubbock was the first to examine the actual operational details of technique. He asked 'how' questions: how is a novel made, how does it work? The following quotation should be seen as a milestone in novel criticism.

> Let us very carefully follow the methods of the novelists whose effects are incontestable, noticing exactly the manner in which the scenes and figures in their books are presented. . . . Our criticism has been oddly

[1] 'A Prediction in Regard to Three English Authors', in *Vanity Fair* (Feb. 1924).

incurious in the matter, considering what the dominion of the novel has been for a hundred and fifty years. The refinements of the art of fiction have been accepted without question, or at most have been classified roughly and summarily – as is proved by the singular poverty of our critical vocabulary, as soon as we pass beyond the simplest and plainest effects. The expressions and the phrases at our disposal bear no defined, delimited meanings . . . we still suffer from a kind of shyness in the presence of a novel . . . we are haunted by a sense that a novel is a piece of life, and that to take it to pieces would be to destroy it . . . it is not a piece of life, it is a piece of art like another; and the fact that it is an ideal shape, with no existence in space, only to be spoken of in figures and metaphors, makes it all the more important that in our thought it should be protected by no romantic scruple.

Lubbock has an intimate knowledge of James's ideas about fiction – he edited the later volumes of the New York Edition and then his letters – and his sensitive grasp of James's sense of the craft of fiction enabled him to write, not only a seminal work for all subsequent novel criticism, but some especially brilliant appreciation of James's own techniques. In a really outstanding section on *The Ambassadors* he scrutinises exactly what that technique is and how it works. With this section we enter – in the most distinguished manner – the modern era of James appreciation. I will run some quotations together to give some sense of the great step forward his work represents.

The world of silent thought is thrown open, and instead of telling the reader what happened there, the novelist uses the look and behaviour of thought as the vehicle by which the story is rendered . . . suppose that instead of a man upon the stage, concealing and betraying his thought, we watch the thought itself, the hidden thing, as its twists to and fro in his brain – watch it without any other aid to understanding but such as its own manner of bearing might supply. The novelist, more free than the playwright, could of course *tell* us, if he chose, what lurks behind this agitated spirit; he could step forward and explain the restless appearance of the man's thought. But if he prefers the dramatic way, admittedly the more effective, there is nothing to prevent him from taking it. The man's thought, in its turn, can be made to reveal its own inwardness.

Let us see how this plan is pursued in *The Ambassadors*. . . . This is a story which must obviously be told from Strether's point of view, in the first place. The change in his purpose is due to a change in his vision, and the long slow process could not be followed unless his vision were shared by the reader. . . . Only the brain behind his eyes can be aware of the colour of his experience, as it passes through its innumerable gradations;

and all understanding of his case depends upon seeing these. . . . Neither as an action set before the reader without interpretation from within, nor yet as an action pictured for the reader by some onlooker in the book, can this story possibly be told. . . .

But though in *The Ambassadors* the point of view is primarily Strether's, and though it *appears* to be his throughout the book, there is in fact an insidious shifting of it, so artfully contrived that the reader may arrive at the end without suspecting the trick. The reader, all unawares, is placed in a better position for an understanding of Strether's history, better than the position of Strether himself.

Lubbock describes exactly how this complex effect is gained without the author intruding on the reader's perceptions and inferences. He points out that James is showing us a man who is 'slowly turning upon himself and looking in another direction'.

To announce the fact, with a tabulation of his reasons, would be the historic, retrospective, undramatic way of dealing with the matter. To bring his mind into view at the different moments, one after another, when it is brushed by new experience – to make a little scene of it, without breaking into hidden depths where the change of purpose is proceeding – to multiply these glimpses until the silent change is apparent, though no word has actually been said of it: this is Henry James's way, and though the *method* could scarcely be more devious and roundabout, always refusing the short cut, yet by these very qualities and precautions it finally produces the most direct impression, for the reader has *seen*.

Lubbock discusses other James novels in this crucial book, but the above quotations can stand as an example of the whole new dimension of objectivity, sophistication, and analytic awareness that he brought to bear on the work of Henry James.

In 1925 Van Wyck Brooks published *The Pilgrimage of Henry James*, which proposed a reading of James's whole career as a writer which was to prove very influential. Brooks conceded the brilliance of James's early work, calling him 'the first [American] to present the plight of the highly personalized human being in the primitive community'. But then James made the fatal mistake of cutting himself off from his native land and the later work declines because he is not at home in the culture where he lives.

The caution, the ceremoniousness, the baffled curiosity, the nervousness and constant self-communion, the fear of committing himself – these traits of the self-conscious guest in the house where he had never been at

home had fashioned with time the texture of his personality. They had
infected the creatures of his fancy, they had fixed the character of his
imaginative world; and behind his novels, those formidable projections of
a geometrical intellect, were to be discerned now the confused reveries of
an invalid child.

And in one resounding sentence Brooks nailed down the failings of the
last three novels (as he saw them). 'Magnificent pretensions, petty
performances! – the fruits of an irresponsible imagination, of a
deranged sense of values, of a mind working in a void, uncorrected
by any clear consciousness of human cause and effect.' Just as expatriate
American writers such as Pound, Eliot and Gertrude Stein respected
James, Brooks made James a symbol of all the dangers of expatriation. Looking back on this important book in a later essay Brooks
wrote:

> And as so many novelists of our own 'twenties lost their substance and
> grasp of life, it struck me that the case of James was really a symbol – I
> mean those novelists who had grown up in the so-called expatriate religion
> of art with a feeling that native lands are not important. Judging by these
> later cases, it seemed to me disastrous for the novelist to lose his natural
> connection with an inherited world that is deeply his own, when, ceasing
> to be 'in the pedigree' of his own country, he is no longer an expression of
> the communal life.'[1]

Brooks's insistence that the writer should have a sense of his own
society, the conscience of his community, prefigures the sort of
criticism which was to become increasingly common in the 1930s.
And his verdict on the subjective derangement and perversity and loss
of human centrality in the last three great novels has been echoed
many times since – it is, for instance, essentially the verdict given by
F. R. Leavis in *The Great Tradition* (1948).

Brooks had made a strong case against James, but it did not go
unanswered. In a long review of *The Pilgrimage* Edmund Wilson made
some very proper qualifying comments on the justness of Brooks's
treatment of James.[2] Wilson indeed admits that 'Mr Brooks has made a
contribution of permanent value toward the criticism of Henry James'.
But he immediately makes the point that 'Mr Brooks has completely

[1] 'The Pilgrimage', in *Days of the Phoenix* (New York and London, 1957).
[2] 'The Pilgrimage of Henry James', in *New Republic*, XLII (6 May 1925) 283–6;
reprinted in *The Shores of Light* (New York, 1925; reprinted London, 1952).

subordinated Henry James the artist to Henry James the social symbol.
. . . It is precisely because Mr Brooks's interest is all social and never
moral that he has missed the point of James's art.' That point, as
Edmund Wilson presents it, is that James is one of those artists who is
basically interested, not in this or that set of social conditions, but in
universal 'conflicts of moral character'. As he says, in some respects
James's art improved: in the later works 'the leaning toward melodrama
that allowed James in his earlier novels to play virtuous Americans off
against scoundrelly Europeans has almost entirely disappeared'. In the
late works we do not find any simple schematisation of characters:
'it is simply a struggle between different kinds of people with different
kinds of needs'. Wilson denies that James became more worldly, more
decadent as he grew older. 'On the contrary, James, in his later works,
is just as much concerned with moral problems, and he is able to see
all around them as he has not been able to do before.' And in warming
to his defence of James (not without making his own qualifying
judgements) Wilson makes one especially pertinent remark about
what he considers to be the basic theme in James – the lasting conflict
between the selfish and the selfless, the worldly and the moral: 'and in
this tendency to oppose the idea of a good conscience to the idea of
doing what one likes – wearing, as it does so often in James, the aspect
of American versus European – there is evidently a Puritan survival'.
With characteristic perspicacity Wilson could see that in many ways
James was a profoundly American novelist, but it was left to later
critics and scholars to explore and discuss in just what ways James's
writing reveals the work of an essentially American imagination. We
have now become more accustomed to the apparent paradox that a
writer may discover more about his own culture by leaving it.

Touching on this paradox, Harry Levin can write in a recent article:
'James demonstrated, as Flaubert had done and Joyce would do, that
retirement can be the most serious commitment.'

E. M. Forster's *Aspects of the Novel*, another notable book on the
novel, appeared in 1927. In underlining the importance of Lubbock's
The Craft of Fiction he helped to secure for it some of the deserved
respect and attention which, initially, it did not receive. 'Those who
follow him', wrote Forster of Lubbock, 'will lay a sure foundation
for the aesthetics of fiction.' However, Forster himself preferred not
to follow him, and his chapter on *The Ambassadors* criticised James for
sacrificing life in the interests of aesthetic form.

The beauty that suffuses *The Ambassadors* is the reward due to a fine artist for hard work. James knew exactly what he wanted, he pursued the narrow path of aesthetic duty, and success to the full extent of his possibilities has crowned him. . . . But at what sacrifice! . . . He has, in the first place, a very short list of characters. . . . In the second place, the characters, besides being few in number, are constructed on very stingy lines. They are incapable of fun, of rapid motion, of carnality, and of nine-tenths of heroism. Their clothes will not take off, the diseases that ravage them are anonymous, like the sources of their income, their servants are noiseless or resemble themselves, no social explanation of the world we know is possible for them, for there are no stupid people in their world, no barriers of language, and no poor. Even their sensations are limited. They can land in Europe and look at works of art and at each other, but that is all. Maimed creatures can alone breathe in Henry James's pages – maimed yet specialized.

Forster sees James as having 'pruned off' all the wantonness and waywardness and deep complexities of people and society which would not fit into his predetermined, aesthetically satisfying pattern. It is a serious accusation, and similar charges against James's work have been voiced by eminent men as different as William James and André Gide and can still be heard today, particularly from those who take Tolstoy to be the ideal type of novelist.

A rather significant spokesman for such a point of view was Vernon Louis Parrington, and it is unusually apt that his disparaging remarks about James should have been published in 1930 – a suitable preface, as it were, to the decade in which James's reputation slumped to its lowest point. Parrington's important book was called *The Beginnings of Critical Realism in America* (*1860–1920*), and he starts his attack on James by citing a comment by Pelham Edgar from his book *Henry James, Man and Author* (1927). Edgar was one of those critics who held up James as a supreme representative of 'civilisation'. 'Civilisation at its highest pitch was the master passion of his mind, and his pre-occupation with the international aspects of character and custom issued from the conviction that the rawness and rudeness of a young country were not incapable of cure by contact with more developed forms.' This condescending attitude towards America infuriated Parrington, and his subsequent comments on James read like a more severe extension of Brooks's objections.

He suffered the common fate of the *déraciné*; wandering between worlds, he found a home nowhere. It is not well for the artist to turn cosmopolitan, for the flavor of the fruit comes from the soil and sunshine of its native fields. . . . Did any other professed realist ever remain so persistently aloof from the homely realities of life? From the external world of action he withdrew to the inner world of questioning and probing; yet even in his subtle psychological inquiries he remained shut up within his own skull-pan. His characters are only projections of his brooding fancy, externalizations of hypothetical subtleties. He was concerned only with *nuances* . . . how unlike he is to Sherwood Anderson, an authentic product of American consciousness!

It is rather crude stuff after Lubbock's criticism, and the sweeping generalised indictments reveal a very imperfect reading of James's actual novels, if not a radical ignorance of them. But the final reference to Anderson – a comparison obviously intended to be to James's disadvantage – makes clear the motive behind the animus. After a decade of expatriates the feeling was growing that American writers should turn their attention to the 'homely realities' and 'sprawling energy' of American life – to the physical local details of the many places in America which were perhaps without any traditional civilisation and culture, but where people's sufferings were no less real for being comparatively inarticulate. Needless to say the varying degrees of Marxism produced in different writers by the economic disasters of the 1930s encouraged this feeling about the responsibilities of the American writer. Speaking very generally, if the key American writers of the 1920s were Hemingway and Scott Fitzgerald and, in a different way, T. S. Eliot and Ezra Pound, then we can see the 1930s as the decade of Dos Passos, John Steinbeck, James Farrell and, in a different way, William Faulkner. In such a decade it is not surprising that interest turned away from Henry James, and that, if his reputation did not exactly disappear, his books were mainly unread. We find an intelligent critic, William Troy, writing in 1931 that 'James is in immediate need of some sort of reinstatement at the moment'.[1] Troy makes an eloquent case for the relevance of James for the young contemporary writer: he explains how James, like any other great artist, worked to impose some sort of order on the 'splendid waste' of life (James's own phrase), and he insists that James did not turn away from the values of life in order to cultivate the values of art. Troy ends his essay trying to persuade contemporary writers that James still has much to give them. 'What they can learn from him

---

[1] 'Henry James and Young Writers', in *Bookman*, LXXIII (June 1931) 351–8.

is the deepest meaning of the phrase "the integrity of the artist". He
can show them to what an essential degree the artist is dependent on
something anterior to himself in life; how the truest values of art
are never to be dissociated from the most potent values of the world
about him.' It was fairly said, but it would be some years before James
was in any way 'reinstated'.

This is not to say that he received no significant attention during
the 1930s: on the contrary, a number of important articles were
published during that decade which no survey of James criticism can
ignore. In 1931 Constance Rourke, in a book of tremendous importance
for the study of American literature – *American Humor* – devoted a
long and brilliant chapter to James and his book *The American*. Dismissing the accusations that James was 'a troubled evasionist without a
country', she established with emphatic directness one of James's
major purposes. 'James was bent upon a purpose that had absorbed
many American fabulists, that of drawing the large, the generic,
American character.' She pointed out that his 'gallery of characters'
provided 'a legible critique of the American character for those who
care to read it', and she showed how very accurately his work reflects
the changes that came over American society in the later nineteenth
century. Miss Rourke was one of the first critics to expand a little on the
distinctly American aspects of James's genius.

> He was grounded in the Yankee fable; his basic apprehension of the
> American character was that which had been drawn there . . . he came
> closer than any of the earlier American writers to that introspective analysis
> which had belonged to the Puritan, closer even than Hawthorne. . . .
> Whether or not James was subject to some untraceable Puritan influence,
> whether he touched popular sources, whether perhaps he gained greatly
> from the initial experiments of Hawthorne and Poe, his novels vastly
> amplified this new subject of the mind lying submerged beneath the scope
> of circumstance, which had long engaged the American imagination.

Miss Rourke makes an interesting comparison between Mark
Twain's *Innocents Abroad* and James's *The American* – just as, later,
Edmund Wilson would suggest a comparison between *A Connecticut
Yankee in King Arthur's Court* and *The Sense of the Past* – and notes
how unthinkable it would be for an English or French writer to write
books simply called *The Englishman* or *The Frenchman*; and she
discusses what James added to the generic portrait of the American
in his first major novel – 'in the spelling of the old fable the outcome

had changed from triumph to defeat. Defeat had become at last an essential part of the national portraiture.' Noting that 'triumph had hitherto been the appointed destiny in American portraiture, except for vagabonds and common adventurers', she shows how 'again and again James pictured this low-keyed humor of defeat'. Her essay stressed that James added depth and subtlety to the portrait of the generic American. 'He showed that the American was in truth what the belligerent Yankee had always declared him to be, a wholly alien, disparate, even a new character.' And she also noted the predominantly unsatisfying or pathetic fate suffered by James's venturing Americans. 'For the most part emotion in these Americans in his wide gallery is frustrated, buried, or lost. Instead, renunciation, tenderness, pity, are likely to be dominant among them.' Miss Rourke finished her essay by noting that subsequent American writers had been influenced only by James's subject – not by his technique. 'In later years other American writers have followed him in using the international scene; yet his other great achievement, that of portraying the inner mind, cannot be said to have given any notable impetus to the American novel.' She notes that the 'portrayal of the inner consciousness' has been developed mainly by European writers – Proust, Joyce, Virginia Woolf and Dorothy Richardson. But Miss Rourke's essay was more important for stressing James's American origins than his European influence.

It was in the mid-1930s that Edmund Wilson wrote the long study called 'The Ambiguity of Henry James',[1] which has since become famous if only because it precipitated a prolonged argument over the meaning of *The Turn of the Screw* which is still alive some thirty years later. Bringing an overtly Freudian approach to bear on James for (I think) the first time, Wilson sees the figure of the governess in *The Turn of the Screw* as a study in hysteria and morbid hallucinations consequent upon deep sexual repression and frustration. 'We see now that it is simply a variation on one of James's familiar themes: the frustrated Anglo-Saxon spinster', and Wilson develops his anatomy of the Jamesian world by pointing out that not only are most of his female characters either 'emotionally perverted' or 'emotionally apathetic', but the men also seldom achieve normal passional fulfilment. 'James's men are not precisely neurotic; but they are the masculine counterparts of his women. They have a way of missing out on

[1] In *Hound & Horn* (April 1934).

emotional experience, either through timidity or caution or through heroic renunciation.' And having found *The Sacred Fount* to contain 'the conception of a man shut out from love and doomed to barren speculation on human relations', Wilson applies his psychological insights about James's work to James himself. 'He seems to be dramatizing the frustrations of his own life without quite being willing to confess it, without always admitting it to himself.' Wilson then develops an interesting contrast between James's attitude to his young protagonists, and Flaubert's: 'whereas in James the young man is made wondering and wistful and is likely to turn out a pitiful victim, in Flaubert he is made to look a fool and is as ready to double-cross these other people who seem to him so inferior to himself as they are to double-cross him'. James is incapable of Flaubert's remorseless and bitter irony. But Wilson goes on to point out that there is an important difference between the two writers: 'there was another kind of modern society which Flaubert did not know and which Henry James did know. Henry James was that anomalous thing, an American. . . . The American in Henry James insistently asserts himself against Europe.' Wilson notes that in the later novels 'it is always the Americans who have the better of it from the moral point of view'. And he paraphrases what seems to him James's final assessment of his Americans. 'Yes: there *was* a beauty and there was also a power in the goodness of these naïve and open people, which had not existed for Flaubert and his group. It *is* something different and new which does not fit into the formulas of Europe.' Again we notice that it is the *American* Henry James that Wilson stresses. And despite his apparently severe psychological comments on James's particular relationship to life, Wilson ends this long essay with the highest praise. 'For Henry James *is* a great artist, in spite of everything. His deficiencies are obvious enough. He was certainly rather short on invention; and he tended to hold life at arm's length.' (Wilson makes the interesting suggestion that his 'censure of Tolstoy for his failure to select is a defensive reflex action on Henry James's part for his own failure to fill in his picture'.) But Wilson goes on to say that 'the objects and beings at the end of James's arm, or rather, at the end of his antennae, are grasped with an astonishing firmness, gauged with a marvellous intelligence', and he ends his essay by equating James with the greatest writers.

> His work is incomplete as his experience was; but it is in no respect second-rate, and he can be judged only in the company of the greatest.

My argument has not given me an occasion to call attention to the classical equanimity, the classical combination of realism with harmony – I
have tried to describe them in writing about Pushkin – which have been
so rare in American and in English literature alike and of which James is
one of the only examples.

Hitherto, roughly speaking, we have seen James appreciated for his
highly cultured intelligence; because he is on the side of true civilisation; and on account of his masterly technical innovations. We have
seen him praised both as one of the great explorers and fabulists of the
American character and also as one of the first great modern novelists
of the world within, the first to dramatise the inward effort and strain
of the unique – and lonely – perceiving consciousness as it seeks to
understand and negotiate new and problematical worlds. Now,
around the mid-1930s, another James was emphasised: the James whose
work was full of intimations of horrible decadence, of imminent social
disorder and chaos, perhaps even war. Instead of the emphasis being on
James's refined sense of civilisation, it now falls on James's profound
vision of evil. I think it is worth mentioning the comments of three
writers to illustrate this new emphasis in James criticism. In 1934 the
American critic Newton Arvin published an article in *Hound & Horn*
called 'Henry James and the Almighty Dollar'.[1] This was one of the
earliest attempts to portray James as a penetrating critic of the society
of his own times. Arvin admits that James seems somewhat reluctant
to embark on any direct indictment of his age, but he points to '*The
Princess Casamassima*, with its hints at the decadence of the privileged
classes, its evocation of the dreariness and hopelessness of life in the
London slums, its intentionally vague intimations of retributive
movements from below', and goes on to claim that James's 'penetrating
ethical insight' served him as well as any detailed historical or sociological knowledge. The point he brings forward is this: 'that Henry
James's world, especially the world of his later fiction, is far from being
a pretty one; that, on the contrary, it is morally as ugly a world as any
in the English novel, up to that point, and that a tiny handful of decent
people wander through it, bravely or timidly as the case may be, like
men astray in a land of condors and boas'. He singles out the 'gross
preoccupation with money' which marks James's characters and says
that 'James's scene is one in which greed plays something like the
same role as snobbishness in Thackeray's scene or sentimentality in

[1] VII (April–June 1934).

Meredith's'. Henry James 'became in his old age the chronicler of a festering society' and lays bare 'a world obsessed by the nervous craving for acquisition and haunted by fear of penury'. This is how Arvin summed up: 'It was a greedy society in the midst of which James found himself living; and, though all the conditions of that greediness were never made clear to him – though he failed to criticize it from a more significant angle than that of a refined individualism – he was too honest, too responsible, too scrupulous a writer to white-wash society as he found it.'

Also in 1934 Stephen Spender published his important book *The Destructive Element*. This contained an extremely penetrating analysis of the world of *The Golden Bowl* and, in particular, Spender emphasised not only that it was a predominantly 'dead' world, but also that it was pervaded by a 'feeling of horror that is entirely modern'. He cites some of the more vivid images of pain, torture, suffering and dread that occur in the book and comments:

> When one considers these examples, one begins to feel certain that beneath the stylistic surface, the portentous snobbery, the golden display of James's work, there lurk forms of violence and chaos. His technical mastery has the perfection of frightful balance and frightful tension: beneath the stretched-out compositions there are abysses of despair and disbelief: *Ulysses* and *The Waste Land*.
>
> What after all do these images of suffocation, of broken necks, of wailing suggest but a collection of photographs of the dead and wounded during the Great War? We remember his phrase, made in 1915: 'to have to take it all now for what the treacherous years were all the while making for and *meaning*, is too tragic for words'.

Having discussed the many felicities in James's art, Spender, like Arvin, emphasises the social criticism implicit in his work – 'his account of our society makes, in effect, an indictment as fierce as that of Baudelaire'. Spender sees a contradiction in James's attitude, for if James loathed the corruption of his society he also relied on the freedom and independence which that society secured for him. 'He saw through the political and social life of his time, but he cherished the privilege which enabled him to see through it.' Perhaps Spender mainly reveals his own political attitude at the time when he mentions Joyce and Wyndham Lewis along with Henry James and says 'the key to the subjectivism of all these writers is an intense dissatisfaction with modern political institutions'. But his picture of James as a writer who was intensely aware of the horrors and abysses in modern society would help to make James seem more relevant to a generation who would have had little time for an artist presented as a sort of Pateresque devotee of 'the beautiful'.

In 1936 Graham Greene added his powerful contribution to the conception of James as a man more preoccupied with a vision of evil than with the refinements of the genteel. In his essay 'The Private Universe'[1] he starts by paying tribute to Percy Lubbock for having described the technical achievement of James and says that he now wants to 'try to track the instinctive, the poetic writer back to the source of his fantasies'. He finds the key to James in one of the last things he wrote. 'I think we may take the sentence in the scenario of *The Ivory Tower*, in which James speaks of "the black and merciless things that are behind great possession" as an expression of the ruling fantasy that drove him to write: a sense of evil religious in its intensity'. Like Spender, Greene sees some sort of intuitive connection between the world of James's late novels and the First World War – 'they are complete anarchists, these late Jamesian characters, they form the immoral background for that extraordinary period of haphazard violence which anticipated the First World War'; but he sees James's preoccupation as one which transcends modern politics. He notes that both James's father and brother had had visionary experiences of utter evil and horror and, having described these visions as reported in their writings, he maintains that they 'are a more important background to Henry James's novels than Grosvenor House and late Victorian society'. 'It is true that the moral anarchy of the age gave him his material, but he would not have treated it with such intensity if it had not corresponded with his private fantasy. They were materialists, his characters, but you cannot read far in Henry James's novels without realising that their creator was not a materialist. If ever a man's imagination was clouded by the pit, it was James's.' Greene understands the emphasis on James as a social critic but insists that

the Marxists, just as much as the older critics, are dwelling on marginalia. . . . His lot and his experience happened to lie among the great possessions, but 'the black and merciless things' were no more intrinsically part of a capitalist than of a socialist system: they belonged to human nature. They amounted really to this: an egotism so complete that you

[1] Reprinted in *The Lost Childhood and other essays* (London and New York, 1951).

could believe that something inhuman, supernatural, was working through the poor devils it had chosen.

Just as we can see Spender revealing his own preoccupations when he writes about James, so we note that Greene emphasises that aspect of James which is most sympathetic to his own view of the universe. Yet it is the mark of a great writer than he can appeal to many different imaginations and many different visions of life: it testifies to the universality of his relevance; the range and variety of experience he has touched on; the encompassing humanity of his awareness. Where Edmund Wilson chooses to stress a balance between realism and harmony comparable with Pushkin's, and Spender emphasises a modern awareness of society analogous to Joyce's, Greene fastens on the pervading pity in James's work, which he compares, in what is perhaps the highest claim ever made for James, to that of Shakespeare: 'it is in the final justness of his pity, the completeness of an analysis which enabled him to pity the most shabby, the most corrupt, of his human actors, that he ranks with the greatest of creative writers. He is as solitary in the history of the novel as Shakespeare in the history of poetry.'

That would seem to provide a good point on which to conclude this brief survey of the changing critical attitude to James up to the Second World War. And, in fact, after these important articles of the mid-1930s not very much was heard about James for a while. Indeed the *PMLA* bibliography of scholarly work, which is printed every year, has no entries under the name of James for the years from 1933 to 1937 (inclusive). A provocative article on James by Yvor Winters appeared in 1938,[1] and a well-known appraisal of his work by L. C. Knights appeared in 1939 (it was reprinted in *Explorations*); then 1940 again seems to be a blank year. But throughout the 1940s, with some fluctuations, interest in James increased steadily (to use the *PMLA* bibliography as a rough guide once more – five entries for 1941, twenty-five for 1949). Faced by this escalation of interest it is perhaps arbitrary to single out any one piece of writing as being particularly influential or significant. Yet one publishing event does seem to mark the real beginning of the modern interest in James. In the autumn of James's centenary year, 1943, Robert Penn Warren edited a number of the *Kenyon Review* which was entirely devoted to James and

---

[1] Reprinted in *In Defence of Reason* (New York, 1947).

contained serious, often brilliant, articles by such distinguished critics as R. P. Blackmur, Francis Fergusson, Austin Warren, Jacques Barzun and David Daiches. This formidable group of essays certainly consolidated James's reputation and probably did much to enhance it. Also in 1943 an essay by another famous critic, Philip Rahv,[1] seems to look both to the past and the imminent future of James criticism. Rahv notes that, at the time, James 'is at once the most and least appreciated figure in American writing', and he gives examples of how James is misinterpreted, particularly in America. On the other hand the intelligence and insight of his own comments on James is indicative of the understanding and respectful treatment that James was to receive at the hands of the leading American critics of the 1940s and 1950s. Perhaps typically of that generation he stressed the 'doubleness' of James.

> His characteristic themes all express this doubleness. The 'great world' is corrupt, yet it represents an irresistible goal. Innocence points to all the wanted things one has been deprived of, yet it is profound in its good faith and not to be tampered with without loss. History and culture are the supreme ideal, but why not make of them a strictly private possession? Europe is romance and reality and civilization, but the spirit resides in America. James never faltered in the maze of these contraries; he knew how to take hold of them creatively and weave them into the web of his art.

Clearly there was some connection between the war and the sudden access of interest in James on a wide scale, though to speculate here would be out of place (I have included one essay from 1943 by William Troy which suggests some reasons). Pretty certainly the Hitler–Stalin pact discredited all kinds of Marxist criticism and thus released James for less doctrinaire handling, but whether it was the 'darkness' or the 'civilisation' in Henry James's work which appealed more when civilisation itself was enduring its darkest hours must have depended on the individual reader. The fact we can be sure of is that the number of people reading James increased enormously and continued to increase after the war. Since 1943 the books, dissertations and articles on James have continued to appear in almost unmanageable numbers (the *PMLA* bibliographies for 1964 and 1965 both have over sixty entries under Henry James). Any summary of the critical work on

---

[1] 'Attitudes toward Henry James', in *New Republic*, 15 Feb. 1943.

James since the war is well beyond the scope of this essay. Every aspect of James has been subjected to numerous approaches. You can find different studies of his themes, philosophy, moral vision, metaphysics, psychological theories; of the different periods of his own life; of the imagery, symbolism, syntax, allegory, fantasy and emblems in his work; of his various narrative and dramatic techniques; of his reactions to America, England, Italy, etc; of his relation to various writers, American, European and English, and to various members of his own family; of the manifold sources for his novels and stories, ranging from the ancient Greeks to his French contemporaries; of his revealing revisions of his earlier work, etc. There is no point in continuing a list which could be extended indefinitely. Inevitably one may sometimes wonder if so much is necessary or desirable. Will not the critics and scholars bury James under their amplifications, explanations, speculations, whatever?

A major James scholar, Oscar Cargill, writing in the early 1960s said: 'Working through the very great mass of commentary on James's fiction, I have been struck by a curious deficiency – nobody apparently reads anybody else – there is no accumulated wisdom, no "body" of appreciation.'[1] It is a just observation; and, of course, unnecessary repetition there has been. But it is possible to see this phenomenon as testifying to the stature of James as an artist. The truly great writers are inexhaustible; they are susceptible to a plurality of interpretations because their imaginative vision has comprehended and preserved so much potential human experience. When the critics and scholars produce new essays and books about Shakespeare year after year, they are not struggling for some definitive solution: they are preserving a heritage we can ill afford to lose; they are, by their ongoing discussions, maintaining a vital contact with one of the most profound imaginations that the human race has produced. James is no Shakespeare, but he is a great writer – one whom every age will appropriate for itself in its own way. The work of a great writer is so much deeper and wider and more inclusive than the mind of any single critic that no one man can, or should, hope to dredge up all the richness and mysteries which the writer has, miraculously, caught and contained in his work. It is worth remembering the dying writer in James's story 'The Middle Years': 'He sat and stared at the sea, which appeared all surface and twinkle, far shallower than the spirit of man.

[1] *The Novels of Henry James* (New York, 1961) p. xii.

It was the abyss of human illusion that was the real, the tideless deep.'
Only the greatest minds, the greatest imaginations can comprehend
something of that 'tideless deep' which is the 'spirit of man' and then
only fitfully. As the writer in the story makes clear in his dying words:
'We work in the dark – we do what we can – we give what we have.
Our doubt is our passion and our passion is our task. The rest is the
madness of art.' It is only an apparent paradox that the sanity of society
is in a crucial way dependent on 'the madness of art'. But the art
cannot be fully explained; it is simply there to be experienced and
appreciated according to our abilities and susceptibilities. As James
said, to criticise properly is 'to appropriate, to take intellectual possession, to establish in fine a relation with the criticised thing and make it
one's own'. The strange promiscuity of a great work of art is such that
it can be appropriated, possessed, made over countless times in countless ways, and yet be still open to another relationship with some new
inquiring mind. I would like to think that the Criticism, Discrimination
and Appreciation of the last twenty years would have seemed somewhat less infantile to James than that of his own age. But having said
that we must guard against any complacency by realising that, with
a writer like James, there is and can be no question of anything like
a final definitive 'appropriation' of his work. Only endless revisits to
an inexhaustible source.

TONY TANNER

Note on the Principles of Selection

CONFRONTED by the vast amount of critical material which has accumulated around the work of Henry James, any anthologist has to take some ruthless decisions about what to omit. For the benefit of any intending reader I should perhaps make mine clear from the start, and if possible explain them. First, since there are so many good and valuable articles which have not been made available in book form I took the initial decision *not* to include any work which had, to my knowledge, appeared in a book. I am well aware that I thereby debarred much of the most distinguished work on James, but the books are readily available, and anyone at all interested will want to read them *in toto*. To select extracts and chapters from various books to make yet another book seemed in this particular case to be unjustifiable repetition. Instead I have added a bibliography which attempts to cover most of the important books on James.

Secondly, I have deliberately avoided including many excellent articles which have been reprinted, included in anthologies and referred to and cited so often that any anthology which offered them to the public once more, albeit in a new context and relationship, would become immediately redundant. Thus, for example, there are no essays by Joseph Conrad, T. S. Eliot, Edmund Wilson, Lionel Trilling, Alfred Kazin, Philip Rahv, Morton Zabel, Richard Blackmur, Stephen Spender, F. O. Matthiessen, Jacques Barzun, Leon Edel, F. W. Dupee, Richard Poirier, Irving Howe and other distinguished writers and critics whose names are rightfully connected with the history of James criticism. I contend that the very distinction of many of the essays by these eminent men has rendered them too well known to require further republication (some I have summarised in my introductory essay).

Thirdly, I have limited my selection to criticism written since 1943. There is enough admirable material to justify this concentration, and I have tried to give a fairly comprehensive picture of James criticism before that date in my introductory essay.

The essays I have chosen, then, are neither particularly famous, nor are they selections from books. But they seem to me representative of the different kinds of intelligence, patient research, imaginative interpretation and sensitive study which have been exercised in the field of James studies in the last twenty-five years or so. And my hope is that this anthology might serve two functions. For those already interested in James it offers itself as a supplement to the better-known James criticism, which they probably possess or know. It seeks to bring together essays, often rather hard to find (for instance, from scholarly American journals not readily available except in the largest libraries), which make a definite contribution to our understanding, appreciation and knowledge of James's work – a contribution not already covered by the available books on James. On the other hand, for those who are just starting to read James, it will serve as a helpful introduction and a continual aid. There are some general essays which contribute to our comprehension of James's fictional world and his whole conception of the writer; then there are essays on different aspects of most of the major novels. It is doubtless too much to hope to please all of the people even some of the time; nonetheless my hope is that anybody with any interest in James will find this collection in some degree helpful, informative, stimulating and enriching. If nothing else, let it stand as an appreciative tribute to the vital attraction which the work of Henry James continues to have for our own age.

Chronology

1843	Born on 15 April in New York.
1855–8	Goes to schools in Geneva, London and Paris before returning to live in Newport, Rhode Island.
1860	While at school at Newport, sustains the strange injury to his back that prevented him from taking part in the Civil War.
1862	Attends Harvard Law School for one year.
1864	His family settles in Cambridge, Massachusetts. James has his first story and reviews published.
1869–70	Travels in England, France and Italy. While he is abroad, his young cousin Minny Temple dies.
1870	Publishes his first novel, *Watch and Ward*.
1872–4	Again in Europe, where he begins *Roderick Hudson*.
1874–5	*Roderick Hudson* published (1875), as well as a book of stories and a book of travel sketches. James in New York doing literary journalism.
1875–6	Spends a year in Paris, where he meets eminent writers, such as Turgenev, Flaubert and Zola. Writes *The American* (published 1877).
1876–7	Settles in London.
1878	The publication of *Daisy Miller* brings James some fame.
1879–82	Publishes *The Europeans* (1878), *Washington Square* (1880), *Confidence* (1880) and *The Portrait of a Lady* (1881).
1882–3	His parents die.
1886	Publishes *The Bostonians* and *The Princess Casamassima*.
1887	Another visit to Italy.
1888–90	Publishes *The Reverberator* (1888) and *The Tragic Muse* (1890).
1890–5	Tries to write for the theatre, finally abandoning the attempt after being booed at the first night of *Guy Domville*.

1897–8   *The Spoils of Poynton* and *What Maisie Knew* (1897). Moves to Lamb House, in Rye, Sussex.

1899–1904   Publishes *The Awkward Age* (1899), *The Sacred Fount* (1901), *The Wings of the Dove* (1902), *The Ambassadors* (1903), *William Wetmore Story and his Friends* (1903) and *The Golden Bowl* (1904).

1905–10   Revisits America after an absence of twenty years. He writes *The American Scene* (1907) and then edits the twenty-four volume New York Edition of his works.

1910   His brother, William, dies.

1913–14   Writes his autobiographical volumes *A Small Boy and Others* (1913) and *Notes of a Son and Brother* (1914).

1915   Becomes a British subject.

1916   Dies on 28 February. He leaves two unfinished novels, *The Ivory Tower* and *The Sense of the Past*, and a third autobiographical volume, *The Middle Years*, all three published in 1917.

WILLIAM TROY

The Altar of Henry James (1943)

THIS is, perhaps, an unfortunate title; it does not refer, for example, to the increasing number of people who have been throwing themselves at the feet of Henry James in the last few years. At least a half-dozen full-length studies of his work are in preparation; not all of his books are easily available on the market; his reputation is higher than at any moment in his own lifetime. It is clear enough that to the present generation he means something more than to the generation of Van Wyck Brooks and Lewis Mumford or to the addled and intolerant generation of the thirties. Also clear is that what he means is something different. To say what this something is in every case is, of course, impossible. What this article undertakes is to suggest that if he makes such a great appeal to so many of us today it must be because there lies at the center of his work something that corresponds to our deepest contemporary needs and hopes. It raises the question of what was James's *own* altar – or, if one prefers, the particular object of piety to which he was able to devote himself at the end.

All this is to strike the religious note; and, indeed, since we have no better word for the kind of passionate and responsible sense of human things that James possessed, he must be accounted a religious man. In this he simply followed his astonishing father, who ached out a lifetime trying to reconcile a heritage of respectability and good sense with a taste for Swedenborgian mysticism. Nor was he essentially unlike his brother William, whose too sudden plunge into the darker cellars of the personality, during the period of his breakdown, frightened him into a loud and quasi-religious philosophy of optimism. All the Jameses were religious. The important thing about Henry is that he was an artist; that is, he had to work in a concrete medium and in a more or less fixed craft which did not permit him the consolations of shaking his head over Brook Farm experiments or becoming the Socrates of the Chautauquas. It meant that he could not evade the really great questions because these questions were stubbornly imbedded in the very materials of his craft—the lived and observed human situation.

For us it means that if we are to look for what is essential in James we are not likely to find it on the surface of his writing. (This is probably what T. S. Eliot means by the remark, 'James had a mind so pure that no idea could violate it.') As in any authentic artist, the 'meaning' in James is contained in the total arrangement and order of his symbols, and in the novel everything – people, events, and settings – are capable of being invested with symbolic value. In only a few novelists like Turgenev, Joyce, and the Mann of *Death in Venice* are meaning and literal statement so indivisible; the great works of the last period, *The Ambassadors* and *The Golden Bowl*, are put together, if not like a vastly exfoliated lyric, like one of the final plays of Shakespeare. And to approach them in the manner of Spurgeon or Knight on Shakespeare is almost certainly to uncover conflicts of feeling that are more often than not belied by the overt urbanity of style. It is also to raise the question of how much is conscious, how much unconscious, in any artist's work – in James's case, the often noted element of ambiguity. Is it merely an accident, for example, that in an early work like *The Portrait of a Lady* all the great climaxes in Isabel Archer's career – from her refusal of the English lord to her final flight from Caspar Goodwood – are made to occur in a garden? If an accident, it was a fortunate one, for the garden-symbol provides a wonderful point of concentration for the widest possible number of associations – the recollection especially of the famous garden in which one of Isabel's ancestresses was also confronted with the fruit of the tree of the knowledge of good and evil. It enables us to arrive at the formula, nowhere explicit in the book, that the real trouble with Isabel is that she is someone who will have none of the bitter fruit and runs from the garden in panic. And it might lead us to an even wider formula regarding James's own attitude toward these matters at this point in his development.

For the symbolic approach to James, besides lifting the mystery of individual works, makes possible a more organic study of his whole growth and achievement than the usual chronological division of his career into three periods. If the garden-symbol began as an accident, for example, it persists with remarkable frequency; and it is submitted to a series of drastic modifications. In *The Portrait of a Lady* it is clearly

ambivalent. On the one hand, it is all that rich if uncertain promise of
beautiful fulfilment that life is opening up to Isabel – wealth, marriage,
Europe. On the other, it is the dwelling place of the unknown terror
that is actually in herself – the terror of experience which at the end
she rationalizes in terms of moral obligation. If the novel ends with
such manifest ambiguity it is because James himself has not yet resolved
certain issues in his mind and temperament. In the novels and tales
of the nineties, the so-called 'middle period', the symbol is first split
wide asunder into its two aspects, then one of them is made to domi-
nate. When the governess in *The Turn of the Screw* begins her afternoon
walk in the garden everything is calm and radiant and peaceful. It
is with the force of a shock, she tells us, that it suddenly becomes
transformed for her into a scene of desolation and death. Once again
we know that this is a case of projection; the garden is all that alarming
and unsuspected side of her nature which she cannot accept because she
believes it to be evil. Nor do we feel that James accepts it; evil, working
in the guise of zeal, is triumphant; and the story adds up to another
terrifying treatment of the Othello motif, the infinite amount of
mischief done in the world, in the name of goodness, by self-blinded
innocence. Even more terrifying perhaps in its nightmarish cancellation
of all normal motives is *The Other House*, in which nearly all the action
occurs in a garden. James did not include this in the New York
Edition; it is the one altogether evil book that he ever wrote. But it
sounds the depths of what must have been in his life a period of the
most torturous metaphysical panic and moral despair. Without such
a sojourn in the abyss as it represents he would never have attained to
the full-bodied affirmation of the last and greatest period. Like Strether,
in *The Ambassadors*, he wins through, by a long and difficult 'process
of vision', to an acceptance of human life as it is lived – qualified, of
course, by a revalidation of the naïvely grasped moral certitudes of his
youth. It is in Gloriani's garden that Strether makes the celebrated
speech with the refrain, 'Live, live while you can!' But life now is to
be lived always with the wary knowledge of the shadows lurking ever
in the dark corners of the garden.

To point out that the full import of James is to be derived only from
some such weighing of his major symbols is not to deny that throughout his work he does let drop explicit judgments and opinions on
important matters, although never like Tolstoy or Proust to the
temporary abnegation of his role. It so happens that in one of the final

stories of the middle period – not one of the best known or most admired – he has given us what may be taken as something like a testament of belief. 'The Altar of the Dead' is unique in the James canon, fluttering on the edge of a morbid emotionalism and sustained only by a marvelous tonality of style. It is also a masterpiece of its kind in English – the long short story or *novella*. But for our purpose it is significant because it is the only one of James's works in which a character is made to come face to face with the problem of religion.

Its hero, one of those sensitive middle-aged gentlemen whom James apologizes for writing about in the nineties, shocked by the callousness of a friend who remarries too soon after his first wife's death, dedicates himself to keeping up the memory of his dead friends.

> What came to pass was that an altar, such as was after all within everybody's compass, lighted with perpetual candles and dedicated to these secret rites, reared itself in his spiritual spaces. He had wondered of old, in some embarrassment, whether he had a religion; being very sure, and not a little content, that he hadn't at all events the religion some of the people he had known wanted him to have. Gradually this question was straightened out for him – it became clear to him that the religion instilled by his earliest consciousness had been simply the religion of the Dead.

Difficulties begin when quite by accident he enters a church and is tempted to light real candles before the real altar of a religion in which he does not believe. For he soon acquires a companion in mourning – a woman given to the same rites for a dead friend. In time it turns out that this friend, who had actually been her ruin, is also the one man among his friends whom the hero cannot commemorate because of some betrayal in the past. This coincidence threatens their relationship; they can no longer pay tribute at the same altar. A resolution is managed only when the hero realizes that the true 'religion of the Dead' requires that we remember even our enemies – just because they were once part of ourselves and helped make us what we are.

What does James intend by this strange and tenuous parable, which he himself refers to as a 'conceit'? It is, as he tells us in a preface, an instance of the 'exasperated piety' of the Londoner of his time: 'an instance of some such practiced communion was a foredoomed consequence of life, year after year, amid the densest and most materialized aggregation of men on earth, the society most wedded by all its conditions to the immediate and finite'. It is a commentary on the pathetic desolation of the individual in our society – a desolation shared by both the living and the dead. Toward the dead it expressed the same kind of sympathy that we find in Baudelaire's

> Les morts, les pauvres morts, ont de grandes douleurs,
> Et quand Octobre souffle, émondeur des vieux arbres,
> Son vent melancolique à l'entour de leurs marbres,
> Certe, ils doivent trouver les vivants bien ingrats.

And in its emphasis on the still potent influence that the dead can exercise on the living it recalls Joyce's fine story, 'The Dead'. As to the living, or the living-dead, it explains their desolation as the absence of any ritual by which some principle of continuity in human experience may be recognized and observed. For it is continuity that it represented as the basis of everything – of personality, friendship, morality, and civilization itself. Without some sense of it the individual is no more than a moment in time and a speck in space; he has nothing by means of which he can define his own identity.

What James tells us, finally, is that we exist only by virtue of the existence of others, living and dead, with whom we have ever had relations. The individual, in the language of modern physics, is only an 'event', to be defined in terms of a given field of forces. These relations or forces bring with them certain obligations, and the greatest of these is the formal act of commemoration. It is not morbidity that prompts James to write: 'The sense of the state of the dead is but part of the sense of the state of the living; and, congruously with that, life is cheated to almost the same degree of the finest homage (precisely this our possible friendships and intimacies) that we fain would render it.' We pay respect to the dead because they enhance the state of the living, and the dead is, of course, a metaphor for the whole tradition of civilized humanity of which we are a part and in terms of which we must ultimately be measured. This sense of the continuum between past and present, between all who share the memory of a common experience, is now known to be at the base of every religion in the world. For James it is a very real religion, although wholly without any theological cast. Or, if we prefer, he emerges as one of our great humanists, the greatest perhaps, because his humanism was grounded in such a rich tragic experience. And, in that case, his altar – what would it be but the sometimes splendid and exultant, sometimes mangled and ignoble, body of humanity stretched out in imagination in time and space? At a moment when loss of continuity is our gravest threat, when personality is everywhere at a discount, when all consequent values dissolve in the general terror, it is probably no great wonder that more and more people are turning to Henry James.

JOHN HENRY RALEIGH

Henry James: The Poetics of Empiricism (1951)

CRITICISM of Henry James in our time is verging into metaphysics. The late works have recently been analyzed in terms of 'dialectic' and 'myth',[1] as products of Swedenborgianism,[2] and as an artistic objectification of William James' philosophical pragmatism.[3] Despite great individual differences these three approaches hold in common the basic assumption that James' inner and final meaning has not yet been ascertained and the corollary assumption that this final meaning is perhaps expressed symbolically, by technique, rather than overtly by subject matter.[4] In this climate of opinion James is conceived of as a kind of nineteenth-century Dante, the architect of a secular *Divine Comedy* for some later-day equivalent of scholasticism, and the legendary 'late manner', once considered merely idiosyncratic, is thought to be an elaborate structure which metaphorically expresses a coherent system of values. The critical problems are, first, to find James' Aquinas, or the rationale for the body of ideas on which the late works constitute a metaphor, and, second, to define the relationship between this logical statement and James' symbolic one.

The following essay will proceed along these lines. Although I have no St Thomas to offer, I should like to point out some broad but unmistakable analogies between the basic characteristics of James' work as a whole and a certain body of ideas, whose ultimate source will be briefly sketched, and to suggest, further, that the late technique is an esthetic embodiment of these ideas. In terms of the evolution of James' art, with which this essay will also be concerned, my thesis is that the mature technique simply makes explicit certain distinctive qualities which are implicit in all the novels, early and late.

James, of all novelists, must be approached obliquely, and his 'distinctive qualities' are best defined in a formal rather than in a subjective manner. As generations of irritated readers attest, James' novels are not case histories of human beings whom one can talk about as of one's friends; but, at the same time, these novels constitute, collectively, a perfectly valid interpretation of and a remarkable metaphor on human experience in general. With James, as indeed with any other novelist, there can be no simple equation of art to life, for characters in a novel are not human and there is no *necessary* direct connection between them and us. A connection may exist, but it is fortuitous rather than logical, since they are motivated not by our own sometimes unique drives or peculiar experiences, but by certain assumptions that the author holds, consciously or unconsciously, as to what constitutes personality, experience, and their interaction. Thus, like a philosopher he is trying with the aid of certain theoretical assumptions to impose form and meaning on the chaos of life; and his characters are not human beings but meaning-functions within this system. It is from their consonance with the system and not ourselves that they derive their validity. In James' novels his most memorable or remarkable characters, like Isabel Archer or Strether, are those who most perfectly body forth his basic assumptions as to the nature of personality and experience.

All this is obvious and, perhaps, presents no great problem in the earlier nineteenth-century novel where the depiction is all done by an omniscient author, who tells you what to think, and where the action is liable to be external rather than internal, making it necessary for the reader himself to supply much of the motivation. But when the author moves out of the way, and the novel itself becomes introspective, as with James, then the subject-matter becomes that most inexplicable of all subjects, human consciousness, and necessarily the author must have fairly definite ideas as to its nature and function or he could bring no order at all to his art.

Using the word 'idea' in connection with James is perhaps misleading. Strictly speaking he had none, or at least he professed to have none. His father's philosophy, in fact any abstract system, possibly excepting his brother William's, left him cold. T. S. Eliot in one of his famous pronouncements has said that James' mind was too fine ever to be violated by an abstraction; and, in a sense, Eliot is right. James did entertain ideas, but they only filtered in obliquely through the maze of personal relationships and feeling-values which for him constituted the basic ingredient of life itself and the subject-matter of his novels. But he did have an abiding conviction, which was that human consciousness was beatitude, the only real value in a complex, almost indecipherable universe, and the sole argument for immortality. This was his real subject-matter, and the late works, in effect, comprise a religion of consciousness. Page after page is given to its exploration; characters are ranked according to how high or how low, in perceptiveness and subtlety, are their conscious minds; and the movement of the story progresses as various bundles of consciousness impinge upon one another, attracted or repulsed or drifting. Thus James' system, since I have now made him a metaphysician, has at its heart a certain attitude towards, and hence certain assumptions about, consciousness. These assumptions determine the generic qualities of life-experience in James' novels. The critical problem then is to comprehend and define as closely as possible the nature of this 'consciousness' which gives meaning to the works.

There are certain fundamental traits in all the Jamesian characters and the life they lead that have been noted by many critics: their passivity, their sensitivity, their acquisitiveness, their individualism, the ambiguous quality of their motivations, which are always concerned with ethical choice, but never have reference to an explicit moral code, their supreme esthetic sense, which seems to encompass all aspects of their personality, their subtle, complex, but constantly shifting interdependence, one with another, and, finally, the tenuous nature of everything, where hardly any problem is completely clear-cut, no relationship ever certain or immutable, no issue ever precisely decided.

Many of these characteristics can be and have been accounted for by critics in sociological terms. For example, individualism and acquisitiveness are pre-eminently American traits and to point this out is to say that the novels of James reflect the culture into which he was born. But the passivity and the tenuous and ambiguous quality of experience are hardly accounted for by a comparison with nineteenth-century American society, and it is these two traits which so distinguish James' vision of life. Very often they are explained away in Freudian terms and are taken to be an unconscious expression of James' own sexual aberration, whatever it was. But the reduction of the novels to an end-product of this condition is as fallacious as the view that holds Dostoevski's works to be solely the eruptions of an epileptic. Both of these great and distinctive novelists wrote as they did because they were so deeply expressive of their respective cultures. By the time of his death Dostoevski was rightly regarded as one of the national prophets. Posthumously, James is beginning to be accorded the same rank, and with some justice, for the distinctive characteristics of human experience in James' novels, passivity and ambiguity, have their root and source in a group of ideas profoundly fundamental to American culture.

As every textbook says, the ideas of British empiricism are basic to most American institutions and to the American life-attitude in its theory, if not always in its practice. The dismissal of absolutes, the political democracy, the social equality, the religious tolerance, the moral relativity, the personal individualism, the respect for property, all these fundamental traits and many more have been shown to be implicit in the thinking of Locke and his successors. It is a gross oversimplification, of course, to say that there is a straight line between Locke's ideas and American culture. Many factors, including the whole history and heritage of Western civilization, the geography of the American continent, the personal motives of the men who founded its institutions, enter in, but it is reasonable to assume that the doctrines of Locke were primary here and found congenial surroundings. And, in spite of Transcendentalism and the other great forces abroad in nineteenth-century America, a substratum of Lockeanism persisted, as Merle Curti[5] has effectively demonstrated. Constantly, in sermons, in Fourth of July orations, and in other public speeches Locke or his doctrines were referred to or quoted. If anything, the extreme individualism of British empiricism, enshrined originally in the Constitution and in various social institutions, became more radical in its American setting. In a Fourth of July oration, delivered at Newport in 1861, Henry James Sr gave voice to the common feeling that in the United States the twin bases of individualism, Protestantism and constitutional liberty, which had been inherited from England and for which Locke was prime philosophical spokesman, would finally reach full fruition in his own native land: 'We inherit Protestantism and constitutional liberty; but there is a vast difference between us and them, *we begin where they leave off* . . . they affirm the inalienable sanctity and freedom of the nation as against other nations; we, the inalienable sanctity and freedom of the subject as against the nation.'[6]

Now behind these familiar democratic sentiments lay certain assumptions about the nature of man, and, as Henry James Sr was a vigorous expositor of these assumptions in political and social terms, so Henry Jr, perhaps quite unwittingly, constructed his novels on their psychological premises. This relationship will perhaps be more clear if I set forth very briefly Locke's fundamental assumptions concerning personality and experience, well-known in a general sense, but not, so far as I know, in this particular context.

In Locke's philosophy[7] the basic entity of man was a mental substance, which was at once different in kind from all material substances, such as the body and the physical universe, and, at the same time, independent of and separate from all other mental substances. On a material level, this mental substance, using an aggregate of material substances, such as the body and tools, acquired other material substances, or property, which then assumed a status coequal to that of the body itself. On the conscious level, the mental substance was a blank consciousness, the tabula rasa, which received impressions from and thus perceived qualities in material objects. These qualities were either primary, inherent in the object; secondary, inherent in the perceptor; or tertiary, inherent in neither. Most of the impressions were secondary or sensory. The blank was nothing in itself, but did have the power of reflection which enabled it to develop epistemologically by the process of abstraction, turning particular impressions into general ideas.

Practically every character trait and every interrelationship in the James novels can be accounted for as the logical outcome of these ideas. For example, if the basic element of man, the mental substance, is different from and independent of all material substances, including its own body, then it follows that here alone a knowable reality exists; hence James' exclusive concern with his characters' consciousness, to the exclusion of anything materially concrete about them, including their own physical passions. Again if all these mental substances are independent of one another and possess no innate ideas in common, then there is no specified or specifiable relationship between them, and their moral relationships become a highly individualistic affair. Each person is his own arbiter and must arrive at moral decisions by an appeal to his own experience, which, in this case, usually means sense impressions, and, finally, morality becomes purely esthetic. The consciousness most sensitive to impressions is liable to be the most moral. So in James there is an equation between the esthetic and the moral sense, and the individual who most appreciates the beauty of a Renaissance painting is also the most moral. Or to consider the attitude toward material things. If material substances, or property, assume a status equal to that of the body, they are then an extension of that body, and ownership becomes sacrosanct. So the Ververs of *The Golden Bowl*, inordinately acquisitive in any literal sense, are presented in the Jamesian context as admirably disinterested people, and, generally, in the world of James no opprobrium attaches to what might be regarded as the most blatant materialism. Very often those that have the most, Newman, Isabel Archer, Milly Theale, the Ververs, are also the most admirable since they are expressing themselves most fully. The characters of *The Spoils of Poynton* are ranked according to how finely they appreciate the 'spoils'. Conversely, evil and corruption usually set in when the dispossessed, like Gilbert Osmond or Kate Croy, reach out for their share. But the corruption is in them, in their lack of perception, not in the fact of materialism itself. There are many other analogies that could be drawn between the assumptions of empirical philosophy and the works of James, and most of them would probably be true of many other English and American novelists as well. But there are two implications of Lockeanism which seem to have been most vividly realized in James' works and which, in turn, give the works their uniqueness, for, without Freudianizing James, one can show that both the passivity of his characters and the ambiguity of their relationships are the logical outcome of the empirical assumptions on consciousness, personality, and experience.

This perhaps sounds too simple to be true but James' beloved consciousness, the chief subject-matter of his works, was nothing more than an artistic presentation of the idea of the tabula rasa being written upon by experience, or sense impressions. If the mind is a blank upon which experience writes, then it follows that personality itself is passive rather than active and that a person is more of an observer than anything else; consequently there is that thin red line of sad young men in the James novels who rise to life's battle only to renounce, and the archetypal figure, Isabel Archer or Strether, is the perfect observer upon whom nothing is lost. Not all the Jamesian characters are atrophied by their passivity; a character such as Newman, who, in Locke's words, has 'mixed his labor with' the wilderness, has a powerful will and a capacity for action, but everybody's inner life, which is the subject-matter of most of the late works, is invariably presented as passive rather than active, as compared, for instance, to the inner life of a Stephen Dedalus or a Raskolnikov. Very often this passivity is liable to encompass the outer life as well.

Ambiguity in human relationships is likewise a logical implication

of empirical psychology. If each mental substance is absolutely independent of every other mental substance and they are all equal, they
can be organized in no objective fashion, such as hierarchially, and
there can be no specified relationship between them. Their relationships
then must necessarily be ambiguous: so in James there are the frankly
ambiguous conclusions to *The Portrait of a Lady* and *The Wings of the
Dove*; a margin of obscurity in most of the relationships of the later
works, as, for instance, in *The Spoils of Poynton* where only omniscience
itself could ever satisfactorily figure out what happened and why; and
finally, an essential isolation of all characters illustrated thematically by
the betrayal motif that runs through all the novels and exemplified
constantly by the conscious processes of the characters, most of whom
are eternally engaged in the ever-changing, never-ending task of trying
to figure out their inexplicable fellow characters.

These general characteristics, passivity of the individual mind and
ambiguity in human relations, are evident in both the early and late
works of James, but they are much more marked in the late. This was
not brought about by perversity on James' part, as has often been
charged, but by the fact that his technique had become completely
functional and spoke these basic characteristics in style and structure
as well as in theme and action. One hesitates to add anything to the
literature about that monumental phenomenon, the late style. Many
explanations have been given, each having a claim to validity. It is
said that the habit of dictation, the theatrical experiences, various literary influences, such as Conrad, Maeterlinck, and Ibsen, all contributed
to the increasing elaboration of the late works. But it is also assumed
that James had somehow arrived at a 'deeper psychology' and that the
late characters are more profoundly conceived or more profoundly
probed than the earlier ones. To the contrary, there is an almost unholy
consistency in the general traits of the Jamesian characters as a whole,
from early period to later. Newman of *The American*, early, and Adam
Verver of *The Golden Bowl*, late, are fundamentally similar in basic
make-up. Both are misrepresentations of the self-made American
millionaire of the nineteenth century, a familiar figure in all of James'
novels – morally superior, extremely sensitive, inordinately curious, a
supreme gatherer of impressions, in short, a superior tabula rasa linked
to an American will and capacity for practical action. Minus the
capacity for practical action and hence the wealth, Strether of *The
Ambassadors* is essentially the same type. This broad equation of

Newman to Verver to Strether is not meant to imply that James did not vary his types; rather it suggests that the infinite variations were played, as they always are, on certain great and basic themes, here the fundamental assumptions of empiricism concerning personality, experience, and the conscious life.

Yet there is an enormous difference between Newman and Verver in their respective contexts, and the difference is, once more, the difference of technique. If there is a change in psychological portrayal, it is one of extension rather than depth; that is, the characters and their reactions to situations are the same, but James has deepened and enriched their *effect* on the reader by all the resources of the late style, and the greater part of the power of the late style results from the fact that the concepts of consciousness which in the early novels were only vaguely implicit in the characters and their situations have now become explicit in the style. This increased immediacy of effect in the late style has been partly accounted for by what is called the method of 'dramatization'. In the mature period, James, instead of analytically describing his characters, presented directly the workings of their minds. This presentation was always carefully controlled and ordered, as he wished to avoid the un-controlled flux of real experience, but it accomplished the aim of presenting a version of experience directly to the reader. Nevertheless, even admitting the gains in immediacy assured by this device, one may still be baffled by the peculiar splendor of the conscious lives and by the subtly shifting relationships of the characters in *The Wings of the Dove* and *The Golden Bowl*.

The point I am trying to make can best be illustrated by a comparison of James' handling of the same psychological process, the conscious mental substance being acted upon, at three different stages of his career, early, middle, and late. Newman of *The American*, Hyacinth Robinson of *The Princess Casamassima* and Maggie Verver of *The Golden Bowl* are all typical in that they operate, psychologically, in the same fashion, and, by a comparison of each in the process of being conscious, the functional nature of the late technique is underlined. *The American* was written early, in a straightforward fashion and a simple style. We are told, directly and initially, of the receptivity of Newman: 'It [Newman's face] had that paucity of detail, which is not yet emptiness, that blankness which is not simplicity, that look of being committed to nothing in particular, of standing in a posture of general hospitality to the chances of life, of being very much at one's own disposal, characteristic of American faces of the clear strain.'[8] Now Newman in a moment of crisis when his intended bride, Madame de Cintre, has told him that she is to become a Carmelite nun: 'The image rose there, at her words, too dark and horrible for belief, and affected him as if she had told him she was going to mutilate her beautiful face or drink some potion that would make her mad' (II 418). There is nothing particularly distinctive about this, and the image comes in on the receptor in conventional terms of horror.

With Hyacinth Robinson of *The Princess Casamassima* the psychological process, while basically the same, is beginning to acquire power and depth. James had not yet arrived at the full-fledged dramatic method; so much about Hyacinth is described rather than presented, but the description is becoming fuller, more elaborate, and more concrete. The comparison between Newman and Robinson is, perhaps, not apt, since they are radically different social types. Newman is an American millionaire and Robinson an impoverished English bookbinder, but Hyacinth demonstrates the general direction in which James was traveling in describing the mind being operated upon. This is Hyacinth's consciousness after he has begun his apprenticeship as a bookmaker:

> For this unfortunate but remarkably-organized youth every displeasure or gratification of the visual sense coloured his whole mind, and though he lived in Pentonville and worked in Soho, though he was poor and obscure and cramped and full of unattainable desires, nothing in life had such an interest or such a price for him as his impressions and reflexions. They came from everything he touched, they made him vibrate, kept him thrilled and throbbing, for most of his waking consciousness, and they constituted as yet the principal events and stages of his career. (V 159).

As the book goes on, Hyacinth's mind begins to get dramatized, in the late manner, and the metaphors of this dramatization begin to dazzle in the late manner. When he returns, dubiously, to his work, after a sojourn on the continent, 'He gave a little private groan of relief when he discovered that he still liked his work and that the thriving swarm of his ideas in the matters of order and books returned to him. They came in still brighter, more suggestive form, and he had the satisfaction of feeling that his taste had improved . . . ' (VI 155). Still later the process begins to sound the organ-note:

> The influence of his permeating London had closed over him again; Paris and Milan and Venice had shimmered away into reminiscence and picture;

and as the great city which was most his lay around him under her pall like an immeasurable breathing monster he felt with vague excitement, as he had felt before, only now with more knowledge, that it was the richest expression of the life of man. His horizon had been immensely widened, but it was filled again by the expanse that sent dim night-gleams and strange, blurred reflexions and emanations into a sky without stars. He suspended, so to say, his small sensibility in the midst of it, to quiver there with joy and hope and ambition as well as with the effort of renunciation. (VI 266).

To move now to *The Golden Bowl* and Maggie Verver *not* having an experience, in a famous metaphor (she is speculating upon her problem, an unfaithful husband and a faithless friend):

> She might fairly, as she watched them, have missed it as a lost thing; have yearned for it, for the straight vindictive view, the rights of resentment, the rages of jealousy, the protests of passion, as for something she had been cheated of not least: a range of feelings which for many women would have meant so much, but which for *her* husband's wife, for her father's daughter, figured nothing nearer to experience than a wild eastern caravan, looming into view with crude colours in the sun, fierce pipes in the air, high spears against the sky, all a thrill, a natural joy to mingle with, but turning off short before it reached her and plunging into other defiles. (XXXIV 236–7).

And, as *The Golden Bowl* progresses towards its climax, the images become successively more savage; thus before one of the great showdowns with her husband's mistress Maggie is shown walking on the terrace: 'The hour was moonless and starless and the air heavy and still – which was why, in her evening dress, she need feel no chill and could get away, in the outer darkness, from that provocation of opportunity which had assaulted her, within, on her sofa, as a beast might have leaped at her throat' (XXIV 235). Or she compares herself to 'the night-watcher in a beast-haunted land who has no more means for fire' (XXIV 299–300).

These three illustrations, chosen, naturally, to prove my point, but not misrepresentative of the general development of James' style, point up the difference between incoming impressions in the early and late novels: formerly they are conventionally imaged; latterly they actually assault, and thus give the effect to the reader of 'depth'. The purest expression of all this is probably in 'The Beast in the Jungle', a late nouvelle, in which experience is pictured as a crouching beast ready to spring. Ironically enough, the beast never springs, until it is too late, on the protagonist, John Marcher, who was 'the man of his time, *the* man, to whom nothing on earth was to have happened' (XVII 125). Marcher's personal tragedy is that he does not take the love offered to him by a woman whom, he realizes too late, he loved. His metaphysical tragedy, in the context of the idea of the tabula rasa, is that since nothing has ever happened to him the blank remains a blank and thus has no meaning; so Marcher, in a sense, does not even exist as a personality, and his impression on the reader suggests precisely that. Of course not all impressions in the late novels leap like beasts at their receptor. Sometimes they caress, as in the great water metaphors when, in stasis, characters sink into a massive sea. The important thing to remember is that they are invariably physically imaged; and thus practically all feelings, love, or hate, or fear, are pictured as a series of sense impressions coming in upon the consciousness.

The idea that the mind is a blank upon which experience writes is certainly not peculiar to British empiricism – it can be found in Aristotle – nor is James the only novelist ever to conceive of experience in these terms. But the stress which empirical philosophy puts on sense impressions, pure and simple, and on the initial blankness and passivity of the mind is unique, and James also is unique in carrying this idea to its logical extreme and poeticizing it in such terms of splendor. As might be expected, James had the defects of his virtues. Gide, among many, has pointed out that the James characters have no subconscious and 'seem never to exist except in the functioning of their intellects'.[9] Thus a Strether compared to a Raskolnikov or a Dedalus may seem thin, and of course he is, the difference between James and such novelists as Dostoevski and Joyce being the distance between the tabula rasa and Freud's subconscious. Against the 'swarm of ideas' that 'return' to Hyacinth Robinson, one might juxtapose the following quotation from Dostoevski's *The Possessed*: it is Lyamshin cogitating: 'A swarm of ideas flared up in Lyamshin's crafty mind like a shower of fireworks.'[10]

But it is significant that James was reaching out, near the end of his career, to a more complex view of personality. In 'The Jolly Corner' the protagonist develops an alter ego and in *The Sense of the Past* he exchanges personalities with a dead ancestor. Edmund Wilson has pointed out that Dickens was working toward the same thing late in his career, especially in the unfinished *The Mystery of Edwin Drood*.[11] Wilson concluded that social pressures prevented Dickens from ever exploring personality in the uncompromising terms of Dostoevski. In James' case, I should say that he would have been prevented the ultimate realization of a depth psychology by his own assumptions about consciousness. So in 'The Jolly Corner' and in *The Sense of the Past* the alter egos have to be actually objectified and placed in other bodies, rather than erupting from within the protagonist himself, as in Freudian psychology. James, like all major artists, carried his medium as far as it would go, and, in the final climacteric, was stretching it to express the inexpressible. It was as if James from the single beginnings of conventional narrative in the early works had gradually sunk deeper and deeper into the personality, empirically conceived. In full maturity he was able to invest this concept with great splendor, as for example in the description of the mind of Frank Saltram in 'The Coxon Fund': 'The sight of a great, suspended, swinging crystal, – huge, lucid, lustrous, a block of light – flashing back every impression of life and every possibility of thought' (xv 300). But James had sounded the limits, and in his late career he seemed to be trying to go beyond. And for the reader there is often in the very late novels, as in *The Sense of the Past*, a sense of strain, as if the medium were being stretched to the point of cracking and were constantly threatening to double back and parody itself. But despite these attempts the consciousness of the characters and their reaction to experience remained the tabula rasa being bombarded by sense impressions and passively reworking these into knowledge.

The most effective demonstration of this is contained in the nouvelle 'In the Cage'. The protagonist, a telegraph-office operator, works, literally, in a cage. She is from the lower classes, but James is careful to endow her with a sensibility superior to her kind, and she is another perfect observer and a superior recording apparatus. Infernally sensitive and infernally acute, she lives a vicarious existence, sitting passively in her cage, in the lives of telegram-senders, most of whom are from the upper classes and are carrying on adulterous intrigues. Outside the cage she has a life of her own, a family and a fiancé, but James makes it clear that her real life goes on in the cage: 'She had surrendered herself moreover of late to a certain expansion of her consciousness; something that seemed perhaps vulgarly accounted for by the fact that, as the blast of the season roared louder and the waves of fashion passed their spray further over the counter, there were more impressions to be gathered and really'– for it came to that – more *life to be led*' [italics mine] (XI 373-4). Later on James describes how these impressions are transmuted into knowledge. The girl is visiting a sea resort with her fiancé, a superior grocer; they go to hear a band concert and the forthright grocer, Mr Mudge, wishes to mingle with the crowd and approach the bandstand, but she, and this is significant, prefers the periphery: 'the far end, away from the band and the crowd; as to which she had frequent differences with her friend, who reminded her often that they could have only in the thick of it the sense of the money they were getting back. That had little effect on her, for she got back her money by seeing many things, the things of the past year, fall together and connect themselves, undergo the happy relegation that transforms melancholy and misery, passion and effort, into experience and knowledge' (XI 452).

Turning from the treatment of individual minds and the question of style to the treatment of individual relationships and the question of structure, one finds, again, that the technique of the late works is an attempt to dramatize most effectively the essential ambiguity of these relationships within which the various characters are, paradoxically, both intimately intertwined and utterly isolated, and where each individual can know another only from moment to moment and then never completely.

This tenuous quality of character relationships is most obviously illustrated by James' practice of sometimes leaving this story hanging in air, with no absolute conclusion. At the end of *The Portrait of a Lady* we know that Isabel is to return to her villainous husband, but at the same time Henrietta Stackpole tells Caspar Goodwood that his cause is not wholly lost. This, however, is of small comfort to Goodwood. The reader does not know for sure whether Henrietta is right or wrong, or whether Caspar will resign or continue his pursuit. Conscious of his own assumptions here, James wrote, in the preface to *Roderick Hudson*: 'Really, universally, relations stop nowhere, and the exquisite problem of the artist is eternally but to draw, by a geometry of his own, the circle within which they shall happily *appear* to do so' (I vii). But even the geometry of the artist is not capable of always drawing a closed circle, as the ambiguous conclusion of *The Wings of the Dove* attests. The ambiguity, to be sure, is not total. When Kate Croy says to Merton Densher in the last sentence of the book: 'We shall never be again as we were!' the reader realizes that their relationship has been altered by the tragic death of Milly Theale, whom they had both betrayed, and that, in some way, her superior morality has mitigated their own amorality. But the exact nature of the change is never described, nor is their future relationship specified. The circle, in other words, is left open. Theoretically, as James himself realized when he used the word 'universal' in connection with human relations, his novels should not have been finite, for relationships always change and never end, barring death, and thus never reach a definite and immutable 'rapport'. Joyce said that, ideally, he should have liked to compress everything he had to say into one word which would then be his total work; working in just the opposite direction, toward infinite linguistic expansion, James, in an ideal situation, should have taken a single set of relationships and have gone on writing about them eternally. In the late novels, according to many readers, he almost achieves this end.

Even when the circle is closed, as it often is, there is generally a margin of obscurity in character motivation in the story itself. One could easily go insane trying to ascertain what has happened in *The Sacred Fount*. To a lesser degree the same is true of most of the later works, where the characters are, in the last analysis, fundamentally isolated from and ignorant of one another. The isolation is symbolized most tragically by the betrayal theme, the 'Judas complex', that runs through all the works, early and late, but which is usually presented most starkly in the late period. Thus Milly Theale, dying, betrayed and alone in a Venetian palace, turns her face to the wall and dies, and Maggie Verver utterly isolated because of her ignorance of life and of the real nature of the people around her, faces for the first time the fact of evil in human relationships.

Nor is it merely coincidental that so many characters in James' novels are solitaries with only the vaguest of antecedents. Even the forthright Newman is given a past of hints and shades, and he, evidently, has no ties or connections. In what I regard as James' masterpiece, *The Wings of the Dove*, each of the principals is carefully introduced as an isolated figure. Kate Croy, to be sure, has friends and family, but on none can she rely. Living in her aunt's house, she is described, in battle terms, as one besieged by her 'lioness' aunt (XIX 29–30). Densher, her lover-to-be, appears upon the scene, a man of rootless bringing-up, vaguely continental. He is a bachelor, having neither family nor friends. Milly Theale is presented as being the very last of a once great family, and she, like Densher, is utterly alone. Her companion and confidante, Susan

Stringer, is a widow and a solitary. A sense of fluidity and isolation
pervades the whole book. Kate and Merton in conversation are
described as occupying a 'small floating island' (XIX 66). Milly is a great
steamer drawing the little boat of Susan Stringer in her wake (XIX 113).
In essence, the novel is set in motion as these more or less isolated
mental substances come together to become interlaced about their
moral problem.

Emphasizing the isolation of the Jamesian characters is their essential
ignorance of one another. This is conveyed structurally by the device of
the point of view, whereby, even if the point of view shifts from one
person to another, no one person is ever in complete possession of all
the facts. The reader may perhaps be able to add everything up, but
not necessarily so, as the conclusion to *The Wings of the Dove* attests.
Very often the late works tend to become, structurally speaking, essays
on the frailty of human intercourse. The movement of *The Golden
Bowl* progresses as various characters make sallies into the vast unknown
which is themselves and their mutual situation. It takes a whole book
for Maggie to realize that her husband and her father's wife are lovers,
another book for her to convey her knowledge of this to all the
principals and bring on the denouement. Within this dimly lit circle,
there are various greater or lesser degrees of ignorance. Mrs Assingham,
the observer, knows more than Maggie at first, but does not know that
Maggie will ultimately rise to the problem and settle it. Charlotte, the
friend, finally realizes that Maggie knows of the situation, but under-
estimates her intelligence and assumes that Maggie can do nothing.
Maggie thinks that her father does not know, but he does and, in turn,
thinks she does not. This stops all real communication between them,
as they protect one another's supposed ignorance. Finally, at the end,
by an esoteric sign – nothing is every explicitly said – they convey
their mutual knowledge to one another, as the novel ends.

Yet, despite their isolation and their ignorance of one another, the
characters of these novels are subtly and intimately interconnected in
an eternally fluid relationship, coming together to shoot impressions at
one another, drifting apart to rework the impressions into knowledge
and coming together again in a different relationship. This sense of
fluidity is often carried over into the physical action itself, and characters
are fluidly attracted and repelled. In *The Golden Bowl* Charlotte is seen
by Maggie as a free-ranging and feline animal: 'The splendid shining
supple creature was out of the cage, was at large; and the question now

almost grotesquely rose of whether she mightn't by some art, just where she was and before she could go further, be hemmed in and secured' (XXIV 239). Later the pair slowly drift together:

> Charlotte, extending her search, appeared now to define herself vaguely in the distance; of this after an instant the Princess was sure, though the darkness was thick, for the projected clearness of the smoking-room windows had presently contributed its help. Her friend came slowly into that circle having also, for herself, by this time, not indistinguishably discovered that Maggie was on the terrace. Maggie, from the end, saw her stop before one of the windows to look at the group within, and then saw her come nearer and pause again, still with a considerable length of the place between them. (XXIV 241)

Needless to say, several pages pass before the slow envelopment is completed and the two confront one another.

The fluid nature of the action, combined with the passivity of the characters, almost gives one the feeling that the only objective and solid entity is the problem itself, whatever it may be, and that it, in a sense, dominates the action. Stransom of *The Altar of the Dead* is described as moving 'round and round' a problem 'in widening circles' (XVII 44) and, in all the late works, the characters continually circle situations which assail them with impressions. The situation or the problem is always themselves and the complex of their relations, but it invariably seems to take on a life of its own. In *The Golden Bowl* the situation is actually symbolized by the bowl with the concealed flaw. So too, in most of the late works, one has the feeling that in the center of the room, dominating all, as it shoots its impressions out to the various mental substances who drift around it, repulsed or attracted, is the sole objective entity, the problem itself. It is somewhat like Locke's primary quality, whose nature the observer arrives at by a succession of sense impressions or secondary qualities.

In short, the action in a late James novel is inherently anarchic, for isolation of the individual and ambiguity in human relationships are but the logical and final outcome of James' fundamental psychological premise, Locke's free-wheeling mental substance. Significantly, although perhaps quite coincidentally, James chose the anarchist movement to portray in his political novel *The Princess Casamassima*, and in his personal life, as his secretary Theodora Bosanquet tells us, he became, in the late years, more and more of an absolute individualist: 'His Utopia was an anarchy where nobody would be responsible for any

human being but only for his own civilized character.'[12] Correspondingly, in the mature technique, personal relationships became more
fluid and ambiguous, understanding of one character by another more
difficult and problematical, and the conscious mental process of each
individual, now thrown back completely on himself or herself, more
spectacular and vivid. The 'late manner' seems to have been an elaborate
subterfuge, sometimes conceived with mathematical precision, as in
The Golden Bowl, to impose order on his human situation which was
continually threatening to dissolve into atomism.

Taken in this sense James' novels are prophetic, an esthetic counterpart to so many American political and social institutions. To state it
negatively, the anarchic individualism, the lack of close and rich social
relationships, the absence of great depth in the version of life portrayed
by the James novels are precisely the same traits so many foreign
visitors have mentioned, disparagingly, in their assessments of American
culture. Indeed many of the social observations of foreign visitors,
especially in the nineteenth century, might well be read as literary
criticism of James. James himself, especially in the famous *Hawthorne*
passage where he laments the insubstantiality of American society and,
by implication, apostrophizes England, was one of the most severe
critics of his native land and its atomistic culture, but, in a deeper sense
than even he realized, he never left home.

These speculations on the relationship between the logical and metaphorical statement of the same complex of ideas are not meant to turn
their subject into a philosopher, but to demonstrate the fact that a completely functional artistic technique is, in a sense, conceptual. In James'
case it is not at all extravagant to say that his true meaning *is* his technique, which has a grammar, rhetoric, and logic beyond and above the
'subject-matter' of his novels and stories.

A concluding reference to philosophy is pertinent. According to
Susanne Langer[13] a habit of thought reveals itself not by the answers it
gives but by the questions it asks. A question is merely an ambiguous
proposition for which a certain number of answers, or completions, is
possible, and to ask a question is to make an assumption. For example,
when the pre-Socratics speculated about the nature of matter, they
necessarily made the basic assumption that there was such a thing as
matter. This mode of asking questions or handling problems is the basic
determinant of a system of thought and is called its 'technique'.

Applying this line of reasoning, by analogy, to literary criticism and to the familiar problem of the relationship between form and content, one might say that James' basic habit of thought was his complex of assumptions about the nature of human consciousness, the way it operated, and the manner in which various entities of consciousness acted upon and were related to one another. In his long career James handled many themes: the struggle of the individual for self-fulfillment and moral certitude, the impact of Europe upon the visiting American, the love between men and women, the plight of the artist, and so on. But he always asked his 'questions' and thus gave his 'answers' in a certain manner – roughly in terms of the assumptions of empiricism concerning personality and experience and their interaction – and this was his 'technique'.

NOTES

1. Austin Warren, *Rage for Order* (Chicago, 1948) pp. 146–61. Warren speaks of the basic ingredients of the late works, dramatic dialogue and highly metaphorical descriptions of states of consciousness, as 'dialectic' and 'myth', respectively.

2. Quentin Anderson, 'Henry James and the New Jerusalem', in *Kenyon Review*, VIII (1946) 515–66. There is neither space nor occasion for a summary of this complex essay. For the minuscule sketch of recent James criticism being given here two quotations will suffice: 'Since the elder James was a theologian and a moralist, it is conceivable that he stood in the same relation to the novelist as Aquinas does to Dante or Kierkegaard to Kafka' (p. 515); 'In the end James is not a tragic poet but the poet of his father's theodicy' (p. 565). Anderson's theories are further elaborated in 'The Two Henry Jameses', in *Scrutiny*, XIV (1947) 242–51, and 'Henry James, His Symbolism and His Critics', in *Scrutiny*, XV (1947) 12–19.

3. Henry Bamford Parkes, 'The James Brothers', in *Sewanee Review*, LVI (1948) 323–8. Parkes says, e.g., that the use by Henry James of a scrupulously observed 'point of view' rather than the customary novelistic convention of authorial omniscience was the artistic counterpart of the pragmatist theory that no truth has absolute validity and, hence, everything is relative to the observer.

4. 'The meaning of his [James's] works has been obscured by its subject matter . . . the deeper significance of his work is to be found not in its subject matter but in its mode of construction' (ibid. p. 326).

5. 'The Great Mr Locke: America's Philosopher, 1783–1861', in *Huntington Library Bulletin*, no. 11 (April 1937) pp. 107–51.

6. 'The Social Significance of Our Institutions', in *American Philosophic Addresses*, ed. Joseph T. Blair (New York, 1946) p. 248.

7. The exposition of the ultimate implications of Locke's doctrines is based generally upon A. N. Whitehead's familiar thesis that Locke effected a 'bifurcation of nature', which broke up any organic relationship between man and nature and man and man, and made each individual an isolated mental substance. I am indebted especially to the detailed working out of this thesis by F. S. C. Northrup, *The Meeting of East and West* (New York, 1947) pp. 80–111.

8. *The Novels and Tales of Henry James* (New York, 1907) II 3–4. Hereafter all references to James will be given in this edition.

9. 'Henry James', in *Yale Review*, XIX (Spring 1930) 641.
10. *The Possessed*, trans. Constance Garnett (New York, 1913) p. 549.
11. *The Wound and the Bow* (New York, 1947) p. 99.
12. *Henry James at Work* (1924) p. 33.
13. *Philosophy in a New Key* (New York, 1948) pp. 1–2.

MAURICE BEEBE

The Turned Back of Henry James
(1954)

In Henry James's most characteristic works the detached observer is
both a technical device and a point of view towards life. Impressions
of exterior reality are fused through a center of consciousness, as
through Coleridge's 'secondary Imagination', to emerge more vitalized
and unified than the 'fixed and dead' elements of real life. This 'lesson
of the Master' became more pervasive as James neared the end of his
career: the much-disputed later style, for example, is the necessary
medium of a highly individualized, subjective consciousness. If the
critic prefers the separateness of the fixed and dead elements, as the
naturalist does, or sees them through his own awareness of spiritual
unity, as Van Wyck Brooks does, he is perhaps justified in saying that
in direct ratio to James's withdrawal from life, he declined as an artist.
But if the critic believes that James's later works are his best, he is
committed to the view that James's art improved as he became more
of a detached consciousness. Most readers, convinced that art depends
on life, are reluctant to concede that alienation can be a cause of artistic
greatness. We are not, however, bound to either sympathetic acceptance or hostile rejection of James's aloofness from life. Several compromise interpretations are possible.

The first compromise, widely accepted, admits that alienation is a
bad thing and that James was a good artist, and tries to reconcile the
paradox by finding that James could not help being aloof from much
normal activity because he was physically or psychologically, or both,
incapable of living a full life. Because his alienation was not willfully
perverse, it may be forgiven him. To accept this compromise is to
assume that the peculiar vision of James was but a form of neurosis and
that his art, good as it may have been, was but a makeshift substitute
for life.

The source of this interpretation is a long and difficult passage in

James's *Notes of a Son and Brother* (1914), in which he describes the injuring of his back while working a fire pump during the early days of the Civil War. This 'horrid even if an obscure hurt' prevented him from enlisting in the Northern Army. The first critic to find in this occurrence the key to James's later emphasis on detachment was Rebecca West:

> In working the fire-engine he sustained an injury so serious that he could never hope to share the Northern glory, that there were before him years of continuous pain and weakness, that ultimately he formed a curious and on the whole mischievous conception of himself. . . . He worked out a scheme of existence . . . in which the one who stood aside and felt rather than acted acquired a mystic value, a spiritual supremacy, which . . . would be rubbed off by participating in action. It was, therefore, with defiant industry, with the intention of proving that such as he was he had his peculiar worth, that he set to work to become a writer.

The best-known later statement of this art-as-compensation theory is an essay published in 1943 by the psychiatrist Saul Rosenzweig. 'The Ghost of Henry James: A Study in Thematic Apperception' first appeared in *Character and Personality*, was reprinted in 1944 in the *Partisan Review*, and was summarized the following year by Clifton Fadiman in his edition of James's short stories, a book often credited with playing an instrumental role in the James revival. The essay has thus received a wide distribution, and its influence on criticism of James has been extensive. Both F. W. Dupee and Leon Edel, authoritative James biographers, reveal in their work the influence of Dr Rozenzweig's essay, though they modify and adapt it to their own interpretations. Because, with the possible exception of Van Wyck Brooks's hostile account in *The Pilgrimage of Henry James* (1925), it is the only attempt to treat analytically the question of James's alienation, it must be taken into account before any new interpretation may be advanced.

The second compromise – the premise with which Dr Rosenzweig's theory may be disputed – is based upon the idea that every great artist as an artist is detached from society. There is an inevitable split between the social being and the creative personality, between the artist in society and the artist at work. Just as no art is entirely independent of life, no artist can entirely deny certain human functions. Yet the creative process is essentially subjective, and if the artist is to be more than a mirror of life or a passive receptor of an exterior 'inspiration', he must, in the act of creating, detach himself from life in order to see it clearly and wholly and to give his work the stamp of individuality. Detachment is an innate characteristic of the creative process in the non-naturalistic artist. The individual may be both a social, carnal being and an asocial, asexual artist.

This is the theory of the artist which James himself held: saturation in life and detachment from life are both required by the artist. In 1888 he wrote to his brother, William, 'The great thing is to be *saturated* with something – that is, in one way or another, with life; and I chose the form of my saturation.' In 1914 James praised in his essay 'The New Novel' a group of younger English writers because they 'come together under our so convenient measure of value by *saturation* . . . a closer notation, a sharper specification of the signs of life, of consciousness, of the human scene and the human subject in general, than the three or four generations before us had been at all moved to insist on'. But he also criticized this group for submerging too deeply and for failing to arrange their materials with conscientious artistry. In his biography of William Wetmore Story, James accused the sculptor of too much saturation; he lacked 'the proper detachment for full appreciation'. One of the 'new novelists' was H. G. Wells, to whom James wrote in 1911: 'There is, to my vision, no authentic, and no really interesting and no *beautiful* report of things on the novelist's, the painter's part unless a particular detachment has operated, unless the great stewpot or crucible of the imagination, of the observant and recording and interpreting mind in short, has intervened and played its part.' It is in this sense that his statement 'It is Art that *makes* life' in a later letter to Wells must be interpreted. For James, the artist is an observer – 'The novelist is a particular window, absolutely, and of worth in so far as he is one' – but what is observed is as important as the observing. Observation is pure and clear only when it is detached and disinterested.

James illustrated this idea frequently in the more than fifty stories in which writers and painters appear. Taken as a group and seen from without, the artists in James's world are almost indistinguishable from the non-artists. They are polite, clean, witty, decent, and as much at home over teacups as at their desks or easels. Many of them can say with Felix of *The Europeans* (1878), 'I have been a Bohemian – yes; but in Bohemia I always passed for a gentleman.' For James, the artistic temperament was not something visible, but a secret thing, to be guarded jealously and revealed only through the production of art.

The ideal artist in James's fiction is the sculptor Gloriani, a character who appears in several different works. In *Roderick Hudson* (1875), Gloriani is one of the several antitheses to the rhapsodical Roderick, for whom art is 'a kind of safe somnambulism'. Gloriani, unlike Roderick, does not make the mistake of confusing his social being with his genius. He lives fully – 'when sometimes he received you at his lodging he introduced you to a lady without art of utterance whom he called Madame Gloriani – which she was not' – and also produces work of significance, perhaps because he 'had a definite, practical scheme of art, and he knew at least what he meant'. He felt that 'the thing to aim at is the expressive and the way to reach it is by ingenuity' and that the prime duty of a work of art is 'to amuse, to puzzle, to fascinate, to report on a real aesthetic adventure'. Since an aesthetic adventure is a matter of vision, this last statement prepares the reader for Gloriani's function in *The Ambassadors*, where, now an eminent and acknowledged master, he becomes a representative of the goal sought by Lambert Strether:

> With his genius in his eyes, his manners on his lips, his long career behind him, and his honours and rewards all round, the great artist, in the course of a single sustained look and a few words of delight at receiving him, affected our friends as a dazzling prodigy of type . . . he was to recall in especial, as the penetrating radiance, as the communication of the illustrious spirit itself, the manner in which . . . he was held by the sculptor's eyes. He wasn't soon to forget them, was to think of them, all unconscious, unintending, preoccupied though they were, as the source of the deepest intellectual sounding to which he had ever been exposed. He was in fact quite to cherish his vision of it, to play with it in idle hours; only speaking of it to no one and quite aware that he couldn't have spoken without appearing to talk nonsense. Was what it had told him or what it had asked him the greater of the mysteries? Was it the most special flare, unequalled, supreme, of the aesthetic torch, lighting that wondrous world for ever, or was it above all the long straight shaft sunk by a personal acuteness that life had seasoned to steel?

Occurring as it does in the emotional center of the novel, the 'germ' from which James is said to have derived his idea for the story, this passage takes on added significance. Gloriani is made to serve as the crowning symbol of the kind of consciousness which Strether tries to attain. Strether discovers in himself 'the oddity of a double consciousness. There was detachment in his zeal and curiosity in his indifference.'

James wrote in his Preface, 'The business of my tale and the march of my action, not to say the precious moral of everything, is just my demonstration of this process of vision.'

Vision or consciousness, Strether comes to realize, is pure only when it is disinterested, when it is motivated by the desire for knowing rather than getting. It is in this way that a certain degree of detachment is inherent in the artistic consciousness. Ralph Pendrel of *The Sense of the Past* (1917) gains a 'second consciousness', but as long as he is immersed in his strange adventure he cannot practice his art: 'Detachment and selection, prime aids of the artist, were the sacred sparenesses menaced by a rank growth of material.' Talent, detachment, and vision are, for James, the basic requirements of the genuine artist. If the artist has these, he may live as he pleases as long as he does not become so saturated in life that, like Roderick Hudson, Frank Saltram of 'The Coxon Fund' (1894), or Neil Paraday of 'The Death of the Lion' (1894), he can no longer produce art.

The exterior trappings of the artist, James felt, are unimportant, because a man is an artist – that is, he creates art – only when he leaves behind him the world of dress and manners to reside in a 'Great Good Place' of his own. James made this the theme of several stories – from the ironic 'The Sweetheart of M. Briseux' (1873) and the parable on the artistic temperament 'Benvolio' (1875) to the stories of the nineties, which R. P. Blackmur has grouped under the heading 'the country of the blue'. A certain group of stories is particularly significant in view of the interpretation of James's detachment advanced by Rebecca West and Saul Rosenzweig. In his Preface to *The Tragic Muse* (1890) James apologized for his failure to make his hero, Nick Dormer, thoroughly convincing as a practising artist:

> It strikes me, alas, that he is not quite so interesting as he was fondly intended to be, and this in spite of the multiplication, within the picture, of his pains and penalties; so that while I turn this slight anomaly over I come upon a reason that affects me as singularly charming and touching. . . . Any representation of the artist *in triumph* must be flat in proportion as it really sticks to its subject – it can only smuggle in relief and variety. For, to put the matter in an image, all we then – in his triumph – see of the charm-compeller is the back he turns to us as he bends over his work.

This passage was written in 1906 or 1907. In at least three of his earlier stories of artists are examples of the turned-back image. Although this may be mere coincidence rather than deliberate symbolism or compulsive association, the several appearances of the image are illustrative of a theme supported by a number of James's writings.

The image appears first in *Roderick Hudson*. The considerable genius of the young sculptor is negated by his failure to secure detachment. When Roderick falls in love with Christina Light and substitutes for artistic creation the pleasures of social intercourse – rather than, like Gloriani, keeping his art distinct from love and society – not only his productivity but even his ability as an artist begins to decline. Shortly before his tragic death, Roderick and his friend Rowland Mallett see a figure on a distant hill which 'in relief against the crimson screen of the western sky . . . looked gigantic'. The figure turns out to be their friend, Sam Singleton, a painter of miniature landscapes and, the antithesis of Roderick in temperament, a patient and humble plodder not given to talk of his art. The rather unsubtle symbolism of the giant on the horizon suggests the moral of the contrast between the two artists:

> Roderick had said to Rowland at first that their friend reminded him of some curious insect with a remarkable instinct in its antennae; but as the days went by it was apparent that the modest landscapist's successful method grew to have an oppressive meaning for him. It pointed a moral, and Roderick used to sit and consider the moral as he saw it figured in the little painter's bent back, on the hot hillsides, protruding from beneath a white umbrella.

The moral, it should be clear, is just the bent back.

James's theory of the split consciousness and personality of the creative artist, apparent in his fiction as early as 1873, was verified by his meetings with living artists. Tennyson in particular, whom he met in 1875, taught him the 'true nature of the Bard'. Describing Tennyson's un-Tennysonian reading of *In Memoriam*, James wrote in *The Middle Years* (1917):

> My critical reaction hadn't in the least invalidated out great man's being a Bard – it had only settled to my perception as not before what a Bard might and mightn't be. The character was just a rigid idiosyncrasy, to which everything in the main conformed, but which supplied nothing outside of itself, and which above all was not intellectually wasteful or heterogeneous, conscious as it could only be of its intrinsic breadth and weight. On two or three occasions of the after-time I was to hear Browning read out certain of his finest pages, and this exactly with all the exhibition of

point and authority, the expressive particularisation, so to speak, that I had missed on the part of the Laureate; an observation through which the author of *Men and Women* appeared, in spite of the beauty and force of his demonstration, as little as possible a Bard.

Nonetheless, Browning was a bard. Around this paradox James wrote in 1892 'The Private Life', in which Clare Vawdrey, James said in his notebooks, stands for 'the idea of . . . R. B.'. The narrator is puzzled by Vawdrey, whose 'talk suggested the reporter contrasted with the bard'. Actually, there are two Vawdreys: one is the disappointingly mundane gentleman of the social scene, while the other is the true bard. 'One goes out, the other stays at home,' says the narrator. 'One is the genius, the other's the bourgeois; and it's only the bourgeois whom we personally know.' The narrator discovers the split in Vawdrey's character when, confident that the great man is downstairs, he enters the poet's room and discovers another person already there: 'His back was half turned to me, and he bent over the table in the attitude of writing, but I was conscious that I was in no sort of error about his identity.'

The turned-back image appears also in 'The Great Good Place' (1900), a more important fantasy on the 'private life' of the artist. George Dane is a celebrated author whose success has driven him beyond the conditions in which he can work. Harried and frustrated by the numerous invitations, requests, and obligations that accompany worldly recognition, he is in danger of submerging in life and losing his art in non-artistic distractions. One morning when Dane is yearning more than usual for a 'happy land' free of interruptions, a young writer whose book has impressed Dane arrives for breakfast. Almost immediately upon entering the room, the visitor guesses what Dane requires. 'I know what you want,' he tells his host: 'It exists – it exists.'

> He suddenly sprang up and went over to my study-table – sat down there as if to write my prescription or my passport. Then it was – at the mere sight of his back, which was turned to me – that I felt the spell work. I simply sat and watched him with the queerest deepest sweetest sense in the world – the sense of an ache that has stopped. All life was lifted; I myself was somehow off the ground. He was already where I had been. . . . He was already me.

Falling asleep while his counterpart sets to work, Dane finds himself in the Great Good Place. Granted the setting of controlled form and arrangement, the complete freedom from distractions, and the aesthetic consciousness of the initiate, the result of a brief stay in the Great Good Place is a return of what Dane calls 'the vision and the faculty divine'.

Four appearances of the turned-back image do not, of course, prove that James used it always deliberately, but it seems significant that the four turned backs represent, in each instance, the same thing. To repeat, it matters not what the artist does in the world, how he dresses, what company he frequents; for when he creates, he inevitably withdraws to a private realm. The detachment of the artist is rooted in an innate consciousness that transforms and vitalizes the objects of normal perception, that actually '*makes* life'. Thus James was able to use the turned back of the artist to symbolize 'the artist *in triumph*'.

A failure to recognize this dual personality in the artist is the basic weakness of the West–Rosenzweig theory. For Saul Rosenzweig, the detachment of James, as it manifested itself in both his life and his fiction, was but a 'fantasied escape from guilt' resulting from his failure to participate in the 'real social world'. Dr Rosenzweig's interpretation is neatly and ingeniously presented and provides a convenient set of materials to reanalyze in the light of the preceding premises on the nature of the artist's detachment as something rooted in an innate 'double consciousness' for which no artist need apologize.

Dr Rosenzweig improves Miss West's account by making the effect of James's injury seem less abrupt. A sense of inferiority, he says, afflicted James from his earliest days and, combined with an Oedipus complex, provided 'fertile soil' for the 'particular infirmity'. Occurring at a time when men were needed, 'the injury even more surely constituted a proof of his powerlessness and crystallized a sense of impotence from which he never recovered'. Associated with this sense of impotence was a 'possible suspicion of unconscious malingering', and 'introversion in which both aggression and sexuality were repressed was now established as a *modus vivendi*'. The immediate effect of the injury, which had a greater psychological than physical impact, was 'a constructive step forward. In the months which followed, James turned to the art of fiction.' For a decade the writing of 'fantasy' was adequate as a means of adjustment, but it yielded to physical withdrawal when 'as if to materialize the "death", James actually left America to take up residence in England in 1875'. Although the repressed pattern of his life explains the increasing peculiarity of his writing – his avoidance of sexual passion and his overqualification of style – it was not until the early 1890s that there occurred 'a return of the repressed'. The ghosts in the supernatural stories of this period represent an 'apotheosis of the unlived life'. The story has a happy ending.

> This fictional attempt to face again the early unsolved problems was followed compulsively by an actual revisit to America. As the criminal returns to the scene of his crime, James now went back to the haunts of his catastrophe. But the neurotic repressions failed to yield, and a severe nervous depression that expressed his sense of defeat ensued.
>
> With the outbreak of World War I soon following, when he was already over seventy, came a final effort at solution – now not by sublimation in fiction, by escape or return, but in relationship to the real social world. It is not surprising that a note of overcompensation was present in these war activities, especially in the assumption of British citizenship, and his end was probably hastened by his profligate expenditure of energy. But in large measure he re-established contact with the realities of his environment by these acts and in the same degree he thus succeeded in laying the ghost of his unlived past before death overtook him.

It is difficult to disagree with certain aspects of this attractive theory. James's own account of his injury in *Notes of a Son and Brother* makes apparent that he felt a close association between his injury and the Civil War. It is probable that the injury was psychosomatic and that it may, to the extent that it made detachment an easier attitude to maintain, have had some effect upon his later career. But at least three of the major conclusions drawn from these premises seem to me untenable. First, the injury was not, as Miss West and Dr Rosenzweig both imply, the cause either of James's detachment or of his decision to become a writer. Second, the injury was followed not so much by regret as by relief, not so much by a sense of guilt as by a conviction of strength. Third, James never repudiated the attitude of detachment.

The weakest link in both Miss West's and Dr Rosenzweig's interpretation of the injury is their ignoring of the detachment inherent in the temperament of James before the injury. Although Dr Rosenzweig improves upon his predecessor by showing that the injury could not have been completely transformatory in effect, the inferiority complex which he discovers in the young James is an awkward explanation of what may be considered but the traditional sensitiveness of the potential artist. The small boy of *A Small Boy and Others* (1913) knew from the first that his primary role in life was that of the observer: 'I really believe I was already aware that one way of taking life was to go in for everything and everyone, which kept you abundantly occupied, and the other way was to be as occupied, quite as occupied, just with the sense and the image of it all, and on only a fifth of the actual immersion.' When the young James attended a stage performance of *Uncle Tom's Cabin*, he did not feel himself stirred to the kind of response one would expect of young Northerners in the days before the Civil War, but simply to 'ironic detachment . . . a great initiation . . . his first glimpse of that possibility of a "free play of mind" over a subject which was to throw him with force at a later stage of culture, when subjects had considerably multiplied, into the critical arms of Matthew Arnold'.

The young James, aloof and introspective of temperament, was more fortunate than most artists-to-be in that he had little family opposition to overcome. If alienation is synonymous with estrangement he was never alienated from his environment; the essence of his domestic environment was complete freedom, the absence of pressure; and he remained for life, as his brother, William, said, 'but a native of the James family, and [he] has no other country'. Henry James, Sr, himself detached from business, profession, the established churches, expedient morality, and active reform movements, was not likely to imbue his children with an appreciation of normal allegiances and aggressive activity.

Considering this singular family environment, it is difficult to understand Dr Rosenzweig's meaning when he says:

> The Oedipus situation of James included a highly individualistic father – a cripple – and a gifted sibling rival (William) who together dwarfed the boy in his eyes beyond hope of ever attaining their stature. A severe inferiority complex resulted. The problematic relationship to father and brother was solved submissively by a profound repression of aggressiveness.

Dr Rosenzweig's interpretation of this situation in the earlier pages of his essay is more confused. With what may be psychological, if not logical, consistency, he seems unable to decide whether James identified himself more closely with his father or with his mother. The implication of the passage above and of several references to Mrs James is that the son, who 'occupied the place of favorite in his mother's affections', became, in reaction against the aggressive (individualistic) father whom he could never hope to equal, passive and feminine. Yet, Dr Rosenzweig also establishes the 'identification' between father and son by suggesting that James's injury was in some sense a repetition of a more serious injury, under similar circumstances, that occurred to the father in childhood. Strangest of the links which Dr Rosenzweig finds between father and son is that the writings of both were neglected by the general public, thus suggesting that though Henry James, Sr, was strong (individualistic) he was also weak (ineffectual). This confusion in the most important part of Dr Rosenzweig's interpretation, its theoretical base, appears also in his analysis of 'The Story of a Year'. For the 'Oedipus situation' to work at all, James would have had to be an extrovert born into a family of introverts and eventually defeated by domestic pressures, whereas the absence of opposition and conflict suggests only an harmonious and innate adjustment to the ideal of family – the supremacy of *being* to *doing* – established by the elder Henry James.

Both Rebecca West and Saul Rosenzweig imply that James did not begin to write until after the injury, which probably occurred in 1861. In the first part of the long paragraph in *Notes of a Son and Brother* describing his injury, James says that even before the accident 'what I "wanted to want" to be was, all intimately, just *literary*'. Before 1861 he translated Alfred de Musset's *Lorenzaccio* and Mérimée's *La Vénus d'Ille*. On 28 May, 1860, Garth Wilkinson James wrote to Thomas Sergeant Perry, 'Harry has become an author I believe, for he keeps his door locked all day long, & a little while ago, I got a peep in his room, and saw some poetical looking manuscripts lying on the table, & himself looking in a most authorlike way.' James's insistence that detachment be an innate characteristic of the sensitive observer was not contradicted by his own life. He was essentially withdrawn before the accident of 1861, and he had already begun to write.

According to Dr Rosenzweig, the injury to James's back, associated in his mind with his failure to participate as a soldier in the Civil War, crystallized a sense of impotence and led to a lasting conviction of guilt. But if James was detached before the accident, it may be seen why, in the pressure of the strongest demand for aggressive activity he had yet experienced, the injury itself provided more relief than regret. At a time when conscription was less democratic, less compulsory than it has since become, it is unlikely that James, convinced as he was that his particular gifts of observation could be devoted to art (in its products, a socially worthwhile activity), would be overwhelmed by his failure to serve in the Army. In times of social emergency it would be difficult for even a Clare Vawdrey to exercise both of his selves; at such a time, the genius-half would be grateful for anything that would permit him to work at the expense of his bourgeois counterpart. The key to the Great Good Place is 'simply the cancelled list'. James's injury may well have performed the same function as the young man who arrived to help Dane escape from his social responsibilities. Like that young man, the injury took care of James's duty. It provided the excuse, the rationalization, for doing what he had always wanted to do.

Even if James did experience some psychological guilt at the time of the injury, it was not permanent, but temporary. In *Notes of a Son and Brother* he wrote of the general period of the Civil War:

> The case had to be in a peculiar degree, alas, that of living inwardly – like so many of my other cases; in a peculiar degree compared, that is, to the immense and prolonged outwardness, outwardness naturally at the very highest pitch, that was the general sign of the situation. To which I may add that my 'alas' just uttered is in the key altogether of my then current consciousness, and not in the least in that of my present appreciation of the same.

James's attendance at Harvard in 1862 helped to speed his recuperation from the psychological effects of the injury.

> I well recall, for that matter, how, when early in the autumn I had in fact become the queerest of forensic recruits, the bristling horde of my Law School comrades fairly produced the illusion of a mustered army. The Cambridge campus was tented field enough for a conscript starting so compromised; and I scarce say moreover how easily it let me down that when it came to the point one had still fine fierce young men, in great numbers for company, there being at the worst so many such who hadn't flown to arms. I was to find my fancy of the merely relative right in any way to figure, or even on such terms just to exist, I was to find it in due course quite drop from me as the Cambridge year played itself out, leaving me all aware that, full though the air might be of stiffer realities, one had yet a rare handful of one's own to face and deal with.

So complete was the cure that James, no longer requiring to compromise himself, was able to leave Harvard in 1863. At most, it had been but 'a modus vivendi workable for the time'. To Dr Rosenzweig, James's 'introversion was now established as a *modus vivendi*', implying a lasting condition, but it is James who uses the term correctly as a temporary arrangement pending settlement of a dispute. In later years he even forgot the date of his injury. Such evidence does not, of course, refute psychoanalytical interpretation, the gist of psychoanalysis being that we do not know the truth about ourselves. In that case, it is curious that James confessed so readily the association in his own mind between the injury and the war. That he had come to grips with it and that he looked back on it more triumphantly than guiltily as his art more and more justified his detachment can be shown only by the consistency with which before and after the injury he made an aesthetic faith of the detached consciousness.

One of James's first stories, 'The Story of a Year', is interpreted by Dr Rosenzweig as a symbolic representation of James's own 'passional death'. The main flaw in this reading of the story is the assumption that James is to be equated with John Ford. According to Dr Rosenzweig, the injury which Ford sustains in a Civil War battle relates him to James in that the wounds which kill Ford are not the product of a bullet so much as his submission to his psychological fate, James's own passional death. There are three aspects of this psychological fate: the unfaithfulness of Ford's fiancée, Elizabeth Crowe; his mother's opposition to the marriage; and his own self-doubt. But Elizabeth's defection does not appear to have a tragic effect upon Ford, who from the beginning insisted on her right to freedom – a point of view that is consistent with James's lifelong attitude towards love as something least defensible when most possessive and aggressive. In discussing the similarity between 'The Story of a Year' and 'Sir Edmund Orme' (1891), Dr Rosenzweig writes, 'There, it will be recalled, the subordination of John Ford to his mother's judgment eventually coincided with his own presentiment of death and made together for what could on the surface well be taken for a jilting by his sweetheart.' A few pages earlier, Dr Rosenzweig said that Ford 'refuses to accept his mother's judgment'. The second statement is true, and though it applies to the beginning of the story, there is no evidence that Ford later bows before his mother's low opinion of Elizabeth. As for the third factor in the 'psychological fate' of Ford, his self-doubt, I do not see that it exists. Ford remains stable and realistic-minded throughout the story. Even his early conversation with Elizabeth, in which he refers lightly to the possibility of his looking like a woman after he returns from battle, does not seem to me to reveal 'certain feminine elements in his personality to which his self-doubt and the anticipated injury may bear some relationship' so much as it testifies to his masculinity: it is as if he were saying to Elizabeth that should he be emasculated in battle they would be of little use to each other.

Actually, all the self-doubt in the story is Elizabeth's, and Dr Rosenzweig overlooks the fact that she, not Ford, is the central character of the story. The changes in Ford's health are necessary to this story of a young girl's inability to make up her mind. James's emphasis on the 'reverse of the picture' permits us to see into Elizabeth and to realize the depth of her indecision, whereas we see the soldierly Ford only from without and *in absentia*. 'The sufferer? It was hardly Jack, after all' is a thought which occurs to her in the moment of greatest uncertainty. In fact, if there is any autobiographical significance in the story, it is to be found in Elizabeth rather than in Ford. The key passage is the following:

> And now it was a relief to have responsibility denied her. Like most weak persons, she was glad to step out of the current of life, now that it had begun to quicken into action. In emergencies, such persons are tacitly counted out; and they as tacitly consent to the arrangement. Even to the sensitive spirit there is a certain meditative rapture in standing on the quiet shore (beside the ruminating cattle,) and watching the hurrying, eddying flood, which makes up for the loss of dignity.

The 'weak' and the 'sensitive' are not quite equal here, despite the 'ruminating cattle' (a curious echo, perhaps, of Hawthorne's *Blithedale Romance*). James was able to relate his own detachment from social responsibility to his innate sensitiveness, his vision. It should be noted that 'The Story of a Year' ends happily, if ironically. Elizabeth, for all the blow to her pride, gets what she really wanted – just as James did.

The later points in Dr Rosenzweig's interpretation depend upon the validity of his initial premises. Unfortunately, it is impossible here, for want of space, to take up in detail the various middle steps: James's expatriation from America in 1875 (for which sufficient reason is found in the social background of the post-Civil War period, the popularity of expatriation among American artists of this time, James's conviction that his art relied on a variety of 'impressions', and the success of his first English publications); the 'return of the repressed' in his supernatural tales of the nineties (Dr Rosenzweig identifies only two such stories – 'Sir Edmund Orme', in which, for reasons already given, the alleged relation to 'The Story of a Year' does not exist; and

'Owen Wingrave', not, as Dr Rosenzweig implies, a glorification of military courage, but an ironic attack on military aggression); the 'compulsive' return to America in 1904–5 (James came, he said, to replenish his supply of impressions, just as he had gone to Europe a quarter-century before; the only evidence that his trip was 'compulsive' is that he came despite the attempt of William to dissuade him); and his nervous breakdown of 1909 and 1910 (for which the failure of the New York Edition of his collected works, the sense of his outlived career, the serious illness of William, and the revival of disquieting memories of the theater are as credible 'causes' as the assumption that his breakdown was a delayed reaction to the 'failure' of the American visit five years before).

According to Dr Rosenzweig, James succeeded, if not in rectifying the past, in re-establishing contact with the 'realities of his environment' and thus repudiating the attitude of detachment. He was moving towards this solution, says Dr Rosenzweig, when he wrote 'The Jolly Corner' (1908).

> The ghost of Spencer Brydon is obviously his rejected self. Moreover, an injury – the two lost fingers – here stands in some relation to the fact that life was not lived or that, in other words, a kind of psychological death had occurred. Finally, the injury and the related incompletion have entailed an unfulfilled love. The hero has fled the heroine because he could not face himself. . . . As Henry James – or Ford – left America to reside abroad, Brydon returns to confront his former self. The identity of the characters is established by the injuries each suffered – James's 'obscure hurt', Ford's wounds, and Brydon's missing fingers. But like James during his visit in 1904–5, Brydon is obviously attempting to rectify the past – to face it again and test the answer previously given. There is thus represented here not merely a harking back with vain regrets but an obvious effort to overcome old barriers and pass beyond them.

Although one need not accept the idea that 'The Jolly Corner' is a complement to 'The Story of a Year' – Dr Rosenzweig even suggests that James, in compiling his collected works, deliberately wrote the later story as a substitute for the first, an hypothesis that overlooks the numerous other stories that James did not, or could not, include in the New York Edition – it is impossible to disagree with the contention that the story deals with an attempt to face the rejected self. That is the surface theme of the story. And James himself could scarcely deny that the story was suggested by his own return to America.

But does it deal with an attempt to 'rectify the past'? Brydon discovers in himself the presence of an alter ego, a split in personality which relates his story to 'The Private Life' or 'The Great Good Place'. Even the turned-back image appears:

> The house within the street, two bristling blocks westward, was already in course of reconstruction as a tall mass of flats; he had acceded, some time before, to overtures for this conversion – in which, now that it was going forward, it had been not the least of his astonishments to find himself able, on the spot, and though without a previous ounce of such experience, to participate with a certain intelligence, almost with a certain authority. He had lived with his back so turned to such concerns and his face addressed to those of so different an order that he scarce knew what to make of this lively stir, in a compartment of his mind never yet penetrated, of a capacity for business and a sense for construction.

Both Brydons are within the one man, just as the two Clare Vawdreys share the same body, and the Great Good Place is located in Dane's study. When Brydon tells Alice Staverton that he will never consent to the desecration of the Jolly Corner property, she replies, 'In short you're to make so good a thing of your sky-scraper that, living in luxury on *those* ill-gotten gains, you can afford for a while to be sentimental here!' The compromise thus suggested is proof that Brydon is both the detached and passive observer and the aggressive participant. He is somewhat taken aback by Alice Staverton's remark, but the story concludes with his reconciliation with his other self. The love of Alice, demonstrated by her willingness to accept both Brydons, permits him to overcome his horror and to recognize the other self.

> 'He has been unhappy, he has been ravaged,' she said.
> 'And haven't I been unhappy? Am not I – you've only to look at me! – ravaged?'
> 'Ah I don't say I like him *better*,' she granted after a thought. 'But he's grim, he's worn – and things have happened to him. He doesn't make shift, for sight, with your charming monocle.'
> 'No' – it struck Brydon: 'I couldn't have sported mine "down-town". They'd have guyed me there.'
> 'His great convex pince-nez – I saw it, I recognized the kind – is for his poor ruined sight. And his poor right hand – !'
> 'Ah!' Brydon winced – whether for his proved identity or for his lost fingers. . . .

The emphasis on sight placed conspicuously in this concluding passage is not, I think, accidental. We noted earlier that much is made of vision in James's stories of artists and detached observers, and if Brydon is a symbolic representation of James himself, the 'poor ruined sight' of the other self is a more important injury than the mutilated fingers. But the two go together: the eyes that see, the hand that writes. It had occurred to Brydon on facing a closed door that he could not have closed it because 'it was against his whole policy . . . the essence of which was to keep vistas clear. He had them from the first, as he was well aware, on the brain.' The other self is, like the worldly Clare Vawdrey, the non-artist half. 'Ah I don't say I like him *better*,' says Alice Staverton. 'The Jolly Corner' certainly represents a confronting of the rejected self, but it is less an attempt to rectify the past than to justify the present. And Spencer Brydon discovers something that James had known for a long time.

It was not until the closing years of his life, says Dr Rosenzweig, that James succeeded in laying the ghost of his rejected life. His activities for the cause of the Allies and his assumption of British citizenship are seen as a form of expiation.

For James, the worst of crimes was the aggressive exploitation or appropriation of another human being. He left no record of a political philosophy, but according to his secretary, 'His Utopia was an anarchy where nobody would be responsible for any other human being but only for his own civilized character.' This Thoreau-like philosophic anarchism, one of James's heritages from his father, was not contradicted by his participation in World War I, any more than Thoreau's philosophy was contradicted by his efforts in the cause against slavery. If every man is to be free, there must be no jailers. Thus James could not have been expected to condone what he called 'the huge immorality, the deep conspiracy of violence, for violence and wrong, of the Austrian and German emperors'. It seemed to him as if the war was but the climax of years of false values, of the triumph of expediency and acquisition over idealism and appreciation, and he took some comfort in the hope that the war would lead to a clearer realization of the true values. On 31 August, 1914, he wrote to William James, Jr:

There is a way of looking at what is taking place that is positively helpful, or almost, when one can concentrate on it at all – which is difficult. I mean the view that the old systematic organisation and consecration of such forces as are now let loose, of their unspeakable infamy and insanity, is undergoing such a triumphant exhibition in respect to the loathsomeness and madness of the same, that it is what we must all together be most face to face with when the actual blackness of the smoke shall have cleared away.

James's participation in the war need not be considered so much expiation as a spirited defense of his lifelong standard of values – the ultimate proof of his detachment in the sense that it was an active defense of the passive against the threat of aggressive exploitation by Germany. There are moments when the detached observer is ethically bound to intervene – for example, Strether's intercession in the life of Chad Newsome, Mr Langdon's protection of Nanda Brookenham, or Mrs Assingham's heroic smashing of the Golden Bowl. Any form of detachment would be a difficult attitude to assume in a police state. In the present day, when we are concerned with the degree to which freedom may be compromised to protect freedom, James's active defense of the passive should seem a credible paradox.

In any case, we need not be over concerned about the paradox if we are willing to assume that there were two Jameses, just as there are two selves of any creative artist. It is the function of the worldly self to see to it that his turned-back counterpart is left free and uninterrupted. The artist James did not participate in World War I. According to Percy Lubbock, James 'spent the eve of his last illness, December 1st, in turning over the pages of *The Sense of the Past*, intending to go on with it the next morning'. In what we have of *The Sense of the Past* there is no evidence of a significant alteration in his ethical or aesthetic creed. James's last novel is another story of a man who, turning his back on the mundane present, enters the timeless and transcendent realm of a second consciousness.

VIOLA HOPKINS

Visual Art Devices and Parallels in the Fiction of Henry James (1961)

No better 'optical symbol' can be found for one aspect of Henry James than the photograph taken in 1906[1] showing him in top hat, cane and gloves in hand, bending slightly forward in the classic Daumier pose, taking in impressions of a painting. This is a portrait, however, not merely of the occasional James – the art critic, friend and befriender of painters, biographer of a sculptor – but also of the essential James – the master of the art of fiction. That his love of pictures and familiarity with the studio world were grist to his mill is evident in stories and novels such as 'The Madonna of the Future' and *The Tragic Muse* in which his depiction of the artist and exploration of aesthetic questions are thematically central. Reflecting his experience of art less obviously but more significantly are the pictorial effects and art allusions permeating his fiction, both early and late. For though James was first and foremost a literary artist preoccupied with the problems of his own craft, his responsiveness to the visual arts was so keen, was so much an integral part of his consciousness, that it inevitably made itself felt in his literary technique. Clearly, a study of the pictorial aspects of his fiction is justified for the light it may cast on his method as well as on individual works.

Aside from his pictorialism, that is, his practice of describing people, places, scenes or parts of scenes as if he were describing a painting or a subject for a painting and his use of art objects for thematic projection and overtone, one may also raise the question whether in structure and style his novels resemble the works of a particular school of painting. What is assumed when this question is raised is either that all of the arts reflect in certain ways the pervasive 'time-spirit' or that there exist certain families of style, for one of which an artist feels an affinity even though it is not contemporary. Thus, in the first instance, we might ask what did James have in common with the Impressionists and in the second, how is his style related to the Mannerists, the art of the past which impressed him most deeply? Just as metaphors communicate with immediacy the feel of experience in a way which abstract or discursive language cannot, comparisons between the arts serve to sensitize the reader to qualities in the works otherwise difficult to define, but each art having its own techniques and traditions, this critical approach necessarily becomes less and less valuable the more one tries to penetrate to the formal structural elements of the works being compared. Therefore, my emphasis in this essay will be on James's pictorialism; only secondarily will I deal with the question of style and period affinities.

An outgrowth of James's habit of seeing a landscape or figures 'composed' so that the scene appears to the spectator as a living picture perhaps recalling a real one or as a subject for a picture is his use of the 'framing'[2] device. Any scene or part of a scene may be considered framed if through visual imagery or description it is circumscribed and set apart from the rest of the narrative. Framing may serve various purposes: it may integrate description with action or with characterization, especially if the scene is presented through the consciousness of a character with a painter's eye; it may convey with great precision the particular tone of the setting or appearance of a character. Most important of all, it may symbolize relationships and underline themes.

Thus, the opening of *Confidence* consists of a series of scenes viewed pictorially, that is, as they are or might be seen by the hero, Bernard Longueville, who, having a 'fancy for sketching', likes to take 'pictorial notes'.[3] For example:

> Longueville, every morning after breakfast, took a turn in the great square of Siena – the vast *piazza*, shaped like a horse-shoe, where the market is held beneath the windows of that crenelated palace from whose overhanging cornice a tall, straight tower springs up with a movement as light as that of a single plume in the bonnet of a captain. Here he strolled about, watching a brown *contadino* disembarrass his donkey, noting the progress of half an hour's chaffer over a bundle of carrots, wishing a young girl with eyes like animated agates would let him sketch her, and gazing up

at intervals at the beautiful slim tower, as it played at contrasts with the large blue air. (1880 ed. p. 8)

Note that though Longueville is said to be strolling about, the scene is described from the point of view of a spectator who remains at a sufficient distance from the market to be able to glance up to see the tower that dominates the scene. In the suggestion of movement – Longueville's walking about, the upspringing effect of the tower, the animation and sparkle of the girl's eyes – the scene is presented as a typical picturesque subject. As Heinrich Wölfflin has pointed out, 'restless architectural forms' and 'real movement' create essentially picturesque effects, and 'there is nothing more picturesque than the busy crowd of the market'.[4] While Longueville is sketching another picturesque scene, the heroine walks into his picture, into his foreground. Description becomes part of the action; the girl he sketches turns out later to be the same one his friend has fallen in love with in Baden-Baden. However, the hero's sketching propensities are not essentially a part of the story. Angela Vivian walks in and out of his life in the same way as she walked in and out of his 'subject', and finally stays in his life just as she became a part of his sketch, but his having an eye for the picturesque is chiefly a device to introduce the local color of Siena into the novel and to show that Longueville is clever and accomplished.

An art object itself sometimes provides the center of James's living pictures: 'Travelling Companions' opens with the heroine, Charlotte Evans, and her father looking at Leonardo's 'Last Supper' while they are being looked at by the hero. Similarly, in the first paragraph of *The American* we see Christopher Newman 'reclining at his ease on the great circular divan which . . . occupied the centre of the Salon Carré, in the Museum of the Louvre' staring 'at Murillo's beautiful moonborne Madonna' (1877 ed. p. 1). In one sharp visual image the theme of America confronting Europe is presented with immediacy and economy. Sometimes the *tableau vivant* comes as a climax to a scene, gathering together in one image its meaning. A striking instance of this kind of framing occurs in *Roderick Hudson* at the conclusion of the dinner party given in honor of Roderick's successful completion of his first works. Coming back to the drawing room after seeing the ladies to their carriage, Rowland

> paused outside of the open door; he was struck by the group formed by the three men. They were standing before Roderick's statue of Eve, and

the young sculptor had lifted up the lamp and was showing different parts
of it to his companions. He was talking ardently and the lamplight covered
his head and face. Rowland stook looking on, for the group struck him
with its picturesque symbolism. Roderick, bearing the lamp and glowing
in its radiant circle, seemed the beautiful image of a genius which combined
sincerity with power. Gloriani, with his head on one side, pulling his
long moustache and looking keenly from half-closed eyes at the lighted
marble, represented art with a worldly motive, skill unleavened by faith,
the mere base maximum of cleverness. Poor little Singleton, on the other
side, with his hands behind him, his head thrown back and his eyes following devoutly the course of Roderick's elucidation might pass for an embodiment of aspiring candor, afflicted with feeble wings to rise on. In all
this Roderick's was certainly the *beau role*. (1875 ed. p. 113)

In the dramatic use of lighting and of expressive posture, this
'picture' suggests a Caravaggio, though given James's dislike of
seicento art the similarity in effect was probably unintended. What
is more to the point is that a synthetic image is presented of the artist
types and of what they represent; through the picture, the major art
themes of the novel presented as table talk in the preceding scene are
recapitulated succinctly and vividly.

In the later fiction, framing devices are used much less literally, more
suggestively. Thinly motivated picture passages like the ones in *Confidence* all but disappear. What a character feels about the scene or
person mingles with his visual impressions. While 'the look of things'
is not neglected, what we see is much more conditioned by the point
of view. Description is presented more indirectly and made to serve
multiple purposes. Thus, our first glimpse of Isabel Archer after her
marriage is as she appears to Ned Rosier: 'dressed in black velvet . . .
brilliant and noble. . . . Framed in the gilded doorway, she struck
our young man as the picture of a gracious lady.'[5] In between the first
visual details, however, and the image of her in her gilt frame, we
are given the impression she makes on Rosier, who had known her
before her marriage. It is as if James were interpreting a great portrait,
touching on visual and decorative qualities but emphasizing the
character that it reveals.

In contrast, the portrait of the Man with the Mask in *The Sacred
Fount* is described in a straightforward objective fashion:

The figure represented is a young man in black – a quaint, tight black
dress, fashioned in years long past; with a pale, lean, livid face and a stare,

from eyes without eyebrows, like that of some whitened old-world clown. In his hand he holds an object that strikes the spectator at first simply as some obscure, some ambiguous work of art, but that on second view becomes a representation of a human face, modelled and coloured, in wax, in enamelled metal, in some substance not human. The object thus appears a complete mask, such as might have been fantastically fitted and worn. (NS XXIX 44–5)

But its meaning is debated by the characters who are grouped before it. Is the man's own face 'Death' and the mask 'Life' or is it the other way around? Is he taking it off or putting it on? Is the mask 'beautiful' or is it hideous with an awful grimace? Does the mask really resemble Mrs Server and the face, 'poor Briss'? The conflicting interpretations which the ambiguous portrait elicits symbolize the central problem of reality and appearance. As Leon Edel has observed about this episode, 'What has been underlined here for us if not the very theme of the book?'[6]

At moments of recognition in which sight merges with insight, the framing device is used to its greatest effect. Faced with the obligation of carrying out his terrible assignment for a cause in which he no longer believes and superseded by Paul Muniment in his relationship with the Princess, Hyacinth Robinson seeks out Millicent Henning in her shop 'as by the force of the one, the last, sore personal need left him'. The futility of his hope of gaining solace from her becomes apparent to him when he comes upon Captain Sholto in the middle of the room, one of two figures in a tableau:

It next became plain to him that the person standing upright before the Captain, as still as a lay-figure and with her back turned to himself, was the object of his own quest. In spite of her averted face, he instantly 'spotted' Millicent; he knew her shop-attitude, the dressing of her hair behind and the long grand lines of her figure draped in the last new thing. She was showing off this treasure to the Captain, who was lost in contemplation. He had been beforehand with Hyacinth as a false purchaser, but he imitated a real one better than our young man, as, with his eyes travelling up and down the front of their beautiful friend's person, he frowned consideringly and rubbed his lower lip slowly with his walking-stick. Millicent stood admirably still – the back view of the garment she displayed was magnificent. (NY VI 423)

Likewise in *The Wings of the Dove*, Milly seeing Kate Croy standing in the French window opening on the balcony 'very handsome and

upright, the outer dark framing in a highly favourable way her
summery simplicities and lightnesses of dress' 'sees' that Merton
Densher has returned from America. 'Kate had positively but to be
there just as she was to tell her he had come back' (NY XIX 272). The
earlier scene centering on the Bronzino is of this same type but more
complex. Unforgettable is the climactic recognition scene of 'The
Jolly Corner' when Spencer Brydon is confronted by his *alter ego*, the
person he would have been had he stayed in America. 'No portrait by
a great modern master could have presented him with more intensity,
thrust him out of his frame with more art, as if there had been
"treatment", of the consummate sort, in his every shade and salience.'
And indeed the figure as presented could easily pass as a description of
one of Sargent's brilliant, slightly dehumanized and sinister portraits,
such as those of John D. Rockefeller and Asher Wertheimer. Brydon
'took him in . . . his planted stillness, his vivid truth, his grizzled bent
head and white masking hands, his queer actuality of evening dress, of
dangling double eyeglass, of gleaming silk lappet and white linen, of
pearl button and gold watchguard and polished shoe' (NY XVII 475).
What is suggested is a pure optical image without depth or outline, all
surface texture and the gleam of light. The framing device is used here
to great effect: Brydon's other self, who represented to him 'the
triumph of life' and who is outwardly as elegant as one of Sargent's
American financiers, when unmasked fills him with horror, so 'evil,
odious, blatant, vulgar' (NY XVII 477) is his face.

The richest, most fully developed of framed scenes in James's fiction
is the thirtieth chapter of *The Ambassadors*, the account of Strether's
excursion to the French countryside 'into which he had hitherto looked
only through the little oblong window of the picture frame'. He has
hopes when he sets out that he may 'see something somewhere that
would remind him of a certain small Lambinet that had charmed him,
long years before, at a Boston dealer's, and that he had, quite absurdly,
never forgotten', He didn't, couldn't have afforded to, buy it but
always remembered it as 'the picture he *would* have bought – the
particular production that had made him for a moment overstep the
modesty of nature' (NY XXII 245–6). The picture itself, he realizes,
might now disappoint him:

> It would be a different thing, however, to see the remembered mixture
> resolved back into its elements – to assist at the restoration to nature of
> the whole far-away hour: the dusty day in Boston, the background of the

Fitchburg Depot, of the maroon-coloured sanctum, the special-green vision, the ridiculous price, the poplars, the willows, the rushes, the river, the sunny, silvery sky, the shady, woody horizon. (NY XXII 246)

When he gets off the train he imagines himself walking into the picture: 'the oblong gilt frame disposed its enclosing lines; the poplars and willows, the reeds and river – a river of which he didn't know, and didn't want to know, the name – fell into composition, full of felicity, within them; . . . it was all there, in short – it was what he wanted: it was Tremont Street, it was France, it was Lambinet'. His past and his present join hands as he wanders about 'boring so deep into his impressions and idleness that he might fairly have got through them again and reached the maroon-coloured wall' (NY XXII 247). Through the work of art which distills the essence of experience freeing it from irrelevant, distracting detail, he is enabled to grasp the essence of the scene before him and in turn through the living scene he recovers the picture. Still staying within the frame of the picture, he finally stops at an inn toward evening, and while resting, waiting for his dinner to be prepared, he perceives that 'at bottom, the spell of the picture – that it was essentially, more than anything else, a scene and a stage, that the very air of the play was in the rustle of the willows and the tone of the sky'. That is, the play in which he has been engaged – the drama of which the main characters are Chad and Madame de Vionnet, he and the other 'ambassadors' from Woollett – has occupied the center of his consciousness here no less than it had in Paris. For on this ramble in the country even more than in Paris he has felt the quintessence of what distinguishes the 'conditions' of life in France from those in Woollett.

The conditions had nowhere so asserted their difference from those of Woollett as they appeared to him to assert it in the little court of the Cheval Blanc while he arranged with his hostess for a comfortable climax. They were few and simple, scant and humble, but they were *the thing*, as he would have called it, even to a greater degree than Madame de Vionnet's old high salon, where the ghost of the Empire walked. 'The' thing was the thing that implied the greatest number of other things of the sort he had had to tackle; and it was queer, of course, but so it was – the implication here was complete. Not a single one of his observations but somehow fell into a place in it; not a breath of the cooler evening that wasn't somehow a syllable of the text. The text was simply, when condensed, that in *these* places such things were, and that if it was in them one elected to move about one had to make one's account with what one lighted on. (NY XXII 254–5)

In short, in this scene framed by the Lambinet, Strether comes to a full realization of the meaning of his decision not to urge Chad to return to Woollett. The Lambinet that he had missed owning recalls the constrictions and deprivations of his past existence, the pleasures of the spirit and senses that had been denied to him. Seeing the landscape through the picture heightens his awareness of the complexities of European experience. In a world which so gratifies the 'lust of the eyes'[7] and stirs the imagination, and in which nature is so inextricably mixed with art, what is clearly seen as immoral in the sharp New England light may have a different aspect and meaning.

It is especially fitting that the picture through which he sees the landscape should have been Lambinet. Guided simply by the desire to be true to history, James could have chosen any other of the Barbizon painters, for this was the French landscape school that discerning Bostonians were beginning to collect in the 1860s. James reviewed an exhibition in 1872 of privately owned paintings that included Rousseau, Daubigny, Diaz, Troyan and was held in the 'rooms' of Messrs Doll and Richards on Tremont Street.[8] Possibly this was the Boston gallery, as John L. Sweeney suggests, that James had in mind in describing 'the sky-lighted inner shrine of Tremont Street' where Strether had his 'aesthetic adventure'.

But why Lambinet? What James said of place names applies here: 'to name a place, in fiction, is to pretend in some degree to represent it'.[9] The naming of, say, Corot or Millet, two of the better known Barbizonists, would have entailed description suggestive of the popular styles of these painters – the blurred foliage and misty groves of the former, the pathos and social message of the latter's reapers and gleaners. In effect any other minor landscapist would have served his purpose just as well, as long as the name did not require the kind of 'doing' that would interfere with the general impression James wished to convey. It is the generic quality of this landscape school – the delight of these painters in the quiet moods of nature and their intimate treatment of it – that matters. Slow moving rivers that reflect a luminous sky and tangled willows, gently undulating meadows and winding forest paths, light filtering through trees – these are their recurring motifs; this is the 'picture' James evokes of French 'ruralism', and this is a typical Lambinet. Also, how much more gently ironic is Strether's having failed to obtain the work of a minor painter like Lambinet rather than of a master like Corot.

To what extent James consciously sought the effect I am about to describe probably cannot be determined, but it seems to me that when Strether enters the village where he plans to have his dinner, it is no longer a Lambinet which is being described, but instead an Impressionist canvas. First of all, the setting – an inn by a river with a pavilion 'at the garden edge' almost overhanging the water, 'testifying, in its somewhere battered state, to much fond frequentation' (NY XXII 255) – is one which the Impressionists were especially fond of painting. The boating party on the river, the open air dance place, the crowd in a cafe or a public garden – these were some of their favorite subjects. (In the synopsis for *The Ambassadors* that James sent to Harpers he refers to the setting as 'a suburban village by the river, a place where people come out from Paris to boat, to dine, to dance, to make love, to do anything they like'.)[10] When, at the opening of the next chapter, Strether sees 'a boat advancing round the bend' containing 'a young man in his shirt sleeves' and a lady 'with a pink parasol', it seems to him 'suddenly as if these figures, or something like them, had been wanted in the picture, had been wanted, more or less, all day' (NY XXII 256). What we have here, however, is no longer, say, Lambinet's 'Le Passeur sur La Seine, près Bougival' but Renoir's 'Canotiers à Chatou' or Manet's 'En Bateau'. Lambinet's figures are peasants, men and women indigenous to the country-side, dressed in rough everyday garb and absorbed in their everyday tasks; Renoir's or Manet's are city folk – the men relaxing in shirt sleeves and the ladies stylishly dressed, wearing charming hats and holding parasols – enjoying the simple pleasures of the picnic excursion.

And it is not subject alone that suggests a difference. A comparison of descriptive phrases in the first part of the chapter with those of the latter part and of the opening of the next one reveals a significant change in Strether's vision: 'sunny, silvery sky, the shady, woody horizon', 'the sky was silver and turquoise and varnish; the village on the left was white and the church on the right was gray' (NY XXII 247) – this is how Strether 'sees' initially. Color is presented through adjectives, and the light is represented as concentrated in the sky, not diffused throughout. That the horizon is 'shady, woody' suggests a traditional aerial perspective in which objects at a distance appear blurred. In contrast, the primary emphasis in the description of the village where he stops for dinner is not on the thing modified by the adjective; instead, adjectives are converted into substantives, a grammatical shift which places the emphasis on the sensory quality of the visual experience rather than on the thing itself. 'The village aspect' affects him 'as whiteness, crookedness and blueness set in coppery green; there being positively, for that matter, an outer wall of the White Horse that was painted the most improbable shade'. Mme de Vionnet's parasol made 'a pink point in the shining scene'. Color details are rendered with greater precision: the church is a 'dim slate-colour' on the outside; the stream is 'gray-blue'. Distant objects are not described as if the perspective were conventional. 'The valley on the further side was all copper-green level and glazed pearly sky, a sky hatched across with screens of trimmed trees, which looked flat, like espaliers' (NY XXII 254-7).

This very subtle shift from the description of Lambinet to that of an Impressionist scene reinforces the thematic development of the episode. The movement of the chapter is from Strether's identification of the picture with the landscape to his grasp of the implications of the identity, from the past to the present. But his understanding and acceptance of its meaning are not tested until the encounter with Chad and Mme de Vionnet; he is confronted with the moral of his 'text', which, as he has just interpreted it, was that if 'one elected to move about' in this kind of world, 'one had to make one's account with what one lighted on'. Strether actually makes his 'account' the next evening in the 'high, clear picture' of Mme de Vionnet's rooms; 'he was moving in these days, as in a gallery, from clever canvas to clever canvas' (NY XXII 273). As can be seen, the movement from the 'special-green vision' of a Lambinet canvas, low toned and idyllic, to the color nuances and pleasure trip theme of the Impressionist canvas corresponds to the evolution of Strether's experience which is climaxed by his discovery that after all 'he was mixed up with the typical tale of Paris' (NY XXII 271).

The foregoing analysis of James's use of the framing technique is not meant to be exhaustive; other instances of this kind of pictorialism should come readily to mind to the alert reader and will be mentioned incidentally in the ensuing discussion. What I have tried mainly to suggest is the variety, richness, and increasingly subtle effects created by it. The same progression from description to evocation and symbolization can be traced in James's treatment of art objects and background in general. Early 'European' stories like 'A Passionate Pilgrim' and 'Travelling Companions' are so overloaded with art description that one almost wonders whether James intended their interest to be in the description or in the story as a whole. Even the more economically constructed 'The Madonna of the Future', reflecting though it does a more critical attitude toward the American who adulates European culture, contains unassimilated and overextended descriptive passages; Howells felt that one of the charms of the story was its 'dissertations on pictures'.[11] Nevertheless, even the works of James's apprenticeship show evidence of an attempt to assimilate art details and action. For example, in 'Travelling Companions' the hero's purchase of a spurious Correggio from a poverty-stricken Italian family serves more than one thematic purpose: the madonna portrayed resembles Charlotte Evans with whom the hero, influenced by the romantic atmosphere of Italy, imagines himself to be in love; and the incident in which the 'so mendacious and miserable' but 'so civil, so charming'[12] Italians sell it to him is worked in with another theme – the painful underside of Italian beauty and picturesqueness. Pictures are also used throughout as a sign of sensibility: Charlotte is moved to recite a dozen verses from St Mark's gospel when standing before a Tintoretto 'Crucifixion'; her father prefers watching the pretty women in the Milan cathedral to climbing to its top. *Roderick Hudson*, in spite of all of its faults, marks a further advance in this direction, for though it still has some of the copiousness of a guide book, the descriptions of places and art objects are much better integrated with the action. The scene in St Peter's, for example, in which Christina is seen kissing the bronze toe of the holy statue is not only a touch of Roman local color but a sign of her capriciousness and flair for the dramatic. She had given no signs earlier of being that devout. By the time of *The Portrait of a Lady*, James was expert in conveying a great deal by a single stroke: when the again rejected Lord Warburton bids Isabel goodbye in Rome, the scene takes place in the gallery of the Capitol with the 'lion of the collection' – 'The Dying Gladiator' – in the background.

While James never exempted himself entirely, not even in his highly poetic and dramatic novels, from the novelist's obligation to satisfy the reader's visual imagination, he soon learned to practice a wise economy in fusing much of what is normally called setting with action and characterization. The art object is an especially important means of achieving this desired fusion, for it can be used simultaneously as a visual detail and as a symbol of a culture, superficially as a plot device and more profoundly as character revelation or as reinforcement of theme. When the allusion is to specific paintings by actual artists or to an artist's style or to that of a particular period, James's ideal of economical richness is most fully realized.[13]

Just as poetic nuances sometimes depend on a reader's recognition of a line or image from other poems, the effectiveness of this kind of art image in James depends on our having a sense of the particular qualities of the painting or style of painting alluded to. Moreover, as his art references reflect his own assumptions about artists and styles, which of course he by and large shared with his cultivated contemporaries, a knowledge of James's taste enhances our appreciation of the image. To know, for example, that he had a 'sneaking relish'[14] for Sassoferrato, 'sneaking' because he considered him basically shallow, an essentially decorative artist, like Decamps, who lacked the 'penetrating imagination' of a Tintoretto or a Delacroix, adds sharpness to the point made in *Roderick Hudson* that this is the one picture which Christina Light and her mother own and display. Fond though he was of the Dutch and Flemish school, James associated 'style' in the grand manner with French and Italian art. Thus, Maria Gostrey's 'little Dutch-looking dining room' with its 'ideally kept pewter' and 'specimens of vivid Delf' (NY XXII 319) speaks for the kind of haven she has to offer Strether. Mme de Vionnet's 'grayish-white salon' with its 'fine *boiseries* . . . medallions, mouldings, mirrors, great clear spaces' and 'consular chairs', 'mythological bronzes', 'sphinxes' heads' and 'faded surfaces of satin striped with alternate silk' (NY XXI 244–5) symbolizes her quite different appeal to his imagination. Similarly, in *The Golden Bowl* Renaissance imagery underscores 'the grand style' of the Prince and Charlotte and classical imagery, the idealism of Maggie and Adam, a reflection of what these art styles represented to James. Appreciation of Italian pre-Raphaelite painting is usually in a story or novel by James a sign of cultivation or an aesthetic temperament: both the diarist and the young man in 'The Diary of a Man of Fifty' like the early Florentines best of all; the painter-hero in 'Mrs Temperly' thinks her daughter was 'like a figure on the *predella* of an early Italian painting' (NS XXVI 269). As an Englishman of his type would, Sir Claude, the step-father in *What Maisie Knew*, regards a taste for primitives as a 'silly superstition' (NY XI 112). Seicento art is generally admired by people without taste: the gentleman painter of 'The Sweetheart of M. Briseux' is doomed to fail if for no other reason than because of his admiration for Guido and Caravaggio. No one but a conventional English gentleman like Sir Arthur in 'The Siege of London' could feel indifferent to French painting and prefer instead the art exhibitions at the Royal Academy.

James's artistry as a novelist and sensitivity as an art appreciator are revealed in the precision with which he selected particular art objects to express shades of meaning. One is rather surprised at first that Henrietta Stackpole's favorite painting should be the tender, almost sentimental 'Virgin Adoring the Child' by Correggio in the Uffizi. But on second thought, doesn't this unexpected preference of hers reveal that for all her crisp, official feminism she has a more personal, feminine side, that side which is expressed in her loyalty to Isabel? But it is *The Wings of the Dove* that deserves the most attention for the rich allusiveness of its art imagery.

The moment when Milly Theale stands before the Bronzino portrait which she is said to resemble marks a climax that has often been critically analyzed. But if we look at the particular Bronzino James described and consider its qualities, we can gain new insight into this passage. First of all, however, we must go back a few pages to the beginning of the Fifth Book which opens with Milly's 'agreeably inward response to the scene'. 'The great historic house had, for Milly, beyond terrace and garden, as the centre of an almost extravagantly grand Watteau-composition, a tone as of old gold kept "down" by the quality of the air, summer full-flushed, but attuned to the general perfect taste' (NY XIX 208).

Carried throughout this chapter and the next is her sense of the occasion as a Watteau picture. 'The largeness of style was the great containing vessel, while everything else . . . became but this or that element of the infusion. . . . Everything was great, of course, in great pictures, and it was doubtless precisely a part of the brilliant life – since the brilliant life, as one had faintly figured it, just *was* humanly led – that all impressions within its area partook of its brilliancy.' For Milly the Matcham reception is '*the* revelation' of her personal success – the 'parenthesis' in her life which had begun with the dinner three weeks ago at Lancaster Gate and which 'would close with this admirable picture' (NY XIX 209–10). Evocative of the delicacy of Watteau,

though by no means descriptive of his palette, is the interwoven blue
and pink and lavender color imagery: 'they were all swimming
together in the blue'; Lord Mark was 'personally the note of the blue';
people 'in your wonderful country' seem to be kept in 'lavender and
pink paper', Aunt Maud says to Milly; Lady Aldershaw 'was all in the
palest pinks and blues'. And when Milly stands before the picture
'the beauty and the history and the facility and the splendid midsummer
glow' melt together in her consciousness: 'it was a sort of magnificent
maximum, the pink dawn of an apotheosis coming so curiously soon'
(NY XIX 213–23).

   Is there any other metaphor that could have conveyed as well the
feeling of Milly's response to the Matcham festivity? Watteau's special
subject was the revels of an aristocratic society – the garden party and
the feast of love. His settings represent the atmosphere of the park
opening into the depths of a misty expanse; the mood evoked is one of
gaiety and refined pleasure. In a review of the Wallace Collection in
1873, James commented on Watteau's 'perpetual grace', his 'elegance
and innocence combined', his 'irresistible air of believing in these
visionary picnics'. His canvases are peopled by 'gentle folks all' and
he 'marks the high-water point of natural elegance'.[15] In comparing
the scene to a 'Watteau-composition', Milly is seeing it as a picture
of social intercourse at its highest pitch. Her vision of English society,
the Watteau image suggests, is an idealization; from another point
of view, for example that of Densher's, instead of 'natural elegance',
English society seems most to exhibit 'natural stupidity'. And its
predatory nature, based as it is on a system in which everyone 'works'
everyone else, is a theme running throughout the book. Milly is not
unaware of the jungle aspects of the social struggle; even in the
Matcham scene, she perceives how Mrs Lauder, 'a natural force', is
'working' Lord Mark; but the point is that it is the beauty of the scene,
all of its elements fusing into a picture of high civilization, that she
responds to.

   But if the Matcham occasion was for her 'then and afterwards a
high-water mark of the imagination' (NY XIX 210), it is when she is
brought by Lord Mark face to face with her 'sister' in the Bronzino
picture that she has her moment of supreme realization.

   Perhaps it was her tears that made it just then so strange and fair – as wonderful as he had said: the face of a young woman, all splendidly drawn,
   down to the hands, and splendidly dressed; a face almost livid in hue, yet

handsome in sadness, and crowned with a mass of hair, rolled back and high, that must, before fading with time, have had a family resemblance to her own. The lady in question, at all events, with her slight Michael-angelesque squareness, her eyes of other days, her full lips, her long neck, her recorded jewels, her brocaded and wasted reds, was a very great personage – only unaccompanied by a joy. And she was dead, dead, dead. Milly recognized her exactly in words that had nothing to do with her. 'I shall never be better than this.' (NY XIX 221)

Lord Mark misunderstands, thinking that by 'this' she is referring to the picture. But still, 'It was probably as good a moment as she should ever have with him. It was perhaps as good a moment as she should have with any one, or have in any connexion whatever' (NY XIX 221). In spite of all of her richness and splendor, the 'personage' in the picture is 'unaccompanied by a joy' *and* dead. Through Milly's identification with her, she at one and the same time feels most fully and sharply the possibilities of life and has the strongest premonition of her doom. But paradoxically, the portrait of the dead woman that has itself endured, also seems to urge her to assert her will to live: ' "I can go for a long time." Milly spoke with her eyes again on her painted sister's – almost as if under their suggestion. She still sat there before Kate, yet not without a light in her face. "That will be one of my advantages. I think I could die without its being noticed" ' (NY XIX 227–8).

In selecting a Bronzino portrait rather than, for instance, a Titian or a Vandyke, James again reveals his sensitivity to overtone and his preference for the 'full-fed statement'. A Titian portrait would suggest splendor and a Vandyke elegance and refinement, but with neither could Milly so readily have identified. It is very likely that James actually had in mind the portrait of Lucrezia Panciatichi in the Uffizi,[16] his description in spirit and in detail is remarkably 'like'. The hair, the neck, the richness of dress, the large hands are all there. The 'recorded jewels' may refer to the legend inscribed on her green beads – 'Amour dure sans fin', not inappropriate as an inscription to *The Wings of the Dove*. But what are the particular qualities of the painting that make it an effective symbol? As is generally true of Bronzino's portraits, the social position of the sitter is apparent: the long nose, the long, thin fingers, the richness of clothing and jewels, the magnificent apartness created by placing the figure in front of a dark background with only a suggestion of an arch or niche – all these characteristics establish the high social status of the subject. However, the painting is not merely a representation of a distinguished, cultivated, and elegant woman. The arms gracefully follow the lines of the body, the right hand touching lightly an open book (as if the sitter had just looked up and was holding her place), the left resting on the arm of the chair. But there is a tautness in the fingers, a slight strain in the posture of the figure, giving an impression of some repressed inner agitation; the stillness and repose are qualified by the imperfectly hidden tension. Almost all of Bronzino's men and women have this air of strain, reserve, containment – a general characteristic of the Mannerists, who, in reaction against the Renaissance celebration of the beauty and vigor of the human body, expressed in their works the spiritual unease of the sixteenth century, its lack of faith in mankind and matter. Typically Mannerist, Bronzino's figures are elongated and distorted; his people appear both over-graceful and ascetic, worldly and spiritual, elegant and sad. What has been said of his men can also be applied to this Panciatichi portrait: 'It is an aristocracy alike of the intellect and the senses that Bronzino has immortalized for us. These men of the Florentine decadence are no mere representatives of a thin refinement of culture. They have known everything and felt everything. They are beyond good and evil.'[17]

Coming after the Watteau image, which conjures up a delicious imaginary world exempt from time and pain, good and evil, the Bronzino becomes a symbol of mortality; the elegance and splendor incompletely mask an all-pervading sadness and sense of mutability.

The Veronese images in the Venetian chapters also illustrate the special economy and richness of particular art references. The descriptions of Palazzo Leporelli are largely based on the Palazzo Barbaro, a fourteenth-century Gothic structure, on the Grand Canal, opposite the Accademia di Belle Arti. James described it as a 'magnificent house – a place of which the full charm only sinks into your spirit as you go on living there, seeing it in all its hours and phases'.[18] The owners were his friends the Daniel Curtises, with whom he stayed in 1887 – this visit was originally planned to last ten days but was extended to five weeks – as well as in the 1890s. Enshrined in *The Wings of the Dove* are James's impressions of its 'pompous Tiepolo ceiling', Gothic windows, and court with a high outer staircase.[19] Perhaps through association the Veronese images sprang to mind; according to a painting representing the interior of one of the Palazzo Barbaro salons there were at the turn of the century two Veroneses – 'The Rape of the Sabines' and 'The Continence of Scipio' – on its walls.[20] But we do not have to try to seek a specific source for the image; James was introduced to this painter of sumptuous feasts and splendid decorations on his first visit to Venice. 'Never was a painter more nobly joyous, never did an artist take a greater delight in life, seeing it all as a kind of breezy festival and feeling it through the medium of perpetual success', James wrote of his wall paintings in the Ducal Palace. Of his famous 'Rape of Europa', he said, 'Nowhere else in art is such a temperament revealed; never did inclination and opportunity combine to express such enjoyment. The mixture of flowers and gems and brocade, of blooming flesh and shining sea and waving groves, of youth, health, movement, desire – all this is the brightest vision that ever descended upon the soul of a painter.'[21]

It is in chapter 28, Milly's 'occasion' in honor of Sir Luke Strett, that the Veronese allusions are clustered.[22] James probably did not have any single Veronese painting in mind, nor is the scene presented in any literal sense as if it were a composite picture. On one level the association of Veronese with the scene contributes to the atmosphere of grandeur and splendor in which Milly is making her life. As the Princess, she was 'lodged for the first time as she ought, from her type, to be', according to Susan Stringham. 'It's a Veronese picture, as near as can be – with me as the inevitable dwarf, the small blackamoor, put into a corner of the foreground for effect' (as in Veronese's 'Feast at the House of Levi',[23] in which a jester, both a dwarf and a blackamoor, crouches on the staircase in the foreground). Densher wonders what part he is to play, 'with his attitude that lacked the highest style, in a composition in which everything else would have it'? Mrs Stringham informs him that he is 'in the picture' – he is to be 'the grand young man who surpasses the others and holds up his head and the wine-cup' (NY xx 206–7), (the pose of the cupbearer in the 'Marriage at Cana' in the Louvre). Later, after dinner, Densher feels 'the effect of the place, the beauty of the scene' acting to transform the guests, who 'during the day had fingered their Baedekers, gaped at their frescoes, and differed, over fractions of francs, with their gondoliers', into figures not out of place in a Veronese canvas. 'Milly, let loose among them in a wonderful white dress, brought them somehow into relation with something that made them more finely genial: so that if the Veronese picture of which he had talked with Mrs Stringham was not quite constituted, the comparative prose of the previous hours, the traces of insensibility qualified by "beating down" were at least almost nobly disowned' (NY xx 213). Milly acquits herself as a hostess 'under some supreme idea, an inspiration which was half her nerves and half an inevitable harmony' (NY xx 214), so well that the Veronese image is almost apt. But while Milly's 'festival' represents an active affirmation of her desire and will to live, to live in the Veronese style, the climax of this scene is Densher's extortion from Kate at last of what it is Kate expects him to do – ' "Since she's to die I'm to marry her?" . . . "To marry her." . . . "So that when her death has taken place I shall in the natural course have money?" . . . "You'll in the natural course have money. We shall in the natural course be free" ' (NY xx 225). Veronese's huge pictures – described by Bernard Berenson as 'cheerful', 'simple', 'displaying childlike naturalness of feeling' and 'frank and joyous worldliness'[24] – are pitched in quite a different key. As can be seen, the association of Milly's occasion with a Veronese canvas is also highly ironic, an irony which becomes apparent only in the light of what Veronese as a painter represents.

Judging by the pictorial effects in his fiction, we must conclude that James's cultivation of his visual sense yielded him rich rewards as a novelist. His poetic allusions to works of art, framing of scenes through pictorial metaphor, evocations of natural scenery, cityscapes, and portraits of people testify to the sharpness and delicacy of his visual perceptions, the depth of his response to art works, and the power of his visual memory. But to what extent and in what way did particular painters influence his writing? This is an extremely difficult, if not impossible, question to answer. There are between the arts, as Wallace Stevens said, 'migratory passings to and fro, quickenings, Promethean liberations and discoveries',[25] but the attempt to isolate an unequivocal 'passage' of painting into writing with regard to technique as well as to subject or theme more often than not results in absurd analogizing. The inescapable fact remains that there are clear boundaries between the arts and that at best what one artist can achieve is a virtual effect of another medium.

James's images and descriptive passages occasionally are traceable to specific paintings, as was seen with the Bronzino. Other examples can be cited. Hyacinth Robinson's vision of the plebeian Millicent Henning '(if there should ever be barricades in the streets of London) with a red cap of liberty on her head and her white throat bared so that she should be able to shout the louder the Marseillaise of that hour' (NY v 164), calls to mind Delacroix's famous 'Le 28 Juillet, La Liberté conduisant le peuple aux barricades', which James, who admired Delacroix above all other nineteenth-century painters, could not have missed seeing in the Louvre. The red-capped figure of Liberty, as Walter Friedlaender observes, 'is no allegory, but a *femme du peuple* with bared breast and blowing hair, holding a flintlock and waving the tricolor'.[26] Hyacinth hardly seems sensual enough even to imagine Millicent with her bosom exposed, but the effect is suggested by 'white throat bared'. The sentence that follows contributes further to the likeness: 'If the festival of the Goddess of Reason should ever be enacted in the British Capital . . . who was better designated than Miss Henning to figure in a grand statuesque manner as the heroine of the occasion?' (NY v 164-5) (The sad, introverted, rather delicately featured young man in the foreground, somewhat dwarfed by the monumental figure of Liberty, could be for all the world a representation of Hyacinth!)

Similarly, the narrator's allusion in *The Aspern Papers* to Sardanapalus – he fears that Miss Bordereau like that Eastern potentate will burn her treasures before she dies – probably originated in James's remembrance of Delacroix's 'Sardanapalus', which greatly impressed him when he first saw it in 1876,[27] rather than Byron's. Likewise, this image in *The Golden Bowl* may very well have had its source in a recollection of a painting: Maggie 'saw as in a picture' why she had not given in to 'the vulgar heat of her wrong'. 'The straight vindictive view, the rages of jealousy, the protests of passion' – these were 'a range of feeling' which 'figured nothing nearer to experience than a wild eastern caravan, looming into view with crude colours in the sun, fierce pipes in the air, high spears against the sky, all a thrill, a natural joy to mingle with, but turning off short before it reached her and plunging into other defiles' (NY xxiv 237). Oriental subjects were a staple of romantic literature as well as of painting, but I think the image came not from a source such as 'Salammbô' but from James's memory of a work by Decamps. 'The picturesqueness – we might almost say the grotesqueness – of the East no one has rendered like Decamps,' James wrote in an art review of 1873. He 'paints movements to perfection; the animated gorgeousness of his famous "Arabs Fording a Stream" (a most powerful piece of water-colour) is a capital proof'.[28] The striking feature of the painting which connects it with James's image is that it represents a moving file of Arabs on horseback, bristling with spears, seeming to come directly at the spectator but in the foreground veering to the right in order to cross the stream at the ford.

A reasonable case can be made for the visual sources of these images, but it should be noted that each image, which we necessarily see with our mind's eye, is only one stroke in James's canvas whereas the assumed prototype may have literary and historical meaning but is essentially self-contained and appeals directly to the viewer's visual and tactile senses. Even more important, though James showed a remarkable ability to suggest the spirit of individual art works, it is the subject that is 'transposed' into fiction; the technique of describing a scene as a picture is intrinsically different from that of painting it.

In my analysis of the Lambinet passage, I tried to show how James's word choice and syntax were attuned to the conveying of sensation and thus produced the effect of an Impressionist vision of the scene. It seems to me highly probable that James's knowledge of Impressionist painting influenced his way of seeing, but only indirectly could it have affected his way of rendering in prose an Impressionist scene, or any other. His was almost to begin with, a picturesque vision; that is, he responded to the play of light and shadow, color and movement detached from the object. The Impressionists, who carried the tendency in painting to detach appearance from object to an extreme and who came to realize that the areas of an object in shadow are not devoid of color or darker than the rest of it but only not as bright, may very well have increased his awareness of atmospheric effects and of the influence of light on color. Through their treatment of contemporary life, he may have come to realize the inherent pictorial qualities of scenes such as the one described at the end of the Lambinet chapter. The scene in which Strether and Mme de Vionnet have luncheon together in the restaurant on the quay in its treatment of textures, light, and color and in the informality of Mme de Vionnet's pose could have been a description in subject and tone of an early Renoir canvas, as F. O. Matthiessen has suggested.

But the proper place to look for possible influences on James's descriptive technique is in the works of Turgeniev, Flaubert, Daudet, Loti. However, the similarities between James's style of 'the major phase' and French literary impressionism is a subject for another study. My point is that if we are concerned with discovering affinities and influences in matters of technique, we have ample evidence here of this kind of relationship in the works of his immediate literary predecessors and contemporaries. Undoubtedly an artist's perceptions of reality, of which his way of seeing the physical world is an important part, shape his method of expression: when inherited techniques are inadequate to express the new vision, new techniques must be created. And in his view of the interrelatedness of all experience, of consciousness not as fixed and stable but as ever in flux, and in his emphasis on the subjective aspects of experience, James had much in common with the Impressionist painter's response to reality. This summary of the Impressionist painter's view of the world could very well be used to characterize one aspect of James's:

> A world, the phenomena of which are in a state of constant flux and transition, produces the impression of a continuum in which everything coalesces and in which there are no differences but the various approaches and point of view of the beholder. An art in accordance with such a world will stress not merely the momentary nature of phenomena, will not see in man simply the measure of all things, but will seek the criterion of truth in the 'hic et nunc' of the individual.[29]

Both William Morris Hunt and John LaFarge had the Impressionist 'eye', though they did not practice the technique of the color spot, rainbow palette, broad brush stroke, and color perspective invented by Pissarro, Monet, Renoir, and the other members of the school, and through his associations with them in the Newport days James was exposed to their belief that 'one should be alive to the crowding impressions of life, instead of arranging one's ideas in any definite or schematic ways'.[30] But it seems to me that the similarity between James's and the Impressionists' perceptions of reality mainly suggests that James was also a man of his time.

More analogous in style, structure, and sensibility than Impressionist painting to James's mature work is Mannerist art. Again, let me make clear that I am not suggesting any direct transpositions or influences, but rather that his relation to Mannerist painting and sculpture is an instance of what Henri Focillon speaks of as

> affinities and accords far more subtle than those which preside over the general historical groupings of mankind. There exists a kind of spiritual ethnography which cuts across the best-defined 'races'. It is composed of families of the mind – families whose unity is effected by secret ties, and who are faithfully in communication with one another, beyond all

restrictions of time or place. Perhaps each style, each state of a style, even each technique seeks out by preference a certain state of man's nature, a certain spiritual family. In any case, it is the relationships between these three values which clarifies a work of art not only as something that is unique but also as something that is a living word in a universal language.[31]

Before we turn to the qualities of James's art which place him in this 'spiritual' family, a brief review of the main characteristics of Mannerist art is in order.[32] The Mannerist style developed in reaction to the High Renaissance ideal of isolation and balance of parts, as reflected most purely in the works of Raphael's mature period. Once thought merely to represent a decay of the Renaissance idea, it is now recognized as a separate style which in painting was fully formed by 1520, by 1550 had degenerated, and by 1590 was sterile and conventionalized.

In Renaissance art, the object in nature was subordinate to established canons of proportion and harmony; it was to be treated not as an optical impression, but as 'heightened and idealized to something objective and regular'.[33] In contrast, the Mannerist approached nature subjectively, defying established rules of perspective, proportion, and composition. For the Mannerist it was not a question of creating the object as one might or should or does see it, but as, to quote Friedlaender, 'from purely autonomous artistic motives, one would have it seen'.[34] Not attempting to represent the object according to what would be viewed as 'natural', the Mannerist stretched limbs and fingers, broke up symmetry, dissolved figures in space – all for the sake of a particular personal rhythmic feeling of beauty. As exemplified by the works of Parmigianino, Tintoretto, Bronzino, the Michelangelo of the Medici Chapel and of the anteroom of the Laurentian Library, Mannerist art lacks both the repose and stability of the Renaissance and the turbulent struggle and triumphant resolution of the baroque; it is an art of preciosity, of intricate asymmetrical patterns leading to no final solution, of subjects treated from unexpected angles, of 'rigid formality and deliberate disturbance, bareness and over-decoration'.[35]

Various theories have been offered to explain the development of the Mannerist style, but the most widely accepted seems to be that it was an expression not merely of dissatisfaction with the perfection of Renaissance art but of the spiritual ferment of the times. As Hans Tietze observes in reference to Tintoretto's emphasis of material phenomena to express spiritual meanings, 'The Renaissance affirmed and achieved reality both in life and in art. The period which followed it endeavoured to discern in this dominated reality an image of metaphysical essence.'[36]

The quality in James's art which has led to his being called a 'romantic metaphysical' by T. S. Eliot,[37] an 'idealistic realist' by Joseph Warren Beach,[38] and a seeker of 'the sacramental sensibility' by R. W. B. Lewis[39] is what relates him to the Mannerist tendency to spiritualize the material world. This is not to say that James was religious in a traditional or formal sense, nor even that he an adherent of his father's idiosyncratic version of Swedenborgianism as Quentin Anderson maintains, but that for him the soul in the sense of man's moral, intellectual, affective life was eminently real. His works represent the attempt to objectify the travails or the creation of the finer conscience, to make vivid and immediate the adventures of the spirit. Not born in a society rich enough in manners and social institutions to engage his imagination and unable to become immersed in the life of an alien culture, at least not in the sense that George Eliot and Balzac were in theirs, he converted his preternatural sensitivity to surface appearances into an instrument for the revelation of moral meanings. In his preface to *The Tragic Muse* James mentions that in pondering over the problem of how to unify his two separate stories – 'his political case' and 'his theatrical case' – he asked himself, 'Were there not . . . certain sublime Tintorettos at Venice, a measureless Crucifixion in especial, which showed half a dozen actions separately taking place? Yes, this might be, but there has surely been nevertheless a mighty pictorial fusion, so that the virtue of composition had somehow thereby come all mysteriously to its own.'[40] But there is another sense, pertinent to our discussion here, in which, as shown in this quotation from an early essay, 'fusion' in Tintoretto spoke to James's imagination:

> Before his greatest works you are conscious of a sudden evaporation of old doubts and dilemmas, and the eternal problem of the conflict between idealism and realism dies the most natural of deaths. In Tintoret, the problem is practically solved, and the alternatives so harmoniously interfused that I defy the keenest critic to say where one begins and the other ends. The homeliest prose melts into the most ethereal poetry, and the literal and imaginative fairly confound their identity.[41]

The parallel in James's art to this Mannerist characteristic of Tintoretto, who as Tietze said 'makes form dissolve into matter and matter into form',[42] is his masterly 'interfusion' of psychological nuances with descriptions of things, so that through the inanimate thing the essence of the spiritual reality is revealed. However, both James's tortuous, involuted later style and Tintoretto's twisted lines and tormented restless forms reflect an unresolved tension in their exaltation of physical and psychical existence.

The irresoluteness of James's endings is suggestive of the Mannerist style – the struggle to repose which lacks a final triumph. By irresoluteness I do not mean that James's works are not rounded off, self-contained works of art, but rather that one is often left with a disturbed feeling because the 'solution' is rarely presented with finality. Isabel Archer returns to Rome, but why and to what? Nick Dormer has indeed given up the political life for the artistic but is his painting of Julia Dallow a sign that he will become the fashionable success that Gabriel Nash predicted? In her renunciation of Owen Gereth and the spoils of Poynton, Fleda Vetch remains true to her finer instincts, but what does Owen's wish for her to have a valuable object from Poynton show about his feelings concerning her moral decision?

This ambiguity is partially attributable to James's approach to his subject. In an essay on Flaubert, James stated that the novelist may stand in two different relations to his subject and the treatment of it: 'The more he feels his subject the more he *can* render it – that is the first way. The more he renders it the more he *can* feel it – that is the second way.'[43] The second way was not only Flaubert's, but the evidence of the notebooks and the prefaces alone testifies to its being James's way as well.

Ever aware though he was of the necessity that fiction be in touch with life, James created his motives for behavior as he worked out his subject, subordinating questions about human actions and emotions that other novelists might feel compelled to treat to his larger artistic purpose. In the detailed work sheets for *The Spoils of Poynton* in the notebooks, for example, Owen's marital fate was a foregone conclusion. As the focus was to be on Fleda's consciousness, his subsequent happiness or misery was inconsequential. As with the Mannerist painter, it is not 'nature' as seen by the ordinary person or by the conventions of another art style that was his concern but rather 'nature' as he 'would have it seem'. Hence the superintelligence and hypersensitivity of James's characters; the probing dialectical conversations which in real life one cannot imagine sustained by even the most perceptive and highly cultivated beings; the omission except through implication of physical drives and passions. What James said in an essay of 1892 about

Tintoretto's 'Marriage of Cana' at the Salute is applicable here: 'There could be no better example of the roving independence of the painter's vision, a real spirit of adventure for which his subject was always a cluster of accidents; not an obvious order, but a sort of peopled and agitated chapter of life, in which the figures are submissive pictorial notes.'[44] For both painter and novelist, the 'schemata' came first; the 'figures' from life are treated as elements in the composition, subordinated to the prevailing artistic rhythm.

James's late style can be called either mannered or Mannerist, depending on whether one views his hesitations and qualifications, his inversions and twisting of syntax, his mingling of literary with colloquial language as an artifice masking an emptiness of content or as a mode of expression reflecting his painstaking effort to communicate with precision refinements of feeling and thought. The mannered style cannot always be easily distinguished from the Mannerist: when a figure in a painting is represented scratching his left ear with the right hand, his arm extended over his head, this may be either a cliché of the style and hence empty of meaning or it may be the only possible way within a design to express a mood. One can in James point out instances in which the style is a beautifully wrought carapace covering a lowly crustacean, but on the whole his late style represents an effort to penetrate meanings deeply and subtly. But while this working out of detail 'with a goldsmith's care . . . makes for an enormous gain in insight and precision . . . the total effect is frequently lost sight of'.[45] James himself did not lose sight of the 'total effect', but though he had a classical feeling for balance and proportion, his tendency toward elaboration often resulted in works with the 'misplaced middle' – overdevelopment in the first half which necessitated radical foreshortening in the second. This asymmetry and preciosity in detail is characteristic of both Mannerist architecture and painting.

As this brief analysis of the Mannerist traits of James's art suggests, Mannerist style is accompanied by a particular sensibility, one which may cherish the ideals of a classical serenity and harmony but which, living in an age of uncertainty and disruption of traditional values, must create out of its own consciousness order and beauty. That James possessed this kind of sensibility I think few will question, and that he felt an affinity for Mannerist art as represented chiefly by Tintoretto is also evident.[46] As to specific 'influences' of the Mannerists on James's style and structure, objective evidence is hard to come by. There is a common frontier of the arts, but communications between the outposts are couched in a language not easy to translate. It is in his pictorialism that the transformation of his visual art experiences into literature can be most clearly seen. But to enter deeply into James's art of the novel, one cannot ignore either the manifest or the latent results of his having cultivated long, lovingly and well the art of seeing.

NOTES

1. This photograph by Alice Boughton was reproduced in *Hound & Horn*, VII (April: June 1934) 478, and is the frontispiece to *The Painter's Eye*, ed. John L. Sweeney (Cambridge, Mass., 1956).

2. Though the definition is my own, I am indebted for this term to F. O. Matthiessen, 'James and the Plastic Arts', in *Kenyon Review*, V (Autumn 1943) 533–50.

3. *Confidence* (Boston, 1880) p. 1. As James's late revisions give a distorted picture of his earlier style, I refer to the earliest editions available of works prior to and including *The Portrait of a Lady*. (All of these editions were published in Boston.) As the revisions after that work do not seem crucial enough to justify using scattered and often difficult to obtain editions, for fiction that followed I refer to *The Novels and Tales of Henry James* (New York, 1907–9) and for works not included in the New York Edition to *The Novels and Stories of Henry James*, ed. Percy Lubbock (1921–3), abbreviated NY and NS respectively and incorporated in my text.

4. *Principles of Art History*, trans. M. D. Hottinger, 7th ed. (New York, n.d.) p. 25.

5. *The Portrait of a Lady* (Boston, 1882) p. 321.

6. 'An Introductory Essay', in *The Sacred Fount* (New York, 1953) xx.

7. James used this phrase in describing his reactions to Paris in a letter of 1899 to his architect friend Edward P. Warren. See John Russell, 'Henry James and the Leaning Tower', in *New Statesman and Nation*, XXV (April 1943), 254–5.

8. *The Painter's Eye*, p. 43.

9. *The Art of the Novel: Critical Prefaces*, ed. Richard P. Blackmur (New York, 1934) p. 8.

10. *The Notebooks of Henry James*, ed. F. O. Matthiessen and Kenneth B. Murdock (New York, 1947) p. 409.

11. See *Life in Letters of William Dean Howells*, ed. Mildred Howells (Garden City, 1928) I 175.

12. *Travelling Companions* (New York, 1919) p. 20.

13. There is a discussion of James's use of Italian art for background and imagery in Robert L. Gale, 'Henry James and Italy', in *Nineteenth Century Fiction*, XIV (Sept. 1959) 157–71. Gale does not analyze in any detail the contextual significance of particular art images.

14. *The Painter's Eye*, p. 58.

15. Ibid. p. 76.

16. This identification was made by Miriam Allott, 'The Bronzino Portrait in *The Wings of the Dove*', in *Modern Language Notes* LXVIII (Jan. 1953) 23–5.

17. Arthur McComb, *Agnolo Bronzino, His Life and Works* (Cambridge, Mass., 1928) p. 9.

18. *The Letters of Henry James*, ed. Percy Lubbock (New York, 1920) I 127.

19. His memory of the 1887 visit is recorded in the preface to *The Spoils of Poynton*. See *The Art of the Novel*, pp. 135–6.

20. This painting, which is in the Boston Museum of Fine Arts, is by Walter A. Gay. Sargent's 'Interior of a Palazzo in Venice' is of the grand sala of the Palazzo Barbaro. With its representation of figures (the Daniel Curtises, their son and his wife) in informal poses, this picture could be a frontispiece to one of James's depictions of 'modern' life in a sumptuous old world setting.

21. *Portraits of Places* (Boston, 1884) pp. 29–30.

22. For a brilliant interpretation of analogies between essentially the subjects of Veronese's paintings and this scene, see Laurence B. Holland, '*The Wings of the Dove*', in *Journal of English Literary History*, xxvi (Dec. 1959) 549–74.

23. James mentions seeing this painting in 'From Chambéry to Milan', in *Transatlantic Sketches* (Boston, 1875) p. 76.

24. *Italian Painters of the Renaissance* (New York, 1957) pp. 47–8.

25. 'The Relations between Poetry and Painting', in *The Necessary Angel* (New York, 1951) p. 169.

26. *David to Delacroix*, trans. Robert Goldwater (Cambridge, Mass., 1952) p. 113.

27. See *The Painter's Eye*, p. 113.

28. Ibid. p. 74.

29. Arnold Hauser, *The Social History of Art* (New York, 1951) I 873.

30. Edward E. Hale, 'The Impressionism of Henry James', in *Faculty Papers of Union College*, II (Jan. 1931) 17. Hale points out that James had much in common with the Impressionist sensibility, but he does not attempt to analyze specific Impressionist characteristics of his work.

31. *The Life of Forms in Art*, trans. Charles Beecher Hogan and George Kubler (New York, 1948) p. 15.

32. My discussion of Mannerist art is based largely on Walter Friedlaender, *Mannerism and Anti-Mannerism in Italian Painting* (New York, 1957); Nikolaus Pevsner, 'The Architecture of Mannerism', in *The Mint, A Miscellany of Literature, Art and Criticism*, ed. Geoffrey Grigson (1946) pp. 116–38; and I. L. Zupnik, 'The "Aesthetics" of the Early Mannerists', in *Art Bulletin*, xxxv (Dec. 1953) 302–6.

33. Friedlaender, p. 5.

34. Ibid. p. 6.

35. Pevsner, p. 136.

36. *Tintoretto, The Paintings and Drawings* (New York, 1948) p. 44.

37. 'Note sur Mallarmé et Poe', in *La Nouvelle Revue Française*, xxvii (Nov. 1926) 525.

38. *The Method of Henry James* (Philadelphia, 1954) p. lxxxvii.

39. 'The Vision of Grace: James's *The Wings of the Dove*', in *Modern Fiction Studies*, III (Spring 1957) 34.

40. *The Art of the Novel*, p. 84.

41. *Transatlantic Sketches*, pp. 91–2.

42. *Tintoretto*, p. 62.

43. *The Future of the Novel, Essays on the Art of Fiction*, ed. Leon Edel (New York, 1956) p. 156.

44. *Italian Hours* (Boston and New York, 1909) pp. 49–50.

45. Giorgio Melchiori, *The Tightrope Walkers: Studies of Mannerism in Modern English Literature* (1956) p. 23. Melchiori considers James a precursor of a twentieth-century Mannerist style.

46. James's taste was eclectic, but it is apparent from letters and essays that the two artists who meant the most to him were Tintoretto and the Michelangelo of the Medici chapel.

WILLIAM J. MASEYCHIK

Points of Departure from *The American* (1967)

JAMESIAN characters may live in a world in which there are numerous social forms to observe and proprieties to maintain, but the bond of decorum is more than social. While it is also true that members of James's Society may appropriate one another and proceed mutually to manipulate and exploit each other, there are bonds besides inter-personal involvement and control upon them as well. The physical environment is equally important. James's characters are under the sway of the places from which they come, and whatever worlds they enter. The lively inter-action between them – the social warfare waged in the interests of wealth and power, must not obscure the strong correspondences between the environment and the consequently limited behaviour in it – the fact of patterned action. For James's work is, above all, composed.

To create patterns in action, characters are flattened. *The American* (1877) provides an excellent example of two-dimensional characters. As an American, Newman's name – Christopher for the explorer, adventurer, and discoverer, Columbus; and Newman for the innocent Adamic man – suits him. It is his first time abroad, and he comes to discover. The same propriety is evinced in the name, Claire de Cintré. In the course of the novel, her life is clearly something of a curve, an arch. She experiences an unhappy marriage, suddenly she rises to a zenith of possibility for Newman, and finally she sinks into the utter abnegation of the convent. 'Arch', moreover, seems entirely appropriate to the world of confinement in which she lives. Arches circle over; they support, but cover too. The people who keep Claire so beautifully are the Bellegardes. Valentin, who has the warmest heart for Newman, does for love. When Newman needs help, he turns to the Duchesse de Outreville. He believes she is relatively uninvolved.

Finally, there is Mrs Bread, a staple whom Newman depends on for the plain facts. These characters are more flat than 'real people'.

The use of emblematic names is not the only way characters are objectified. They are frequently compared, and sometimes even equated, to things; most often to art objects and ornaments. 'Madame de Cintré is a great white doll of a woman . . . a prize.' She is exquisitely pale and does not talk much. Néomie Nioche is 'extremely perfect; as hard and clear-cut as some little figure of a sea-nymph in an antique intaglio'. When the lady copyist is re-met in Hyde Park, she has become a painted object. Mrs Bread, whose name is itself a thing, presents a more oblique example of the relationship of people and things. The only sure sign of life in the gloomy Bellegarde house, she was once attacked by Madame Bellegarde because she wore a red ribbon in her cap. Madame Bellegarde said it was a device to attract her husband, M. Bellegarde. The red ribbon stood for Mrs Bread's attractive vitality.

A strain is felt when characters are likened to inert things. They lose something called 'life'. But there are, in fact, other examples of 'life' disappearing to be found. Newman and his American friend, Tristram, are in the Louvre. They look at the Van Dykes and Titians, wondering if they are originals. In doing so, they suggest that a masterpiece conveys nothing more than a copy: in a great painting there is no feeling given form that would be missing in a copy. But when Newman commissions Néomie to copy the Louvre's most difficult paintings, he finds she cannot. He cannot understand what the fact that she is not a real artist has to do with this.

Having established the relationship between characters and things, and noticed Newman's tendency to overlook the life-like quality in art, we can now return to our idea of a controlling environment. As the vitality of the characters wanes, the physical environment grows powerful. Newman is subject to his environment. One day he leaves his work in the city, and takes a carriage to look at the green leaves on Long Island. From the exhilarating openness and greenness comes the new idea that he will go abroad. The place creates the controlling idea. He soon arrives in Paris and there behaves *comme il faut*, as Americans are supposed to behave in Paris. He goes to the Louvre with his guide books. Again the place creates the controlling idea. Newman is utterly subject to the new environment. In it, he is powerless. He is, at last, locked out of Paris when Claire enters the convent;

he is, that is, summarily locked out of the Parisians' Paris into the Americans' Paris. He leaves and resumes his place in America.

Americans are not the only characters who suffer in a tyrannical environment. The Bellegardes live in a world of concentrated privacy. Newman goes through 'gray and silent streets of the Faubourg St Germain, whose houses present to the outer world a face as impassive and as suggestive of the concentration of privacy within as the blank walls of Eastern seraglios. . . . The place was all in the shade; it answered to Newman's conception of a convent.' From the house, the story unfolds. The Marquis and his mother prove as impassive and suggestive – Newman always sensed something sinister in them – as their house. They keep secrets also. Significantly, the house is situated on the Rue de l'Université. Universities preserve intricate forms and ancient knowledge, which is what the Bellegarde house represents for Newman: old traditions, history, things to be learned. The place resembles a convent; and this is *the* European fact – that Claire can be locked away in a convent – which becomes Newman's central experience as the American in Europe. 'There's a curse upon the house' which none of its members will escape. Valentin's uniqueness as the romantic Bellegarde need not be emphasized. Though he lives apart on the Boulevard Haussmann, his rooms are 'low, *dusky, contracted*, and *crowded* with curious bric-à-brac'. They are 'pervaded by the odour of cigars, mingled with perfumes more *inscrutable*. Newman thought it a damp, gloomy place to live in, and was puzzled by the *obstructive* and fragmentary character of the furniture' (my italics). Valentin's death is as much the result of the curse upon the Bellegardes' house, a world he cannot leave even on the Boulevard Haussmann, as it is the result of *Don Giovanni* at the opera. He may die in a duel for love, but he is cursed as an old member of the house. The environmental romance of the opera, which Newman also sees in that curious Bellegarde house, and the house's gloom are one. The cursed environment continues to control its creatures wherever they are.

The characters in *The American* are not merely subject to their environment; more, they wait upon it and learn from it. James created an aesthetic of crystallizations and 'impressions', important stillnesses and revelatory moments. His is an aesthetic of the *trouvaille*, the *bon mot*, and the *aperçu*, moments when something new is glimpsed and found in a detail, caught in a word, perceived and apprehended through the surface of a still scene before the elements in that composition shift and all fades. In the composed Jamesian scene, new meaning is seen in a single detail, in the relative position of the compositional elements, in forms. People may also be forms or details, compositional elements. There is, for example, the moment when Newman watches Claire de Cintré speaking with Lord Deepmere:

> The end of the conservatory was formed by a clear sheet of glass, unmasked by plants, and admitting the winter starlight so directly that a person standing there would have seemed to have passed into open air.

Conservation, plants and clarity are the keynotes of the passage. The ideas and things attach themselves respectively to the secret saved, the curse which flowers from Fleurières, and the first revelation of mystery. Newman sloughs off the mystery. He doesn't like mysteries, he says, and yet the moment stays with him. He remembers it when he is told of the curse. The physical environment was entirely suited to the disclosure. This is also true when Mrs Bread reveals the exact nature of the curse to Newman. She does so among ruins – a place in which the past endures, silent and disfigured. Newman's final revelation comes to him when he returns from America to the Rue d'Enfer to gaze a second time at the place of Claire's confinement: 'The barren stillness of the place seemed to be his own release from ineffectual longing. It was told him that the woman within was lost beyond recall . . . somewhere in his mind, a tight knot seemed to have loosened.' Once again it is the place which tells. When Newman at last *sees* the convent, he goes.

At this point the importance of the physical environment becomes clear. It articulates, and has a definitive value. In the first place, it exercises certain controls over its inhabitants whether they be Europeans or Americans. Everyone has his place in his world. Secondly, and more important, the environment reveals the quintessential conditions of its inhabitants' lives, though this is only apparent during those revelatory moments when the genius of the place appears.

In *Washington Square* (1880), James continues this interest in people as 'objects', and in the containing environments. Characters are again two-dimensional. The most striking thing about simple Catherine Sloper is her garish clothing. Catherine's father is simple too. His daughter will never have his sanction to marry Morris. With his will stubbornly fixed, he is as inevitable as a problem in geometry. Morris

himself is most like an inanimate object. Dr Sloper speaking anatomi-
cally calls him 'a beautiful structure'. And Morris lives in a kind of
'doll-house'.

Washington Square, like the worlds we saw in *The American*, is a
tyrannical environment. It may be the 'ideal of quiet and genteel
retirement'; the Sloper house may be 'devilish comfortable . . . a
perfect castle of indolence' for Morris, but the ideal quality and
comfort are deceptive. It is as impossible for one of its inhabitants-to
escape the Square as it was for the Bellegardes or Newman to escape
their worlds. Catherine's world is no bigger than a brownstone. She
receives Morris's proposal, not in the park as intended, but in her
father's parlour. The promise of new life elsewhere does not extricate
her. Before she goes to Europe with her father, she is counselled to
appeal to him in some celebrated spot – perhaps on the Grand Canal
some night. She does just this, but the old man remains obdurate.
Nor is a way found in the Alps. In fact, away from the Square,
Catherine and her father become lost. Old Sloper looks at the Alpine
scene, but he sees no romance. Even Catherine finds 'the place ugly and
lonely'. The doctor asks, 'Should you like to be left in such a place as
this, to starve? . . . That will be your fate – that's how he will leave
you.' In Switzerland now, Catherine and her father have never really
left the Square. After their return to America, Catherine discovers
Morris is leaving her and, for the first time, abandons Washington
Square and goes out to find him. But he's gone. There is nothing
beyond the Square. What of the city? The scheming Mrs Penniman
and Morris meet at various places in the city to discuss his marriage
to Catherine. But note how desolate and void these places are. They
usually meet at the Greenwood Cemetery, the 7th Avenue oyster
saloon (its floor would typically be covered with sawdust and shells),
and by an empty lot. And Mrs Penniman says virtually nothing.

The Square is where we last see Catherine, after Morris has gone.
'Catherine, meanwhile in the parlour, picking up her morsel of fancy-
work, had seated herself with it again – for life as it were.' Here is
another still, revelatory moment: Catherine is working on a pattern,
what her life has always been and always will be. She comes to rest,
composed in her place. Action tends to pattern.

Characters continue to remain immobilized under the sway of place
in *The Portrait of a Lady* (1881). What marks the development here are
the many comparisons between characters' imaginations, and structures

and places. They are natural to James's aesthetic. If one can glimpse the essence of a situation in a detail or the patterned surface of a scene, it follows that the scene itself expresses something significant: a state of mind, a certain disposition or general nature. Isabel Archer (is a beautiful arch) is described in terms of architecture and landscaped gardens. The room in Albany where she once played was bolted and shut off from the street. 'But she had no wish to look out, for this would have interfered with her theory that there was a strange, unseen place on the other side – a place which became to a child's imagination, according to its different moods, a region of delight or terror.' The closed room prompts this way of thinking – no less than it would if it were the imagination itself. Elsewhere, 'Isabel's nature had, in her conceit, a certain garden-like quality, a suggestion of . . . shady bowers and lengthening vistas, which made her feel that introspection was, after all, an exercise in the open air, and that a visit to the recesses of one's spirit was harmless when one returned from it with a lapful of roses'. The mind is a house or garden; ideas are roses in it. From this harmony of mind and physical environment in the imagination comes a sense of great repose.

Ralph Touchett's 'places' are similarly restful. Like a work of art, tea at Gardencourt has about it the stillness of 'a little eternity . . . an eternity of pleasure'. Here Ralph sits quietly drawing the world into himself, dreaming of Isabel's future, interiorizing reality and imagining how it will compose itself with one light touch of his plan. Gardencourt is as shadowy as the imagination. Here is no 'real dusk'. 'Real dusk would not arrive for many hours; but the flood of summer light had begun to ebb, the air had grown mellow, the shadows were long upon the smooth, dense turf.' An envelope with which the novel opens and ends, Gardencourt contains and locks away a world of experience even as a work of art locks away and contains its certain life. Gardencourt has as much life as people. Mme Merle says of it, 'I don't venture to send a message to the people, but I should like to give my love to the place.' Isabel says, 'it's too enchanting . . . it's just like a novel'.

But enchantment can bind and hold, creating sometimes a terrible stillness. When old Touchett died, 'Isabel kept her place for a half an hour; there was a great stillness in the house'. When Ralph dies, 'The house [is] perfectly still – with a stillness that Isabel remembered; it had filled all the place for days before the death of her uncle.' As the book progresses, the stillness of eternity in the scene becomes the hush of death. A ghost attests to the element of death in that beautiful state of mind, Gardencourt. Ralph tells Isabel she cannot see this ghost until she has suffered. After her disastrous marriage to Osmond, she returns to Gardencourt where Ralph is dying. Before his death, Isabel sees a wraith – sees at last the *spiritus loci*.

But Ralph was a positive, life-giving character. He had a portion of his inheritance left to Isabel to create new possibilities for her; to provide materials for composition (if not to attempt one light stroke). For she should have this inheritance freely so that her life should take its own course. Yet it is also true that life-giving Ralph is dying from the moment we see him. He is a paradox, something rather like a work of art, at once alive and dead. It is as though a portraitist had looked at Ralph, selected certain lights and shadows on his face, detected a unique disposition of bones and flesh, and then fixed his vision in line, color, and form – as though he had killed his live subject to make his dead canvas live.

The mind of the aesthete Osmond, and the places associated with it, return us to this question of life and death in the world of art. Osmond's world is more negative than Albany and Gardencourt, but the difference is of degree, not kind. His world is also still, shadowy, and exclusive; as private as thought and imagination. It too presents a picture well-composed. Osmond's Florentine villa has one of those far-projecting roofs which make 'so harmonious a rectangle with the straight, dark cypresses that usually rise in groups of three and four beside it'. A group of people there 'might have been described by a painter as composing well'. Isabel, however, soon learns that the villa 'was the house of darkness, the house of dumbness, the house of suffocation. Osmond's beautiful mind gave it neither light nor air; Osmond's beautiful mind indeed seemed to peep down from a small high window and mock at her.' (One of those high windows, 'in their noble proportions . . . [whose] function seemed less to offer communication with the world than to defy it to look in'.) The villa's façade 'was the mask, not the face of a house'.

Osmond wants to live perfectly, but his criterion, perfection, is too narrow. As Ralph observes, 'When I saw this rigid system close about [Isabel], draped though it was in pictured tapestries, that sense of darkness and suffocation . . . took possession of her, she seemed shut up with an odour of mould and decay.' Attracted by the still beauty of Osmond's world, Isabel watches in pain as the aesthetically controlled environment becomes, for the girl who so loves freedom, a *hortus conclusus* in which nothing can stir. Unlike Ralph, who is chary of tampering with life in the interests of composition, Osmond is totally dedicated to composing. He treats people like objects, the better to compose them. 'He found the silver quality in this perfection in Isabel; he could tap her imagination with his knuckle and make it ring.' Osmond places people even if it means figurative or literal death for them. He wants to place Pansy in a convent, and dying Ralph into an unhealthy climate. '[Touchett] ought never to have come; it is worse than an impudence for people in that state to travel; it's a kind of indelicacy.' While Osmond is for delicacy and propriety, everything in place, Ralph travels for his health. Osmond wants to sort things out; he wants to put them in their places; to compose things, or people, as the case may be. He is the sinister 'artist', and his world is skeletal.

There is a deceptively striking similarity between Osmond's aesthetic and what James presented as his own in the introduction to *The Portrait*. He too likes to place people, or characters: 'I see them placed.' He describes Isabel as 'the image of the young feminine nature that I had for so considerable a time all curiously at my disposal'. What does James do with these 'women' he has at his disposal? He often locks them up. If Bellegarde locks up Claire, and Osmond Isabel and Pansy, who but James himself has locked up Catherine Sloper, and Mrs Touchett, who is always for some unknown reason 'locking herself away'? In writing, James 'piled brick on brick', but the novel itself shows he is in fact more a life-giving Ralph than an Osmond.

James may continue to liken people to things, specifically *objets d'art*, in *The Portrait*, where Pansy is a 'Dresden-china shepherdess . . . an Infanta of Velasquez'; but, unlike Osmond, James knows what Merle tells Isabel: 'I've a great respect for things! One's self – for other people – is one's expression of one's self; and one's house, one's furniture, one's garments, the books one reads, the company one keeps – these things are all expressive.' The species of wisdom here is beyond Osmond. He does not think things express others' selves (for him there are none besides his), but that things are all that those other selves are. For him, things cannot be expressive because as far as he is concerned there is nothing to express.

James, on the contrary, sees that things expressing no life are grotesque. When his characters step back for a moment, thus surrendering something of their vitality, the lifeless physical environment quickens into a monstrosity.

> It was perfectly *still*; the wide quadrangle of *dusky* houses showed lights in none of the windows, where the *shutters* and *blinds* were *closed*; the pavements were a *vacant* expanse, and, putting aside two small children from a neighboring slum, who, attracted by *symptoms of abnormal animation in the interior*, poked their faces between the rusty rails of the *enclosure*, the most *vivid* object within sight was the big red pillar-post on the southeast corner (my italics).

'Putting aside two small children', the composed London dusk becomes a state of psychopathology. The scene, as at Albany, Gardencourt, and Osmond's villa, is again shadowy and still. The quiet dark corresponds to an interior darkness in the mind. But now the language is clearly, strangely, clinical. Contrasted to young Isabel's healthy imagination, 'symptoms of abnormal animation in the interior' might describe the mind of an agitated patient, as well as of an empty square. The emptiness teems with psychological life. The red pillar-post becomes a vivid object – alive, as it were. But it is pathological: the red pillar-post expresses nothing. With the death of that rare subject, Ralph Touchett, such a grotesque reversal – subjects dying, objects living – occurred: 'Isabel grew nervous and scared as if the objects about her had begun to show for conscious things.'

When 'scenes of life' are too nicely composed, when their 'life' is removed, they become sterile still-lifes, environments in which subjects turn into objects, and vice versa. But James has also shown the importance of form and of composition for revelations. As one example from *The Portrait*, Isabel watches Osmond and Merle standing motionless together. 'She had received an impression'; she took 'in the scene before she interrupted it'. We are reminded of Newman watching Claire de Cintré and Lord Deepmere in the conservatory; and of Catherine Sloper at her needlework. The scene again holds the key to the life of its inhabitants, this time hinting at the relationship between Osmond and Merle. Something is newly discovered through a chance arrangement of compositional elements. 'Their *relative positions*, their absorbed mutual gaze, struck her as something detected.' Through contemplation of the nature of the environment, we detect the 'life' of its inhabitants.

The environment is the key which unlocks the life of *The Wings of the Dove* (1902). This novel is notable for the variety of places it presents. There is the 'vulgar' world we first associate with Kate Croy, where one tastes 'the faint, flat emanation of *things*, the failure of fortune and honour'. There is the materialistic world of Aunt Maud, where we take in 'the *message* of her massive, florid furniture, the immense *expression* of her signs and symbols . . . so almost *abnormally* affirmative, so aggressively erect [are] the huge heavy *objects*' (my italics). There is the world of Lord Mark's Matcham, and 'the storied ceilings of Venice'.

Merton Densher moves through these worlds, and others, freely. He moves through Kensington Gardens to Lancaster Gate; from Matcham to America to the Palazzo Leporelli; and so to the little Venetian quarter. Densher was educated in Switzerland, Germany, and England. 'Never was a man in so many places at once.' Though he is connected with numerous places, he remains indifferent and restive in them because he wants to find *the* place. He does not know where he belongs really, and cannot act decisively until there is a revelation and he finds the place which is marked.

During Milly's final sickness, her door is closed to Densher. There is a storm over Venice, and he goes to St Mark's Square. ' . . . in the high arcade [of the Piazza] half Venice was crowded close, while, on the Molo, at the limit of the expanse, the old columns of St Mark and of the Lion were like the lintels of a door wide open to the storm . . . the palace had *for the first time* failed of a welcome' (my italics). Like St Mark's open to the storm, the Palazzo Leporelli admits a darker element than Densher, namely the element of Milly's death. Significantly, it is Lord Mark who has come to Venice to reveal Kate's and Densher's secret engagement to Milly, and so cause the disturbance which precipitates her death. 'The weather had changed, the rain was ugly, the wind wicked, the sea impossible, because of Lord Mark. It was because of him, a fortiori, that the palace was closed.' Who or what is Lord Mark? His presence will not be separated from St Mark's, from Densher's rejection and Milly's Venetian death. When Lord Mark, Densher's rejection, the storm, and Milly's death come quickly together, Densher glimpses something new. People who are like things such as marks, or scenes *aperçues* such as St Mark's, help to make the message clear and precise.

But the central figure in *The Wings*, the dove Milly Theale, has no clearly marked place. Her nature is too contradictory. She is the 'real thing', and in novels so concerned with subject and object, and life and death, this makes her more complex than an heiress. She is 'real', has life; but is also a 'thing', and so is dead. (The dead metaphor, 'real thing', lives.) She is a paradox, and as the other characters say, has illimitable possibilities. She lives in the Palazzo Leporelli; more than a 'temple to taste', also a house of death. The rich 'apartment of state' embodies the moribund state of its owner. Because her entire family is dead, she always wears a seemly black. But one evening she appears stunningly in white. That one extreme suits her as well as another attests to her paradoxical nature. She turns her face to the wall to die, but then Densher calls, and she receives him looking vibrant. A special environment is required for such a 'thing' to be 'real'.

Milly sits on the Alpine cliffside above the abyss. 'Grey immensity is her element.' She belongs to some wonderful undefinable realm. As she tells Susan Stringham, 'So you see, you'll never really know where I am. Except indeed when I'm gone; and then you'll only know where I'm not.' Her place is defined negatively: it is not in this world. The young heiress who possesses such 'fine materials' is herself of 'fine material', of some incorporeal realm. She represents a characteristic Jamesian refinement on that early subject–object fusion in *The American*; the human still as art object, but now a living–dead object – the 'real thing'. For Milly belongs to the world of art. (Her name, Theale, comes from 'Thing' and 'Real'.)

The most mobile figure in a world of great social mobility – (like Ralph, travelling for her health), Milly fits nowhere in that world. From lower- to middle- to upper-class worlds, *The Wings of the Dove* extends from a foreground of low-life to the more remote world of Matcham. Despite this comprehensiveness, Milly has no place in any of these worlds. She belongs to a more eternal realm. Her Palazzo Leporelli is a 'museum'; Milly a 'Bronzino'. At Matcham, there is a Bronzino portrait of a lady which suits Milly perfectly. As Lord Mark observes to her: 'But you're a pair. You must surely catch it.' Everyone there agrees.

> The lady in question, at all events . . . was a very great personage – only unaccompanied by joy. And she was dead, dead, dead. Milly recognized her exactly in words that had nothing to do with her. 'I shall never be better than this.'

'The lady in question' and the pronoun 'her' are ambiguous. Does the painted subject say, 'I shall never be better than this', or is it Milly herself? If Milly has 'immense possibilities' and if she 'shall never be better than this', perhaps at most she will be just this – a work of art. And that will best answer her promise. Soon she will be dead as the 'Bronzino', and yet – and this is most important – capable of moving after she is dead. Capable, that is, of moving Densher, inspiring his moral growth. (And as Ralph does for Isabel, she leaves Densher money to free him at last.) Milly, dying, gives life.

This is the value of expressive places and animated objects. Milly Theale, a very rare 'subject' to begin with, dies and with her death stirs more certainly than ever before. She acquires a more unique 'life'. Looking back towards *The American*, James articulates a new environment for what are now his 'subjects', and creates new 'things' to live in that world. It is as if Milly were a painting which conveys some sense of life even as it is being painted but never as much as when completed. No longer becoming, the still canvas has vibrant being. Milly's life does not *really* begin until she is finished.

The portraits of Bronzino – who had a 'gift of incisive vision, never of the whole of reality, but of surfaces and fragments'[1] – have always been known for their life-like quality.

NOTE

1. *Encyclopedia of World Art* (New York, 1960) II p. 631.

J. A. WARD

The Europeans and the Structure of Comedy (1964)

ANY analysis of the structure of *The Europeans* should begin with the observation that it is essentially a comic novel. For one thing, it owes much to the well-made dramatic comedies of such nineteenth-century playwrights as Dumas *fils*, Augier, and Sardou, and also to the narrative romances of Feuillet and Cherbuliez.[1] Not only do the wit, the grace, and the situation of *The Europeans* suggest such works, but also the rigid construction, the careful balancing and juxtaposition of character types, and the rigorously logical progression of events (rendered scenically) to an inevitable conclusion. Also James draws freely upon much older comic patterns, such as the conversion of a traditional society by a group of young intruders to a fresher view of life and the triumph of the young lovers over the objections of their obtuse and narrow-minded elders.[2] In addition, *The Europeans* uses such venerable devices as the comic intrigue and the complicated and neat rounding-off. The atmosphere is pastoral, and the spirit is predominantly gay.

The clash of opposing social groups provides the central comic situation, and since the clash is for the most part resolved harmoniously, the prevailing view of life in the novel is comic, that is, faults exist to be laughed at, and errors exist to be corrected. In *The Europeans*, James gets closer to a purely comic vision of the international conflict than in any other novel, but it is a mistake to force the work into an exclusively comic pattern. Finally the novel is *sui generis* in its design. It has a conventional comic foundation, but the total effect is something different. James's conception of structure in this novel is organic, so that while he uses many of the usual motifs and compositional devices of comedy, he rejects those demands of a mechanical form that either misrepresent or have no bearing on the idea he wishes to develop.

The New England setting is of first importance in the comic mood of *The Europeans*. Though James frequently uses Europe for comic and satiric purposes – as when he exposes the provincialism of Henrietta Stackpole against the background of St Peter's Cathedral – he never makes it the setting of a predominantly comic story. Even in the stories in which James invests Europe with the picturesque coloration of travel literature, he is unwilling to isolate the beauty of the past from the evil he usually associates with the past. But America in *The Europeans* is mainly a pastoral scene – a Forest of Arden or 'green world'[3] suggesting the Golden Age not only to Felix Young, but also to the reader. Here is a world in which evil can exist only as something temporarily disagreeable. If the pastoral scene makes the gloom of the Americans additionally quaint and groundless (they are seen as Calvinists in Eden), it also provides an atmosphere in which young lovers can achieve bliss and in which innocence can never be sullied. The setting also colors our estimation of the Europeans; it prevents us from associating them with any Old World corruption. The casual, semi-rural Arcadia that James wishes us to accept as a Boston suburb of the 1840s[4] is in every way congenial to a humorous treatment of the international theme.

The comedy of *The Europeans* blends gentle, urbane satire of the Puritan temperament with a modulated evocation of the charms of innocence. The relaxed, mildly ironic tone lends an easy grace to the novel. The tone itself is a perfect vehicle – perhaps the principal reason for the excellence of the book. It is detached yet genial, sympathetic yet neither serious nor sentimental, and it falls well short of either frivolity or cynicism. The narrative approach is old-fashioned, recalling Thackeray and Trollope rather than forecasting the later James. Throughout we hear the voice of the author gracefully and even ceremoniously telling his story and commenting on his characters. This voice is exceedingly tolerant, and yet it is witty at the expense of the characters; it gives a steady and barely perceptible control over our own judgment of the action, counseling us to refrain from both harsh judgments and suspicions that the story is merely trivial.

The experience which James renders in *The Europeans* is rather graver and less purely amusing than we commonly expect in comedy, and yet not grave enough to be something else – such as tragedy, melodrama, or even romance. James deliberately mutes the moral issues that he lingers over in other novels. If the tone is slightly unsteady, the reason is James's reluctance to falsify certain deeper realities that the situation seems to bring forth. For example, Gertrude Wentworth occasionally overreaches the simple role that James assigns her; she is hard-hearted and callous of others' feelings. This is a quality James often reveals in the American heroine,[5] but it is out of place in the translucent scheme of *The Europeans*. The novel softens and almost conceals the suggestions of unresolvable difficulties, but it does not omit them. The rigid structure and essential artificiality of classical comedy, the leisurely flow of the prose, and the unhurried lives of the characters make *The Europeans* a nearly perfect comic performance, but the novel remains something both more and less than comic. Even the neat resolution of the plots in the final half-dozen pages – in which four marriages are recorded, with Shakespearean finality and ceremony – does not disguise the special quality of the experience of the novel.

As in most comedy, James's principal technique is to represent his characters as undeviating simplifications. *The Europeans* is thus roughly an allegory, with each of the major characters representing a large aspect of the culture which has produced him. Yet a sense of complexity is achieved through James's characteristic technique of implying contrasts among characters and events. With the possible exception of Robert Acton, no single character is very complicated, but we can understand their significances only by perceiving how James has dramatically related each to each. For instance, Felix Young is an extremely simplified creation – in the mold of the gay young man of the well-made play – but to estimate his character we must consider his relation to the characters who frame him, not merely to his obvious foils, Mr Brand and Mr Wentworth, but also to Gertrude and to Eugenia. The structure follows from a revelation of complex inter-relationships among simple characters, all latent within the obvious and basic contrast between Europe and America.

Superficially it would seem that the Europeans – Felix and Eugenia – are to be admired, and the Americans – the Wentworths, the Actons, and Mr Brand – are to be pitied. Freedom is preferable to oppression, a positive view to a negative one, culture to barbarism, intelligence to irrationality, happiness to gloom, and art to a distrust of art. Read solely in such terms, the novel shows the gradual conversion of Gertrude and the final resistance of Robert Acton to the European temperament, and as a flat background to this central action the utter rigidity of all the other Americans. The mechanics of character selection and the logical movement of the plot are obvious.

Yet it is a distortion of the experience of the book to suggest where our sympathies should lie or to demonstrate which way of life 'wins'. The Europeans have a larger role than to expose the limitations of the Americans. Critics do not widely disagree in their assessments of the New Englanders, but there are extreme differences of opinion as to how Felix and his sister are to be regarded. Felix is usually accepted as a thoroughly congenial embodiment of European *joie de vivre*, but Eugenia has been judged both a selfish schemer for wealth and position[6] and a charming, graceful woman whose faults are essentially minor.[7] Certainly the title characters are the major figures in the novel. Everything that happens is an effect of their plotting; the Americans merely react to them. As the causes of the action, they create the structure of the novel. In the opening chapters their mere presence provides a means of contrasting two cultures, but afterwards everything develops from their various intrigues and sub-intrigues. We witness not merely a static contrasting of opposing national views, but the direct and conscious influence of the Europeans upon the Americans.

James's characterization of the two Europeans largely accounts for the structure as well as the tone of the novel. Eugenia and Felix are essentially different from most of the other Europeans in James's fiction. Their distinctiveness consists in the apparent lightness with which they are handled; they seem – at least to the tastes of critics who share some of the Wentworths' bias – to get off too lightly. Detached as they are from the vaguely malignant European scene, Felix and Eugenia are remote from the evil atmosphere that shrouds such European characters as the Bellegardes and Richard de Mauves. It is not just that the genial tone and the pastoral vision of things prohibit any strong suggestion of the sinister and the portentous. The European background of Felix and Eugenia is only faintly and indirectly conveyed, and then it is suggestive of either Graustarkian fable and comic opera (how else is the reader to regard Eugenia's situation as morganatic wife of Prince Adolph of Silberstadt-Schreckenstein?) or of fancifully picturesque travel posters and provincial misconceptions of the bohemian life (Felix, we are told, has strolled through Europe with a band of carefree musicians). When Gertrude first sees Felix, she glances upward from a volume of *The Arabian Nights*, and the vision she beholds is as miraculous as the story she has been reading. Gertrude is naïve, but the Europeans consistently behave in a manner in keeping with her fantasies. Also the Europeans are purged of ancestral evil. The connivances of Eugenia's remote brother-in-law are clearly not to be lingered upon; this is but a quaintness as extravagant and as charming as the childlike view of the Old World that fascinates Gertrude.

In one respect it is characteristic of James to represent Europe through such a pair as the good-natured Felix and the worldly Eugenia. In *The American*, for example, Valentin de Bellegarde has the same zest for life as Felix Young, while his brother and mother, like Eugenia, are much devoted to traditional manners. In *The American*, of course, the burden of manners is considerably heavier than in *The Europeans*, eventually oppressing even the frolicsome Valentin. Still the schematic arrangement of European characters in *The American* has much the same effect as in *The Europeans*.

Since Felix and Eugenia are removed from the hereditary guilt and rigid social apparatus that weigh upon the Bellegardes, they appear not only unusually free (more like Americans than Europeans) but also unusually simplified. Felix is the least credible character in the novel. He is childishly good-natured, singlemindedly bent on happiness, and thoroughly engaging and charming – a man with neither temper nor guile, seemingly incapable of thinking any but the most flattering of thoughts about anyone. Not only is he unrestricted by the demands of class that finally inhibit Valentin de Bellegarde, but he is free from the demands of any class or society, and yet at the same time highly civilized. He stands virtually alone in James as a man who has all of the benefits of worldliness but none of the faults.

With the Baroness, who likewise stands for a part of the generic European character, James has a more difficult artistic problem. For his intention seems to be to draw a thoroughly attractive kind of Madame Merle, and by extension to represent artfulness as an un-equivocal good. But it is part of James's technique in sketching the Baroness to make her slightly ridiculous: she is so absurdly out of place in the world of the Wentworths that some of the amusement is at her expense – as in mock-heroic poetry the epic devices used to satirize must appear foolish in themselves.

What both Europeans embody is a highly refined form of oppor-tunism, and they become involved with a group of Americans who embody the contrary quality of discipline. This opposition is the subject of *The Europeans*, the central idea that gives the novel its dramatic unity. The terms of this opposition are represented in their abstract essence in a dialogue between Gertrude and Felix. Felix remarks:

'You don't seem to me to get all the pleasure out of life that you might. You don't seem to me to enjoy. . . . You seem to me very well placed for enjoying. You have money and liberty and what is called in Europe a "position". But you take a painful view of life, as one may say.'

. . . .

'I don't think it's what one does or one doesn't do that promotes enjoyment' [Felix continues]. 'It is the general way of looking at life.'

'They look at it as a discipline – that's what they do here' [Gertrude replies]. 'I have often been told that.'

'Well, that's very good. But there is another way,' added Felix, smiling: 'to look at it as an opportunity.' (pp. 103–5)[8]

The clash of 'ways of looking at life' obviously accounts for the make-up of a number of the characters and for their roles in the drama. Thus to Gertrude Mr Brand represents discipline and Felix represents opportunity. Robert Acton's sense of duty is concentrated in his devotion to his mother, and the Baroness personifies the life of self-gratification he is tentatively inclined to. But James's dramatic representation of the conflict of discipline and opportunity has a more pervasive role in the design of the book. For both opportunism and discipline are many-sided characteristics, particularly when they are regarded as cultural rather than merely personal attributes. The central characters in *The Europeans* together manifest the complexities implicit in these abstract qualities, and the action which engages these characters tests the assumptions about life which impel them.

Felix and his sister express the various meanings latent in the principle of opportunism. In its simplest and most apparent form, their opportunism is a capacity for experiencing pleasure. Felix with his comic imagination finds everything delightful – even muddy roads. Though he may speak of the benefits of a high civilization, he is most often seen as a man fully responsive to the less obvious pleasures of life. His painter's eye is his dominant faculty, and life as he sees it is gayly colored and fundamentally amusing. The Baroness, on the other hand, converts raw experience into traditional forms. Felix delights in the harsh simplicity of the Wentworths' house – 'it looks like a magnified Nuremberg toy' (p. 46), he remarks – but the Baroness elaborately decorates the neighboring cottage where she and Felix stay. The accumulated artifices of a traditional culture 'make' life. Money, style, and tradition together transform the dreary into the pleasurable.

Both the responsiveness of Felix and the social art of the Baroness are to be held in high regard; each reflects 'imagination', which the Wentworths sadly lack. The Europeans introduce the Americans to a way of seeing life and a way of refashioning life, and for doing so they are to be admired. But if their opportunism is a source of happiness and enrichment – for themselves and others – it is at the same time based on selfish motives.

Each is seeking economic gain from the New England relatives, Felix by painting their portraits and Eugenia by marrying one of them. If the Baroness is depressed and Felix is gay in the first chapter, their different moods should not conceal the similarity of their ambitions. Soon however their self-interest blends with a general benevolence. Even the Baroness feels a deep affection for her newly met kin. The plot of the novel develops from the gentle aggressions of Felix and Eugenia. Each is quickly paired with a New Englander – Felix with Gertrude, the Baroness with Robert Acton. Though we never lose sight of the essential self-interest that governs the two foreigners as they intrigue for fortune and status, their separate operations are viewed sympathetically. Gertrude, after all, needs Felix, who will be the best of husbands for her; nor is there any suggestion of hypocrisy in his expressed love for her.[9] Similarly the Baroness's graces attract Acton, who would certainly profit from marriage to such a woman. Furthermore, if the Baroness is a schemer or adventuress, as some have claimed, she conducts herself with such delicacy that it is Acton, if anyone, who appears crass and self-centered.

The sub-intrigues which the Europeans concurrently undertake also show that their self-interest is in no way incompatible with good will. By the middle of the novel, Felix and Eugenia extend their operations. Felix, who alone sees the obvious affection between Charlotte and Mr Brand, delicately suggests to Gertrude and to her former suitor that such a match would be a happy one. By directing Mr Brand's attention to Charlotte, Felix of course eliminates a major obstacle to his own marriage to Gertrude. He additionally profits by asking the obliging Charlotte to plead his own case before her father.

The sub-intrigue engineered by the Baroness is equally a combination of disinterested benevolence and shrewd self-interest. Clifford Wentworth, recently suspended from Harvard for drinking, is a difficult problem for his father. As the scion of the family, he desperately requires reformation. The Baroness, 'a woman of finely-mingled motive' (p. 173), undertakes to civilize Clifford, but at the same time she feels that Clifford may be kept in reserve as a potential husband, should her relation with Acton come to nothing. 'A prudent archer has always a second bowstring . . . ' (p. 173), she tells herself.

Although the Baroness and Felix seem most suited to experience life in its fullness, they are also shielded from certain dimensions of reality because of their special talents and perceptions. Felix, who is called a child by his sister, has a spontaneity that is refreshing in the chilling atmosphere of New England, but those problems which cannot be viewed in a cheerful light he either flatly ignores or else brushes away with irrelevant jests. His good nature is indeed a tonic to the Went-worths – when they submit to it – but it depends upon a fundamental shallowness of vision. He can successfully disarm Mr Wentworth and even Mr Brand by refusing to recognize their distress, but in the significant closing scene with his sister he fails utterly to help her. After an exasperating meeting with Acton, during which she guesses that his reluctance to marry her will eventually lead to her rejection, she guardedly asks Felix to help her. But Felix, the only person capable of influencing Acton to propose, conveniently dodges the veiled message. He does nothing for his sister, choosing to evade a problem in which good humor might prove inadequate. And when he speaks with his sister following her defeat, he can contribute neither advice nor sympathy. In the end he is nearly as pathetic as Acton in his weak attempt to salvage a hopeless situation by incongruous jollity.[10]

In a different way, the Baroness is also shielded from certain kinds of experience by her devotion to forms. She is not so intolerant of depression as is Felix – and thus she can express a wider range of attitudes and emotions than he – but she is at a loss when feelings are expressed directly, unembellished by conventional graces. It is worth noting that the one person whom she cannot deal with at all is Lizzie Acton, whose 'dangerous energy' (p. 132) makes her a natural enemy to the Baroness. Clifford is merely gauche and ill-bred, but Lizzie, who finally 'civilizes' Clifford, while the Baroness fails, has an immediate sexual and emotional expression of herself that the Baroness partly envies and partly despises.

The Baroness's artfulness cannot compete with Lizzie's vitality, and to that extent it is a limitation. But her relation with Lizzie is counter-weighted by her relation with Acton's mother, whose directness reveals social ineptness rather than refreshing honesty. Understandably, the Baroness is irritated by the dull tactlessness with which Mrs Acton, whom she has met only once previously, announces that she is dying and requests Eugenia to remain in the community because 'it would be so pleasant for Robert' (p. 233). In the exchange between the two women, art surely shows itself as superior to artlessness. In her ignorance of the rules of conversation, the old woman is unintentionally rude and offensive; the Baroness through intelligence, self-control, and a respect for decorum, prevents the unpleasantness of the situation from coming to the surface. With the single exception of her relation to Lizzie (which is important, because Lizzie defeats her plans with Clifford), the Baroness's artificiality is an expansion, not a repression of herself. Her manner, her conversation, even her clothes and her furnishings fully express her. Robert Acton, on the other hand, most often uses his acquired finesse to conceal his deeper feelings – even from himself. His quasi-worldliness, like his conscience, protects him from reality.

The Baroness has mastered the art of knowing how to be looked at. For her, appearance not only takes on more importance than reality, appearance is reality. She feels it is preferable to carry one's self like a pretty woman than to be a pretty woman. Pathetically and ironically she is regarded by the New Englanders as hardly a person at all, rather a spectacle to be gawked at, or to be paraded before friends and neighbors, like an exotic and unintelligible work of art. Eugenia is crudely rebuked by Acton, who acts as though manners and wit are in themselves sufficient bases of friendship, not requiring the further connection of marriage. Thus his relation to the Baroness remains that of an audience to a theatrical performer. Nor do the Wentworths ever acknowledge the Baroness's existence as a woman:

> They were all standing around [Eugenia], as if they were expecting her to acquit herself of this exhibition of some peculiar faculty, some brilliant talent. Their attitude seemed to imply that she was a kind of conversational mountebank, attired, intellectually, in gauze and spangles. (p. 63)

The distinguishing qualities of both Felix and Eugenia point simultaneously to the special virtues and special limitations of both the Europeans and the Americans. Eugenia's artistic self-representation accounts for her own civilized grace, but it is also a measure of her failure to deal with life directly, particularly in its more vigorous aspects. Her grace exposes the severe deficiency of a Mrs Acton, but it is the reason for her own inferiority to a Lizzie Acton. Correspondingly,

Felix can experience a pleasure beyond the capacity of an American, but he cannot recognize the pain which they so exaggerate as an element of life.

But it must be said that there is very little of pain in the novel. Thus the Americans are exposed as quixotic in their fear of a nonexistent evil. Finally what oppresses them is a fear of the unconventional and a fear of pleasure. As representatives of these qualities, the Europeans are harmless. Their suggested faults – their plotting for self-gain, Felix's inability to acknowledge pain, the Baroness's inability to face raw experience – are in no way inimical to the Americans. The Europeans offer only the possibility of happiness to the entire group. If anyone suffers, it is the Baroness, though she is no less admirable than Felix. The reason is simply that Felix's bonhomie proves less difficult for the New World to endure than the Baroness's courtliness.

But Eugenia's failure is not the only unpleasantness in the book. Through symbolism James suggests grave realities underlying the experience of the novel, though the suggestion is too mild to distort the genial tone. Mainly the setting, the dialogue, and the witty narrative voice blend; the discordant notes remain beneath the surface, to be perceived, but not to offset the comic mood.

For instance, James casually develops a complicated symbolism of youth and age – a rhetorical and scenic set of paradoxes that strengthens the dramatic ironies involved in the conjunction of the two cultures. These ironies are simultaneously frivolous and meaningful. New England, represented in the imagery of both youthful vitality and of death, is at once young and old. The book begins with a view of a dismal graveyard and ends with the death of Mrs Acton. To the Baroness, 'Gertrude seemed . . . almost funereal' (p. 54); and to Felix, 'there was something almost cadaverous in his uncle's high-featured white face' (p. 52). But if these and other comments reflect something life-denying in the New Englanders, many others reflect their comic youthfulness. Just as Mr Wentworth regards his eighty-year-old house as a 'venerable mansion' (p. 47) and as James speaks of Boston as an 'ancient city' (p. 1), so not even the Puritan temperament can conceal the youthfulness of the American civilization. The New Englanders are untried and rather timid children. The Wentworth house is not really old, but very fresh; and America is 'a comical country' (p. 8).

The Wentworth circle is both young and old – as young and old as the Golden Age. And in a different way, the same paradox applies to the Europeans. In the first chapter the Baroness tells Felix (whose last name is 'Young'): 'You will never be anything but a child, dear brother.'

> 'One would suppose that you, madam,' answered Felix, laughing, 'were a thousand years old.'
> 'I am – sometimes,' said the Baroness. (p. 21)

Felix's youth – a freedom from suppressions – and the Baroness's antiquity – an absorption in the manners of a very old civilization – help define their combined character. The two are not greatly different, for Felix's childishness differs only in degree from the Baroness's age; both exult in the promises of life. Age is wisdom for the Baroness, but only decay for the Wentworths; youth is gayety for Felix, but only inexperience for the Wentworths.

The Europeans are both younger and older (happier and wiser) than the also young and old (innocent and decayed) Americans, specifically because they are opportunists. And – to compound the paradoxes – their opportunism is characteristic of Americans rather than Europeans, especially as it is also associated with their freedom and their youth. James exploits the reputation of America as the land of opportunity (of course, in other of his works it is rather the land of opportunists, and Europe is the land of opportunity). If the notion of opportunity that motivates the Europeans is not exactly a standard American one, James nevertheless identifies the enterprises of the Europeans with the promises latent in America. At one point Felix thinks, 'this was certainly the country of sunsets. There was something in these glorious deeps of fire that quickened his imagination; he always found images and promises in the western sky' (p. 217). Even Eugenia, who is considerably less absorbed in nature than Felix, responds to the promise symbolized by the primitive American scene. Walking through the streets of Boston, 'she surrendered herself to a certain tranquil gayety. If she had come to seek her fortune, it seemed to her that her fortune would be easy to find. There was a promise of it in the gorgeous purity of the western sky . . .' (p. 19).

The suggestion that the Europeans are more archetypically American than the New Englanders is recurrent.[11] It establishes an additional relationship between the sets of characters and thus further refines the shape of the novel. In *The Europeans*, incidents, characters, and places become significant because they correspond to and yet contrast with other incidents, characters, and places. Thus the three prominent houses in the Wentworth neighborhood are each implicit criticisms of each other and of the kind of people who live in them: the Wentworths' is chaste and austere; the Baroness's is lavishly decorated; and Robert Acton's is an awkward compromise between the other two.[12] A less obvious pattern in the novel is formed by the repeated episodes in which lies are told or are commented on. The lie is a regular occasion for moral ambiguity in James; he nearly always employs the lie to differentiate the rigid moralist from the free spirit. To regard the telling of lies as *per se* heinous is to mark one's self as narrow and self-righteous. Thus one of the clearest indications that Gertrude is imaginative is that she tells harmless fibs. A lie is partly responsible for the downfall of Eugenia, though to her (and to our) mind when she lies to Mrs Acton in her son's presence she is only being courteous. In effect, the Baroness is regarded as a living lie; to the New Englanders she is performing a role rather than living a life. And Felix's flattering portraits of the Wentworth circle are at bottom lies. The New Englanders can regard forms of artfulness only in terms of ethics, because they can express themselves only by a moralistic rhetoric. But the Europeans convert moral questions to aesthetic ones. Thus to Mr Wentworth Clifford's alcoholism is a moral failing, while to Eugenia and Felix it represents a deficiency in manners.

Gertrude Wentworth is the only New Englander who accepts the offerings of the Europeans. James represents her as a kind of potential Eugenia, with the same tastes and habits though in a cruder, less articulate form. They are the only characters who tell 'lies', who respect appearances, and who are described as 'restless' and 'peculiar'.[13] But the main effect of these resemblances is to throw their differences into relief. Thus Gertrude's mistaking the high cultivation of the Europeans for naturalness is evidence that she is at center merely rebellious. The novel implies that one is never so natural – in the sense of giving full expression to the imagination – as when he is endowed with the manners of a rich civilization; but such a perception is certainly beyond the capacity of Gertrude. Gertrude actually fails to respond to the civilizing influences of the Europeans; her main reason for wishing to be like them is to free herself from her 'obligations' and 'responsibilities' – such as attending church, marrying Mr Brand, and telling the truth. She has not mastered the tact, the courtesy, and the geniality of Felix; she wants only his freedom. In her various self-assertions she is flippant and inconsiderate. Yet James does not present Gertrude in a harsh light; he simply reveals her as a rather ill-tempered and irritable girl who, in spite of her yearnings, has no real understanding of the life she has determined to lead.

But it is Eugenia rather than Gertrude who is excluded from the harmonious resolution of difficulties at the end. In the language of ancient comedy, Eugenia is what Northrop Frye calls the *pharmakos* – the rascal inimical to the well-being of society who is driven out in the comic resolution. Such an expulsion 'appeals to the kind of relief we are expected to feel when we see Jonson's Volpone condemned to the galleys, Shylock stripped of his wealth, or Tartuffe taken off to prison'. But the rejection of Eugenia pleases only if *The Europeans* is read as a total approbation of the New Englanders. As the novel stands, however, Eugenia's repudiation is somewhat like those 'most terrible ironies known to art' such as 'the rejection of Falstaff' and 'certain scenes in Chaplin'.[14]

In permitting the expulsion of Eugenia, James not only allows himself his only severe judgment of the New Englanders, but he gives a rather harsh turn to the otherwise genial tone of the novel. Eugenia dominates the final chapter, and if her dismissal does not nullify the gayety of the multiple weddings it at least counterbalances the mood of joy with one of unpleasantness. Indeed the seasonal backdrop of the novel is attuned to Eugenia's spirits. Her early gloom is complemented by a late spring snowstorm, but the climate improves and summer arrives as Eugenia's mood lightens; but as Eugenia perceives that Acton will fail her, summer gives way to winter. 'Les beaux jours sont passés' (p. 208), the Baroness says, contradicting her brother, and her words reflect both the climatic conditions and her own prospects. Eugenia is rejected not only by Acton, but by Clifford, by Lizzie, and by the Wentworths, and even by her brother, whose jollity in the end is an obvious limitation. Since the Baroness is an imaginative and resourceful woman, she resists mere pity, but there is a sense of loss and a mood of somberness in her departure.[15] We feel that the society which dismisses her is seriously deficient.

The artistic effect of Eugenia's failure is certainly not to tighten the structure and enrich the texture of the novel. Rather the ending extends the small dimensions of the 'sketch' – as James subtitled the novel – into a less restricted and conventional area. It would have been a simple matter for James to arrange the marriage of Acton and Eugenia (as he arranges the benign, yet unconvincing, acquiescence of Mr Brand to Gertrude's marriage to Felix), but instead of granting his readers the fulfilment of their expectations, James forces them to revise their estimate of the entire affair. James seems unwilling to submit totally to the demands of comedy. He refuses to make the final sacrifices of his artistic freedom to the *a priori* requirements of an artificial form.[16] Though he employs innumerable conventional comic techniques in *The Europeans*, he refuses to employ any for its own sake. Everything in the novel is carefully calculated to develop a central idea – the clash of a life based on responsibility with one based on opportunism – so that even the most mechanical of devices subserve an organic scheme. That there are many such devices may explain why James deprecated the novel. Never again was he to be so reliant upon such contrivances, and significantly *The Europeans* is the last novel of its type that James wrote.

NOTES

1. See Oscar Cargill, *The Novels of Henry James* (New York, 1961) pp. 67–8. James's admiration for the French dramatists of the 1870s is amply reflected in his essays on the Parisian stage collected in *The Scenic Art*, ed. Allan Wade (New York, 1957). Leon Edel, in *The Complete Plays of Henry James* (Philadelphia, 1949), discusses the general influence of the well-made play on James's novels (pp. 34–40).

2. Here and elsewhere in this essay I am indebted to the analysis of comic modes in Northrop Frye, *Anatomy of Criticism* (Princeton, 1957) pp. 43–52, 163–86.

3. The phrase is Professor Frye's (p. 183).

4. It seems probable that James intentionally made the New England scene considerably less urban and cosmopolitan than it actually was. In misrepresenting Boston of the 1840s, James aroused the civic loyalty of Thomas Wentworth Higginson, who reviewed *The Europeans* unfavorably in the *Literary World*, x (22 Nov. 1879) 383–4. The anachronisms are discussed by Cargill, pp. 62–3, 69.

5. See R. P. Blackmur, Introduction to *Washington Square* and *The Europeans* (New York, 1959) pp. 5–12.

6. Notably by Edward Sackville-West, Introduction to *The Europeans* (1952) p. viii; Joseph McG. Bottkal, Introduction to *The Aspern Papers* and *The Europeans* (Norfolk, Conn., 1950) p. xix; and Osborn Andreas, *Henry James and the Expanding Horizon* (Seattle, 1948) p. 45.

7. For example, by Rebecca West, *Henry James* (New York, 1916) p. 42. Richard Poirier identifies the viewpoint of the Baroness with that of James in *The Comic Sense of Henry James* (New York, 1960) pp. 109, and devotes most of his essay on the novel to a demonstration of the admirableness of Eugenia.

8. Page references are to *The Europeans* (Boston, 1878).

9. Also, as F. W. Dupee remarks, Felix 'actually rescues the family from possible disruption by this somewhat threatening daughter'. See *Henry James* (New York, 1951) p. 103.

10. Thus Felix is rather less than the 'person of radical responsibility' he is called by F. R. Leavis, 'The Novel as Dramatic Poem (III): *The Europeans*', in *Scrutiny*, XV (Summer 1948) 212.

11. See Poirier, pp. 139–40, for further evidences of this irony and for illuminating observations regarding it.

12. See Edwin Bowden, *The Themes of Henry James* (New Haven, 1956) pp. 48–50, for a detailed analysis of the symbolic values of the three houses.

13. Here I am summarizing Poirier, pp. 112–16, though, as I suggest subsequently, the differences between Gertrude and Eugenia are as striking as the parallels: the differences are striking precisely because of the parallels.

14. Frye, p. 45.

15. It is typical of James to decrease gradually the comic mood of his novels. *The American*, *The Spoils of Poynton*, *The Awkward Age*, and *The Ambassadors*, in particular, are novels in which the casualness and high-spiritedness of the opening chapters give way to tense seriousness.

16. One of James's most recurrent critical principles is his belief that the novelist should remain uninfluenced by external rules and theories and should devise his own restrictions according to his sense of the needs of the novel he is writing. In 'The Future of the Novel', for instance, he writes, '[the novel] has the extraordinary advantage . . . that, while capable of giving an impression of the highest perfection and the rarest finish, it moves in luxurious independence of rules and restrictions'. See *The Future of the Novel: Essays on the Art of Fiction*, ed. Leon Edel (New York, 1956) p. 36.

TONY TANNER

The Fearful Self: Henry James's
The Portrait of a Lady (1965)

I

THE feeling which Isabel Archer most consistently experiences is fear. She is frightened by Warburton's offer, of Caspar Goodwood's persistence, and Gilbert Osmond's anger; she is frightened of sexual passion, of her unexpected wealth, of her 'freedom'; but beneath all these specific apprehensions there is, she admits, a deeper, radical fear – fear of herself. Seeing that it is a self which can misread Osmond so disastrously and make such a profoundly mistaken choice then, we may say, she has good grounds for her fear. But her fear, her error, and her final resolution are, it seems to me, crucial stages on a psychic journey which forms the very heart of the novel. This journey is the journey of an uncommitted, undefined self which sets out to find the right house to live in and the right partner to live with. A house – because the undefined self needs a defining shape: a partner – because the self can only realise what it is, by seeing itself reflected in the chosen and respected eyes of another; in selecting a partner it is selecting the gaze and regard which will assure it of its own reality and value. Putting it very crudely, Isabel Archer chooses the wrong house and the wrong partner. It is the full nature of this error – and her subsequent actions – that I wish to explore. But first I should like to make it clear that if I tend to treat characters, events and buildings as being 'emblematic' (Quentin Anderson's word), this does not mean that I am insensitive to the more realistic qualities of the novel which are praised, for example, by F. R. Leavis in *The Great Tradition*. I certainly do not wish to suggest that the book is something aridly schematised and drained of the opaque complexity of life in the interests of abstract meanings. The life is there: Isabel remains a hauntingly authentic and elusive character moving through vivid and tangible territories. But

James has so selected and arranged his realistic data, and has so saturated
it with deeper implications, that Isabel's journey is also an analogue
of the journey of the inquiring self-seeking realisation and identity.
Everyone she meets, every house she enters, all are detailed, plausible,
recognisably of the world. But they are also significant steps of an
inward quest which far transcends the social realism of a young
American girl living in late nineteenth-century Europe. In this essay I
shall be stressing the inner quest more than the outer realism – but of
course, either without the other would be an immeasurably poorer
thing. To suggest the full significance of Isabel's error I shall be considering some of the characters and then some of the architecture. But
first I want to make a general point about the Jamesian world which
I can best clarify by introducing a quotation from Kant (not, indeed,
suggesting any direct influence, even though Henry James, Senior,
studied Kant fairly thoroughly). Kant asserts that 'in the realm of ends
everything has either a value or a worth. What has a value has a
substitute which can replace it as its equivalent; but whatever is, on
the other hand, exalted above all values, and thus lacks an equivalent
. . . has no merely relative value, that is, a price, but rather an inner
worth, that is, dignity. Now morality is the condition in accordance
with which alone a reasonable being can be an end in himself, because
only through morality is it possible to be an autonomous member of
the realm of ends. Hence morality, and humanity, in so far as it is
capable of morality, can alone possess dignity.' This idea is compactly
summarised in his second categorical imperative. 'So act as to treat
humanity, whether in thine own person or in that of any other, in
every case as an end withal, never as a means whereby.' And this key
statement was probably influenced, as Ernst Cassirer has suggested, by
Rousseau's maxim: 'Man is too noble a being to serve simply as the
instrument for others, and he must not be used for what suits them
without consulting also what suits himself. . . . It is never right to
harm a human soul for the Advantage of others.'

I have introduced these quotations because I think they offer useful
terms with which to outline James's moral universe. Imagine two
worlds. One is the world of ends in which everything and everyone
has an intrinsic worth and they are all respected for what they are.
That is, literally, they are regarded as ends in themselves. This is the
moral world. In the other world, everything and everyone is regarded
as a means, nothing is considered as having a fixed inherent worth but

only what Kant calls a 'value'. This is misleading since we tend to use 'value' to imply 'worth', so let us say 'price', i.e. a market value which may change as appetites change, as opposed to an inner spiritual value, a permanent immutable worth. In this lower world of means, people only look at each other in the light of how they can use people, manipulate them, exploit or coerce them in the interests of some personal desire or appetite, or indeed mutilate and shape them to fit the dictates of a theory or a whim. In this world people see other people only as things or instruments, and they work to appropriate them as suits their own ambition. The world of means is a world of rampant egoism, while the world of ends is the realm of true morality and love. These two worlds are effectively the upper and lower parts of James's moral world. And what happens to Isabel Archer is that while she thinks she is ascending towards the world of ends, she is in fact getting more deeply involved in the world of means. The shocking knowledge she has to confront after her marriage is that she is 'a woman who has been made use of' as the Countess Gemini puts it. She who thought herself so free, so independent, a pure disciple of the beautiful, now has to face up to the 'dry staring fact that she had been an applied hung-up tool, as senseless and convenient as mere shaped wood and iron'. She, of all people, finds herself trapped in the world of instruments and things. Seeking a world of disinterested appreciation, she falls into a world of calculating appropriation. How does an error of such magnitude come about?

II

Isabel Archer's character has been amply analysed by many other critics so all I want to do is stress that from the outset her approach to life is very romantic, idealistic, and theoretic. 'Isabel Archer was a young person of many theories; her imagination was remarkably active' as James tells us clearly enough. And Henrietta Stackpole is certainly correct when she says to Isabel: 'The peril for you is that you live too much in the world of your own dreams.' What these dreams consist of we know right from the start: 'she spent half her time in thinking of beauty and bravery and magnanimity; she had a fixed determination to regard the world as a place of brightness, of free expansion, of irresistible action . . . she was always planning out her development, desiring her perfection, observing her progress'. Thus, she views the world as a benevolent sphere which will be plastic to her

theories of 'free expansion' and 'irresistible action'. She seems unprepared for any harsh encounter with all that indifferent otherness
which is not the self, which is not amenable to the self, and which may
well prove cruel and hostile to the self. More dangerously, it is hard to
see how she intends to put her theories of self-development into
practice. What will that expansion and action consist of? As we soon
realise, her most characteristic response in the real world is one of
refusal and rejection. Like many another character in American fiction
much of her energy goes into avoiding any commitment which might
serve to define and arrest her. She is generally in favour of 'the free
exploration of life' and yet she shrinks from any of the solid offers
that life holds forth. Caspar Goodwood suggests oppression, coercion
and constraint on the plain physical level. Lord Warburton, with his
complex social relations and obligations, suggests immobilisation on the
social level. If she rejects the first out of a distinct disinclination to enter
a firm physical embrace, she rejects the second on 'theoretic' grounds
because what he offers does not tally with her vague notions of
indefinite expansion. So we may say, summing up, that she rejects the
physical and the social in her theoretic pursuit of freedom, knowledge,
and self-realisation. Why, then, does she go on to accept Osmond?
As she realises, 'The world lay before her – she could do whatever she
chose' – the Miltonic echo is deliberate, it recurs again. And out of the
whole world to choose Osmond! Notice that she is the only character
in the book who is remotely taken in by this 'sterile dilettante' as Ralph
so cogently calls him. Why? When we first see her she is reading a
history of German thought; that is to say, drinking from the very
source of American transcendentalism. And when, later, she imagines
her future married life with Osmond, she feels assured of 'a future at a
high level of consciousness of the beautiful'. This implies a sort of
romantic Platonism which she might well have found in her youthful
reading. She wants to exist at the heights of sheer communion with
ideal beauty. As opposed, we may say, to involving herself with the
lower levels of un-ideal actuality, From the start she tests things and
people by whether they please her 'sublime soul'; and when she
receives her fortune, the vast amount of money gives her 'to her
imagination, a certain ideal beauty'. Isabel's instinct for the actual is as
curtailed as her longing for the ideal is exaggerated. She rejects the
sexual and social life. In marrying Osmond she thinks she is embracing
the ideal. She idealises herself, her motives for marrying, her ambitions,

and Osmond himself. It is all pathetically wrong. But as Mrs Touchett shrewdly says: 'there's nothing in life to prevent her marrying Mr Osmond if only she looks at him in a certain way'. Looking at him in her own way – romantically, theoretically (she 'invented a fine theory about Gilbert Osmond'), consulting her yearning for a life lived on the ideal level – Osmond seems perfectly suited to Isabel's needs.

Among other things, then, her mistake is the result of a radical failure of vision: idealising too much, she has perceived all too little. But more than that, Osmond is exactly what a large part of Isabel wants. He seems to offer release from the troubling life of turbulent passions; he seems to offer a life dedicated to the appreciation of ideal beauty. As we well know, Osmond merely regards Isabel as worthy 'to figure in his collection of choice objects'; but consider how Isabel feels about herself just before her marriage and at the height of her confidence in herself: 'she walked in no small shimmering splendour. She only felt older – ever so much, and as if she were "worth more" for it, like some curious piece in an antiquary's collection.' And she enjoys this feeling. It is hard to resist the conclusion that a part of her – the theorising, idealising part – is quite prepared to be placed in Osmond's collection. The lady is half willing to be turned into a portrait. And, given her temperament, there is much to be said for becoming a work of art. It offers a reprieve from the disturbing ordeals awaiting the self in the mire of the actual. Osmond is a student of the 'exquisite' and we discover how cruel and sterile that can be. But in her own way so is Isabel. She speaks honest words about their marriage: 'They had attempted only one thing, but that one thing was to have been exquisite.' In some ways Osmond is as much a collaborator as a deceiver.

Although there are hints of the proper villain about Osmond (James perhaps goes a little too far by revealing that Osmond's favourite author is Machiavelli), he is in fact a curiously hollow, insubstantial man: 'no career, no name, no position, no fortune, no past, no future, no anything' as Madame Merle says. Perhaps this apparent lightness, this seemingly empty detachment from the world is more attractive to Isabel than the solid identity, the heavy actuality of Goodwood and Warburton. Certainly his claim that he has renounced passional life and ordinary human attachments to pursue his high-minded study, his 'taste', echoes something in Isabel. The paradox, of course, as Ralph sees, is 'that under the guise of caring only for intrinsic values Osmond lived exclusively for the world. Far from being its master as he pretended to be, he was its very humble servant, and the degree of its attention was his only measure of-success.' He pretends to be a devotee of the ideal, to have renounced the base world. This is what draws Isabel. But to care so totally and uncritically for forms, taste, convention ('I'm convention itself' he revealingly admits) is to be absolutely enslaved to mere appearances, never questioning essences or the intrinsic worth of things. This, precisely, makes him a dedicated inhabitant of the world of means. He has renounced the lived life of instinct and action not, like Ralph, the better to appreciate its intrinsic values, but in order to give himself over entirely to calculated surface effects. How far he will take this is of course revealed by what he does to his daughter, Pansy. It is the same thing as what he wants to do to Isabel – to turn her into a reflector of himself, utterly devoid of any spontaneous life of her own. Isabel, of course, having stronger and richer stuff in her, can resist. But Pansy shows the process all but complete. All her natural vitality and spontaneity have been quietly suffocated to be replaced by a perfected puppet-like behaviour which does not *express* Pansy's own inner life, but simply *reflects* Osmond's taste. Such a total appropriation of another person's life for egotistical ends is of course the cardinal Jamesian sin. But there is something in Isabel herself which is not so remote from Osmond's disposition. At one point we read that she was 'interested' (a neutral word) to watch Osmond 'playing theoretic tricks on the delicate organism of his daughter'. She should be interested, for she has spent her whole life playing theoretic tricks on her own organism. Osmond is an egotist, but so, we are told, is Isabel: he is cold and dry, but so is she: he pays excessive attention to appearances rather than realities, and up to a point so does she (I will return to this): he prefers art to life, and so does she: he has more theories than feelings, more ideals than instincts, and so does she. He is a collector of things, and she offers herself up to him as a fine finished object. Isabel accepting Osmond's proposal of marriage is the uncertain self thinking it is embracing the very image of what it *seeks* to become. Her later shock and revulsion is the self discovering the true worthlessness of what it *might* have become. Osmond is Isabel's anti-self. This is why, I think, James made Osmond American when he might well have made him a cynical European ensnaring American gullibility. He is American because Isabel is American. She, of course, has qualities which differentiate her sharply

from Osmond. But she also has tendencies which draw her straight
to him. He is an actualisation, a projection, of some of the mixed
potentialities and aspirations of her questing, uncommitted self. He is
part of her self writ large, and when she learns to read that writing
properly (she actually refers to not having 'read him right'), she is not
unnaturally appalled.

I must here say a little about the other American 'parasite' and plotter,
Madame Merle. As Osmond is 'convention itself' so she is 'the great
round world itself'. She is totally devoted to the world of things – she
thinks of it in terms of 'spoils' – and she has subjected the unruliness of
authentic nature to the surface perfection of contrived manner. Isabel
is not so blind as not to be able to detect her occasional cruelty, her
subtle dishonesty, the sense she gives of 'values gone wrong'. But
unlike Osmond, there is something pathetic about her, and something
which also offers a warning to Isabel. For clearly Madame Merle was,
like Isabel, first used and then abused by Osmond, and she has not
gained anything from the world even though she has devoted herself
to it. She keeps herself going by 'will', forcing, always, the right mask
for the right occasion. But she ends up utterly dried up, unable to cry:
'you've dried up my soul' she says to Osmond (it is worth recalling
here that no less a writer than Shakespeare habitually depicted evil as a
state of desiccation, a complete lack of the very sap and tears of life).
Perhaps the saddest cry in the whole novel is Madame Merle's lament:
'Have I been so vile for nothing?' It at least attests to a vestigial moral
sense which she has deliberately subverted for the world's ends, only
to see no gains. She has been a disciple of appearances and indeed has
mastered the art, but she is rewarded by being banished to America
(apparently the worst fate James could conceive of for an erring
character). She is a sadder case than Osmond because she knows that
she is doing bad things to Isabel. Her effects are as calculated as
Osmond's, but at least she winces at perpetrating them. She is an almost
tragic example of the scant rewards and plentiful shames awaiting
those who live only for 'the world'. And it is Madame Merle who gives
perhaps the most succinct expression of living in the world of means
to be found in the whole book. 'I don't pretend to know what people
are for,' she says, 'I only know what I can do with them.' She exactly
fits Kant's (and Rousseau's) definition of the immoral world. She sees
people as instruments but has no sense of their intrinsic worth: means
to her hand, not ends in themselves.

In the world of Osmond and Madame Merle, self-seeking and simulation go together. They have to calculate effects: what *is*, is neglected; what *seems* is paramount. Now Isabel herself is a partial devotee of appearances. I will quote a few references to this. She has 'an unquenchable desire to please' and 'an unquenchable desire to think well of herself': thus she is 'very liable to the sin of self-esteem'. More subtly, we read of 'her desire to *look* very well and to *be* if possible even better'. A similar crucial distinction is made later: Isabel's chief dread 'was that she should *appear* narrow-minded; what she feared next afterwards was that she should really *be* so'. (My italics in both cases.) These fine hints reveal a problem of great importance for the novitiate self: which will receive more attention – appearance, or essence? For much of the early part of her travels Isabel falls into the subtle and understandable error of devoting herself to appearances. She wishes to emulate Madame Merle. She contrives to appear to Osmond as she thinks he wants her to appear; like a fine finished work of art which re-echoes and reflects his ideas and taste. In this sense Osmond *is* a man deceived, and Isabel is right to realise that she did mislead him by appearing to be what in fact she was not. That is why Isabel has a true instinct when she says she is afraid of her self. Realising the depths of her error with regard to Osmond is also to realise that she does not know what her self is, nor what it may do. (After all there is Madame Merle, a terrible example of how the self may mutilate the self from a sense of misplaced devotion and ambition.) And indeed this is the crucial difficulty for the self. Only by engaging itself in a situation, projecting itself into the world of things and appearances, can the self realise the self (i.e. transform latent potentialities into visible realities). But once in that situation, it may find that it has chosen a position, a role, which falsifies the self. We don't know what is in us until we commit ourselves in a certain direction: then we may find that the commitment is utterly wrong. Thus all choice may turn out to be error and in this way the self may ruin the self. Certainly Isabel exacerbates her chances of choosing wrong by coldly consulting her theories, her imaginative ideals, her book-fed romanticisms; and that wrong choice does seem to threaten years to come of waste and disappointment. Seen thus, Isabel's difficulty, her error, her fate, form a journey on which we must all, in our different ways, go. For it is only through choice and commitment that we can find out what we are. In this sense error is also discovery. Isabel has to close with Osmond in order to arrive at a deeper knowledge of her self, of her distorted values, of her egotism, and of the real pain and cruelty of life. By marrying Osmond she suffers in good earnest, but she thus earns the right to see the ghost of Gardencourt. Her consolation – and it is the supreme one in James – is truer vision.

III

To bring out more clearly Isabel's journey as the journey of the developing but all-too-often erring self, I now want to move from the characters she meets to the buildings and settings she moves through. And first I must quote from a crucial exchange between Isabel and Madame Merle: it comes near the end of chapter nineteen and is really central to the whole book. Talking of an earlier suitor Isabel says: ['I don't care anything about his house', and Madame Merle replies: 'That's very crude of you. When you've lived as long as I you'll see that every human being has his shell and that you must take the shell into account. By the shell I mean the whole envelope of circumstances. There's no such thing as an isolated man or woman; we're each of us made up of some cluster of appurtenances. What shall we call our "self"? Where does it begin? where does it end? It overflows into everything that belongs to us – and then it flows back again. I know a large part of myself is in the clothes I choose to wear. I've a great respect for *things*. One's self – for other people – is one's expression of one's self; and one's house, one's furniture, one's garments, the books one reads, the company one keeps – these things are all expressive.']

Now this idea that the self is only the self that we consciously create and play at being, the self that we visibly express and project, is still being explored by existential psychologists like Sartre (for instance in *Being and Nothingness*, where he discusses the waiter 'playing at being a waiter . . . the waiter in the cafe plays with his condition in order to *realize* it'), and by such imaginative sociologists as Erving Goffman (his brilliant book *The Presentation of Self in Everyday Life* is very relevant here). So Madame Merle's attitude expresses a deep truth about our society. She has gone the whole way. She is concerned only with the agents of expression – things, clothes, appearances, appurtenances. She reconstructs a false self to show the world. She is what she dresses to be. This is extreme: it entails the death of the soul and the ultimate disappearance of the individual inner self. As Isabel says to herself, it is difficult to imagine Madame Merle 'in any

detachment or privacy, she existed only in relations . . . one might
wonder what commerce she could possibly hold with her own spirit'.
She is rather like Lord Mellifont in 'The Private Life' who disappears
when he is on his own. If you care only for appearances, you exist only
when there are people to look at you.

However, in this key conversation, Isabel's answer to Madame
Merle is also extreme. She says: 'I know that nothing else expresses
me. Nothing that belongs to me is any measure of me; everything's on
the contrary a limit, a barrier, and a perfectly arbitrary one. . . . My
clothes may express the dressmaker, but they don't express me. To
begin with it's not my own choice that I wear them; they're imposed
upon me by society.' To which Madame Merle wryly answers:
'Should you prefer to go without them?'

This is a classic formulation of a basic American attitude. Lionel
Trilling once noted that there is something in the American temperament which wishes to resist all conditioning, all actual society, and
aspires to a life which will permit the spirit to make its own terms.
'Somewhere in our mental constitution is the demand for life as pure
spirit.' (See his essay 'William Dean Howells', in *The Opposing Self*.)
Emerson's 'Self-Reliance', Thoreau by Walden Pond, Whitman celebrating the self – these, of course, are the classic types for the American
imagination. They certainly did believe there was such a thing as the
'isolated' self, and welcomed the fact. And characters like Bartleby and
Huck Finn and Augie March reveal the ineradicable suspicion of all
conditioning forces, all actual fixed social situations. They refuse, opt
out, move on. Like Isabel they see barriers and limits everywhere, and
much of their energy goes into avoiding the shaping pressures (and
appurtenances) of society. Isabel's retort is, thus, in a great American
tradition. And up to a point she is right. Things and appurtenances are
not identical with the self, as Osmond and Madame Merle make them.
We are not what we wear. But to see everything in the actual world as
sheer barrier, hindrance, and limit is also dangerous. For without any
limits the self can never take on any contours, cannot become something real. The pure spirit of the self has to involve itself with the
material world of things and society in order to work out an identity
for itself, indeed in order to realise itself. To that extent the self must
dress itself and must choose its clothes. In laying the responsibility for
her clothes (i.e. her appearance, her situation, etc.) on society and calling
it an arbitrary imposition, Isabel is being dangerously irresponsible. For

it is her error in thinking that life can be lived as pure spirit in contempt of things that leads her to mistake Osmond's attitude. The ironic result is that she puts herself in the power of a man who wants to treat *her* as a thing. James's insight here is profound. For there is indeed a dangerously close connection between an idealistic *rejection* of 'things' and an idealising *of* 'things'. This is why Osmond is such a telling figure. In the appearance of living for the spirit in disregard of the material, he has in fact spiritualised the material. And James must surely have been one of the first to see into this particularly modern malaise which other American critics have mentioned in discussing modern society; namely, the confusion of the spiritual and material realms, the spiritualising of things. James knew that things and sur-roundings (the shell) *were* important: there was a way of being among things which manifested the quality of the self, which enabled it to realise itself. But of course there was also a way of being among things which menaced and could destroy the self. Isabel Archer's journey is hazardous but representative: and her error no less than human.

We first see Isabel – as we last see her – in a garden. This is always an important setting in James (usually indicating a place of meditation and appreciation). Gardens are certainly important in this book. At the start of her European journey Isabel regards her inner world as a garden and indeed many of her happiest moments are spent in them. She is happiest, in particular, at Gardencourt, and the very name points to the fact that this is the locale in the book which most exudes a mood of mellow reciprocity between the civilised and the natural. But Isabel is far from appreciating it at the start of her adventures. She sees it only as romantic and picturesque. It is only much later that she appreciates that it is something more real and indeed more sacred than that. After this opening glimpse James takes us back to the house in Albany, New England, where Isabel started on her travels. The most important of many suggestive details about this house is the 'condemned door', the entrance which 'was secured by bolts which a particularly slender little girl found it impossible to slide'. It is to be Isabel's later fate again to be locked in. Also, the windows are covered, but 'she had no wish to look out, for this would have interfered with her theory that there was a strange, unseen place on the other side – a place which became to the child's imagination, according to different moods, a region of delight or terror'. This of course expresses Isabel's whole attitude to life: her theories and imagined versions of reality are generated behind

closed doors and covered windows. Instead of venturing forth she sits
poring over books. One more detail is particularly prophetic: she 'had
the whole house to choose from, and the room she had selected was the
most depressed of its scenes.' James often used the metaphor 'the house
of life' and indeed, of its many rooms, Isabel is yet to choose the darkest
and most imprisoning.

If you see Isabel's quest as being at least in part a search for the right
house then her reactions to Warburton and Osmond become even
more revealing. When she rejects Warburton after visiting his house,
Lockleigh, she puts her rejection in this way: she says she is unable
'to think of your home . . . as the settled seat of my existence'. As
though the main thing about him was the fact that he doesn't have
what she regards as the right house. Osmond's house is brilliantly
described. First of all, it is on a hill-top, the best place for a person who
wants to put the claims of the base world behind and live a life of ideal
appreciation and detached observation. Clearly Isabel is attracted to
this degree of rarefied removal. But we note that in the first, perfectly
plausible, topographical description, the front of the house is deceptive.
'It was the mask, not the face of the house. It had heavy lids, but no
eyes; the house in reality looked another way. . . .' This, I need hardly
point out, is entirely true of its owner. Even the windows bespeak
Osmond: 'their function seemed less to offer communication with the
world than to defy the world to look in'. Isabel's approach to this key
dwelling is laced with subtle portent, and I must quote at some length
here. 'The companions drove out of the Roman Gate . . . and wound
between high-walled lanes into which the wealth of blossoming
orchards overdrooped and flung a fragrance, until they reached the
small suburban piazza, of crooked shape, where the long brown wall of
the villa occupied by Mr Osmond formed a principal, or at least very
imposing, object.' They drive into the courtyard. 'There was something
grave and strong in the place; it looked somehow as if, once you were
in, you would need an act of energy to get out. For Isabel, however,
there was of course as yet no thought of getting out, but only of
advancing.' The whole drive provides a compressed analogue for
Isabel's venture into life so far. The blooming promising beginning, the
flung fragrance (Touchett's unlooked-for bequest perhaps), then the
crooked square, the preventing wall, and the enclosing courtyard – the
whole passage subtly prepares us for what becomes explicit only much
later when Isabel realises that 'she had taken all the first steps in the

purest confidence, and then she had suddenly found the infinite vistas of a multiplied life to be a dark, narrow alley with a dead wall at the end'. And note the geography of the following image. 'Instead of leading to the high places of happiness, from which the world could seem to lie below one, so that one could look down with a sense of exaltation and advantage, and judge and choose and pity, it led rather downward and earthward, into the realms of restriction and depression where the sound of other lives, easier and freer, was heard as from above, and where it served to deepen the feeling of failure.' Isabel thinks Osmond lives on the heights of meditation and free appreciation, but really he dwells in the depths of calculation and constricting appropriation. Her life seemed to lead up to the world of ends; instead she was plunging down into the world of means. Osmond's palace of art turns out to be 'the house of darkness, the house of dumbness, the house of suffocation'. But it was the house she chose. James knits his imagery together in the famous description of Isabel's reaction when Osmond proposes. She feels 'a pang that suggested to her somehow the slipping of a fine bolt – backward, forward, she couldn't have said which'. Is she about to be released or immured? In her most testing moment she is unable to distinguish what presages liberation and expansion, and what threatens detainment and constriction. Her radical confusion is all there in the image.

I will not here describe the many galleries and museums and other houses and rooms Isabel passes through, but all repay careful study. For in this book all the architecture means something of specific importance to Isabel, as of course it must to the self-seeking, both freedom *and* form. Pansy's convent, for instance, has all the appearance of a prison to Isabel's clearer vision. On the other hand, some architecture can offer consolation. For example there is a beautiful passage describing a ride she takes in Rome – 'the place where people had suffered' – some time after her discovery of the truth about Osmond. 'She had long before taken old Rome into her confidence, for in a world of ruins the ruin of her happiness seemed a less unnatural catastrophe. She rested her weariness upon things that had crumbled for centuries and yet were still upright; she dropped her secret sadness into the silence of lonely places.' It is a most moving description of the bruised and erring spirit absorbing strengthening reminders and consoling clues from the marred but splendid debris of human habitations of the past. And one of the reasons why Isabel returns to Rome at the end, renouncing the refuge of Gardencourt which she now does appreciate as sacred, is that the self has to return to the place where it made its most defining, if mistaken, choice. That is where the work of re-habilitation and re-education must go on. It is where knowledge is earned. I think this is why, in the last scene of the book, we see Isabel running from the darkening garden of meditation back into the well-lit house of life. But before exploring that decision I want to discuss the significance of Ralph.

IV

Ralph is of course a recurring Jamesian figure – the subtly debarred spectator who enjoys everything in imagination and nothing in action. Thus Ralph has 'the imagination of loving' but has 'forbidden himself the riot of expression'. All his happiness consists of 'the sweet-tasting property of the observed thing in itself'. To appreciate the 'thing in itself' is precisely to be an inhabitant of the world of ends. Ralph is wise, he is dying: 'restricted to mere spectatorship at the game of life', banned from participation, addicted to appreciation. A true Jamesian artist figure. Suitably, he is most often seen sitting in gardens. On one occasion in particular the contrast between 'house' and 'garden' is used to good effect. This is when Ralph tells Isabel the real truth about Osmond. She, with her theories, rejects his visions – and leaves the garden. She ends the conversation 'by turning away and walking back to the house'. But Ralph cannot follow her: it is too cold for him in the house, he is too susceptible to 'the lurking chill of the high-walled court'. It does not seem to me excessive to see Ralph as the artist-meditator, who cannot function in the house of life, but who indulges his imagination and speculation in the garden. He sits; he does not act. He is content to watch and appreciate Isabel; he has no thought of dominating or manipulating her. In his own way he is also an aesthete, someone who stands back and relishes the beautiful. But where Osmond is a false aesthete, Ralph has the true artistic instincts. Osmond wants to turn Isabel into a work of art (we see her at his home 'framed in the gilded doorway' already adjusting to her status as portrait); Ralph appreciates her living qualities artistically. Osmond hates Ralph because he is 'an apostle of freedom'. But, as Isabel comes to see, Ralph is more intelligent, more just, better. Not egotistic, as Osmond always is. This leads up to the deathbed scene. Isabel is back at Gardencourt, happy at least that she is no longer having to act and falsify. At Gardencourt she can be herself, her true self. And, dying, Ralph comforts her: 'But love remains.' He tells her she has been adored and her response is revealingly simple. 'Oh my brother.' In Osmond Isabel thought she recognised a soul mate. She was very wrong. At last, having suffered, she realises who is the true image of what her self wants to be – Ralph. 'Oh my brother.' Having seen through the false approach to life, she now appreciates the true artistic attitude: a vision based on love, on generosity, on respect for things in themselves and a gift of unselfish appreciation.

In taking the measure of Osmond, Isabel has started to move towards Ralph's point of view. The great chapter, forty-two, when she takes stock, is really the beginning of her deeper knowledge and clear vision. She is starting to read things properly, as Ralph does. And with this new access of vision, Isabel becomes less active externally and more active internally. She has started on what James later called 'the subjective adventure': the adventure of trying to understand, to sound out depths, to appreciate qualities, to transcend the importunities of the ego. By the end of the book Isabel Archer has started to become a Jamesian artist.

Just before the end we see her in the garden at Gardencourt: this time pensive and quiet, much closer to a knowledge of true values than when we saw her stride so confidently on to that lawn at the start. It is now twilight: she is sitting on a bench alone. This stance, this setting, becomes a dominant one in James's later work – not only in the last great story 'The Bench of Desolation', but in such works as *The Ambassadors* as well as in many stories like 'Crapy Cornelia' and 'Mora Montravers'. In that last story, for instance, we see the self-effacing Traffle, excluded, estranged, sitting staring at the approaching evening with only one consolation. As the night comes down on him he has, for company, his Jamesian mind: 'exquisite, occult, dangerous and sacred, to which everything ministered and which nothing could take away'. Clearly James had a recurring vision of a person who has somehow failed to realise him (or her) self in the physical world, who has renounced all active participation, and who withdraws into sedentary isolation, consoling himself with the fruits of a finer, if sadder, consciousness. Isabel, we feel, is drawing towards her truer role as she sits in the darkening garden. But she is interrupted by Caspar Good-wood, who comes to disturb her on her bench in the garden: she cannot yet enjoy Ralph's invalid immunity from the challenge and

threat of engagement. Goodwood kisses her, and in a curious cluster
of images James implies that she is both wrecked and then freed.
Goodwood brings a possessive lightning, 'but when darkness returned
she was free'. I am not fully certain of James's intention here, but the
effect is this. For a long time she has wondered if her true fate, the true
realisation of her self, should not have been with Goodwood. Now for
the first time she is subjected to the full force of his sexual claims. It is a
shattering experience, but it is also a release. She was not made to go
that way. There is no going back to the simple level of life he represents.
He tries to prevent her from returning to Rome where, as he says,
she has to 'play a part' and maintain a false 'form': but it is precisely
this that she must, at this stage, do. She runs back to the house: 'there
were lights in the window of the house; they shone far across the lawn'.
She reaches the door. 'Here only she paused. She looked all about her;
she listened a little; then she put her hand on the latch. She had not
known where to turn; but she knew now. There was a very straight
path.' James has annoyed readers by not saying what that path is. But
I think the wonderful suggestivity of this last scene tells us all we need.
The last pause and lingering look surely imply that she is reluctant to
leave the garden – a refuge and a place of meditation. But she cannot
opt out of her fate so easily, just as even more she cannot return to
American innocence and physical simplicity with Goodwood. She
chose her room in the house of life and she must return to it. She must
return to the chill and ruins of Rome: for the self cannot back out of a
mistaken course but only push through and move beyond. But she
takes back with her a new vision, a deeper understanding, a capacity
for modest unegotistical contemplation which all promise a richer
future – a future in which she will come to a true realisation of what her
real self is. It is beside the point to ask whether she will divorce Osmond.
When she has attained her new vision, he simply shrinks into insignifi-
cance, just as Madame Merle melts away to America. We do not even
hear his voice for the last seventy pages or so of the book, and by the end
of the book we feel that Isabel has attained the most important kind of
freedom, an internal one. She is liberated from her twisted vision and
her confused values. She can see through all false appearances. She
returns to Italy, to the 'ruins' she herself was partly responsible for.
But she will not, we feel, ever again be subordinate to the deceptions
and calculations of a worldling like Osmond. Even if she does not break
out of the house and kick over the traces, and even if she never again

indulges in any more passions, her future will be quite other. For her way of looking has changed. Now I think one might fairly suggest that James, in fact, could not see exactly what sort of future such a person might have, how she might take up her place again in the social scene. We can admire Isabel's fine stoicism and admit at the same time that it is hard to visualise the details of her future. And this, I think, is because James is already feeling the necessary connection between the artistic observation of life *and* the renunciation of active participation in it. As Isabel becomes more the artist, in her mind, so she will withdraw from social involvement, if not physically then at least psychologically. If she never returns to sit in the garden of Gardencourt, then we may be sure she will spend many later years reposing in the garden of her mind. With James's later artist figures or observers, the attempt at any active participation is all but abandoned from the start. Hyacinth Robinson finds no satisfying role or niche for himself in society and shoots himself. Lambert Strether develops a new complex comprehensiveness of vision and appreciation, but to retain it, it is essential that he must not get 'anything for myself' – no spoils, no physical relationships. The narrator of *The Sacred Fount* is the conscience of society, at the cost of never enjoying its actual embrace. There are other such figures, but none perhaps so humanly comprehensible as Isabel Archer, in whom we can see the erring self emerging into the incipient artist. With later characters the divorce between action and observation is almost accepted as inevitable from the start. It would seem that James, in his own way, came to share Goethe's reflection that 'the acting man is always without conscience; no one has conscience but the observing man'. If nothing else, *The Portrait of a Lady* shows us the birth of a conscience out of the spoiling of a life.

WILLIAM McMURRAY

Pragmatic Realism in *The Bostonians* (1962)

SOME recent readers of *The Bostonians*, Lionel Trilling and Irving Howe for example, have stressed the novel's political aspects. Henry James himself would seem to have invited such an emphasis when he said that he wished to write 'a very *American* tale'[1] dealing with our peculiar social conditions, especially with the decline in the 'sentiment of sex'. Sex and politics, certainly, are everywhere in the novel. The way that they are there, however, urges a consideration of moral and philosophical matters that describe a larger framework than a sexual and political one in which to examine James's intention and attitude. Public and private experience are both dealt with by the novelist as complementary aspects of what he perceived as a uniquely American conduct of life; and it is this conduct, dramatically focused in a conflict among characters who, James said, were evolved from his 'moral consciousness',[2] that is the subject of *The Bostonians*.[3]

While both Howe and Trilling concern themselves primarily with the novel's political aspects, they nevertheless do contribute to our understanding of some of the moral and philosophical issues it raises. Howe, especially, understands James to be asking how a sense of 'personal uniqueness' may be kept in the midst of 'limiting and treacherous social relationships'.[4] He sees James as supposing 'that the ideological obsessions which form so constant a peril for public life will leave their mark, not merely on social behavior, but also on the most intimate areas of private experience' (p. xiv).

Behind the varying modes or appearances of James's drama, Trilling perceives 'the conflict of two principles, of which one is radical, the other conservative. The two principles are constant, although circumstances change their particular manifestations and the relative values they are to be judged to have. They may be thought of as energy and inertia; or spirit and matter; or spirit and letter; or force and form; or creation and possession; or Libido and Thanatos.'[5] The dualism that Trilling finds pervades the novel. On the other hand, may not the many different kinds of dualism be regarded as the pluralistic experience of the novel's world? What James shows, I suggest, is that pretensions to absolutism in such a world are destructive of the spirit of life in both private and public spheres of human activity.

Olive Chancellor claims first place among James's reforming Bostonians because it is she who tries hardest of all to make life be a thing that suits her self. Her habit of conduct is characterized by a strenuous egocentricity that she mistakes for idealistic altruism. How much of Olive's personality is a result of temperament (Basil Ransom sees that she is the kind who takes things 'hard' while he takes them 'easy'),[6] and how much is a result of her Boston upbringing is moot. With James, we take Olive as we find her, watching to see what she will do. Olive's way, however, is to take nothing as she finds it. A pathological selfishness impels her to try to make the world reflect her own image. Inevitably, the essence of her life is conflict: she thrives on it. One of the reasons she asks Basil Ransom to call on her in Boston is her anticipation that, as a Mississippian, he will not see things as she does. 'If she had supposed he would agree, she would not have written to him' (p. 15). Olive's personal identity has its psychological basis in a rigorous selfishness that solidifies in conflict. In a pluralistic and opposing world, Olive stands for a monistic absolutism in the name of Chancellor.

Since Olive lives largely for the future, her life is one of intention rather than of actuality. Things as they are in themselves must be changed into things as she wills them to be. Her radical reformism leads her, on the political field, to campaign for the emancipation of women in a world governed largely by men. What Olive does not see is that the freedom she would win for women is pitched at an absolute level that strikes at the heterosexual basis of human existence. When Olive enlists in the service of her cause the sympathetic and generous Verena Tarrant, any normal or usual relationship between the two women is perverted by the tyranny of Olive's pathological personality. In Verena, Olive believes she has found 'what she had been looking for so long – a friend of her own sex with whom she might have a union of soul' (p. 80). Homosexuality in Olive is the biological evidence of a rigid self-centeredness that has blinded itself to the heterogeneous character of reality. We are not surprised that Olive needs to keep Verena from marrying, that she needs to pledge her to 'an absolute sanctity' that would 'bind them together for life' (p. 113). Together, Olive and Verena prepare themselves for Verena's coming out, the mystical moment when Verena's transcendentalism will inspire in her sex their glorious emancipation. Whenever Verena's absolute bent for experience leads her astray into activities other than those for the cause, Olive suffers them only by dismissing them as 'phases' to be gotten through on the way to the supposedly 'real' life which beckons from a distant but triumphant future.

Basil Ransom is the chief foe to Olive's cause. As a southern gentleman of the old stamp and as a reactionary, he is eminently suited to challenge Olive's point of view. In a hysterical feminine age, he conceives it as his mission to preserve 'the masculine tone'. Women, as Basil sees them, best fulfill their destinies in the private circle of the 'domestic affections', the circle into which he seeks to draw Verena Tarrant. Basil offers Verena a private and particular love rather than an abstract union of soul. When he first hears Verena's inspirational speaking at Miss Birdseye's, Basil cannot help smiling 'at the sweet grotesqueness of this virginal creature's standing up before a company of middle-aged people to talk to them about "love"' (p. 64). Rooted in conservatism, Basil Ransom is as narrow in the point of view he opposes to Olive as she is in hers – though he prosecutes it less strenuously than she.

The conflict among competing absolutisms is reflected in Verena Tarrant. In her, Olive's rule is challenged not only by Basil Ransom, but by Verena's thoroughly selfless indulgence of experience. Having come to believe that she is devoted to Olive and the cause, for example, Verena later admits to herself that she has fallen in love with Basil. What, then, about Olive and the cause? What, indeed, about the truth Verena had pledged herself to live by?

> It was simply that the truth had changed sides; that radiant image began to look at her from Basil Ransom's expressive eyes. She loved, she was in love – she felt it in every throb of her being. Instead of being constituted by nature for entertaining that sentiment in an exceptionally small degree (which had been the implication of her whole crusade, the warrant for her offer of old to Olive to renounce), she was framed, apparently, to allow it the largest range, the highest intensity. It was always passion, in fact; but now the object was other. (p. 396)

That her love for a person of the opposite sex, and for Basil Ransom in particular, should now seem to Verena to be love's 'largest range, the highest intensity', is an ironic testament to how far round Verena's passion for selflessness has brought her from Olive Chancellor. Verena's 'wheel . . . of experience' (p. 398) has come full cycle; and it is at this point, when 'her desire to keep on pleasing others at the time when a force she had never felt before was pushing her to please herself' (p. 398),[7] that Verena enters that 'state of moral tension' which is to be her lot – even though Basil Ransom acts to wrench her from it at the close of the novel.

Verena's state of moral tension is one created by conflicting views of truth in experience, both of which struggle in her to assert supreme authority at the same time. Which one does Verena choose? Neither one. If she is to be true to her nature of an absolutely open and selfless consciousness, Verena cannot exercise nor act upon any exclusive and discriminatory self-reference or self-intention. Verona's 'gift' is her selfless capacity for experience (its specific mode being love), which renders her self-transcendent nature incapable of acting upon any mundane impulse originating in self. Yet, in her way, Verena is a passionate *femme fatale* (with flaming red hair) in James's story: her ardent selflessness is charming but treacherous. It wants the saving grace of an enlightened self-interest. If Verena gives herself effortlessly, it is because she is – as near-sighted Doctor Prance sees – 'anemic' of any self to give. Early in the novel Verena protests that her gift is 'not me' (p. 56); and it is this not-Verena creature who, when questioned about her attitude toward the marriage tie by Olive, answers that she prefers 'free unions' (p. 85).

In the end it is Basil who must act, as the selfish male force, to take Verena into his life. When James writes of Verena's tears that 'It is to be feared that with the union, so far from brilliant, into which she was about to enter, these were not the last she was destined to shed' (p. 464), we understand him to be forecasting the inevitable tension which will mark the union between Basil's closed and private love in the marriage tie, and Verena's open and universally public love in a 'free union'. Verena's strength and her weakness is that she loves not wisely but too well. If Olive and Basil are too selfish in their different ways, Verena fails in not being selfish enough.

Basil Ransom's victory over Olive Chancellor brings to a climax in the novel a metaphysical impulse that emerges as a concept of reality in which competing absolutisms are relatively integrated within an organic totality of experience. The primary appearances the competing absolutisms take are as love and politics. However, they are but particular vehicles for a larger moral and philosophical meaning. The major problem raised by James's drama – what attitude, in a various world, is most likely to bring us into harmony with the actuality and potentiality of life? – is answered in the fate of the three central characters. The narrow and exclusive worlds of Olive and Basil are opposed to the boundless one of Verena Tarrant. In her selflessness the worlds of both Olive and Basil are contained. Verena's crisis comes when she is driven to choose between them. But the psychological and moral condition for exercising such a choice – a consciousness of self as the basis for discriminatory action – is what Verena lacks in her make-up. If Verena is to fulfil the range of her potentiality and be furnished with a sense of self, the union between her and Basil must take place. It does; but only by virtue of Basil's forceful action in the critical moment when Verena is torn between her opposite experiences of life and love. As the embodiment of conflicting absolutisms, Verena (at least, at the stage of development she reaches in the novel) cannot act to exclude a part of her experience in favor of another. Her state of moral tension is one born of a reality in which the truth of experience is seen to be plural rather than single. The union between Basil and Verena telescopes James's vision of the character of reality as one emerging out of experience itself. As such, reality is conceived of as dynamic and changing rather than static. It stands for life in actuality and potentiality. It means freedom to live. Verena's task henceforth will be to learn how to live in that freedom – an emancipation of a kind that neither she nor Olive had ever dreamed of.

What James's realism offers us in *The Bostonians*, I suggest, is a dramatic illustration of pragmatism.[8] Reality in the novel is such that all absolutisms, when tested by experience, either must yield their claims to sanctity or fall in disaster. Disaster in the novel ranges all the way from private to public catastrophe. The framework for disaster is established in the conflicting 'set' of relationships existing among its central characters; and it is this set of relationships that breaks into discordant strife in the climactic scene at, ironically, the Boston Music Hall. In her suffering and defeat, Olive Chancellor discovers a depth of understanding and courage that is admirable. The pathos of her fate is that it should turn out to be not the triumphant victory of her cause, but a humiliation of all she had stood for.

American life, as portrayed by Henry James in *The Bostonians*, shows the conduct of that life to be marred by an absolutist psychology that has significant moral and philosophical meaning for our private and public experience. Morally it means that, in pretending to absolutist forms in our activity, we risk spiritual death. Philosophically it means that, in limiting reality and truth to our narrow experience, we falsify them at our peril. A pragmatism that would free us of these things by keeping life 'open' is what James urges instead.

NOTES

1. *The Notebooks of Henry James*, ed., F. O. Matthiessen and Kenneth B. Murdock (New York, 1947) p. 47.

2. Ibid. pp. 67-8.

3. Daniel Lerner and Oscar Cargill – in 'Henry James at the Grecian Urn', in *PMLA*, LXVI (June 1951) 316-31 – say that the real subject of the novel 'is the conflict itself, the clash of characters' (p. 321). [See pp. 166-83 of this volume.]

4. Henry James, *The Bostonians*, with an Introduction by Irving Howe (New York, 1956) p. viii. Subsequent quotations from this work are parenthetically cited in the text.

5. Lionel Trilling, *The Opposing Self* (New York, 1955) p. 108.

6. It is interesting to compare William James's observation in 'The Moral Philosopher and the Moral Life' (1891): 'The deepest difference, practically, in the moral life of man is the difference between the easy-going and the strenuous mood.' See *Essays in Pragmatism* ed. Alburey Castell (New York, 1948) p. 84.

7. Morris Gedge in 'The Birthplace' wrestles with a similar problem.

8. Joseph J. Firebaugh in 'The Ververs', in *Essays in Criticism*, IV (Oct. 1954) 400-10, examines James's pragmatism in *The Golden Bowl*.

DANIEL LERNER and OSCAR CARGILL
Henry James at the Grecian Urn (1951)

I

THE myth of the cultural 'limitations' of Henry James appears to have been the creation of two British journalists, Ford Madox Hueffer* and Rebecca West, who, while they rendered to James the service of publicity, were not sufficiently read in either James or the classics to generalize as freely as they did on both his riches and his deficiencies. Hueffer led off in 1913 in this fashion:

> Classicism . . . has quite extraordinarily little part in Mr James' pages. It is not, again, only that you will find almost no mention in all the works (from *Roderick Hudson* to *The Finer Grain*) of Diana, Pasiphae, Diodorus Siculus, Theocritus, or even a writer whom, if he had ever mentioned him, Mr James would certainly have called 'poor dear old Euripides'. . . . It is not, however, only that; it is that, right up to *The Golden Bowl*, in all the writings, you will discern no trace of the Latin or Greek classical spirit. . . . But even in *The Golden Bowl*, which we may regard as containing the maturest fruits of our subject's philosophy, we have the singular remark that the banks of the Thames seemed, for the Roman prince, to have much more of the atmosphere of Imperial Rome than the banks of Rome's Tiber. And the singularity of this remark lies in attributing this imperialism not to the peoples but to the places.[1]

Impelled, as a devout daughter of the British Empire, to pick up and to expand Hueffer's singular observation that James was 'a purely non-historic personality', Rebecca West expresses displeasure at James's 'nagging hostility to political effort' and expatiates on his ignorance of past cultures: 'He had a tremendous sense of the thing that is, and none at all of the thing that has been', she complains, and she 'burns with shame' at James's remarks about the Franco-Prussian

---

* Hueffer is better known by the name he assumed in 1923: Ford Madox Ford. *Editor*.

War, the French Revolution, and – this above all – the Roman Empire. She finds James 'so deficient of that general [classical] culture' as to be 'incapable of forming a philosophy'.[2]

This Hueffer–West theory of James's 'limitations', unchallenged since they wrote, neglects the fact of his broad, cosmopolitan education: before he was fifteen Henry had studied at a dozen schools in five countries. Miss West's specific complaint against his ignorance of Roman culture overlooks the plain statement that he had read 'a very fair amount of Latin literature'.[3] It ignores also the recondite allusions to classical lore that recur in James's letters[4] and the brilliancy of his specific commentaries on classical subjects.[5]

More important, the theory fails to consider the possibility that James deliberately suppressed classical allusion in the bulk of his fiction, feeling perhaps that it was inappropriate to the contemporary tone he wished to give his writing, thinking that it would associate him as a novelist with Scott or Bulwer-Lytton. There can be no doubt, since he could and did handle classical allusion expertly elsewhere, that his general suppression of it in his fiction was artistically motivated and deliberate. But if we accept this conclusion, we must also be ready to believe that when James actually employed classical allusion or built on the analogy of one of the ancient classics, he did so with equal calculation. Such a view is consistent with our knowledge of the care with which this master worked out every effect, of the discrimination with which he chose or rejected.

There are two very important novels by James – *The Bostonians* and *The Other House* – to which neither Mr Hueffer nor Miss West refers but which seem to bear such relation to the *Antigone* of Sophocles and the *Medea* of Euripides, respectively, as to upset the theory of James's cultural limitations and to provide not merely proof of his knowledge of ancient literature but also of that fond familiarity which leads to expert use. We intend in this paper to explore these seeming relationships with the hope of establishing these plays among the important sources of the two fictions. We are encouraged to do so at the outset by the scattered classical allusions in the first of these novels which any reader may pick up[6] but which must have special significance here, since James usually suppressed such allusions elsewhere. That significance may be merely, however, the appropriateness of such allusion to the atmosphere of arid and unnatural intellectuality that James was trying to create in *The Bostonians*, but we think not wholly so.

II

The Bostonians is one of the few novels for which Henry James acknowledged a literary source. On 8 April 1883, the novelist transcribed into his *Notebooks* 'part of a letter I have just written J. R. Osgood, my publisher, in regard to a novel'; the detailed outline, which is given, is that of *The Bostonians*, and James adds, 'Daudet's *Evangéliste* has given me the idea of this thing.' That he adhered to this source might be inferred from the fact that, over a year later when he was worrying about getting started on his novel, he rejected such titles for it as 'The Newness – The Reformers – The Precursors – The Revealer', since 'people will say they are taken from Daudet's *Evangéliste*' – as if he did not wish the relationship of the two works to be known. Yet the editors of the *Notebooks*, after comparing James's outline of his prospective novel with his own synopsis of Daudet's work, venture the opinion that 'James could hardly have taken more than an initial impulse from *L'Evangéliste*, which had just appeared in 1883, and which he analyzed in his essay on Daudet in the same year'.[7] Turning from James's synopsis to the French novel itself, we are struck by the correctness of this judgment upon the use that James made of it. Here, to be sure, is a woman with a fixed idea, a religious fanatic who persuades a young girl to follow an unnatural course to the sorrow of her fiancé and her mother, neither of whom has force enough to oppose her cruel mentor. Dramatic conflict, a salient feature of *The Bostonians*, is almost wholly lacking. Charles Lorie-Dufresne, the fiancé, a meek widower with two small children, never faces Madame Autheman or sets in motion any opposition to her will; in the end he drifts feebly out of the story. Madame Ebsen, mother of the victimized girl Eline, has the strength only of an injured suppliant, though her fate, and not she, induces the venerable Dean Aussandon to deny Madame Autheman the sacraments, an act costing him his position. Because Daudet invents no proper opposition to his protagonist, because her sway is complete, her characterization is superficial and unconvincing. James saw this, holding that in *L'Evangéliste* Daudet had 'got up' his material 'solely from the outside', and that Madame Autheman in particular was 'quite automatic' and 'psychologically . . . a blank'.[8] Contributing no more than 'the idea of the thing' – by which James would seem to have meant only the idea of a strong woman enslaving a less experienced member of her own sex – *L'Evangéliste* truly can be said to have supplied only the 'initial impulse' for *The Bostonians*.

If Daudet did not supply the dramatic conflict and the psychological depth which make *The Bostonians* an engrossing novel, from what source did these things come? Partly from the novelist himself, surely, for he brought to the writing ten years of practice in the form and more years of reflection on it. But partly also from his reading. Though we believe that this reading was more varied for even *The Bostonians* than hitherto supposed, we have perhaps a clue to a classical source in the fact that James in his essay upon Daudet very aptly calls Madame Autheman (who corresponds to Olive Chancellor in his own fiction) 'a Medusa of Calvinism'. May not this be a hint of an association which had already begun to form in his own mind? We seem to be on the right track when we encounter this sentence in *The Bostonians* concerning its protagonist, Olive Chancellor: 'The unexpected temperance of her speech on this subject of Verena's accessibility to matrimonial error seemed to the girl to have an antique beauty, a wisdom purged of worldly elements; it reminded her of qualities that she believed to have been proper to Electra or Antigone.'9 Perhaps a comparison of the *Antigone* and *The Bostonians* may reveal parallels quite as important as those that exist between *L'Evangéliste* and the novel.

What are the Greek and English works about? Both, in general terms, are about a young, unmarried woman seen in the process of trying to accomplish an end she has set for herself. The end for each is a major one, and the whole life of each woman is identical in the story with her efforts for her Cause. The Cause involves, in each case, a conflict of traditional morality and conventional assumptions with restless discontent and aspiration as embodied in the 'heroine'. The embattled young woman is vanquished in each case, and with her aspiration ends her life (Olive Chancellor, for reasons we shall see, only figuratively). Antigone's Cause is the burial of her brother Polyneices, to whom the sacred burial rites have been legitimately forbidden by the king, Creon, because the slain youth had led an army against the state. The play begins immediately after Creon has issued his edict and Antigone has resolved to defy it. In the first scene Antigone tries to persuade her sister Ismene to share the virtuous crime with her. Ismene will not help her, and in the second scene we learn by 'report' that Antigone has performed the rite alone. This single act is the logical focus of the play, and the remainder is concerned with the dramatic clash of will and personality between Antigone and Creon, each representing, however, a philosophical position. Through the clash of personalities, the single act is tested against the basic ethical views represented in the major figures, with supplementary data supplied for each view: by Haemon and Tiresias for Antigone; by Ismene and Chorus for Creon. The very structure of the play resembles the procedure of a debate, with two main speakers and a rebuttal for each side. First Antigone engages Ismene, then she takes on Creon; Creon goes far beyond the arguments of Ismene, finishes with Antigone and meets Haemon. There is an impasse, then Tiresias appears with a grand summation and rebuttal for Antigone's side. Creon's side yields to the rebuttal (which is enhanced by the deaths of Antigone and Haemon) in a concluding concession and apologetic. It is a striking reversal of modern artistic practice in that, to use I. A. Richards' term, the specific act serves as 'tenor' and the ethical argument conveyed through representative personalities as 'vehicle'.

In *The Bostonians*, as in the *Antigone*, the heroine devotes her life to a Cause. And, like Antigone, she tangles with a male whose views on the subject are quite different. Olive Chancellor, the heroine, is a consecrated feminist. Basil Ransom, her cousin from Mississippi and her antagonist, holds for male superiority. But their conflict can hardly be due to their views, for they never discuss the subject together. As contrasted with the Antigone–Creon debates. Olive and Ransom are merely *ever aware* of their differences. Further, Verena Tarrant is at the outset a feminist equally with Olive, yet Ransom falls in love with Verena, and, after rescuing her, finally marries her. Verena, if we pause to examine her, has a complexity of relationship and motivation far beyond that of her simple prototype Eline of Daudet's novel. She serves the function of a foil to Olive Chancellor, as Ismene does to Antigone. At the same time she is dependent on Olive: 'The fine web of authority, of dependence, that her strenuous companion Olive had woven about her, was now as dense as a suit of golden mail' (1 201). As Ismene, as a weaker 'sister' foil to the stronger,[10] Verena should be swayed by sentiment and loyalty to Olive, while responding with every essential fibre of her being to the opposite point of view. And so, in subtle way, she does. But Verena parallels also, in the formal situation, the position of Haemon. She actually occupies the role of Olive's chief defender in debate against Basil Ransom (the counterpart of Creon) throughout the novel. In this way, being linked with both Olive and Ransom, she takes a central position in the book. So central, in fact, that Mr Edmund Wilson has written: 'The subject of *The Bostonians* is the struggle for an attractive daughter of a poor evangelist [Verena] between a young man from the South who wants to marry her [Ransom] and a well-to-do Boston lady [Olive] with a Lesbian passion for her.'[11]

This is Mr Wilson's view of what the struggle is about – a forthright but not very subtle statement. His analysis is accurate (the struggle, Verena as its object, the Lesbian passion), except for one important emphasis. Though Verena is the direct object of the struggle, the struggle *for her* is no more the 'subject' of James's novel than Antigone's act of ritual is the subject of Sophocles' play. Antigone's act is simply the occasion for the explicit conflict between her and Creon, just as Verena Tarrant is the occasion for the struggle between Olive and Ransom. But we must not confuse the occasion with the conflict: the real 'subject' of both works is the conflict itself, the clash of characters. With this difference: in the *Antigone* each antagonist is the bearer of an ethic; with the fall of either, a moral viewpoint falls. For James such a procedure was impossible; to freight a character with an ethic was to load him out of human shape, to make an 'all-knowing immortal' out of a 'flurried human'. In *The Bostonians* the subject is a struggle of personalities instead of a conflict of characters; not ethical justification for human behavior, but human motivation as the source of behavior, is what we are invited to consider. Nothing more weighty (and few things are more weighty) is James's 'subject'.

Having noticed these basic similarities and differences, we may turn briefly to the major figures. In the main struggle within each story there is a sexual conflict, the male ultimately destroying the female. Creon and Basil Ransom both believe that man must rule *physis*, by his very nature (the Chorus asserts: ' 'Tis now as it hath ever been, and still in years to come the old order will not change.'[12] But there is a clear divergence. Creon begins with plain statements of male dominance: 'No woman, while I live, shall master me' (p. 66); and, 'From this time, women they needs must be, and range no more' (p. 68). But when he gets down to cases, his utterance takes this form:

> We must defend
> The government and order of the state,
> And not be governed by a wilful girl.
> We'll yield our place up, if we must, to men;
> To women that we stooped, shall not be said. (p. 71)

Whatever the motivation (and Sophocles pays it no heed), Creon's ultimate argument is from political ethics; the final two lines of the last quotation are quite clear on this point. Ransom, too, has general views on the subject. We find him 'thinking that women were essentially inferior to men, and infinitely tiresome when they declined to accept the lot which men had made for them. He had the most definite notions about their place in nature, in society' (I 232). That he finds them 'infinitely tiresome', rather than subversive elements (as in Creon's view), gives us a lead as to what to expect when *he* gets down to cases. Compare Creon's weighty discourse with Ransom's treatment of Verena and her 'ideas', in their first meeting: ' "Now I want you to tell me this. . . . Do you really believe all that pretty moonshine you talked last night? I could have listened to you for another hour; but I never heard such monstrous sentiments. . . . Confess you meant it as a kind of *reductio ad absurdum* – a satire on Mrs Farrinder [the feminist leader]?" he spoke in a tone of the freest pleasantry, with his familiar, friendly Southern cadence' (I 108).

Perhaps this is better compared with Creon's ideological contempt for Ismene. The precise parallel to Creon–Antigone is Ransom–Olive. And here we find that Ransom's distaste for Olive grows out of a preference in personalities, not in political ethics. Ransom's theory (so local, so Mississippian, so 'human', as against Creon's universal ethical criteria) 'was to the effect that the simplest division it is possible to make of the human race is into the people who take things hard and those who take them easy. He perceived that Miss Olive Chancellor belonged to the former class' (I 12). Ransom himself belongs very clearly to the latter class. So, we come to see, does Verena Tarrant; and, given the congenial temperament, Ransom finds *her* sociological views no bar to falling in love. But with Olive, whose views Verena shares, the case is different. Ransom's struggle with Olive comes clearly out of their innate personal antipathy: 'little by little, she gave him an uneasy feeling – the sense that you could never be quite safe with a person who took things so hard' (I 21).

The sex-conflict between Creon and Antigone had been integrated with the opposition of their 'views' by Sophocles, in advance of his play's opening scene. With Ransom and Olive, the difference in 'views' gradually subsumes itself under the sex-conflict *in response to* the developing situation (and it remains on the personality level, but intensified). Says Ransom: 'I don't object to *old* old maids; they were delightful; they always had plenty to do and didn't wander about the world crying for a vocation. It is the new old maid you have invented from whom I pray to be delivered' (II 240).

How about the heroines – does James consistently develop the parallels and dissimilarities we have been noting in constructing Olive Chancellor? Is Olive really Antigone reshaped by a modern hand? Quite evidently she is, and more. We recall that Verena found in her qualities 'proper to Electra *or* Antigone'. Perceptible, too, is a quality represented most distinctively by Cassandra. And given James's conception of personality, this is neither strange nor eclectic. We think of Cassandra as the prophetess of evil (a kind of ancient Calamity-Jane); Electra represents the derangement of the singleminded pursuit of revenge; Antigone is the model of consecration of Will to Idea. James could scarcely concede that such characterizations do ample justice to the human personality as conceived in modern times. So, though Olive Chancellor is modelled on Antigone, there is no incompatibility, but rather an added complexity and interest, James felt, in enriching her personality with traits drawn from other tragic heroines. The result, we shall see in the following quotations, is the personality of a tragic female compounded on Sophoclean models but one that Sophocles never conceived.

The likeness to the prophetic Cassandra comes out in crucial places, as in Olive's last words to her dying friend, Miss Birdseye: ' " I shall see nothing but shame and ruin!" Olive shrieked' (II 217). And James's intention is clear from his references to her as 'the little prophetess' (I 113). The likeness to the haunted and vengeful Electra comes out chiefly in the wildness of Olive's behavior in the final scenes. But we detect it throughout in her own words, as (regarding the want of a vote): 'I always feel it – everywhere – night and day. . . . I feel it as a stain that is on one's honor' (I 187). Or with reference to the coming victory of feminism, in her relish of 'the revenges of the future' (I 191). We detect it, too, in Verena's plaintive cry: 'I do tell her, sometimes, that what she desires is not only justice but vengeance' (II 10). (Compare the plight of Chrysothemis.)

But the dominant strain in Olive's personality remains Antigone's: the yearning for consecration, even unto death, to some great ideal. John Jay Chapman notes that the prospect of death as punishment 'does not terrify Antigone: she welcomes it. She almost seems to fear lest, neglecting these rites over her brother, she may miss the chance of dying nobly.' And he translates thus her words to Ismene in the opening scene: 'Be what you list! But I will bury him; and Death shall add a beauty to my deed.' A moment later Antigone cries, 'Nothing in death is dreadful, save the fear lest Death be robbed of his nobility.'[13]

Precisely this quality is found in Olive throughout. 'The most secret, the most sacred hope of her nature', James tells us, 'was that she might some day have such a chance, that she might be a martyr and die for something' (I 14). And again, later, James writes: 'Sacredly, brightly single she would remain; her only espousals would be at the altar of a great cause' (I 204).

The latter remark introduces a note which broadens our perspective on Olive. She is more than a composite of several Greek tragic heroines whom she resembles; she is a personality in which qualities of the three are thoroughly integrated and a different whole emerges. Consider, for example, the sexual question in regard to the classical females. Much has been made of their celibacy, and rightly. But their actual situation is this: Electra is forbidden to marry (lest she raise up children hostile to the murderers) and Antigone is *prevented* from marrying by Creon's fiat. Antigone laments:

'Unwept and unfriended,/ Cheered by no song Hymenæal . . . /
Lo, I am led, heavy-hearted.'

'O tomb! O nuptial chamber! O house deep-delved/
In earth, safe-guarded ever.'

'And now, made captive thus, he leads me hence
No wife, no bride for ever . . . of marriage-joy
And nursery of children quite bereft.' (76–7)

Electra, too, bemoans her 'Wasting away without children, and over me no kindly husband stands'. But the connection is not, in James's phrase, 'worked-in'; these lines just quoted seem almost inconsistent with what we conceive as the 'real' character of Antigone and Electra. Compare how beautifully the sexual aspect is 'worked-in' by James in creating the personality of Olive: ' "Priests – when they were real priests – never married," she tells her proselyte Verena, "and what I dream of doing demands of us a kind of priesthood" ' (I 164). Here the consecration and its object ('what I dream of doing') are integrated with the celibacy in a single sentence. And this sort of integration we find throughout, as in the sentence previously noted, 'Sacredly, brightly single she would remain; her only espousals would be at the altar of a great cause.'

As contrasted with the regretful wails over their celibacy uttered by Antigone and Electra, Olive's celibacy is the outcome of a deep-rooted will (she is 'unmarried by every implication of her being', 120). And James, with a sense of tactics equal to his great grasp of strategy, develops this consistently. Olive's Cause is Feminism, and the objects of her consecration are women. That she should fix her devotion upon the most striking concrete embodiment of her aspirations seems natural; that she does actually develop a Lesbian passion for Verena is, as Edmund Wilson claims, patent. The connection in the *Electra* is nearly as bare; even granted for a moment Electra's Lesbian drive toward Chrysothemis (which, curiously enough, was not brought out until the nineteenth-century neo-Freudian translation of Hofmannstal), the connection is not very important. But in *The Bostonians* these items are little master-strokes; the conceptual connections of Sophocles become dramatic interrelations in James. See how the sexual aspect is worked in with the moral aspect in this passage about Olive: 'She has an immense desire to know intimately some very poor girl. This might seem one of the most accessible of pleasures; but, in point of fact, she had not found it so. There were two or three pale shop-maidens whose acquaintance she had sought; but they seemed *afraid of her*, and the attempt had came to nothing. She took them more tragically than they took themselves, they couldn't make out *what she wanted them to do*, and they always ended up by being odiously mixed up with Charlie' (141).

Achieving the intimacy she desired 'with some very poor girl' by attaching Verena to her, Olive Chancellor becomes an unnatural figure for a comedy of manners, such as is *The Bostonians*. Indeed, unless James were willing to burlesque her, to make her a female Malvolio, he must develop her as a tragic character – a woman helpless in her compulsions, capable of eliciting our sympathies while repelling us by her intrinsic violence, her *un*womanliness, with a presentiment of her fate. From this point of view, Olive Chancellor is almost a synoptic version of the Sophoclean tragic female. Nearly every sensible generalization that can be made about them fits her too. Thus A. R. Chandler's contention that 'Pugnacity, pride, erotic passion, and the tendency to lamentation are their four chief motivating forces'. Thus T. B. L. Webster's remark, regarding these females, that 'frankness, fortitude, and sensitiveness to shame' are 'distinguishing characteristics'. And finally, F. H. Prye's sense in these females of 'a consciousness of rectitude which can neither surrender its convictions without shame nor persist in them without ruin'.[14]

It is probably unnecessary here to labor the closeness of the parallels. Merely to read over the final chapter of the novel is to see each of these points embodied in Olive Chancellor and her situation. The last chapter, we recall, is laid backstage in a great Boston auditorium; Verena is scheduled to make her major address on behalf of the feminists. It is to this end that Olive's devoted plans and best-laid schemes have moved – for to have Verena make this speech now is to win her for ever. Basil Ransom appears;[15] he has discovered the plot – with him also it is to win Verena now or never. Verena leans toward him, but Olive's influence is still strong. This is a showdown between them, with Ransom carrying the fight: 'Olive meanwhile, was literally praying to her kinsman. "Let her appear this once: not to ruin, not to shame! Haven't you any pity . . . ?" ' (Note the very words 'ruin' and 'shame' used above by Prye.) 'Her face and voice were terrible to Ransom', James tells us. Yet Ransom obdurately persists, 'She's mine, or she isn't, and if she's mine, she's all mine.' The struggle continues, others backstage taking up for Olive. But her fight is a losing one. Verena the woman is too much for Verena the feminist; and as Olive recognizes this her spirit is steeled: 'As Ransom looked at her he became aware that the weakness she had just shown had passed away . . . she was upright in her desolation. The expression of her face was a thing to remain with him for ever; it was impossible to image a more vivid presentment of blighted hope and wounded pride. Dry, desperate, rigid, she yet wavered and seemed uncertain; her pale, glittering eyes strained forward, as if they were looking for death.' And as Ransom receives these impressions, Olive does indeed gather herself up for a death plunge. Her death is an emotional suicide, a fatal violation of her personality. For Olive, the shy, inhibited, mortally sensitive, rushes out on the stage to face Verena's audience herself: 'If he had observed her, it might have seemed to him that she hoped to find the fierce expiation she sought for in exposure to the thousands she had disappointed and deceived, in offering herself to be trampled to death and torn to pieces. She might have suggested to him some feminine firebrand of Paris revolutions, erect on a barricade, or even the sacrificial figure of Hypatia, whirled through the furious mob of Alexandria.'

James's intention is clear: the phrases are those of tragedy – 'fierce expiation', 'trampled to death and torn to pieces', 'sacrificial figure of

Hypatia'. But the situation is out of joint. Our protagonists are not a king, a prince, and the daughter of a king, struggling over a great ethical problem. Instead they are an overzealous, undersexed spinster, a lawyer from Mississippi who can't make a living, and the pretty, rather stupid daughter of a dowdy, pushing couple – all backstage haggling over whether the girl shall or shall not make a speech. And after Olive's frantic exit to her 'tragic' emotional suicide, we find Ransom leaving the hall with Verena, 'relieved to know that, even when exasperated, a Boston audience is not ungenerous'. The Back Bay 'Hypatia' meets, instead of 'the furious mob of Alexandria', merely the polite, though scattered, handclapping of a wellbred Boston audience. And as they gain the street, with Verena in tears, James ends the book: 'It is to be feared that with the union, so far from brilliant, into which she was about to enter, these were not the last she was destined to shed.'

But her tears are bathetic, compared to the heavy, inescapable woe at the end of a Greek tragedy. James has failed to unite the essentially comic and essentially tragic elements in his impossible synthesis of Yankee materials, Daudet's *L'Evangéliste*, Sophocles' *Antigone*, and what-have-you. It is a great, and from a modern point of view, a very interesting effort, but it is none the less a failure. Either Olive should have been burlesqued, which James could not do, granted his perceptions and his sympathy, or Ransom and Verena should have been elevated and destroyed with her. The stuff is not the stuff of tragicomedy.

III

The multiple points of resemblance between the *Antigone* and *The Bostonians* might lead us to look for contacts between the *Medea* of Euripides and *The Other House* as numerous as those between the suction cups of some giant cephalopod and the sea-floor. Here, however, there is little parallelism, albeit such parallels as exist are especially forceful; nevertheless *The Other House* has far more of the character of a Greek play than has *The Bostonians*. It is as if James, after acknowledging the commercial failure of the earlier novel, returned to the Greek analogy to discover if a piece more in harmony with the mood of classical tragedy might produce the success denied to his previous effort.

No clearly stated purpose of this sort is discoverable in James's *Notebooks* or his published correspondence, though the notebook entry of 26 December 1893 in which James sketches his first outline of *The Other House* is by now probably known to every devotee of the novelist: 'I have been sitting here in the firelight – on this quiet afternoon of the empty London Xmastide, trying to catch hold of the tail of an idea, of a "subject". . . . The prudent spirit makes a punctual note of whatever may be the least indistinct – of anything that arrives at relative concreteness' (p. 138) – so James clears his idea of any suggestion of literary ancestry. It is a thing that came to him *de novo* out of the flickering firelight. To assume more distant origins is to impugn the testimony of the novelist – or is it? James does not speculate from what source came the 'flutter of impalpable wings' that brushed across his face 'with a blur of suggestion' on this occasion. His business was to get down his *donnée* as quickly as possible, not to analyze himself to see how he came in possession of it, what reading had gone before, what hardly suspected meditation.

That James had received suggestions before *The Other House* commenced to jell in his mind is the thesis of Leon Edel, his editor.[16] The latter traces James's inspiration for Rose Armiger, 'the Bad Heroine', back to the time, two years prior, when he had witnessed Elizabeth Robins interpret the role of Ibsen's Hedda Gabler. 'Her motives', James had written of Ibsen's heroine, 'are just her passions. . . . She is infinitely perverse. . . . One isn't so sure she is wicked and by no means sure . . . that she is disagreeable. She is various and sinuous . . . complicated and natural; she suffers, she struggles, she is human, and by the fact exposed to a dozen interpretations.' There are reflections also in the composition of Rose, the same authority believes, of Rebecca West of *Rosmersholm* and of Hilda Wangel of *The Master Builder*. He continues:

The Other House, because it was in origin dramatic, and because the central character derives from the Ibsen heroines, comes closest to being an 'Ibsen play'. Its provincial setting, the retrospective method employed at the outset, the small cast, the use of Dr Ramage as a family advisor (an Ibsen type recalling Judge Brack or Rector Kroll) and Mrs Beever as the objective outsider able to view the struggling characters with reason and judicial calm – these suggest at every turn the Ibsen externals. The plot has elements in common with *Rosmersholm* with which James was familiar as far back as 1890 and which was played in London in 1893, the year he planned *The Promise* [his first title for *The Other House*]. Both the James and Ibsen works are haunted by a dead wife: Beata's suicide in *Rosmersholm*, before the play begins, contributes a barrier of psychological guilt to Rebecca's and Rosmer's love, even as the promise Julia extracts from her husband before her death interposes a barrier to Rose Armiger's love for Tony Bream, against which she acts with such violence. In this, Ibsen and James used a situation, common enough in literature and life, that Freud later was to study and analyse – that of a young woman in a strange household who 'consciously or unconsciously weaves a day-dream about the disappearance of the mistress of the house and the master taking the newcomer to wife in her stead'. But where the situation between Rosmer and Rebecca constitutes the principal focus of *Rosmersholm*, the plot of *The Other House* is rendered complex by the introduction of the Good Heroine, who is, in a sense, to substitute for the dead Julia, since she loves Tony and he reciprocates her love. Hence Rose's motive in killing Effie is not only to release Tony from his vow: she must make Jean Martle 'disappear' (to use the Freudian word) and this she can achieve only by incriminating her. (pp. xvii–xviii)

Edel's thesis is reinforced by his surmise that James intended the part of Rose Armiger – had he cast his material in dramatic form (as he was later to do) – for Miss Robins, his friend and chief exponent of Ibsen on the London stage.

But, as in the case of *The Bostonians* and the *Antigone*, one source need not exclude another; even if James made large use of Ibsen materials, it does not follow that he drew solely upon Ibsen for his inspiration. This conclusion would too much simplify a master who is generally acknowledged to be somewhat complicated, if not recondite. Presuming that James may have read widely in the drama as a preparation for his 'dramatic years', we have fortified that presumption by a demonstration that he made some use of Sophocles in constructing *The Bostonians*. May not he have been reading another Greek dramatist prior to sketching his plot on that December afternoon when he first drafted the outlines of *The Other House*?

Indeed, in the sketch are one or two elements, hardly traceable to Ibsen, out of which the story may have been born. In the three Ibsen dramas, for example, there is no murdered child. True, Rosmer's Beata could bear him no children and this fact might, by some obscure process of association, have suggested Tony Bream's child to James and then the destruction of that infant by the wife's friend with the object of pinning the guilt upon her rival. But this seems rather farfetched. A more likely source would show either a passion-driven mother destroying her own children or a female friend destroying them for her advantage. The former situation obtains in the *Medea* of Euripides. Medea had been as 'infinitely perverse' as Hedda Gabler – and for love. She had helped Jason get the Golden Fleece from her father and had murdered her own brother for Jason's sake, we must remember, before the beginning of the play which bears her name. Still subject to the same violent emotion, now turned to hate, she murders her own children, as well as Jason's new wife and father-in-law. Grimly she reveals her motivation to her former husband:

> Thy sons are now no more,
> This will afflict thee.[17]

It is perverted love that makes this 'detested lioness' set her fangs in her own children. And it is her uncontrollable passion that induces Rose Armiger to drown the child of her best friend and the daughter of the man she aspires to wed.

But drowning was not the original device James meant his Bad Heroine to employ in doing away with the child. In his sketch 'she determines to poison the child – on the calculation that suspicion will fall on her rival'. It is 'a strange and little known poison . . . brought from a far country' by a returned lover whom the Bad Heroine casts off. 'It is in a locket, say: some woman gave it to him. *He* gives it to the Bad Heroine *before* she throws him over.'[18] This intent to use a strange poison ties *The Other House* to the *Medea*, for Medea dispatched poisoned ornaments to Jason's new queen through Jason's little sons. Creon, the rival's father, was slain by the same poison when he clasped his daughter to him. The fact that James first intended the murder to be by poisoning rather than by drowning may be indicative of the order of his sources. Even after he had begun serialization of *The Other House* in the *Illustrated London News* he clung to poisoning as the child's mode of murder! 'The illustrative design that figured at the head of each instalment remained unchanged throughout the serialization: a horrified Rose Armiger holding at arm's length a cup – presumably filled with poison – while, in the shadows behind her, Satan whispers into her ear. It seems clear from this that when the first instalments appeared James still retained the original idea of making Rose poison Effie; he altered his *dénouement* before the serial came to its end.'[19] This alteration leads us to suppose that James re-read *Rosmersholm* as he worked on *The Other House*, and that, when he came to the climax of that play in which Rebecca and Rosmer drown themselves, he was induced to change the device by which the child dies in the novel.

Again, James's initial indication of the roles played by Dr Ramage and Mrs Beever suggests the prior inspiration of the Greek drama. 'There are two persons to figure as the *public*, the judging, wondering, horrified world, the doctor and a convenient older woman who has been in the first act.'[20] These commentators on the action suggest the chorus of a Greek play in this first setting forth of their function, rather than characters invented on such models as Ibsen's Judge Brack or Rector Kroll. Is it not amplification which makes them like the latter?

But *The Other House* is more like the *Medea* than it is like any play of Ibsen's in its *dénouement*. The murderess goes scot-free. In the Ibsen plays the sinner is punished before the curtain falls. The ruthless Hedda, whom Rose Armiger most resembles, kills herself with the pistol with which Lövberg had been slain after Judge Brack recognizes it as having belonged to her and threatens to expose her. Rebecca West, of *Rosmersholm*, who, at the beginning of Ibsen's drama, somewhat resembles Rose Armiger, is transformed into a noble person (with no resemblance to Rose) but as a consequence of her early will to evil is so involved in Rosmer's downfall that she can only prove her love to him by committing suicide with him. In the *Medea*, however, the murderess, despite the curses Jason calls down upon her, takes her departure, physically unscathed –

> To Erectheus' land
> I am now on my road, where I shall dwell
> With Ægeus, great Pandion's son. . . . (ii 114)

Like Ægeus, Dennis Vidal serves as a way of refuge for the defeated Bad Heroine of *The Other House*. Attempting to explain in his Foreword to the stage version of *The Other House* why James permits the criminal ostensibly to escape punishment, Leon Edel recalls an observation of James's when he 'was writing his precocious book reviews, in his early twenties. In *Orestes* or *Macbeth*, he wrote, the dramatic interest of crime "lay in the fact that it compromised the criminal's moral repose". . . . He is concerned with Rose's "moral repose" and he makes it clear when she walks "free" from "the other house" that her punishment will be greater than any the law can devise.'[21]

This is correct, but in citing *Orestes* by way of analogy, Edel has unconsciously testified, with that intuition given to the scholar who is close to his subject, to the Grecian atmosphere in which Rose Armiger is swathed. However much she may owe to Hedda Gabler and to

Rebecca West in conception, and we freely admit the greatness of that debt, there is as much, surely, that she owes to the *Medea*. Unifying *The Other House* by her presence, she makes it the closest analogue to the Greek drama in James's writing. In fact, the novel is a modern contrivance out of the stuff of the ancients, largely supplemented by readings from Ibsen and probably others. Indeed, if this study has any merit it is in its revelation of the distance and scope of James's search for materials. He knew more than Hawthorne, Eliot, Turgenev, Balzac, Daudet, and other French realists. He knew Ibsen, and he knew the Greeks.

NOTES

1. *Henry James: A Critical Study* (1913) p. 101.

2. *Henry James* (London, 1916) pp. 27, 60–2, 65.

3. *Letters of Henry James*, ed. Percy Lubbock (New York, 1920) I 8.

4. For example, in a letter to Jusserand, the French Ambassador: 'Dear Athenian, For once in my life I am more Attic than Alcibiades! I am living on the honey of Hymettus while you eat Spartan broth in Pall Mall.' Quoted in Marie Garnier, *Henry James et la France* (1927); see 'Une lettre inédite'.

5. For example, his discussions of Epictetus and of William Morris' 'Earthly Paradise' and 'Life and Death of Jason', in *Notes & Reviews* and *Views & Reviews*.

6. *The Bostonians* (London and New York, 1886) pp. 6, 47, 91, 101, 138, 141, 162, 173, 236, 257, 429.

7. *The Notebooks of Henry James*, ed. F. O. Matthiessen and Kenneth B. Murdock (New York, 1947) pp. 46, 47, 67, 48. 'Alphonse Daudet' appeared in *Century Magazine*, Aug. 1883. See Le Roy Phillips, *A Bibliography of the Writings of Henry James* (New York, 1930) p. 192.

8. *Partial Portraits* (New York, 1911) pp. 237, 199.

9. *The Bostonians* (Boston, 1921) I 167. All further quotations from this work are followed by parenthetical page citation.

10. W. N. Bates, *Sophocles* (Philadelphia, 1940) p. 133.

11. 'Ambiguity of Henry James', in *Hound & Horn* (April 1934) p. 391.

12. Robert Whitelaw's translation, nearest in time to the publication of *The Bostonians*. Subsequent parenthetical *page* references are to Gilbert Murray's *Ten Greek Plays* (New York, 1929).

13. *Antigone*, trans. J. J. Chapman (New York, 1930) pp. 68, 69.

14. Chandler, '. . . Sophocles, Analyzed According to Freudian Method', in *Monist*, XXIII (1913) 77; Webster, *An Introduction to Sophocles* (New York, 1936) p. 60; Prye, 'Theory of Greek Tragedy', in *Nebraska Univ. Studies* (Oct. 1913) XIII 37.

15. Circumventing the policeman, whose presence may have been suggested by that of the guard at the tomb in *Antigone*.

16. *The Other House* (Norfolk, Conn., 1948) pp. xiv–xviii.

17. *The Plays of Euripides* (Everyman ed.: New York, 1908) II 114 (Woodhull's translation).

18. *Notebooks*, pp. 140–1.
19. *The Other House*, p. xiii.
20. *Notebooks*, p. 140.
21. *The Complete Plays of Henry James* (Philadelphia, 1949) p. 679. The reader will be interested in the suggestion made us by Mr Edel that the motivation of Rose is slightly influenced by that of the mother in 'The Author of "Beltraffio" ' (1884), who allows the child to die under the guise of 'protecting' the child from the father.

SISTER JANE MARIE LUECKE, O.S.B.

The Princess Casamassima: Hyacinth's Fallible Consciousness (1963)

HYACINTH ROBINSON's sensitive consciousness is the mirror which controls the shape of Henry James's *The Princess Casamassima*. As in so many of his other novels, this consciousness is the aesthetic device that reflects the experience of the people involved, and is responsible to some degree for the value attached to that experience. But Henry James's happily chosen term, 'consciousness', has been given such complicated treatment by scholars as would seem to be directed only to aesthetics or metaphysicians, whereas his novels actually adhere to Marianne Moore's more accessible dictum: he created 'imaginary gardens with real toads in them'. Hence, anyone who wishes to read him aright must know something about 'toads' as well as about aesthetics lest he take the reality of the life portrayed for artifice, or worse still, the 'imaginary gardens' for the 'real toads'.

The danger in such an error is not so much that one applies a Paterish scheme of morality to human life as that one misses the very human significance that enriches James's fine art. For the consciousness in a Jamesian novel may very well be the artistic center, the 'jar in Tennessee' or 'the blue guitar' through which 'things as they are' are transformed before they are seen or heard; it is nevertheless also the element which makes James's report of people's experience most true to the actual and most painfully human – what stamps it as moral realism.

Little Robinson's consciousness, then, is an aesthetic device that reflects, indeed, the 'imaginary gardens' of *The Princess Casamassima*. The moral realism of the novel, however, derives from the fact that Hyacinth's consciousness is humanly fallible with a dangerous affinity for seeing only what it wants to see. His is what the psychologists call 'selective perception'. And this fallibility is the 'real toad' that gives the novel its significantly human vision.

The idea of a selective or fallible consciousness seems not to have been explored by critics who stress the value of its being intelligent, imaginative, and sensitive. But James himself, although he insists on all the above qualifications, recognizes also 'the danger of filling too full any supposed and above all any obviously limited vessel of consciousness'. James may not say in theory that a perfectly clear, mirror-like consciousness is too superbly amoral in the human situation to be interesting or dramatically real, but he does say that 'if we were never bewildered there would never be a story to tell about us'; and he warns novelists against making characters 'too *interpretative* of the muddle of fate, or . . . too divinely, too priggishly clever'.[1]

The importance James attached to the creation of a limited, erring, or fallible consciousness can be traced through the Prefaces. He says about Rowland Mallet's in *Roderick Hudson* that 'the beautiful little problem was to keep it connected, connected intimately, with the general human exposure, and thereby bedimmed and befooled and bewildered, anxious, restless, fallible' (p. 16). On the other hand, Isabel Archer gave him 'as beautiful a difficulty as you could wish' in a consciousness, because hers was so largely 'her relation to herself'. James relates that he told himself while planning *The Portrait of a Lady*, 'Make her only interested enough . . . in the things that are not herself, and this relation needn't fear to be too limited' (p. 51). In speaking of Lambert Strether (whom I consider his pre-eminent achievement of a selective consciousness) James never mentions his fallibility, saying only that he 'rejoiced in the promise of a hero so mature'. Nevertheless, it seems to me he implies Strether's limitations when he immediately recognized that the speaker in the Paris garden 'would have issued . . . from the very heart of New England – at the heels of which matter of course a perfect train of secrets tumbled for me into the light' (p. 314).

That the distinctly human failing of the central consciousness is its selective perception is not found in the Prefaces; the novels, however, provide ample illustration, as I will show from *The Princess Casamassima*. In the three referred to above (chosen because with *The Princess* they represent the early, middle, and late James) Rowland Mallet, Isabel Archer, and Lambert Strether share. Hyacinth Robinson's propensity for seeing only what he wants to see in others – the desire or ability of each depending on whether his intelligence or imagination is wrongly or inadequately informed, or uninformed, whether it has temporarily lost its moorings, or whether it is simply too limited to see all that is perceptible – and they fill in from their own imagination and desires the missing details of the mental images. Because these images are more real to them than the actual reality, they suffer bewilderment and often real sorrow when the imaginary constructions are finally destroyed by the reality.

The early helpless plea of Roderick Hudson, 'You don't understand me' (helpless because he must make it to the man to whom he owes the most), and his late despairing but perceptive thrust, 'What I resent is that the range of your vision should pretend to be the limit of my action', could be repeated by all the victims of inaccurate mental images in these novels. However, it is only in *Roderick Hudson* that the central selective perceiver is placed in a position to harm seriously another person. In the others, the central characters themselves suffer most from having forced imaginary constructions upon their friends' differing realities. Perhaps Rowland's error took in a wider circle because he was, as he admitted to Cecilia, 'too reasonable'; he simply couldn't 'see it any other way'.

Isabel Archer and Hyacinth Robinson err as idealists: Isabel has an ideal image of herself, and she accepts anyone who enters her life only as he or she relates to that personal ideal; Hyacinth's dominating ideals are outside himself, and his torment is to relate himself to these outside ideals. The destruction of the mental image by reality had different effects in each case, although no one can say with certainty what kind of a person Isabel was when she returned to Osmond. Hyacinth's bewilderment turned to despair. It might just as well have brought him to hatred and separation, or to the coolly respected isolation that would seem to have become Rowland's lot. But more happily, such an experience can lead to the enlargement that depends on man's surviving just such confrontations and becoming thereby detached and poised in his own self-consciousness. And this seems to have been Strether's outcome (as it may have been Isabel's), perhaps because he was initially mature and his fine imagination was only temporarily unmoored in a totally new experience where all the old guidelines necessarily failed him and he had to flounder – as only a sensitive intelligence and imagination can do – until new guidelines could be fashioned from the pain of his mistakes and consequent bewilderment.

The above references to the Prefaces and novels serve only to fit my treatment of Hyacinth Robinson's selective consciousness into a body of Jamesian theory and practice. An awareness of this fallible element, this 'toad', in *The Princess Casamassima* not only enlarges the human vision in that novel but also reveals, as I hope to demonstrate, that in the totality of that vision Hyacinth is not necessarily heroic. I realize, of course, that in making this last statement I am challenging the views of Lionel Trilling, who states that Hyacinth 'dies of the withdrawal of love' and that his death 'is not his way of escaping from irresolution' but 'an act of heroism';[2] of Elizabeth Stevenson, who calls him 'the victim of a triple betrayal'; of Oscar Cargill, who makes it a quadruple betrayal; and of Louise Bogan, who makes his consciousness 'a cool and undistorted mirror' that 'will always give him the clue about everything'.[3]

The Princess Casamassima and Paul Muniment are the two characters in the novel who seem most responsible for Hyacinth's fate. However, their responsibility is far more passive than active, for the simple reason that Hyacinth has made them fit ideals he had long cherished. Paul is met first of the two, and the key to Hyacinth's fatal idealization of him can be found in such carefully placed comments as this: 'Our hero treated himself to a high unlimited faith in him; he had always dreamed of some grand friendship and this was the best opening he had yet encountered. No one could entertain a sentiment of that sort more nobly, more ingeniously than Hyacinth, or cultivate with more art the intimate personal relation' (I 202).[4] When the same ideal is repeated much later in the novel ('he had dreamed of the religion of friendship' [II 126]) it is taut with the reader's knowledge of all that Hyacinth has consciously refused to see in his friend.

From the first he had been 'immensely struck' (I 99), and although he recognized in Paul that which 'would be paid' even if it would make 'society bankrupt' (I 101), nevertheless, because he 'had a great desire to know superior persons' (I 102) Hyacinth felt 'the desire to go with him till he dropped' (I 106). He had to begin immediately to 'explain' away the crudities and apparent lack of interest Paul exhibited, and he came close enough to reality to see that it was an effort 'to keep the tears from his eyes' when 'he saw himself forced to put such a different construction on his new friend's hospitality' (I 134); still, he would not permit himself to see what he did not want to see, because he 'had dreamed of the religion of friendship' (II 126).

When the proper importance is attached to such pointed comments by the narrator as the above, it can be inferred that the social or anarchistic cause was never more than the ostensible provocation of Hyacinth's vow. Paul and the Princess said this explicitly for us when they referred to 'his feelings, his attachments', since 'he never had any opinions' (II 204). But this was not a surprise since we had just heard Hyacinth himself declare to Paul: 'It's no use your saying I'm not to go by what you tell me. I'd go by what you tell me anywhere. . . . I don't know that I believe exactly what you believe, but I believe in *you*, and doesn't that come to the same thing?' (II 195).

Perhaps the effort Hyacinth made to maintain his image of this friend was never so great as at just this point since it followed so closely his asking Paul how he will like it 'when I'm strung up on the gallows', and his catching in Paul's casual evasion of the question a tone that 'cast a chill on Hyacinth's spirit . . . like the touch of a hand at once very firm and very soft, yet strangely cold' (II 189). Yet he finally 'dismissed the sentimental problem . . . he condoned, excused, admired – he merged himself, resting for the time, in the consciousness that Paul was a grand person, that friendship was a purer feeling than love, and that there was an immense deal of affection between them'. And the narrator pointedly adds, 'He didn't even observe at that moment that it was preponderantly on his own side' (II 195).

Paul Muniment then is a determining force in Hyacinth's life principally because Hyacinth imagined him to fit his ideal of that 'grand friendship' he had 'dreamed' about all of his life. Furthermore, the revolution had been something he could hear discussed and 'cease to pay attention' (I 95) until he met Paul who struck him 'as such a fine embodiment of the spirit of the people' (II 194). And it is significant that as they drove to Hoffendahl where Hyacinth vowed away his life, Paul 'passed a strong arm around him, holding him all the way as if for a tacit sign of indebtedness'. Although Hyacinth was often bewildered by Paul's refusal to take him seriously, he rejected those insights that might impute anything but the most admirable qualities in his friend, and rather blamed himself, as he did at that moment when the arm around him 'gave Hyacinth pleasure till be began to wonder if it mightn't represent also the instinct to make sure of him as against weak afterthoughts' (I 320-1).

Whereas Paul Muniment represents to Hyacinth first of all the intimate relationship he is looking for in a friend, and secondarily the general social cause, the Princess on the other hand pre-eminently embodies his preconceived general ideal and then gradually becomes a personal matter. This is caught by the narrator in the report of the very first impression Hyacinth received on meeting her in the theater box. 'That head . . . suggested to Hyacinth something antique and cele-brated, something he had admired of old – the memory was vague – in a statue, in a picture, in a museum' (1 183). She represented all of art and culture and riches and refinement, but what made him most vulnerable to her was the fact that she also embodied for him all of beauty, and this quality determined the selective lens through which he would continue to perceive her. 'She was too beautiful to question, to judge by common logic' (1 187), even though he simultaneously wondered 'if he were not being practised on for some inconceivable end'. At the end of this first meeting, he characterized all his consequent attitude toward the Princess when he answers Millicent's declaration that she is a 'bad 'un' with 'Well, I don't care', and says to himself 'that he didn't believe a word of it' (1 199).

It would be asking too much to expect an inexperienced young man as sensitive to beauty as was Hyacinth not to be overcome by the beauty and capricious charm of a Princess Casamassima. This is certainly one of the reasons why James has at least four persons warn Hyacinth of the danger her friendship might lead him into: Paul Muniment, Mr Vetch, Sholto, and most important, Madame Grandoni. Among them they read her character and actions for him about as accurately as it is possible to do; but even when Hyacinth himself recognized that she regarded him 'as a curious animal', her face became 'more nobly, tenderly beautiful' (1 258).

Later, when the Princess asked him to remain at Medley, 'there was something in her light fine pressure and the particular tone of her mentioned preference that seemed to tell him his liberty was going' (II 19). He had still the self-poise to say, 'I've been strongly warned against you' (II 34), but finally the temptation, 'purple with the wine of romance, of reality, of civilization', was too great, and any 'considerations of verisimilitude' became 'as nothing to him' (II 37).

Because the Princess was so many more things to Hyacinth than simply a beautiful woman whom he adored, he felt she would have been 'all cruelly, all abominably dishonest' if he 'mightn't count on her' when he returned from abroad (II 135). But he was able to count on her and she gave him a rich experience through that winter of their visits to the poor and of their fireside companionship that made Hyacinth feel 'at times almost as if he were married to his hostess, so many things were taken for granted between them' (II 241).

The crisis or climax of Hyacinth's relationships with the Princess and with Paul occurred when he stood in the street with her husband and, with 'the state of feeling of those who love in the rage of jealousy', watched the two descend from a hansom and enter her house together (II 288). Although he reacted so violently, this scene cannot accurately be called his awakening to reality, or his confrontation with truth and betrayal. It does not fulfil either of these phrases completely if one takes into consideration very much about human nature, about Hyacinth, and about Henry James.

The question is, how much of the reality did Hyacinth really confront or admit, and how much of this was a change or turning on the part of his friends? What he confronted remained a question in his mind: What were 'the relations of the two persons who had descended from the cab'? And his resolution of the immediate situation was to laugh and say, 'He may be with her fifty hours!' (II 288–9). Actually, what he was witnessing he had conceived months before as a natural development when he told the Princess, 'You'd like him much better than me' (II 36). He had heard Rosy Muniment state unequivocally about Paul, 'He's in love with the Princess' (II 185); and he himself had tried to get Paul to admit as much when he suggested that the reason Paul did not visit the Princess was 'that you're in danger of falling in love if you go in for a more intimate acquaintance'. Whereupon, Paul's answer, 'It's a rum go, your wanting me to make up to her. I shouldn't think it would suit your book', had brought out what Hyacinth probably thought was his own altruistic and realistic view, 'Why the devil should I care now?' (II 188). Even now in his jealousy, Hyacinth admits 'he wanted Paul to know her months and months before' (II 310).

Of course, none of these realistic conjectures had been as real to Hyacinth as his own imaginary construction of the kind of deep friendship he thought he shared with each of these important persons in his life. And in this sense the climactic scene is an awakening for him – he is confronted with the reality that these friends did not reciprocate in kind. But that is only a negative awareness. He cannot reach a positive realization of the actual situation because he now can perceive only what his new selective lens, jealousy, permits; and jealousy narrows the vision rather than enlarges it.

His resulting view of the Princess is one of bewilderment because he cannot hate her – she still fits his pre-eminent image, since she is still only too beautifully 'purple with the wine of romance, of reality, of civilization'. He had reminded himself often that she was a 'capricciosa' and this made no difference in his adoration, so it cannot now. It is his own position in their personal relationship that he thinks changed, so he feels the desolation of the 'superseded' who cannot blame his beloved for being different from what she always was. He had passed in his relationship with the Princess from exalted idealization, to adoring companionship, to a friendly (never amorous) familiarity, to raging jealousy. In his final scene with her he returns gradually to his initial position: when she spoke passionately again about the 'people', her tone 'made his heart beat fast, and there was something so inspiring in the great union of her beauty, her sincerity and her energy', that he could imagine no greater horror than 'dearest Princess, if anything should happen to *you* – !' To her haughty question why? he could only answer, 'Simply because there's no one in the world and has never been any one in the world like you' – an answer that lifted her, in a show of indifference and contempt for his opinion, right out of his personal life and into the realm of exalted idealization. But since he had changed from what he was when he first met her, he is left now in tears (II 360).

His reaction to the reality of Paul's position is not so complicated. He can, at bottom, hate him because 'a man shouldn't turn against his friends' (II 308), although strangely enough he tries to maintain still that 'he's as fine a man as stands' (II 307). Nevertheless, he has learned one awful truth – Paul was not worthy of the 'religion of friendship' – and since this was the primary image Paul had assumed in his life, the effect on Hyacinth of his 'failure' is different from that of the Princess's. It leaves him nothing but curiosity as a reason for going 'near Muniment' again (II 310), and leaves him, furthermore, without an embodiment for the cause to which he had pledged his life.

Just as Hyacinth Robinson had previously perceived more than was really present in the characters of both his friends; so now, after his shock, he sees less than is there – he is again selecting his vision to a preconceived notion. But it is just this human propensity that makes for the dramatic tension present during his last meeting with the Princess, when he would not recognize (as the reader does) that if he had told her of his receipt of the 'call' she probably would have shown more sincere interest than he had ever enjoyed from her before. Since he read only what his lonely, self-pitying, and self-punishing vision permitted, the 'most vivid impression' he carried away was that 'she had done with him . . . forever' (II 371). How far he is from the truth only the reader, and Paul, are left to learn from her reaction to Paul's message that the billet had been received, and from the fact that she finally seeks him out.

Paul is misread differently in that Hyacinth thinks he has 'turned'. Paul was never previously what Hyacinth had thought him, and he remained himself throughout. He is typically 'generous' when he tells the Princess he would not go near Hyacinth because 'I wish to leave him free'. Since he has just said, 'If he doesn't like it he needn't do it' (II 369), the reader is left to infer that Hyacinth may well have risen in Paul's complacent estimation if he had taken a 'living' stand against fulfilling his vow.

Hyacinth's suicide is no resolution of his problem, and no decision—or at best a decision based on false assumptions. Besides, it prevents his ever learning the truth about his friends.[5] He needed to live long in order to learn about things as they are, and to cut off that life himself when the confrontation could have been most enlarging and ennobling was the choice of the weak. When Lyon Richardson was capsulating a Jamesian philosophy of life as drawn from his major characters, he expressed much the same idea: 'Only the strong have the full power to choose wisely between two goods, to discard things of price for the priceless things, to conquer the self-weakening force of blind hate and to show their strength by showing mercy.'[6] James realized that 'life enjoys playing unpredictable dirty tricks on mankind', but, as Basil Ransom says in *The Bostonians*, human beings 'are born to suffer – and to bear it, like decent people'.[7] Such a view does not imply that Henry James has reference to an explicit moral code when he inflicts far-reaching ethical choices on his characters.[8] But it does imply that James was enough of a realist to know that, although what human beings think and feel is more real to them than reality, it is just the confrontation of the dichotomy between imaginary construction and actual existence that constitutes the most dramatic – enlarging or devastating – experience in human life. Hence, he could choose no better subject matter for his novels than 'consciousness', no more human world, no better field for moral realism.

The danger is that his readers become sentimental, and call such a character as Hyacinth Robinson heroic. When all is said, it is rather the Princess Casamassima who, at the end of the novel, is left with her experience in the typically Jamesian 'heroic' position.

NOTES

1. Henry James, 'The Preface to *The Princess Casamassima*', in *The Art of the Novel* (New York, 1946) pp. 63–4. Citations from the Prefaces in the following paragraph, where page references are given in the text, are to the same edition, but in each case the Preface is the one to the novel named.

2. *The Princess Casamassima* (New York, 1948) pp. xxvii and xl.

3. The last three authors are cited in Oscar Cargill, '*The Princess Casamassima*: A Critical Reappraisal', in *PMLA* LXXI (March 1956) 112–13.

4. Citations from the novel in my text are to the two-volume edition documented in n. 2.

5. I have not considered Millicent Henning in this paper because I think Hyacinth takes her pretty much for what she is. The need she fills in his life is in the real, rather than the ideal order. He can leave her entirely alone when the Princess or Paul is near him, for then his life 'was pervaded by an element of romance which overshadowed, though by no means eclipsing, the brilliant figure of Miss Henning' (I 143). But, as the narrator so adroitly implies even in that statement, Hyacinth, nevertheless, probably would have found sufficient comfort in her generous-bosomed body to go on living longer if she had been available at the crisis – faithful or unfaithful. But her unavailability, although it precipitated the suicide, is overrated if it is looked upon as a prime cause for it. Since she was part of his real past and present, his mind could juggle her variability without losing its balance. Not so for Paul and the Princess.

6. *Henry James: Representative Selections with Introduction* (New York, 1941) p. lxxxviii.

7. See A. L. Goldsmith, 'Henry James's Reconciliation of Free Will and Fatalism', *NCF* XIII (Sept. 1958) 114.

8. See J. H. Raleigh, 'Henry James: the Poetics of Empiricism', in *PMLA* LXVI (March 1951) 109. [This essay is reprinted in this volume, pp. 52–70.]

LYALL H. POWERS

James's *The Tragic Muse* – Ave Atque Vale (1958)

THE comparatively recent appearance of a new edition of *The Tragic Muse* might in itself justify a re-examination of the novel with a view to a somewhat fuller understanding of its significance in the development of Henry James's literary career. We might recall two biographical facts that also encourage reinvestigation of the novel of 1890. First, James intended to write no more novels after *The Tragic Muse*. He wrote succinctly to his brother, William: 'The Tragic Muse is to be my last long novel. For the rest of my life I hope to do lots of short things with irresponsible spaces between them.'[1] Thus, we might not unreasonably expect to find in this farewell to the large form a final expression of his ideas on the art, or at least something of an apologia for his life as a novelist. Second, James had decided while at work on this book to begin a career as a dramatist and thus realize what he had called 'the most cherished of all my projects'. (In December 1888, Edward Compton urged him to dramatize *The American*.) We might then also look in the novel for an indication of James's real attitude to this new phase of his career as an artist. The expression of these two will, of course, take the form of metaphor, since *The Tragic Muse* is neither a literary essay nor an autobiography, but a novel.

These two reasons for what I would call the crucial significance of *The Tragic Muse* also account for what has been regarded as one of the novel's principal aesthetic failures: its cluttered and unduly complex appearance. James himself was well aware of its complexity: the preface he later wrote for the novel refers to 'my theatrical case' (of which Miriam Rooth is the subject) and to 'my political case' (which includes Nick Dormer, Julia Dallow, Mr Carteret, and Peter Sherringham), and confesses the fear that his canvas would lack unity, would be two pictures instead of one. A further complication is the announced central theme of the novel:

> some dramatic picture of the 'artist-life' and of the difficult terms on which it is at the best secured and enjoyed, the general question of its having to be not altogether easily paid for. To 'do something about art' – art, that is, as a human complication and a social stumbling-block – must have been for me early a good deal of a nursed intention, the conflict between art and 'the world' striking me thus betimes as one of the half-dozen great primary motives.[2]

In *The Tragic Muse*, the conflict between art and 'the world' is presented as Nick Dormer's problem of choosing between a political career and the life of a painter – a problem made dramatic by the fact that his choice also apparently involves a woman – Julia Dallow, virtually the goddess of politics in the novel, or Miriam Rooth, the tragic muse herself.

Even such a brief summary as this should indicate that James's central theme serves to draw together the 'theatrical case' and the 'political case', and so impose a unity on his creation. But there remains yet another objection to the structure of the novel – that its conclusion is simply a contrived happy ending. One gets the impression, so it is maintained, that everybody is married off to everybody else and that all live happily ever after. There is even some reason to suspect that James may have intended a pleasantly sentimental ending – contrary as it would have been to all his aesthetic theories. Early in his career, in an attempt to satisfy the many critics who complained of his failure to provide pleasant endings for his stories, James rounded off *The Europeans* (1878) with no fewer than three happy marriages. Even then he failed to please his countrymen. It may be argued that in *The Tragic Muse* James was making a last attempt to please.

In answering this rather damning argument we shall be led to a discovery of that crucial significance I have mentioned. We have seen that James regarded the central theme of *The Tragic Muse* as an extremely important one, and that he admitted he had always intended to do something about it in his work. He mentions the difficult terms on which the artist-life is at the best secured and enjoyed, 'the general question of its having to be not easily paid for'. He then refers to art as 'a human stumbling-block'. Even had we not his personal admission here, we should realize that this exactly describes the case of James himself. At the outset of his career he had examined the problem of the American artist in *Roderick Hudson* (1876), where Roderick Hudson and Roland Mallet serve as James's *hic* and *ille*. His giving up his native land for Europe – as Roderick Hudson had done – and his very celibacy are indicative of James's conception of the sacrifice and self-denial demanded of the artist. And it is here that we begin to touch upon the apologia that runs through the novel. This brings us to the first point in our analysis of *The Tragic Muse:* the relation between the artist and his inspiration.

The artist's devotion to his art is typically expressed in terms of the love – usually, indeed, extremely passionate love – of the artist for his muse. But this was not the relationship which James conceived of as existing between artist and muse; rather, the love he felt for his muse was severely chaste – perhaps romantic or chivalric. The reason behind this attitude is that James regarded passionate, carnal love (even as metaphorical expression) as a thief of individual integrity; and respect for individual integrity predominates in James's ethic.[3] Many of his novels and tales are metaphorical reiterations of the belief that marriage or carnal love symbolizes denial for the artist, in one way or another, of his absolute devotion to his art. The treatment is evident in such stories as 'The Author of "Beltraffio" ', 'The Lesson of the Master', and 'Nona Vincent'; and the novel *The Wings of the Dove*, for example, extends it beyond the realm of artists. And then, of course, we find the very same pattern in James's own life: the early death, in 1870, of his beloved cousin Minny Temple had a profound effect on him, and in a sense she continued to inspire him throughout his long career. (Her resemblance – even in name – to Milly Theale, the heroine of *The Wings of the Dove*, is certainly striking.) James's reaction to Minny's death is significant; his letter to William on this occasion has as its constant refrain that Minny can now be translated from reality to an image of the mind. And his other letters of that period are punctuated with such remarks as: 'the more I think of her the more perfectly satisfied I am to have her translated from this changing realm of fact to the steady realm of thought. There she may bloom into a beauty more radiant than our dull eyes will avail to contemplate.'[4] Certainly Kate Croy's statement to Merton Densher about Milly Theale, in *The Wings of the Dove*, might with equal justice have been applied to James himself regarding his attitude to Minny Temple: 'Her memory's your love. You want no other.'

This, then, is the prevailing pattern in James – the celibate artist, the chaste muse, and their incorporeal, spiritual intercourse. And it is this pattern that *The Tragic Muse* manifestly follows with remarkable fidelity. The career of Nick Dormer is marked, first, by his success in the political arena, success to be crowned by his marriage to Julia Dallow. His renunciation of the political life is emphasized by his consequent loss of Julia – she is jealous of Nick's attention to art, specifically to Miriam Rooth, the actress whose portrait he is painting. And we see that Miriam, the tragic muse of the title, comes close to being Nick's muse of painting: it is she who inspires him artistically and who becomes the model for his first important canvas. If Nick has left politics for art, on another level he has lost Julia and all the promise of married life (so fatal to the artist), and apparently gained Miriam and all the chaste delights of artistic celibacy. Thus, in James's metaphorical expression of the artist's devotion to his art, love for the muse is rather chivalric, romantic, quasi-platonic, and the intercourse between artist and muse is conceived of as quite uncarnal. There is no *consuming* passion: the individual integrity of the artist is not disturbed.

Although Miriam Rooth is recognizable as the traditional muse-figure in the novel, there is something ambiguous about her role: there is a side to her which is not unequivocally appealing to Nick, for she is likewise the representative of the art of the theater. It is this duality in Miriam which prevents her from being completely satisfactory to Nick. His refusal to do a second portrait of her is indicative of his dissatisfaction. Regarded simply as a personage in the story, Miriam Rooth has an interestingly mixed background. The mother, by her own re-iterated admission, is a high-born lady (a Neville-Nugent of Castle Nugent). The father, originally a Mr Roth, is in his way a more interesting specimen. We learn that he was 'a Jewish stockbroker, a dealer in curiosities', that he was also something of a musician and had a quick aesthetic faculty. He emerges as a complex mixture of the artistic and the commercial. And Miriam was 'visibly her father's child', a fact emphasized by such scenes as that in which Nick, working at her portrait, is 'troubled about his sitter's nose, which was somehow Jewish without the convex arch'.[5] Thus Miriam Rooth is, in James's terms, a Jewish muse – at once mercenary and aesthetic.

And it is here, perhaps, that we begin to find intimations of James's private attitude to his new venture in the arts. In a way, the Nick-Miriam situation in the novel may be regarded as James's projection of his problem of turning to the theater – there was both an artistic and a mercenary impetus involved, perhaps an insoluble paradox. We remember that he had long cherished the idea of writing for the stage, that he had made an unsuccessful attempt in 1882, but that he had just recently accepted a commission to try again. There is a change, however, in the reasons now given by James for this return to the theater. Now a commercial consideration appears uppermost. Leon Edel points out that, impressed by the substantial earnings of successful playwrights in contrast to the limited returns from the sale of his books, James saw a bright opportunity in writing for the stage. He would devote the time usually spent on novel writing to 'pot-boiling' for the theater. Here was a solution to his financial problems.[6] Nevertheless, James must have suffered a twinge of conscience in contemplating what would amount almost to an act of prostitution. This aspect of the situation is clearly represented in the ambiguity of Miriam Rooth's character: she is Nick's muse, but as mercenary as she is aesthetic.

There is yet another side to the question which further supports this interpretation. Although James had long desired to try his hand as a playwright, a certain apprehensiveness had touched him in recent years: he came to dislike – if not the theater itself – at least the conditions of its existence, and consequently perhaps to fear it somewhat. In a little article of June 1889, called 'After the Play', he wrote bitterly of this situation – 'the grossness and brutality of London . . . its innumerable demands on the attention, its general congregation of influences fatal to the isolation, to the punctuality, to the security of the dear old playhouse spell'.[7] These very sentiments are repeated almost verbatim by Gabriel Nash in the early pages of *The Tragic Muse*. Even Miriam herself is awake to the degrading conditions of the theater and to the almost evil circumstances in which she is obliged to practice her art. It was evidently with mixed feelings that Henry James regarded the new step he was about to take in his career, feelings that must have haunted him constantly during the writing of this, his intended farewell to the novel.

If he mistrusted the immediate muse he was courting (part mercenary and part aesthetic), he must have sought some ultimate author of artistic inspiration – a divinity which breathed into him not the particular spark for creating for the stage, but one which filled him with the more general impulse to lead the artist's life, to do the artist's work in whatever form. This divinity is symbolized in the figure of

Gabriel Nash. He is the inspirer of artists, as responsible for Miriam's career as he is for Nick's: in both cases he provides an initial impetus. In fact, Gabriel has a really exalted rank in the hierarchy of the gods of art – he is, as regards Nick, the ultimate inspiration while Miriam is rather the immediate inspiration. His very name, Gabriel, is significant, for it is Nash's annunciation that makes the artist aware of the artistic burden he bears.

Yet there is something capricious about this fascinating character as he last appears in the novel: after serving as the means to get Nick Dormer to renounce his political career and devote himself to painting, Nash seems to criticize Nick for going ahead with his painting – indeed for *doing* anything at all. This, we realize, actually sums up the core of Nash's consistent personal philosophy: that *doing* is of secondary importance, that *being* is all. Nash means simply that what one *does* – for instance in art – matters little in comparison with what one *is* – say, an artist; or that one can *do* without *being* – a sort of hypocrisy. In being an artist, one *participates* in the eternal Being of Art. And Nash is obviously the manifestation of that timeless essence. 'I shall never grow old', he tells Nick, 'for I shall only *be*, more and more . . . I daresay I'm indestructible, immortal.'[8] It is significant that this exchange, on the occasion of Nick's painting Gabriel's portrait, is introduced by a description of the subject's discomfiture at being fixed on canvas: 'it was new to him to be himself interpreted. . . . From being outside the universe he was suddenly brought into it, and . . . reduced to [the position] of humble ingredient and contributor' (VIII 410). And the chapter concludes with other significant allusions to Nash's relation to the stream of time: 'punctuality was not important for a man who felt that he had the command of all time', and 'Nick now recalled with a certain fanciful awe the special accent with which [Nash] had ranked himself among imperishable things' (VIII 412). After sitting to him for his portrait Nash disappears from Nick Dormer's life. However, it is quite apparent that Gabriel Nash has served as the temporal manifestation of the eternal essence in which Nick as artist participates. Nash is James's symbol of the spirit of art.

This interpretation of the functions of Miriam Rooth and Gabriel Nash in *The Tragic Muse* permits us to return finally to a consideration of the actual conclusion of the novel. Such a consideration will enable us to test again the value of the interpretation and will perhaps cast a different light on the apparently artificial aspect of the dénouement.

We have seen that the novel seems to marry off all the pairs of characters – at least by implication – and to hang out a 'happily-ever-after'
sign. But let us examine these pairings-off. Surely there can be no
objection to Peter Sherringham's marrying Biddy Dormer; and then
what actually does Miriam's marriage to Basil Dashwood mean?
Miriam's words to Nick at the close of their last interview give us the
clue. Referring to Basil she says, 'Don't talk about trouble – what's
he meant for but to take it?' And in answer to Nick's congratulations
she adds: 'What will you have? . . . It was clear there had to be some
one' (VIII 428). In other words, Miriam's marriage to Dashwood merely
symbolizes her being wed to her art – the liaison with Basil was already
a *fait accompli* which in no way detracted from Miriam's life as an artist.
The actual marriage really only confirms her devotion to the theater.

The reunion and apparently imminent marriage of Nick and Julia
Dallow, however, presents a somewhat more complex problem. They
finally spend some time together at her country place, Harsh; and
Nick does paint her portrait and hangs it in an exhibition. Everything
seems to point to a complete union of these two characters. But there
remains the fact of the portrait, a key symbol in the novel. To put it
simply, the effect of a portrait is to assure the disappearance of the
subject from the artist's life: Nick paints Miriam, who marries another,
refuses to sit to Nick again, and bids him a pleasant farewell; he later
does Nash, who literally disappears from his life. It would seem likely
that Nick's painting Julia would have a similar result. Indeed. Nick
seems always to have been aware of this peculiar law of the portrait.
Upon their original engagement to be married Nick answered Julia's
offer to sit to him with the startling and apparently inexplicable
'Never, never, never!' (VII 283). Finally there is direct reference to this
law of the portrait late in the novel. Miriam refuses to sit again to
Nick, but adds,

> 'You'll find other models. Paint Gabriel Nash.'
> 'Gabriel Nash – as a substitute for you?'
> 'It will be a good way to get rid of him. Paint Mrs Dallow too,' Miriam
> went on . . . 'paint Mrs Dallow if you wish to eradicate the last possibility
> of a throb.'
> . . . 'The last possibility? Do you mean in her or in me?'
> 'Oh in you. I don't know anything about "her".'
> 'But that wouldn't be the effect,' he argued with the same supervening
> candour. 'I believe that if she were to sit to me the usual law would be

reversed.'

'The usual law?'

'Which you cited a while since and of which I recognised the general truth. In the case you speak of,' he said, 'I should probably make a shocking picture.'

'And fall in love with her again? Then for God's sake risk the daub.' Miriam laughed out as she floated away to her victoria. (VIII 398–9)

Here, then, the question, simply phrased, is: Will Nick reverse his original decision by painting Julia badly, forsaking art, and marrying the goddess of politics; or will he adhere to it by painting her well, remaining faithful to his art, and retaining his celibacy?

A putative answer to this question is given shortly after by Gabriel Nash in the form of a prophecy. His prophecy begins by assuring Nick that Julia will send for him to do her portrait and that he will comply:

> she'll recapture you on that basis. She'll get you down to one of the country houses, and it will all go off charmingly – with sketching in the morning, on days you can't hunt, and anything you like in the afternoon, and fifteen courses in the evening. . . . You'll go about with her and do all her friends, all the bishops and ambassadors, and you'll eat your cake and have it, and everyone, beginning with your wife, will forget there's anything queer about you, and everything will be for the best in the best of worlds. . . . That's the sort of thing women do for a man – the sort of thing they invent when they're exceptionally good and clever. (VIII 406–7)

And the dangers sketched by Gabriel in this speech do indeed seem to have materialized in the subsequent pages. Shortly after Nash's departure Nick accepts Julia's invitation for Christmas: 'When nothing else was forward Nick "sketched" the whole company . . . all save Julia, who didn't clamour; and, growing rather red, he thought of Gabriel Nash when he bent over the paper' (VIII 416–17). Nash's prophecy seems at least partially fulfilled – although Nick has not yet married Julia.

But the case for Nash's prediction that Nick would eventually 'sell out' on art is strengthened by the fate of Nick's portrait of his mentor. Nick had asked to do the portrait as a sort of memento: 'Let me at any rate have some sort of sketch of you as a kind of feather from the angel's wing or a photograph of the ghost – to prove to me in the future that you were once a solid sociable fact, that I didn't invent you, didn't launch you as a deadly hoax' (VIII 408). He was obviously thinking of the law of the portrait – but how much more serious for Nick would be the loss of this subject, his ultimate inspiration. It sounds almost as though Nick were begging permission to make for himself a graven image.

However, not only does Nash disappear, his portrait also fades away to nothing but a blur resembling the roughest preliminary sketch. Nick explains this to Biddy by saying that his model is dead: 'Nash has melted back into the elements – he's part of the great air of the world' (VIII 419). And the faded portrait seems to symbolize Nash's abandonment of Nick, to suggest that Nick has sold out as an artist and so no longer has a right to Nash's inspiring influence.

But before we accept all this at face value with the rather damning interpretation it would dictate, let us recall what has been made of Nash earlier in the novel: something of an eternal being who thus would never grow old, who ranked among imperishable things, who might be said to have appeared momentarily in the stream of time without being subject to its effects; we have seen, in short, that Nash is very like the embodiment of the eternal essence of art – especially so for Nick. Surely his disappearing from Nick's view does not mean that the eternal being has ceased to exist – even if Nick may momentarily think so. I would suggest that we might understand this turn of events as something of an analogy to the Christian story, in which the temporal manifestation of an eternal power appears briefly before the eyes of men to inspire some by his presence, to save all who would be saved, by his apparent death and subsequent resurrection. Thus Nash's death, for Nick, need be no tragedy ultimately, provided his spirit is kept alive, the cult maintained. And an indication, surely, that Nash's inspiration has remained alive for Nick would be his ability to recover and carry on the celebration of that cult. In a word, his works as an artist would resemble the work of a priest of the cult – each work of art the celebration of a mass. The fact that Nick does recover from the disappearance of Nash, at least to the extent of being able to paint a rather successful portrait of Julia Dallow, would perhaps indicate, then, not the imminence of marriage, but indeed the very opposite – that he was again working as the devoted, celibate artist, celebrating the cult of Gabriel Nash, the religion of art.

Thus understood, the theme of the conflict between art and the world seems to be worked out to its logical conclusion – the persistent triumph of art. This triumph, of course, means sacrifice for the artist, the renunciation of certain material goods – in this case, of a wife. And this, it seems to me, is the interpretation dictated by the development of the novel. If my interpretation is correct – that Nick held firm to his renunciation of 'the world' and to his decision to follow the true divinity – then it enables us to understand *The Tragic Muse* as the metaphorical expression of James's attitude of bidding farewell to the novel and hail to the theater. It is the expression of his fear that he might suffer irremediably as an artist by 'pot-boiling' for the theater, but likewise of his trust that an exalted and ultimate inspiration would see him through, would enable him to continue *being* an artist regardless of the kind of thing he might be *doing* at any given time. This, then, was the basic biographical stock simmering in the crucible which produced *The Tragic Muse*. If not one of James's greatest novels, it nevertheless has its peculiar and significant value.

NOTES

1. *The Letters of Henry James*, ed. Percy Lubbock (New York, 1920) I 163.

2. *The Novels and Tales of Henry James* (New York, 1907–17) VII Preface p. v.

3. See Osborn Andreas, *Henry James and the Expanding Horizon* (Seattle, 1948), esp. ch. 1.

4. From a letter to his mother, quoted in Leon Edel, *Henry James: The Untried Years, 1843–1870* (Philadelphia and New York, 1953) p. 325.

5. *Novels and Tales*, VII 49.

6. *The Selected Letters of Henry James* (New York, 1955) p. 111.

7. In *The Scenic Art: Notes on Acting and the Drama, 1872–1901*, ed. Alan Wade, Introd. Leon Edel (New Brunswick, N. J., 1948) p. 239.

8. *Novels and Tales*, VIII 411 – hereafter referred to in the text by volume and page.

ROBERT C. McLEAN

The Subjective Adventure of Fleda Vetch (1964)

WHILE most recent critics praise Henry James's *The Spoils of Poynton* as heralding the triumph of his 'major phase', they disagree about the moral substance of the novel.[1] To some, Fleda Vetch's renunciation of Owen Gereth and the spoils is an heroic act in a sordid world; it ennobles Owen and establishes Fleda as the embodiment of the moral sense.[2] Others find Fleda's sacrificial act one of 'moral hysteria', destroying not only her own life but the happiness of Owen and his mother, Mrs Gereth.[3] But both of these ethical readings are based upon the dubious assumption that Fleda, the register and center of the novel, is a reliable reflector who acts according to a high moral standard and whose evaluation of herself and others is beyond question. The doubtfulness of such an assumption, I think, is suggested by the qualifications with which critics spice their interpretations of Fleda, one, for example, arguing forcibly that Fleda is admirable but admitting that her 'character will not perfectly stand scrutiny',[4] and another conceding that, though 'Fleda alone is willing to sacrifice no one but herself', she is disconcertingly often a sophist.[5]

James's tantalizingly brief and enigmatic critical discussion of *The Spoils* in the prefaces provides grounds for a different reading – one which explains in richer terms the quality of the novel and its inscrutable heroine. On the manner of narration he is explicit. From the moment Fleda ingratiates herself with Mrs Gereth in chapter 1 – 'positively, from that moment', James says, 'the progress and march of my tale became and remained that of her understanding'.[6] And early in the novel itself James avers that Fleda is the person 'in whose intenser consciousness we shall most profitably seek a reflexion of the little drama with which we are concerned' (ch. 1, p. 10).

James's most interesting prefatory pronouncements concern the quality of the reflector – of the person whose mind is itself the 'action' and the 'story' (Preface p. xiii). James pairs Fleda with Laura Wing, the central figure of 'A London Life', a companion piece to *The Spoils* in the New York edition. Like *The Spoils*, 'A London Life' reaches the 'spectator's consciousness' 'only through the medium' of its heroine's 'own vision, own experience, with which all the facts are richly charged and coloured' (Preface p. xxii). Although the characterization of Laura Wing resembles a photograph, and Fleda's a painted portrait, richly ambiguous and subtly colored, the two highly imaginative 'free spirits' have – as their emblematic names suggest – an intensity of fancy, a tendency to flee from reality, and a willingness and ability to live according to a romantic, subjective code in place of a realistic, objective one. Each assumes that she is more perceptive, more moral, even more practical than anyone about her. Since 'free spirits' encounter a world different from what they conceive to be ideal, whether 'heroic, ironic, pathetic or whatever', they are 'always much tormented, and by no means always triumphant . . .' (Preface p. xv).

I

We first see 'slim, pale and black-haired' (ch. 1 p. 5) Fleda at Waterbath, where she meets Mrs Gereth. Fleda, 'who hadn't a penny in the world nor anything nice at home, and whose only treasure was her subtle mind' (ch. 2 p. 13), is the plain daughter of an eccentric widower. She is, we learn from the comments of society, a sort of professional house guest, avoiding the unpleasant home of her heavy-drinking father. Her sister Maggie escapes the Vetch household by marrying a dull and poor clergyman and in her mean suburban home reserves a room for Fleda, should the latter fail in *her* quest for security.

Fleda, who has armed 'herself for the battle of life by a course with an impressionist painter',[7] has ambitions far beyond Maggie's. Although she learns from Maggie that 'people *were* saying that she fastened like a leech on other people – people who had houses where something was to be picked up' (ch. 6 p. 60), Fleda is determined to make something big of her meeting with the Gereths. At its most modest level her aim is to enjoy the graciously furnished Gereth home as a companion to Mrs Gereth, whose remaining at Poynton offers her 'an apology for a future' (ch. 3 p. 23). But Fleda also tastes of 'the bitter tree of knowledge' (ch. 13 p. 144) – sees, that is, the possibility of marrying Owen – and her wish, ultimately, is to become Poynton's mistress.

In the Waterbath garden, Fleda, already informed about Poynton's riches, encourages Mrs Gereth to talk about her collection. Sensing that Mrs Gereth might want to match her with Owen, as she symbolically does in their walks to and from church, Fleda is quietly but quickly acquiescent. The 'absolutely beautiful and delightfully dense' Owen, she thinks at first meeting, would be grateful for the 'cleverness' she is prepared to bring to a marriage. On that Sunday Fleda's 'meagre past fell away from her like a garment of the wrong fashion' (ch. 1 pp. 10-11). The next day, as she travels to London, her mind's eye roves lovingly over Poynton which, if she is clever and ingratiating, may be hers.

But to say that Fleda is merely opportunistic is at best incomplete. Although largely responsible for the awkward predicament in which she finds herself – as a false confidante and adviser for both Mrs Gereth and Owen – Fleda is also the victim of Mrs Gereth's machinations. Intoxicated as she is by Mrs Gereth's idea that she can allure Owen away from Mona Brigstock, Fleda nevertheless is an inadequate villainess on several counts. She is, for example, amazingly naïve about and considerably repelled by sex. Doubtful about what men and women do together, she envisions physical contact between the sexes as 'romping'. When she sees the 'tall, straight and fair' Mona with Owen on the Waterbath lawn she is shocked. Mona has been 'laughing and even romping', and Fleda is convinced there was 'intimacy as well as puerility' in the 'horse-play' on the hill bank (ch. 1 p. 9). Later in London when Owen invites her to lunch she withdraws, fearing a 'romp in a restaurant' (ch. 6 p. 65). Fleda goes to West Kensington under explicit instructions: 'Only let yourself go, darling – only let yourself go!' (ch. 12 p. 142). For Mrs Gereth, as Fleda later learns to her dismay, 'letting go' means doing 'what a healthy young woman must like' (ch. 17 p. 202), what leads to a quick marriage at the Registrar's. But Fleda attaches a different meaning to the command.

No suggestion of seduction taints her plan for winning Owen. Her aim is to overwhelm him with her moral fastidiousness and worldly tact, so that he 'would admire her, adore her, exactly in proportion as she herself should rise gracefully superior' to the bungling Brigstocks (ch. 15 p. 170). She is, she believes, the kind of girl who 'could never . . . be drawn in; . . . could never lift her finger against Mona'. Rather she sees her function in the heroic, magnanimous performance

of 'some high and delicate deed' (ch. 9 p. 106) which would arouse
even Owen's dulled wit. In emulation he 'should be superior, be
perhaps even sublime' (ch. 16 p. 180) in provoking Mona to break the
engagement.

Aside from her maneuvers to show herself to moral advantage,
Fleda is remarkably passive and ineffective. In the face of a job to be
done, she most often shuns action and instead gives herself over to
the workings of her unusually fecund imagination. After she undertakes to persuade Mrs Gereth to move peacefully from Poynton, for
example, Fleda, unwilling or unable to act, creates in her 'subtle mind'
(ch. 2 p. 13) the tale of Cinderella: 'She dodged and dreamed and
fabled and trifled away the time. Instead of inventing a remedy or a
compromise, instead of preparing a plan by which a scandal might be
averted, she gave herself, in her sacred solitude, up to a mere fairy-tale,
up to the very taste of the beautiful peace she would have scattered
on the air if only something might have been that could never have
been' (ch. 4 pp. 44-5). Again, in West Kensington, her 'only plan was
to be as quiet as a mouse' (ch. 13 p. 144). She 'judged nothing so
imperative as the gain of precious time', and she 'lost herself in the
rich fancy' of what would happen 'if *she* were mistress of Poynton'
(ch. 13 pp. 146, 147). Mrs Gereth, regarding Fleda as one more
collected object, one of her 'best finds' (ch. 21 p. 245), nurtures her
delusions. From the time she shows her the spoils, thus sweeping
away the girl's 'preoccupations and scruples' (ch. 3 p. 22), she works
to convince Fleda of her superior powers. At Ricks when Mrs Gereth
is trying to screw up Fleda's courage 'to let herself go', Fleda hears
herself 'commended . . . for attractions new and strange: she figured
suddenly in . . . queer conversations . . . as a distinguished, almost as
a dangerous, beauty' (ch. 12 p. 140).

One of the rare passages in which the first person narrator interrupts
the flow of the subjective narrative offers valuable commentary on the
operations of Fleda's moral and imaginative faculties. After her talk
with Owen at Ricks, Fleda turns over the thought that Owen must
really love her, yet only recently held the beautiful Mona in his arms.
By contrasting 'Mona's permissions' with her own 'stony stares', she
feels so virtuous and generous that she determines not to entice Owen
away. 'We may not', says the narrator, 'perhaps too much diminish
the merit of that generosity if we mention that it could take the flight
we are considering just because really, with the telescope of her long

thought, Fleda saw what might bring her out of the wood.' Mona herself would break with Owen without Fleda's intervention. 'If the rupture should come from Waterbath they might all be happy yet' (ch. 9 pp. 107-8). Fleda's scruples and magnanimity toward her rival, James points out, increase with her hope for success. Her ethics are far from absolute.

A second example includes interesting commentary on Fleda's imagination, while dramatizing it at work creating something from an apparent void. On receiving Owen's answer to her letter from Ricks, Fleda fears he has written a love-letter - 'let himself go on paper' - yet is disappointed to find his note merely 'a short profession of friendly confidence' (ch. 12 p. 135). With her ability to 'fill out blanks' (ch. 12 p. 140) by means of her agile mind, she provides a satisfactory explanation for the note's shortcomings.

> Fleda had awaited his rejoinder in deep suspense; such was her imagination of the possibility of his having, as she tacitly phrased it, let himself go on paper that when it arrived she was at first almost afraid to open it. There was indeed a distinct danger, for if he should take it into his head to write her love-letters the whole chance of aiding him would drop: she should have to return them, she should have to decline all further communication with him; it would be the end alike of dreams and of realities. This imagination of Fleda's was a faculty that easily embraced all the heights and depths and extremities of things; that made a single mouthful in particular of any tragic or desperate necessity. She was perhaps at first just a trifle disappointed not   find in the risky note some syllable that strayed from the text; but the next moment she had risen to a point of view from which it presented itself as a production almost inspired in its simplicity. It was simple even for Owen, and she wondered what had given him the cue to be more so than usual. Then she admirably saw how natures that are right just do the things that are right. He wasn't clever - his manner of writing showed it; but the cleverest man in England couldn't have had more the instinct that in the conditions was the supremely happy one, the instinct of giving her something that would do beautifully to be shown to Mrs Gereth. This was deep divination, for naturally he couldn't know the line Mrs. Gereth was taking. It was furthermore explained - and that was the most touching part of all - by his wish that she herself should notice how awfully well he was behaving. (ch. 12 pp. 135-6)

The flight images in the cited passages run throughout the book and are a major means of delineating Fleda's character. To Patrick Quinn[8] the metaphors symbolize Fleda's idealistic withdrawal from

reality, and to Alan Roper[9] her aspiration to rise above the sordid
world of egoism about her. I suggest that these metaphors of height
and flight, depth and diving, are chiefly indicative of Fleda's winged
imagination – her self-delusion and wishful thinking. On one occasion,
for her to believe she is the object of Owen's desire is to give herself
'wings that she felt herself flutter in the air' (ch. 9 p. 105). Again, when
she learns from Owen that Mona denounces her, 'it was a sudden drop
in her great flight' (ch. 14 pp. 164-5). When she does not hear from
Owen that he is 'free', she feels 'a deep sense of failure, the sense of a
sudden drop from a height at which she had had all things beneath her.
She had nothing beneath her now; she herself was at the bottom of the
heap' (ch. 17 p. 199).

A related pattern of religious images adds a yet deeper penetration
of Fleda's character. Mrs Gereth stands as the leader in a holy war
against the Brigstocks, whose home, a center of barbarism, is filled
with 'maddening relics' and pieces of 'household piety' (ch. 2 p. 19),
which it would be a 'pious duty to forget' (ch. 1 p. 7). Since Mrs
Gereth crusades against the introduction of 'abominations' (ch. 2 p. 19)
into the shrine of Poynton, her religion has an aesthetic orientation.
But it has, more importantly, an ethic based on the domination of the
female over the male, the mother over the son. Owen's great wrong
was not taking up with Mona, though that was 'disgusting', but 'his
failure from the first to understand what it was to have a mother at all,
to appreciate the beauty and sanctity of the character'. A mother, Mrs
Gereth instructs Fleda, should receive the obeisance accorded the
'consecrated Madame de Jaume', whose sons give her 'the supreme
word about everything' (ch. 5 pp. 49-50). Owen's heretical rebellion is
directed against the established authority at Poynton, the center of
female worship, where he has been allotted but one room – 'the one
monstrosity' of the house, according to Mrs Gereth. There he conducts
the business of the estate 'with men red-faced and leather-legged';
there he collects his 'tobacco-pots and bootjacks', his 'arms of aggression
and castigation' – 'eighteen rifles and forty whips' (ch. 6 p. 59). At
Waterbath, on the other hand, Owen finds a society dedicated to the
comfort of men who find entertainment in billiards and hunting and
pleasure in the women who serve them. The conflict between the two
ways of life is dramatized as Mrs Gereth pitches back the 'female
magazine' brought to Poynton by a Waterbath Brigstock. Fleda sees
the publication as one more token of Brigstock barbarity, but it also

is symbolic of the Brigstock ability to accommodate the male, containing as it does patterns for antimacassars – 'greasecatchers' (ch. 4 p. 36), Mrs Gereth calls them – which threaten to adorn Poynton's antique velvet chairs and sofas.

At the outset Fleda willingly subscribes to Mrs Gereth's creed. After serving a week of 'initiation' (ch. 3 p. 22) at Poynton, where she is cared for as a 'priestess of the altar' (ch. 4 p. 37), she attends Mrs Gereth as an acolyte. But rigorous authoritarianism cannot long satisfy a 'free spirit', and Fleda's antinomianism leads her to establish a new sect with a membership of one. Her cult imitates her erstwhile mentor's in having as its center of devotion Poynton Park and as its aims the manipulation of other people and the domination by the female. The differences, however, are greater than the similarities. Mrs Gereth purposes to coerce the unwilling to her standard and, in theory at least, recognizes the efficacy of sexual attraction in ruling the 'weak' male; but Fleda tries to make others desire to do what she wills and is blind to the power of sex. She is guided, moreover, not by the established authority by which Mrs Gereth governs, but by intuition, a kind of inner light. Most important, while Mrs Gereth is satisfied with tangible success without regard for the morality of the means by which it is achieved, Fleda requires the semblance of ethical perfection, both for others and for herself. For such an appearance she is prepared, even eager, to suffer, renounce, and be martyred.

Fleda's apostasy is born of her talks with Owen at Poynton, when she undertakes to find a peaceful settlement with him, rather than to wage war, as his mother has determined. But the only satisfactory solution requires the amicable withdrawal of Mona. As the family squabble deteriorates and the engagement endures, Fleda relies more and more on her inner resources, less and less on outside guidance. To face Mrs Gereth after seeing Owen at Ricks, she is sure she should find adequate courage 'if she could only be equally sure that what she should be called upon to do for Owen would be to suffer' (ch. 10 p. 113). By the time her defeat is certain, Fleda has traveled still further from the world of reality. She so closely involves herself with Poynton that she can find satisfaction in having provided the means by which the spoils (relics) are returned to the shrine. She sees herself as a saint and indulges in a state of ecstasy, above the toils of this world – 'like any other of the passionately pious she could worship now even in the desert' (ch. 20 p. 235). With support from this feeling of exaltation, she accepts her penance with Mrs Gereth with calm, promising never to desert her aging companion: 'She said nothing, but her silence committed her as solemnly as the vow of a nun' (ch. 20 p. 243).

II

Because of her ethical relativism and her tireless imagination, Fleda is a thoroughly unreliable interpreter of her experience, and on the reader is placed the burden of extricating the truth from what James labels the girl's 'contributive and participant view' (Preface p. xv). To do this, the reader must rely heavily on objective, provable statements and happenings. At the same time, he must conjecture the thoughts and feelings of other characters in order to evaluate Fleda's distortions and counter her delusions. Such a task admittedly has its hazards, but its rewards are great.

Four crucial dramatic scenes between Owen and Fleda provide rich material for our scrutiny of Fleda's subjective adventuring. These meetings – in London, at Ricks, in the Vetches' West Kensington flat, and at Maggie's house – are significant for two reasons. First, they are the most important confrontations between representatives of the Poynton 'wiseheads' (ch. 2 p. 20) and the Waterbath 'barbarians' (ch. 12 p. 140) and form the dramatic structure of the novel. Fleda's meeting with Mona in the garden at Poynton is not fully dramatized but presented in retrospect, as Fleda recalls it. Of the bitter, private meetings between Mrs Gereth and her son – when Owen announces his engagement and when Mrs Gereth visits Poynton after the return of the spoils – we know only what Fleda surmises or what little Mrs Gereth is willing to reveal to her. Second, in the interviews we are allowed to see and hear Owen and to judge the dependability of Fleda's interpretation of his words, silences, and gestures: here James most fully implicates his reader, forcing him to isolate the objective situation from the subjective imaginings of the central consciousness.

In preceding shorter encounters James provides sufficient preparation for judging these scenes intelligently. Before the battle lines are drawn up between Waterbath and Poynton, for example, Fleda sees Owen at Cadogan Place. Owen merely says 'It's awfully nice of you to look after poor Mummy.' To Fleda, however, 'his child's eyes in his man's face put it to her that, you know, this really meant a good deal for him and that he hoped she would stay on' (ch. 2 p. 20). This early we see

Fleda, who wants to remain with Mrs Gereth and also wants Owen to want her to, finding justification for her desires by reading into Owen's mind – a device she later employs to extremes. Another opportunity to judge Fleda's reliability occurs when Owen announces his impending wedding, 'absolutely fixed' (ch. 4 p. 41) for three months hence. Owen makes clear his position: the 'furniture' and the house are his – Mrs Gereth must leave. Fleda, who pointedly speaks 'of the contents of the house only as "the works of art" ', however, refuses to believe that Owen himself would deprive his mother of 'her seat by the Poynton fire', and she 'easily guessed' that Mona, in spite, is using Owen to injure Mrs Gereth. Although a family acquaintance of only a few months, Fleda becomes 'aware of being charged with . . . seeing Mrs Gereth safely and singly off the premises' (ch. 4 pp. 43, 44). How conscientiously she discharges this self-imposed obligation is problematic. Owen allows his mother to remove to Ricks 'a dozen pieces, chosen absolutely at will' (ch. 5 p. 52); but so far as the reader knows, Fleda, who considers such an offer unfair to her benefactress and believes that any selection would be 'wholly subject to Miss Brigstock's approval' (ch. 4 p. 44), never forcefully presents Owen's compromise. We know only that, before retreating to London under cover of duties for Maggie's wedding, Fleda could tell 'herself that she had let Owen know of her having, to the best of her power, directed his mother in the general sense he desired . . .' (ch. 6 p. 60).

The first major encounter occurs in London just before Mrs Gereth's strategic theft of the spoils. On the day after she receives Mrs Gereth's letter informing her that the ex-mistress has moved temporarily to Ricks and will soon settle there, Fleda is stopped by Owen on Oxford Street. Owen evidently has heard of Mrs Gereth's preparations and is jubilant, insisting that he wants to give Fleda a 'ripping' present as a 'tribute of recognition of all she had done for Mummy'. Owen's offer is certainly intended as a reward, since he tells Fleda that 'perhaps the Brigstocks would contribute' to the gift which would commemorate her 'cleverness'.[10] But Fleda is troubled by Owen's high-pitched hilarity and concludes that, while not exactly 'thinking of anything so vulgar as to make love to her', he is acting strangely for an engaged man. She rejects all the rich gifts tendered, accepting only 'a small pin-cushion, costing sixpence, in which the letter F was marked out with pins' (ch. 6 pp. 64, 65).

When Fleda also refuses lunch – 'a romp in a restaurant' – Owen walks with her across the park in puzzled silence. Fleda 'knew Mona would have considered she ought now to take the "penny bus" again; but she had by this time to think for Owen as well as for herself – she couldn't think for Mona. . . . He wanted to stay with her – he wanted not to leave her: he had dropped into complete silence, but that was what his silence said' (ch. 6 p. 65). Still filling the emptiness, her thoughts soar: 'She had read in novels about gentlemen who on the eve of marriage, winding up the past, had surrendered themselves for the occasion to the influence of a former tie; and there was something in Owen's behaviour now, something in his very face, that suggested a resemblance to one of those gentlemen.' At this point, Fleda is able to admit that she can't be a 'former tie', and by a twist of logic assigns that role to Mona (ch. 6 p. 66). Within a few minutes, moreover, Fleda associates herself with 'some thoughtless girl who finds herself the object of an overture from a married man' (ch. 6 p. 68), and she scrambles away from Owen, apparently fearful of a romp on the grass.

In this meeting Owen's actions are easily accounted for. He is delighted at his mother's impending removal to Ricks, grateful to Fleda for her services, and, later, perplexed by her rejection of his friendly offers. The scene reveals more about Fleda. We see her here audaciously reading into Owen's silences assertions simply never made. And we see her, against all probability, putting these unspoken declarations in melodramatic contexts, with herself as the object of desire.

The second interview, at Ricks, is of great importance because it abruptly alters the course of the action and gives Fleda new hope for success. Bitter at the swindle perpetrated by his mother, Owen appears at the dower house to present a strong ultimatum. If the spoils, with the exception of a dozen pieces picked by *him*, are not returned in a few days, he will resort to the law. Although Owen is baffled by Fleda's ambiguous loyalties and her failure to follow the trend of his conversation, he is happy to use her as a mediator.

Convinced that Owen loves her, Fleda is at first reconciled to losing him to her rival. But when Owen, under pressure of her merciless questioning, admits that Mona refuses to marry him until the spoils are returned, Fleda finds her position altered. The 'dumb exaltation . . . she felt rising' (ch. 8 p. 92) is accompanied by a flight of imagination, launched by Owen's solicitous inquiry about her future. Fleda blinks 'a little at the immensity' (ch. 8 p. 98) of the question and completely leaves the objective for the subjective world. She becomes 'wound up', her mind is 'excited' (ch. 8 pp. 98, 99), and her face reflects her mental turmoil, for Owen, hand on the door, smiles at her strangely, saying nothing. Guided by her belief that it is 'the rule of communication with him for her to say on his behalf what he couldn't say' (ch. 8 p. 91), Fleda interprets 'those seconds of silence': 'When I got into this I didn't know you, and now that I know you how can I tell you the difference? And *she's* so different, so ugly and vulgar, in the light of this squabble. No, like *you* I've never known one. It's another thing, it's a new thing altogether. Listen to me a little: can't something be done?' (ch. 8 p. 99). On parting Owen breaks the silence to remark that the dower house is 'awfully nice' and could be put up with 'just as it was', an innocent assertion, the reader feels, since Owen has already told Fleda that both he and Mona admire it. To Fleda, however, 'this would imply the installation of his own life at Ricks, and obviously that of another person. Such another person could scarcely be Mona Brigstock.' As he silently shakes hands in farewell Fleda 'hears his unsounded words. "With everything patched up at the other place I could live here with *you*. Don't you see what I mean?" ' (ch. 8 pp. 100, 101). Many readers have also heard the 'unsounded words' with Fleda. But clearly Owen has said nothing to support her interpolations – he has struggled to have Fleda understand his position, and he has failed.

Most significant about the Ricks encounter, however, is not that Fleda hears in Owen's silences avowals of love, but that she betrays her trust, thus actively involving herself in treachery. To Owen's repeated pleas not to tell Mrs Gereth that Mona demands the spoils as a precondition for marriage, Fleda gives ready assent, agreeing that such information would strengthen Mrs Gereth's obduracy. But Fleda reflects that Owen for 'the first time . . . had intended the opposite of what he said', that he means 'it just *would* do to tell her' (ch. 8 p. 102). Reasoning that 'if the rupture should come from Waterbath they might all be happy yet' (ch. 9 p. 108), Fleda with almost unconscious connivance delivers up two of her three 'secrets' to Mrs Gereth, giving her benefactress the proper facts to act upon, yet preserving the mark of her own innocence. The first 'secret' – Fleda's love for Owen – Mrs Gereth easily deduces as Fleda hotly defends Owen's kindness and sincerity. And Fleda deftly points the way to Owen's 'secret' by observing that Mrs Gereth must return the spoils because Owen 'has his engagement to carry out' – he must keep faith 'on an important clause of his contract', whether it's 'with a stupid person or with a monster of cleverness' (ch. 10 p. 116). Given the clue, Mrs Gereth, who again is not told that Owen allows her a dozen pieces, recalls that Owen's wedding date is past and guesses that by withholding the spoils, she may kill the marriage. Fleda confirms the suspicion: 'Their delay . . . may perhaps be Mona's doing. I mean because he has lost her the things' (ch. 11 p. 128) Searching for the third 'secret' – that Owen loves Fleda – Mrs Gereth asks her companion if Owen has expressed 'no feeling on *his* side'. ' "For me?" Fleda stared. "Before he has even married her?" ' (ch. 11 pp. 127-8). Applauding Fleda's 'wit' and convinced that Owen *must* love her, Mrs Gereth grooms Fleda and sends her to London to seduce her son. Fleda whitewashes the cheat she is abetting by rationalizing that she could at least lend 'herself to this low appearance' (ch. 12 p. 139).

At West Kensington Fleda suffers from her bleak surroundings and from the knowledge that Mrs Gereth 'had made a desert round her' (ch. 13 p. 144), isolating her from old acquaintances. She delays action well aware that every passing day is 'a nail in the coffin of the marriage' (ch. 12 p. 142) and dreams her Cinderella story, losing 'herself in the rich fancy' of how she, as Owen's wife, would reign at Poynton, retaining the 'queen-mother' as custodian of her kingdom (ch. 13 p. 146). Just before the third interview opens James dramatically presents the contrast between reality and dreams, between Fleda's present state of dependent poverty and her possible place as Poynton's princess. As she looks into a dull shop window at the wretched paintings, of some poor girl like herself, finding a 'warning to a young lady without fortune and without talent' (ch. 13 p. 148), she turns to find Owen, the Prince Charming of her fairy tale.

Owen's remarks clearly indicate that he is near the end of his patience. The 'day or two' (ch. 8 p. 93) he allowed Fleda to work upon his mother has lengthened into a month without progress, and Mona has been denouncing Fleda's meddling. Why, Owen wonders, has Fleda left Ricks for West Kensington? And what is the import of his mother's letter commanding him to go to Fleda? 'She means of course that you've something to tell me from her, hey? But if you have why haven't you let a fellow know?' (ch. 13, 151). Fleda is in a dilemma, unable to explain her absence from Ricks or her silence without revealing her hand. With nothing to report but that if Owen will marry her he can have his property, she can only assert lamely – and falsely – that she has 'made an impression' (ch. 14 p. 155) in delivering his ultimatum and has postponed contacting him simply in the hope she might 'hear more from Ricks' (ch. 14 p. 157), from which she fled shocked by Mrs Gereth's theft.

At this point Owen must realize Fleda's ineffectiveness, if not her dishonesty. He probes for an admission of her inability to cope with his mother, asking if it isn't true 'that you've had a row with her and yet not moved her' (ch. 14 p. 157). Fleda, wondering whether or not she has dropped 'into his mind the spark' (ch. 14 p. 155) that will cause him to become amorous and believing he 'might mean many things' which 'should mean in their turn only one' (ch. 14 p. 157), gives such a devious answer that Owen, exasperated, asks what he really needs to know in order to plan his future strategy. 'Then he put it plain. "If [Mona] does break will mother come round?"' This query and Fleda's reply are crucial for understanding not only this interview, but also the final one. Before answering Fleda hesitates between telling the 'truth' and protecting Mona, finally deciding in favor of 'truth' (ch. 14 p. 159). Mrs Gereth, she says, unknowingly giving the necessary information to dupe his mother, will surrender all if the marriage is off.

Having delivered the stroke she believes will separate Owen and Mona, Fleda can afford generosity, and she immediately asserts that Owen must nevertheless keep faith with Mona – a statement which argues for her good faith and puzzles Owen. 'His bewilderment visibly increased. "You think then, as she does, that I *must* send down the police?"' Fleda's answer to this seems to be the test by which Owen judges her. An affirmative reply, an admission of her obvious defeat, would prove her integrity. But Fleda fails. ' "No, no, not yet!" she said, though she had really no other and no better course to prescribe' (ch. 14 p. 160).

The balance of the conversation ricochets from Fleda's aggressive and persistent interrogation concerning Owen's love for Mona to Owen's repeated question of the need to appeal to the law. To Fleda's query '*Have* you been kind to her?' Owen begins to reply, then breaks off to demand a straightforward answer:

'Why rather, Miss Vetch! I've done every blessed thing she has ever wished,' he protested. 'I rushed down to Ricks, as you saw, with fire and sword, and the day after that I went to see her at Waterbath.' At this point he checked himself, though it was just the point at which her interest deepened. A different look had come into his face as he put down his empty teacup. 'But why should I tell you such things for any good it does me? I gather you've no suggestion to make me now except that I shall request my solicitor to act. *Shall* I request him to act?' (ch. 14 pp. 163–4)

'Fleda scarce caught his words' (ch. 14 p. 164). Again she probes into his relations with his betrothed. Do you tell Mona 'you love her'? she asks, and Owen replies: 'I say nothing else – I say it all the while. I said it the other day about ninety times.'[11] Before Fleda can choose a rejoinder to this, he repeats his question of a moment before. '*Am* I to tell my solicitor to act?' (ch. 14 p. 165).

Still Fleda is evasive, rationalizing that to answer would hurt Mona. Instead she asks if Owen is not merely *saying* he loves Mona. Forced to extremities, Owen determines to follow the lead of his adversaries in practicing deception. He decides that only a profession of love for Fleda will get him the spoils. He is just asserting 'there's only one person on the whole earth I *really* love, and that . . . person –' (ch. 14 p. 167), when Mrs Brigstock is announced. Whether or not Owen stops short because he hears the approach of a visitor is not certain. What is clear is that he has concluded that Fleda cannot or will not help him, and he is taking bold steps on his own to regain mastery of Poynton and its spoils.

Fleda flees to Maggie's dismal suburban home, extravagant in her desire for Owen to 'be superior, be perhaps even sublime', hopeful 'that superiority, that sublimity mightn't after all be fatal'. While she waits 'in the mere beauty of confidence' (ch. 16 p. 180), Owen, we may be sure, is polishing his plan to recoup the spoils. Knowing now the conditions imposed by his mother, he will propose to Fleda, while Mrs Brigstock takes on the task of convincing Mrs Gereth of his defection.

The resulting and fourth and final confrontation between Owen and Fleda is perhaps the most moving scene in the novel for its dramatization of human duplicity and anguish. The reader understands Owen's impatience, yet also knows enough about Fleda and the quality of her imagination to commiserate with her. Owen directly announces his freedom from Mona and declares his love for Fleda, assuming this is what a cunning Fleda Vetch has been waiting for.

To his dismay, Fleda rejects him, her mobile moral sense now directing her to suspect Owen's freedom. But Fleda falters on an adverb – 'You see, Mr Owen, how impossible it is to talk of such things yet!' – which Owen, 'like lightning', seizes. 'You mean you *will* talk of them? . . . You *will* listen to me?' (ch. 16 p. 188). At this Fleda's defenses crumble. Her confession of love leaves her with a 'sense of desolation', while it forces on Owen the realization that the person he has so cruelly to deal with is herself a victim. ' "Ah all the while you *cared*?" Owen read the truth with a wonder so great that it was visibly almost a sadness, a terror caused by his sudden perception of where the impossibility was not. That treacherously placed it perhaps elsewhere' (ch. 16 p. 189).

'When', asks Fleda, 'did you say Mrs Brigstock was to have gone back?' (ch. 16 p. 193). As Fleda perceives, if Mrs Brigstock had relayed the news of Owen's inconstancy, Mona would have acted by now. The situation is tense, but Fleda eases Owen's position and preserves for herself her moral shine by insisting he leave until his freedom is demonstrable. Owen has achieved his aim – as has Mrs Brigstock – and the spoils will soon be wending their way back to Poynton Park. But he has also learned to his sorrow the extent of Fleda's involvement and is amazed at a girl whose actions represent so complex a blend of scrupulosity and opportunism.

The ten days' uneasy silence following Owen's departure disconcerts Fleda. 'What game are they all playing?' she wails, with the conviction that Owen was now at Waterbath, and this lament is followed by a signal of the truth – the muddled enthymeme: if Owen was 'under the roof of his betrothed', reasons Fleda, that 'was stupefying if he really hated his betrothed; and if he didn't really hate her what had brought him to Raphael Road and to Maggie's?' (ch. 17 p. 200). In London under the fierce cross-examination of 'her terrible dupe and judge' (ch. 18 p. 216), Fleda searches ineffectually for answers to this question. Owen's blunt response to his mother's telegram – 'We are here – what do you want?' (ch. 20 p. 237) – annihilates all hope for the success of the 'wiseheads'. Mrs Gereth has an explanation for her failure in 'the great gawk of a fact' (ch. 20 p. 239) she learns from Owen at Poynton – the fact, I believe, of Owen's ruse to regain his property. But Fleda is free for a time to find her own resolution. Adamant in her belief in Owen's love, at first she cherishes the fear that he will come to her. 'I mustn't', she tells Mrs Gereth, 'put myself in your son's way, you know.' Mrs Gereth, better informed, 'gave a laugh of bitterness.

"You're prodigious! But how shall you possibly be more out of it? Owen and I – " She didn't finish her sentence' (ch. 20 p. 243). After it becomes evident that Owen and Mona are living happily together, Fleda finds satisfaction in having helped Owen stick to a marriage that had, after all, turned out well. But her great solace comes from the belief that her act of abnegation has sanctified her. Owen's letter requesting her to take from Poynton any one of its spoils is a work of delicacy. In its blessed ambiguity, it denies none of Fleda's illusions – neither Owen's love for her, nor his gratitude, nor her moral perfection – and in suggesting she take the Maltese cross, it hits upon the symbol. of Fleda's interpretation of her experience.

The final chapter, one of the most discussed endings in James's fiction, seems to some readers if not anticlimactic[12] at least melo-dramatic.[13] But seen in terms of Fleda's consciousness, it is artistically inevitable. For, as James states in the preface, 'the progress and march' of the tale 'became and remained' Fleda's 'understanding' (p. xiii), and it is not until the conclusion that Fleda is disabused of her illusions, brought down from her high-soaring flight to her place in the harsh real world of treachery.

Fleda's train ride to Poynton, like her ride from Waterbath to London after first meeting the Gereths, is symbolic of her imaginative quest for the spoils. What Fleda saw in the suburban fields on her first journey 'was a future full of the things she particularly loved' (ch. 1 p. 11). Now, though defeated, she sees in her anticipated visit a triumph of mind and morals over events. Looking off into the bleak countryside she sees shimmering 'a brightness that was the colour of the great interior she had been haunting. That vision settled before her – in the house the house was all; and as the train drew up she rose, in her mean compartment, quite proudly erect with the thought that all for Fleda Vetch then the house was standing there' (ch. 22 p. 263). Just as earlier, the 'meagre past' seemed to fall away from her 'like a garment of the wrong fashion' (ch. 1 p. 11), so now does Fleda in her mind leave the dreariness of the coach to reign over the beauty of Poynton.

But as soon as Fleda leaves the train she learns that the great house with all its riches is destroyed. The fire, a symbolic equivalent for the burning away of illusion and the lighting up of the truth, makes her – and coincidentally the reader – realize that her quest was illusory: Owen never loved her and Poynton could never be hers, neither for a lifetime nor for an hour. The cross, symbol of selfless sacrifice, she does not deserve. Tempted by the 'bitter tree of knowledge', Fleda fell, victim of pride and ambition. Now expelled from her private Eden, she is forced, literally, to worship in a barren desert. She crawls with broken wing to a bleak existence as companion for an aging woman, bereft of the beliefs that could have made such a future tolerable. 'I'll go back' (ch. 22 p. 266), she utters, as the 'story' and the 'action' close.

By means of the 'sublime economy' (Preface p. vi) of refracting all through Fleda's consciousness, by completing the story only with the last line of text, James modeled a masterful work of irony. Fleda, the victim of Mrs Gereth's intrigue, also victimizes her benefactress. Planted in London as bait to tempt Owen, Fleda is the means of trapping the huntress. Similarly, she deceives and is deceived by Owen. More importantly, though Fleda dupes herself as she attempts to deceive others, she has a short-lived triumph. With no real claim to Poynton's spoils, she nevertheless so succeeds in identifying her life with them that their disposition turns for a moment upon her destiny. Owen, who appears to be ineffective and morally weak, proves to be the strongest as well as the most humane figure in the book.[14] Forced to emulate his adversaries, he carries all before him, destroying forever his mother's ability to wage war. Yet, if he is harsh with her, he is gentle with Fleda, a battle casualty. Finally understanding her as a 'free spirit', he not only offers her a choice of the spoils but does his best to keep her from learning the humiliating truth.

A reader's initial temptation to take Fleda at her own evaluation is great. A second reading of the novel, though it does not destroy sympathy for the self-deceived 'free spirit', does make all-apparent her weaknesses. Because Fleda does gain in understanding at the very close, we may pity, not despise her. For the world she lived in, the world James wrote about, was a harsh one, its struggles occurring in an atmosphere of the tea table but in the spirit of the jungle.

NOTES

1. See Oscar Cargill, *The Novels of Henry James* (New York, 1961) pp. 218–43, for a survey of the most important criticisms of the novel.

2. See, for example, F. W. Dupee, *Henry James* (New York, 1951) pp. 186–91; and James W. Gargano, '*The Spoils of Poynton*: Action and Responsibility', in *Sewanee Review*,

LXIX (Autumn 1961) 650–60. Gargano says Fleda's heroic renunciation must be seen 'as the culmination of a series of acts defined by a social situation . . .' (pp. 650–51). Edmund L. Volpe, 'The Spoils of Art', in *Modern Language Notes*, LXXIV 601–8 (Nov. 1959), believes that in the first sixteen chapters Fleda is a 'moral idealist' but in the last six 'inconclusive and confused' chapters acts as a 'moral prig' (pp. 603, 607). John C. Broderick, 'Nature, Art, and Imagination in *The Spoils of Poynton*', in *Nineteenth-century Fiction*, XIII (March, 1959) 295–312, on the other hand, treats *The Spoils* as 'another of James's "fables of the artist" '.

3. See Yvor Winters, 'Maule's Curse: Seven Studies in the History of American Obscurantism', in *In Defence of Reason* (New York, 1947) p. 319; and Patrick F. Quinn, 'Morals and Motives in *The Spoils of Poynton*', in *Sewanee Review*, LXII (Autumn 1954) 563–77.

4. Cargill, p. 232.

5. Alan H. Roper, 'The Moral and Metaphorical Meanings of *The Spoils of Poynton*', in *American Literature*, XXXII (May, 1960) 193–4, 196.

6. Preface to *The Spoils of Poynton, A London Life, The Chaperon*, x (New York, 1908) xiii. All references to James's work, hereafter cited in the text, will be to this volume, and references to *The Spoils* will be given by chapter and page number.

7. ch. 2 p. 14. James here comments ironically both upon Fleda's pathetic presumption that a year's 'course' might equip her for a career in art and upon her lack of practical preparation for the struggle in which she engages. James's judgment of impressionism at the time he wrote *The Spoils* is not known. In 1876 he disparaged impressionists for their amorality and artistic ineptitude (*Henry James: Parisian Sketches, Letters to the New York Tribune 1875–1876*, ed. Leon Edel and Ilse Dusoir Lind (New York, 1961) pp. 109–10. But by the turn of the century he was at least appreciative of their talents: *The Painter's Eye: Notes and Essays on the Pictorial Arts by Henry James*, ed. J. L. Sweeney (Cambridge, Mass., 1956) Introduction pp. 28–9.

8. 'Morals and Motives', pp. 575–6.

9. 'Moral and Metaphorical Meaning', pp. 191–2.

10. ch. 6 pp. 63, 64. That 'the Brigstocks would contribute' to Fleda's gift was added by James for the New York Edition. Like other revisions, this one clarifies Owen's estimation of Fleda as a mediator, not a girl he loves.

11. ch. 14 p. 165. In the Houghton Mifflin edition (Boston and New York, 1896) Owen says he declared his love 'the other day a dozen times' (ch. 14 p. 197). Gargano ('Action and Responsibility', p. 657 n.) says James heightened the passage to stress 'Owen's triviality'. But surely James is here, as elsewhere, sharpening the idea that Owen loves Mona, not Fleda.

12. Charles G. Hoffmann, *The Short Novels of Henry James* (New York, 1957) p. 67.

13. Cargill, p. 239.

14. Critics who judge Owen as an obtuse masculine child confuse Fleda's evaluation with James's. Fleda's amazement at Owen's stylish London dress (ch. 13 p. 159) and his ability to use such a word as 'perpetrated' (ch. 14 p. 163) strengthen the idea that he is not the 'rather simple organism' which Cargill, for example (p. 237), assumes he is. The handsome and virile Owen may be contrasted profitably with the boy-man Lionel Berrington of 'A London Life', whose hair grows 'in curious infantile rings' and who 'had lost one of his front teeth' (ch. 4 p. 308).

JAMES W. GARGANO

What Maisie Knew: the Evolution of a 'Moral Sense' (1961)

HENRY JAMES'S *What Maisie Knew* presents from a complex point of view the initiation of a young girl into a world of vortical activities and emotions. The novel, moreover, as an example of James's celebrated 'dramatic' method, contains ambiguities resulting from the special techniques (not to speak of stylistic eccentricities) he developed from 1896 to 1901, the period the *The Awkward Age* and *The Sacred Fount*. It is not surprising, therefore, to find critics in radical disagreement as to what Maisie learns from the disruptions, reunions, and chance encounters that nourish her consciousness. Does she, as Beach maintains,[1] learn nothing, or does she, as Dupee declares, 'know at last . . . that she is in fact an instrument of badness among [her parents and step-parents] and a not unwilling one so long as she goes along with them in her desire for support and affection?'[2] Are we to adopt the ambiguous view of Pelham Edgar, who, after insisting that the novel traces the development of Maisie's moral sense, confesses that 'as we close the book we are in the same predicament as Mrs Wix, and ask ourselves what, after all, did Maisie really know'?[3] Or is Canby right in assuming that in *Maisie* James, as a rather headstrong virtuoso, was concerned with 'stage effects, not character and personality'?[4]

Of the most recent studies of the novel, those of Bewley and F. R. Leavis are discerning and occasionally analytical.[5] Unfortunately, the controversy between the writers turns on the question of *Maisie's* kinship to *The Turn of the Screw*. Yet, when they specifically discuss *Maisie*, they are, characteristically, almost completely at odds: Bewley finds in Mrs Wix's desire to keep Maisie an 'erotic' interest in Sir Claude, while Leavis assails this view as the 'oddest of . . . perversities'.[6] The disputants also differ as to why Maisie finally chooses to return to England with Mrs Wix, and more importantly they put forth

conflicting opinions concerning the 'tone' of the novel. Both writers
agree, however, that Maisie herself is untainted by the evil that festers
around her. Not until 1956 was it suggested (perhaps on the basis of
Bewley's attempt to relate the novel to *The Turn of the Screw*?) that
Maisie herself is so vitiated by the evil of her 'protectors' that she seeks
to resolve her dilemma by offering to become Sir Claude's mistress.[7]
If it can be substantiated, this interpretation of Maisie's character would
further contribute to the element of 'horror' Bewley discovers in
What Maisie Knew.

In spite of the disparity of critical opinion concerning *Maisie*, the
novel has not been examined with the care that it merits. Generally,
it has been praised, patronized, and explained in a few discursive
paragraphs or pages. In attempting to determine what Maisie knows
at the end of the novel, I shall examine the book's internal logic of
episode and authorial commentary in the hope of capturing its staged
revelations. For, despite obscurities, *What Maisie Knew* does possess
an order and a lucidity in the precisely articulated preparatory scenes
that consummate in the superficially ambiguous final chapters. In this
study my aim has not been to promote another doctrinaire thesis, but
to show, with a measure of documentation that critics of *Maisie* have
avoided, the sure and deliberate architectonics through which James
reveals his theme.

James's preface to *Maisie* emphasizes three aspects of the novel that
should help direct the reader to its meaning. First of all, by describing
his youthful heroine as endowed with 'an expanding consciousness',
he establishes the novel's concern with the theme of growth. Second,
he insists that Maisie must 'for the satisfaction of the mind' be 'saved';[8]
this comment, enforced by his allusions to the child's moral insights
and by his observations on the moral value of two scenes, declares
James's intention to deal affirmatively with Maisie's development.
Finally, James's reference to 'our own commentary [which] constantly
attends and amplifies',[9] calls attention to the authority of his interpolations – some of them surprisingly explicit – which explore and
occasionally fix the significance of Maisie's thoughts and actions. I do
not mean to imply that James mechanically glosses the difficulties of
the dramatic scenes in set passages of exegesis. Instead, the wealth of
authorial explanation is in a sense made integral by the basic technique
of the novel – a central intelligence not altogether capable (as Strether
is finally capable in *The Ambassadors*) of assessing and conceptualizing

the value of her experiences. James, then, in his own words compensates for Maisie's limitations by 'going so "behind" the facts of her spectacle as to exaggerate the activity of her relation to them' without violating the unique sense of the child's response to those facts.[10]

Unless his preface is deliberately misleading, James puts on record how in a general way he intended *Maisie* to be read. I believe that his hints can be taken as serious guides to the meaning of the novel. In confessing this, I admit impatience with the sophistical arrogance that denies a writer, especially one with James's critical acumen, any authority to explain his own creations.

That the heroine's consciousness expands to self-understanding and moral awareness is proved both by her increasingly sensitive response to the events in which she plays a part and by James's comments on her development. The first important scene which shows the direction of Maisie's initiation occurs early and announces with singular clarity the motif of moral growth. At the outset of the novel, Maisie is caught in the continuing hostilities between her divorced parents, with each of whom she spends, in turn, six months of the year. Condemned to carry insults from one parent to another, she achieves her first 'expansion' when she refuses to report their abusive messages and thus thwarts their plans to make her a 'centre of hatred'. Almost too pointedly, James interprets her feigned stupidity as a 'great date in her small still life: the complete vision, private but final, of the strange office she filled. It was literally a moral revolution and accomplished in the depths of her nature' (p. 15). Clearly then, Maisie acquires 'vision', undergoes a profound spiritual alteration, and, by frustrating her mother and father's perverted sport, functions as a force for good. This scene alone, it seems to me, undermines Beach's argument that Maisie learns nothing from her experiences. Since James is here speaking *in propria persona*, the reader must accept the passage as incontrovertible evidence that Maisie is launched under fair auspices.

A favorable start, however, does not insure a safe arrival at distant ports. As Maisie grows older she must confront, with pathetically little assistance, the enigma of her situation. Her mother's marriage to Sir Claude and her father's marriage to Miss Overmore (now known as Mrs Beale) require from her a subtle allocation of loyalty that taxes her youthful ingenuity. To add to the confusion, her step-parents are soon involved in a 'relationship' strongly condemned by Mrs Wix, Maisie's comical but sturdily moral governess. Moreover, her mother's second marriage is followed by a series of 'attachments' to Mr Perriam, Lord Eric, and the Captain, while her father's denigration of conventional codes culminates in his being the paid lover of the Countess. But Maisie, in addition to being exposed to the sordid intricacies of her guardians' amours, is often present at uninhibited adult discussions of them. Nevertheless, her innocence remains surprisingly unsmirched in the immediate proximity of pitch.

And yet, as James shows in *The Awkward Age*, a close cousin to *Maisie*, innocence is not necessarily defiled by knowledge. Aggie's antiseptic education is a ludicrously inept preparation for life in a world with little resemblance to Eden, while Nanda's exposure leads to knowledge, growth, and self-sufficiency. Maisie, like Nanda, is 'a sort of drain-pipe with everything flowing through', and like Nanda too she remains uncontaminated. Less squeamish than many of his readers and critics, James did not subscribe to the Duchess's formula for creating in Aggie the perfect child, a paragon who should be nurtured 'privately, carefully, and with what she was *not* to learn – till the proper time – looked after quite as much as the rest'.[11]

That Maisie's exposure to infection does not lead to paralysis, stasis, or corruption is apparent if the novel's basically simple focus, by no means simply achieved by the artist, is recognized: no matter how devious the adult intrigues, the center of interest always remains fixed in the child's acquisitive sensibility. In his preface, James himself warns against taking the Faranges and their associates as his subjects, for they are lacking in inherent interest because they are 'figures of too short a radiation'; they can only be invested with meaning by 'the child's own importance, spreading and contagiously acting'.[12] Beach's quaint derogation of Maisie's role seems to me to limit the novel's radiation and to reduce it to sparkling but empty virtuosity: 'Maisie herself has really no story. She is hardly more than an observer eagerly following from her side-box the enthralling spectacle of the stage.'[13] Far from being shunted to a side-box, the girl is constantly on stage in the midst of actions too urgent to be dismissed as mere spectacle.

There are at least four scenes (in addition to the episode describing her moral revolution) which dramatize Maisie's journey toward knowledge and maturity. The first scene occurs when Sir Claude, about to turn Maisie over to Mrs Beale, asks her if she dreads seeing her father. In this situation, in which she might easily have condemned her father, she colors with 'an odd unexpected shame at placing in an inferior light . . . so very near a relative as Mr Farange' (p. 119). As interpreter of her increasing sensitivity, James characterizes her emotion, as 'more mature than any she had yet known'. He further indicates that at this moment Sir Claude, who is capable of fine discrimination, 'caught his first glimpse of her sense of responsibility' (p. 120).

In other words, the child does not assume the facile irreverence that her stepfather too casually expects. Instead, with an unusual exhibition of propriety and force of character, she compels Sir Claude to take her conduct seriously. Once again she resists the adult tendency to make her a counter in an irresponsible game of hate. Her self-conscious integrity attests that her moral revolution has not proved abortive. Indeed, it has the subsidiary effect of modifying the cynicism and obtuseness of her adult associates; like Morgan Moreen in 'The Pupil', she contributes significantly to the education and refinement of those who should be enlightening her.

Of course I am not suggesting that Maisie can translate her reactions into abstract concepts; after all, though almost inordinately impressionable and discerning, she often lacks the maturity to understand what, in fact, is happening to her. As she unconsciously stores up sensations and insights, she is naturally less concerned with what she learns than with the wonder of the phenomena she observes; moreover, as the Preface warns, the experiences 'that she understands darken off into others that she rather tormentedly misses'.[14] The imaginative collaborator whom James assumes as his reader must then, with the author's assistance, supply the normative terms that describe her progress. The reader will not be disturbed, however, when after what seems a startling stretch of intelligence and feeling, Maisie lapses into childish naïveté. To expect an arbitrarily consistent development of all her faculties is to treat her as if she were a geometrical proof and not a child. Her mistakes, which are many and sometimes amusing, make her in James's words 'the ironic centre', but they do not nullify her slowly expanding vision.

A second incident showing the deepening of Maisie's nature is that in which her unbelievably stupid father takes her to the splendid house of the Countess. Here the girl's quick perceptions detect behind her father's attentions a desire to give his projected abandonment of her the best of appearances. The scene is triumphantly Jamesean in its

rich and ingratiating evocation of Maisie's diversity, complexity, and
not incongruous innocence. The child's aesthetic sense is vividly
awakened; the daughter experiences filial palpitations and responsibilities; the imperiled little identity maturely considers her own
interests; and her groping moral nature – never given a harsh pro-
minence – slowly builds up to a vision of the ugly implications of what
she has been exposed to. The gradual progression of the scene toward
éclaircissement subtly illuminates James's moral intention, for though
Maisie is child enough to feel enjoyment in the presence of the Countess's expensive possessions, she 'all in a moment' – her knowledge
invariably comes in flashes – admits her father's degradation in allying
himself with someone whom 'neither her mother, nor Mrs Beale, nor
Mrs Wix, nor Sir Claude, nor the Captain, nor even Mr Perriam and
Lord Eric could possibly have liked' (p. 196). It might not be too
extravagant to say that Maisie enters the house a child and leaves it
precociously wise, for her initial pleasure in discovering herself in the
enchanted world of the Arabian Nights is dissipated by the recognition
of 'something in the Countess that falsified everything' (p. 196). That
she betrays, at the end of the scene, a juvenile delight in the money
lavished on her by the Countess does not detract from James's moral
purport; on the contrary, it is evidence that his moral sense does not
interfere with the aesthetic rigor which demands that he be true to the
child's nature.

   Certainly a child who undergoes a moral revolution, learns responsibility, and rejects a revolting father is making rather wholesome
progress. James never intimates that she is crushed or arrested by her
experiences or that she is acquiring the calculated immorality to
attempt to become her stepfather's mistress. In scene after scene,
Maisie's accumulated insight is brought into play, but never more
tenderly than when, with the Captain in Kensington Park, she desperately urges her companion to be loyal to her mother. With the
'small demonic foresight' James attributes to her in the preface, she
envisions her mother's potential disaster.

      'Good-bye.' Maisie kept his hand long enough to add: 'I like you too.'
   And then supremely: 'You do love her?'
      'My dear child – !' The captain wanted words.
      'Then don't do it only for just a little.'
      'A little?'

'Like all the others.'

'All the others?' – he stood staring.

She pulled away her hand. 'Do it always!' (p. 155)

Although a rigid moralist may condemn her encouragement of an illicit affair, she 'supremely' reveals a deep passion for loyalty and an understanding of the moral consequences of promiscuity. Her sense of responsibility, whose birth Sir Claude witnessed, has by now confronted those bitter realities not easily resolved by resort to simple moral fiat. Maisie's allegiance is obviously not to a restrictive code; unlike other James characters, notably Winterbourne, Mrs Newsome, and Mrs Pocock, she is emancipated from – or has never made – the narrow commitment that prevents humane action. Perhaps to act with responsible freedom is necessarily to transgress. Certainly, however, Maisie's earnest, even embarrassing approval of the Captain's love can seem immoral only to those who subscribe to the unbending dogmas of Woollett.

The scene with the Captain, in spite of its immediate impact – James saw in it, on rereading, an 'effect of associated magic' – is in a sense completed by the perfectly wrought episode dealing with Maisie's last meeting with her mother at Folkestone. The child, with almost motherly solicitude, tried to 'adopt her ladyship's practical interests and show her ladyship how perfectly she understood them' (p. 222). Unfortunately, the battered but still arrogant parent is outraged at having the Captain – now 'the biggest cad in London' – recommended to her. Maisie matches her mother's angry explosion, but even anger is accompanied by a terrible prevision of tragedy:

> in the midst of her surge of passion – of which in fact it was a part – there rose in her a fear, a pain, a vision ominous, precocious, of what it might mean for her mother's fate to have forfeited such loyalty as that. There was literally an instant in which Maisie fully saw – saw madness and desolation, saw ruin and darkness, and death. (p. 225)

Such a dark vision – perhaps the key word in the novel is 'vision' – proves that the child has traveled a surprisingly straight course from the moment she decided not to feed her parents' mutual hatred. Without Mrs Wix's moral sense – which, though by no means contemptible, assesses human action by doctrinal requirements – Maisie wrests from the urgency of each of her predicaments a moral vision or a moral imperative.

Despite its inclusiveness, nevertheless, Maisie's vision is not complete until she has focused a true image of Sir Claude. For all her maturity, she would like to find in him not only a father-substitute, but the Prince Charming who, through the largess of treats, outings, and affection, instills romance into her life; their activities release her from the constricting classroom into the glamorous world of parks, restaurants, and foreign travel. His constant avowals of love and loyalty and his easygoing acceptance of her precocity, charm her into a state of devotion. Yet, James compels her to learn, a lesson terrible to a child, that her fairy-tale hero is incapable of ideal behavior in the real world. Her childhood dies with the death of her delusion. Maisie's most impressive act – the real measure of what she knows – is her precipitation of the situation which divests Sir Claude of his specious attractions and exposes his obsessively compromising nature.

Maisie does not, however, suddenly begin to judge Sir Claude at the end of the novel. From the beginning of their association, she occasionally observes in him a shiftiness with which she (like Mrs Wix) attempts to compromise. For example, when he asks if she might help him hide Mrs Beale from Mrs Wix's vigilance, she is described as gaining a 'first glimpse of something in him that she wouldn't have expected' (p. 85). At another point, fear of leaving Mrs Wix drives her to tears, but she 'couldn't have told you if she had been crying at the image of their separation or at that of Sir Claude's untruth' (p. 118). Still, she delusively believes that Sir Claude has been saved when, submitting to Mrs Wix's moral pressure, he flees with her to Boulogne. When the governess joins them, Sir Claude seems momentarily to have 'embraced his fine chance' and risen to ideal action. But Sir Claude proves himself a most unheroic hero when, accepting the first pretext, he announces his decision to return to England. In the ensuing debate with Mrs Wix, he confesses his fear of Mrs Beale and ultimately counters righteous arguments with a princely manner whose 'excess of light' draws 'depraved concession' from Mrs Wix. Though Maisie fails to support her governess's high-flying morality, she astutely notices with 'slight oppression . . . that [Sir Claude] has unmistakeably once more dodged' (p. 264).

Sir Claude's defection is the prelude to a series of events that round out Maisie's education: Mrs Wix's desperate attempt to infuse a moral sense into her charge, Mrs Beale's dramatic appearance in Boulogne, and Sir Claude's return, as a 'different' man, into a situation likely to prove explosive. James's technical daring keeps the action moving, with imaginative brilliance and poise, through surprises, ironies, and charged, elliptical dialogue. Apart from its thematic function, the cluster of scenes displays a mastery of dramatic nuance, spectacle, and timing rarely equalled in James's work. Finally, however, the scenes mass the important characters in Boulogne and prepare for the show-down leading to Maisie's disenchantment with her hero.

Since the three events have a cumulative value, it is necessary to indicate their importance. In Mrs Wix's intense campaign to indoctrinate Maisie, the child performs like a dull student indeed. Her egregious 'stupidity' has persuaded many critics that, even after all her opportunities for 'accumulations', she knows next to nothing. These critics forget, however, that Maisie confronts Mrs Wix's query as to whether she 'really and truly' has any moral sense with clever dissimulation:

> Maisie was aware that her answer, though it brought her down to heels, was vague even to imbecility, and this was the first time she had appeared to practice with Mrs Wix an intellectual inaptitude to meet her – the infirmity to which she had owed so much success with papa and mamma. The appearance did her injustice. (p. 279)

In addition to her feigned ignorance, Maisie gives the appearance of childishness because she has no ready-made Sunday-school code to mouth with impressive facility. Almost pragmatically but most sensitively, she picks her way through the disorder and complexity of a world that Mrs Wix interprets in simple Biblical terms. Yet though the pupil does not, like her tutor, know the answers in the back of the book, she is not without values. Indeed, her life with depraved parents has ironically served to teach her 'one of the sacred lessons of home', that 'there were things papa called mamma and mamma called papa a low sneak for doing and for not doing' (p. 260). In a sense Maisie is a more searching practical moralist than the literal-minded instructor whose formidable moral stance continually awes her. Moreover, through all of her disingenuous sallies, Maisie is motivated by the ideal of loyalty to Sir Claude – an ideal that Mrs Wix cannot sustain.

Mrs Beale's appearance in Boulogne demonstrates that Mrs Wix's moral sense can be rather easily trifled with. When Maisie's stepmother breathlessly courts the governess's support, Mrs Wix is so taken in by the extravagant display of kindness that she practically agrees to accept the woman she had earlier reviled. No wonder Maisie 'became on the spot quite as interested in Mrs Wix's moral sense as Mrs Wix could possibly be in hers' (p. 301). Yet, strangely, in spite of James's persistently ironical view of Mrs Wix, most critics continue to accept her as the moral norm of the novel, forgetting that she is often actuated by materialistic considerations. Though it would be foolish to deny Mrs Wix a measure of comic grandeur – her heroic speeches are always slightly preposterous – she is too high-pitched, narrow, and unsophisticated to embody James's sense of moral vision. On the whole, she has an old-fashioned, grandmotherly rectitude, but she is no vessel of wisdom. Her light is bright enough for the nursery, but it is no radiance. Her own complaint (perhaps her most touching utterance) that Maisie's affairs have led her into moral quicksands is a gauge of her limitations: 'I ask myself where I am; and . . . say to myself that I'm too far, too far, from where I started.' (p. 282). I cannot agree with Bewley's contention that Mrs Wix is the only adult in the novel 'capable of being educated into fineness',[15] for 'fineness', with its suggestion of sensitive discrimination, is just what Mrs Wix will never achieve. Though she can, at times, burst into grotesque displays of moral energy, she rather resembles Mrs Micawber – as Mrs Beale cruelly points out – in her decision to 'never, never, never desert Miss Farange' (p. 126). To the end she remains, in spite of her nagging and doctrinaire morality, 'peculiarly and soothingly safe; safer than anyone in the world' (p. 26). It is indeed most characteristic of her that even after Maisie's sacrifice of Sir Claude she still wonders what the child really knows.

Mrs Beale's descent upon Maisie and Mrs Wix is for her the climactic event in a long struggle for security and power. The onetime governess, whom both Maisie and Sir Claude confess they fear, has designedly achieved status through her marriage to Maisie's father. Then, having quickly calculated that with Farange she is on a sinking ship, she attaches herself to the susceptible Sir Claude. The acute Maisie, reacting with childlike ambivalence, recognizes her stepmother's combination of beauty and strength: 'it took [Mrs Beale] but a short time to give her little friend an impression of positive power – an impression that seemed to begin like a long bright day. This was a perception on Maisie's part that neither mamma, nor Sir Claude, nor Mrs Wix . . . had exactly kindled' (p. 124). This 'power' is, in the Boulogne scenes, hurled with tremendous force against Mrs Wix's long-standing moral 'prejudice'

concerning Mrs Beale's sinister influence on Sir Claude. Almost
completely ignoring Maisie, who is only a pawn in her game, she
wrings important concessions from her former enemy, but her masterful diplomatic *coup* gives Maisie a vivid sense of a cold-blooded,
intriguing nature: she lost 'herself in the meanings that, dimly as yet
and disconnectedly, but with a vividness that fed apprehension, she
could begin to read into her stepmother's independent move' (p. 300).
It is precisely the maneuver which subverts Mrs Wix's opposition that
begins to enlighten Maisie and to prepare her to reject her stepmother.

Sir Claude's return to Boulogne after the grand entrance of Mrs
Beale affords a picture of the indecisive man awaiting the moment
of decision. Unlike the energetic and even dazzling Mrs Beale, he
dreads the consequences that his sexual passions and moral shiftlessness
have logically created. He torments himself with the necessity of
accepting Mrs Beale (as he had earlier accepted Maisie's mother) as a
terrible fate. Obviously, he is morally and psychologically capsized in
a world where even hesitant action leads to commitment. His single
free and seemingly responsible deed, his escape with Maisie to
Boulogne, was a noisy and scared retreat, and not the 'miracle' she had
supposed. For all Mrs Wix's rhetorical excesses, she accurately characterizes him as a soul lost by his slavery to passion. Even with his doom
upon him, he continues to dodge, protesting to Maisie that since his
return to France he has not seen his mistress. It is the beginning of
Maisie's disenchantment that 'there settled on her, in the light of his
beautiful smiling eyes, the faintest purest coldest conviction that he
wasn't telling the truth' (p. 319). When desperately he asks Maisie to
sacrifice Mrs Wix, the child, with an ineluctable vision of his equivocal
character, forces her life to its crisis by proposing escape from both
Mrs Beale and Mrs Wix. Sir Claude's refusal to act enables Maisie to
see the half-heartedness of his conversion and the inveteracy of his
evasive, devious behavior.

Unmistakably, Maisie's proposal to Sir Claude and his reaction to
it have all the ingredients of a climactic scene. Nevertheless, it must be
granted that James presents the scene in a maddeningly elusive manner.
In attempting to realize every emotional nuance of the charged
situation, he resorts – to use favorite words of his – to audacious 'jumps'
and 'leaps' that make less for precise accounting of motive than for
dramatic tension. Emotional intensity is achieved by short questions,

exclamations, and broken sentences; the insistence on Maisie's 'whiteness' and 'fright' and on Sir Claude's 'whiteness' and 'fright', and the
recurrence of words like 'temptation' and 'weakness' give an impression
of agitated rather than minutely discriminated feelings. In short, the
passage is affective and connotative; it is a tense dramatization and not
a clarification. In a sense it is incomplete, and needs the illumination
later shed on it by Sir Claude.

I do not believe that the 'obscurity' of the scene in terms of meaning
(not as drama) is intended to disguise a naked appeal by Maisie to Sir
Claude's sexual passion. Rather, the incident is the consummation of
the novel's design in that the child rises above Sir Claude (and thus
loses her hero) and above Mrs Wix, who before her final heroics shows
that she too can compromise. Maisie's fear of herself, which can be
misread as a fear of her rising sexual feelings, stems from her need to
create an exigency which will prove or expose Sir Claude. Such a crisis
will complete her vision, for her stepfather's reaction to it will, for all
time, clear the troubled moral atmosphere. In asking no less than
heroism from him she becomes herself heroic. And like other innocent
heroines of James, she is doomed to ask too much. No wonder James
says that she experienced 'something still deeper than a moral sense'
(p. 354).

My reading of this difficult and crucial passage is supported by
Sir Claude's answer to Mrs Wix's accusation that he had destroyed the
child's moral sense. In a spirit of revolt against the narrowness and
tyranny of her views, he refuses to be 'treated as a little boy' (for Mrs
Wix has a sort of moral arrogance) and finely declares:

> 'I've not killed anything,' he said; 'on the contrary I think I've produced
> life. I don't know what to call it – I haven't even known how decently to
> deal with it, to approach it; but whatever it is, it's the most beautiful thing
> I've ever met – its exquisite, it's sacred.' (p. 354)

I maintain that Sir Claude cannot be referring to an intended seduction.
No amount of ingenuity concerning James's 'obliquity' or 'ambiguity'
can evade the apparent significance of this speech.

The sum of Maisie's knowledge is not like the answer to a problem
in addition, for in the Jamesean sense she knows 'everything'. But to
be less oracular, Maisie reaches maturity when, by requiring her idol
to satisfy her most strenuous spiritual demands, she refuses to accept
life as a compromise. She has learned that Sir Claude's self-deceptive

hopes to 'square' people – to work out with them convenient arrangements involving no moral decision – never actualize. Before taking
her stand at the end of the novel, she had been abandoned by a father
whose mistress 'falsified everything' and by a mother whose promiscuity may end in 'ruin and darkness and death'. When on the high
ground of principle she provokes the situation which betrays Sir
Claude's temporizing nature, Maisie surrenders her last childish fantasy.
That her expanding consciousness has brought her a ripeness, a kind of
perfection, is shown by Sir Claude's final panegyric:

> [Sir Claude speaks] with a relish as intense now as if some lovely work
> of art or of nature had suddenly been set down among them. He was
> rapidly recovering himself on this basis of fine appreciation. 'She made
> her condition – with such a sense of what it should be! She made the
> only right one.' (p. 356)

Ironically, the deflated hero, the man who prefers to be lost with
Mrs Beale rather than 'saved' with Mrs Wix and Maisie, is the most
sensitive appreciator of his stepdaughter. (Mrs Wix only dimly
perceives what she has gained.) Yet, though he can fully evaluate his
loss, the logic of events has stripped him of all illusions about his own
character. Even when he pronounces Maisie to be free and laughingly
proclaims her too good for himself and Mrs Beale, he accepts his own
inescapable indecision as the queer law of his life. In the end, I am sure,
this constantly frightened playboy is more afraid of Maisie's simple
but intense heroism (as Vanderbank is of Nanda's in *The Awkward
Age*) than he is of Mrs Beale's sexual power. When Maisie looks back
from the steamer and fails to see him on the 'balcony', she must know
that he knows his doom.

NOTES

1. Joseph Warren Beach, *The Method of Henry James* (Philadelphia, 1954) p. 239.
2. F. W. Dupee, *Henry James* (New York, 1951) p. 192.
3. Pelham Edgar, *Henry James: Man and Author* (Boston and New York, 1927) p. 127.
4. Henry S. Canby, *Turn West, Turn East* (Boston, 1951) p. 216.
5. Marius Bewley, *The Complex Fate* (London, 1952) pp. 96–144. This book contains two 'interpolations' by F. R. Leavis.
6. Ibid. p. 128.
7. Harris W. Wilson, 'What Did Maisie Know?' in *College English*, XVII (Feb. 1956) 279–81.
8. *The Novels and Tales of Henry James* (New York edition) XI vi–vii.

9. Ibid. p. x.
10. Ibid. p. x.
11. *The Novels and Tales of Henry James* (New York Edition) IX 53.
12. Op. cit. p. xiii.
13. Beach, p. 239.
14. Op. cit. p. x.
15. Bewley, p. 101.

H. K. GIRLING

'Wonder' and 'Beauty' in
The Awkward Age (1958)

IN one of his theatrical reviews, Max Beerbohm gives an impression of Johnston Forbes-Robertson rendering a line from a play of Henry James, *The High Bid*. Captain Yule, an impecunious philanthropist, returns to repurchase his ancestral home at the cost of marriage to the daughter of his opulent tenant. Chivers, the butler, as ancestral as the mansion, is interrogated by Captain Yule.

> YULE. She isn't merry-like, then, poor Miss Prodmore? Ah, if you come to that, neither am I! (*He throws up the subject, however, without further pressure; he drops for the present* MISS PRODMORE.) But it doesn't signify. (*He's really more interested in* CHIVERS *himself.*) What are *you*, my dear man?
> CHIVERS. (*As if he really has to think a bit.*) Well, sir, I'm not quite *that*. (*Appealing to his friend's indulgence.*) Whatever in the world has there been to *make* me?
> YULE. (*Washing his hands of it.*) I mean to whom do you beautifully belong?
> CHIVERS. (*Who has really to think it over.*) If you could only just *tell* me, sir! I seem quite to waste *away* – for someone to take an *order* of.
> YULE. (*Looking at him in compassion.*) Who pays your wages?
> CHIVERS. (*Very simply.*) No one at all, sir.

Max Beerbohm in *Around Theatres* directs attention to the way in which Mr Forbes-Robertson delivered: 'to whom do you beautifully belong?'

There, in those six last words, is quintessence of Mr James; and the sound of them sent innumerable little vibrations through the heart of every good Jacobite in the audience. . . . The words could not have been more perfectly uttered than they were by Mr Forbes-Robertson. We realised at once to whom *he* beautifully belongs. It is to Mr Henry James. Mr Walkley,

I notice, [in his review] places the word 'beautifully' between two parenthetic dashes; and certainly this way of notation gives the true cadence
better than the way that I have used – the way that Mr James himself
would use; but it is still very far from the perfection of Mr Forbes-
Robertson's rendering of the words. 'To whom do you – beautifully
belong?' is nearer. But how crude a medium print is – or even hand-
writing – for expression of what such a face and voice as Mr Forbes-
Robertson's can express! In his eyes, as he surveyed the old butler, and in
his smile, and in the groping hesitancy before the adverb was found, and
in the sinking of the tone at the verb, there was a whole world of good
feeling, good manners, and humour. It was love seeing the fun of the thing.
It was irony kneeling in awe. It was an authentic part of the soul of Mr
James.

'Beautifully' and 'beautiful' occur so frequently in the writings of
Henry James that their appearance in a sentence is almost equivalent
to his signature. As Max Beerbohm indicates, the idea of the 'beautiful'
is an important part of James's view of life and art; indeed the whole of
his work could be taken as a commentary on it. This 'beautifully',
according to Beerbohm, expressed affection, graciousness and pleasure,
and, going further, 'It was love seeing the fun of the thing.' This is not
the vision of Forbes-Robertson, but of James. All his 'love' James gave
to the craft of letters; here he rejoiced in the 'fun' of applying his
symbol of complete insight to a trivial interchange. If an idea of
'beauty' which includes moral aspiration an ʹ social grace can convey
a gentle humour of incongruity, it can in its confidence dispense with
the protection of irony. The constant reappearance of 'beautiful' in the
novels affirms James's confidence in his aesthetic and in the discretion
of his style.

In spite of the importance of his themes, and the delicacy of his
artistic scruples, James often seems to distil the essence of his literary
purpose through words scarcely worthy of it. Prepositions: 'in', 'out',
or 'there' have to assume crucial significance; and large imprecise
adjectives: 'wonderful', 'beautiful', 'perfect', 'magnificent', 'good' and
'bad' often serve as the vehicles of complex and subtle judgments.
James seeks to exploit the ambiguity of such words, particularly their
ambiguity in fluent conversations, where in certain situations, polite
and 'empty' phrases, or familiar and hard-worked colloquialisms may
be filled with subtleties of meaning and depths of pathos for those
who can decode them.

In *The Awkward Age,* the social figures often give the impression of enclosing themselves in desperate chatter because their sureties are crumbling beneath them. In some contexts, by his deliberate manipulation of multiple meaning, and by his pressure upon words which become more expressive than their common usage warrants, James is enriching the colloquial, indeed giving it an incisive force which is comparable with the impact of words in poetry.

Two epithets in *The Awkward Age*, 'wonderful' and 'beautiful', stand out, in different situations, so prominently that they come to be regarded as opposite poles, although their primary meanings are contiguous; and if all their connotations in the novel are associated, they emerge as complementary parts of a total assessment. The two words have in common a general content of approval, the preservation of which is consistent with James's regard for even the imperfections of human speech. Yet 'wonderful' and 'beautiful' are gradually perceived to express almost opposite ways of being. The people described and placed by these words enact almost opposite values, yet all of them if not admirable, remain fascinating. James exploits the significant distinction between the common usages of the two words. 'Wonderful', which is often used as casually as slang, nearly always carries some irony. In colloquial usage, its very frequency may twist it by unconscious irony into meaning the essence of ordinariness. 'Beautiful', on the other hand, rarely sheds all its dignity. It is difficult to make it ironic without making it crudely sarcastic. 'Wonder' can be expended on unrewarding objects, but 'beauty' can hardly be named without conveying a suggestion, however fleeting, of the ideal, and of a state of aspiration.

On one occasion after another Mrs Brookenham appears to her friends 'indeed, as they always thought her, "wonderful" ' (book VI, ch. 2). Their wonder is perpetually excited by the bold flights of her imagination and the vivacity of her intellectual dissections. She is poised on the extreme edge of the unsayable, flaunting her 'candour' in committing the most personal – which are of course the most interesting, though sometimes almost illicitly interesting – situations to words. Shortly after meeting Mr Longdon, 'the *oncle d'Amérique*, the eccentric benefactor, the fairy godmother', she discusses with Vanderbank, her most intimate friend, the reasons why Mr Longdon dislikes her, in spite of his devotion to the memory of her mother, Lady Julia. When she hurls her consciousness of her own fascination, her acknowledgment of her mother's supreme gifts, and her recognition of Mr

Longdon's fidelity to an ancient love, into a single crucible of relentless analysis, Vanderbank is dazzled.

'Oh I know that if [Mr Longdon] deplores me as I am now [Lady Julia] would have done so quite as much; in fact probably, as seeing it nearer, a good deal more. She'd have despised me even more than he. But if it's a question,' Mrs Brook went on, 'of not saying what mamma wouldn't, how can I know, don't you see, what she *would* have said?' Mrs Brook became as wonderful as if she saw in her friend's face some admiring re-flexion of the fine freedom of mind that – in such a connexion quite as much as in any other – she could always show. 'Of course I revere mamma just as much as he does, and there was everything in her to revere. But she was none the less in every way a charming woman too, and I don't know, after all, do I? what even she – in their peculiar relation – may not have said to him.' (IV 2)

The 'fine freedom' of Mrs Brook's analysis has reduced her mother's charm and Mr Longdon's devotion to component parts in an examina-tion of her own problem – how to gain the good opinion of Mr Longdon. She has claimed a regard for her mother not less than his, and a perspicuity much greater. For she suggests that she can imagine things, perhaps, that Mr Longdon, in his day, never perceived, or that he now no longer chooses to remember. To carry off her original confession of failure, Mrs Brook has belittled Mr Longdon's memories, and has, in effect, brought Lady Julia down to her own moral level, in the innuendo of 'their peculiar relation'. The adroit manipulation of an avowed deficiency so that it becomes a means of self-congratulation, is the 'wonder' of her performance. The taint of this kind of dexterity is the stain on her brilliance; it grows in a monstrous form to devour her and her daughter and her salon. 'Wonderful' first informs the reader that she is extraordinary; gradually that she is so extraordinary as to be outrageous, and, finally, that she is so defiantly and persistently outrageous as to be loathsome. But after the contagion of her voice has destroyed friendship and reduced her salon to a solitude, when 'wonderful' has advanced to 'prodigious', even then she still exacts her due allocation of fascinated interest, anxious attention, and in quite a strict sense, 'wonder'.

The word 'beautiful' has a very different history in the novel. It is so often reiterated that it comes to epitomise, in a single word, all the tragedy of delicacy and excess of scruple which overwhelms Nanda, and with her, Mitchy and Mr Longdon. These three are the people to whom the ascription 'beautiful' is characteristically given.

On occasion the word is used in its simplest senses, colloquial and complimentary. In the most vulgar colloquial sense, Van, spending some time at his toilet, can be said to be 'making himself beautiful'. Nanda, Mrs Brookenham's eighteen-year-old daughter, described merely as 'pretty' by Van – 'there's a great question whether Nanda's pretty at all' – is celebrated as 'beautiful' by Mr Longdon, who traces the style of her beauty through Lawrence and Gainsborough to Raphael. These sufficiently normal uses, however, give no direct indication of the meanings which James wishes the word to convey in other contexts.

The light of 'beauty' is first shed on Mrs Brookenham's circle by the arrival of Mr Longdon. 'Beautiful' even in his 'narrownesses' or 'prejudices', he stands apart from their self-approbation; his devotion to memories of Lady Julia has kept him unpolluted by modernity. For Mrs Brook, standards march with the times; for him they are fixed and unalterable. As an agent of James's own judgment, he asserts both the inflexibility and the power of absolute moral values. Mr Longdon, in surroundings of confusion, is intensely himself.

More than this, Mr Longdon is the cause of this kind of intensity in others, particularly in Nanda. She comes to a realisation of her own integrity by a comparison of what she thinks she is and what Mr Longdon would wish her to be. He appeals to her not to dissimulate with him.

> 'If you were to try to *appear* to me anything – !' He ended in simple sadness: that, for instance, would be so little what he should like.
> 'Anything different, you mean, from what I am? That's just what I've thought from the first. One's just what one *is* – isn't one? I don't mean so much,' she went on, 'in one's character or temper – for they have, haven't they? to be what's called "properly controlled" – as in one's mind and what one sees and feels and the sort of thing one notices.' Nanda paused an instant; then, 'There you are!' she simply but rather desperately brought out.
> Mr Longdon considered this with visible intensity. 'What you suggest is that the things you speak of depend on other people?'
> 'Well, everyone isn't so beautiful as you.' (v 2)

Mr Longdon has appealed to Nanda to disregard discrepancies of years and tastes and standards and to accept 'her original assumption that there was to be a kind of intelligence in their relation'. He requires more than honesty; the charming simplicity of her astonishment requires that her whole being shall be exposed to his loving appreciation and tender criticism. Only the fundamentally innocent can be frank with him. So while Nanda and Mitchy are prepared to reveal themselves to his scrutiny, Mrs Brook and Van are obliged to cover themselves by evasions. They prefer to acknowledge no more than the eye can see – Mrs Brook is not obliged to admit that her son borrows money from her guests and Van, with greater delicacy, chooses not to know how much Mr Longdon wishes to settle on Nanda. On the other hand, Nanda, confronted by the bleached purity of little Aggie, feels herself contaminated by her upbringing and way of life. But she is courageous enough to see herself as she appears in the eyes of Mr Longdon. And this for James is truth. The penetration of Mr Longdon's observation and his inflexible rectitude are the qualities that make him 'beautiful'. Nanda's phrase is a recognition of her surrender to his judgment.

Nanda's first recognition of the existence of these standards of judgment has come, earlier in the novel, when the same word 'beautiful' is presented to her by Van. At her first meeting with Mr Longdon, Mitchy and Van both remark on the way he is impressed by Nanda.

> Mitchy, with his eyes on her, became radiant to interpret.
> 'He knows that he's pierced to the heart!'
> 'The matter with him, as you call it,' Vanderbank brought out, 'is one of the most beautiful things I've ever seen.' He looked at her as with a hope she'd understand. 'Beautiful, beautiful, beautiful!'
> 'Precisely', Mitchy continued; 'the victim done for by one glance of the goddess!'
> Nanda, motionless in her chair, fixed the other friend with clear curiosity.
> ' "Beautiful"? Why beautiful?' (III 2)

After her first conversation with Mr Longdon, Nanda discovers what Van means.

> Detaching herself from Mr Longdon, she got straight up to meet him.
> 'You were right, Mr Van. It's beautiful, beautiful, beautiful!' (III 3)

Mr Longdon did not need to explain to Nanda 'Why beautiful?' She has found it out for herself. James in his elliptical way does not explain it to the reader either. But what Nanda has immediately discovered is that she may also enter into the kind of 'goodness' which Mr Longdon has attained because of his dedication to the memory of Lady Julia, her grandmother. His example is of a line of conduct consistent and pure, sharply distinguished from the amalgam of daring tentatives and shuffling compromises in her mother's 'modern' circle.

The discovery is catastrophic. The elements in her nature are already so composed that experience may alter the proportions in the mixture, but will never affect the substance. In Mr Longdon's judgment, she is a lamb which even in its innocence 'struggl[es] with instincts and forebodings, with the suspicion of its doom and the far-borne scent, in the flowery fields, of blood' (v 3). Her doom awaits her, and her knowledge leads her to it. She has imbibed too much of her mother's devotion to fair appearances and the charm of surfaces to allow her to marry Mitchy, who, both intelligent and good, is marred by the grotesque appearance he flaunts in the face of aesthetic propriety. She knows too that, in the eyes of Van, the object of her love, she is stained by her knowledge of good and evil, and hence her own fair front is also marred, not comically like Mitchy's, but tragically. For Van's prejudices overcome his sympathies; he would choose little Aggie in preference to Nanda. His intelligence, like the talk of the charmed circle, may range wide, but his love for Nanda cannot cast out his fear of her knowledge because he lacks 'the excuse of passion'. 'Bleak as a chimney-top when the fire's out', as her mother calls her, Nanda falls below the aesthetic standard required in the drawing-room at Buckingham Crescent, where Lady Fanny in her beauty and dumbness is idolised. Nanda is not acceptable to Van, and she cannot accept Mitchy.

Both in rejecting and being rejected, Nanda has to bear the burden of her mother's pursuit of the aesthetic rather than the moral good. Her leaning towards the moral, supported by Mr Longdon's approval, makes her aware of all the consequences of her divided preferences. She is innocent, in that none of the sins are of her committing, but as a 'full vessel of consciousness', she is ripe for tragedy. If she were only a lamb tossed by the forces of evil, like Maisie, or the children in *The Turn of the Screw*, or even little Aggie in a large part of *The Awkward Age*, Nanda could not be a tragic figure. Not only does she suffer, she takes upon herself the responsibility for her suffering, and therefore makes of it something nobler than disaster. James's epithet is still – or again – 'beautiful', but now we are called upon to feel in this 'beauty' a sense of nobility and completeness, and to compare it with the glories of inevitable journeys towards doom demonstrated in

Shakespearean tragedy. Within the tragedy, and within the novel, there is no room for the label 'tragic'. If the author wishes to use a summing-up word, it must be a less formal and intrusive one. But it must be a word which stretches from the imperfection of human aspirations to the sublimity of divine judgments; it must be capable of application to whatever situation, high or low, satisfies the highest moral and aesthetic impulses. Such a word, in James's context, is 'beautiful'.

The state of tragic acceptance reached by Nanda is demonstrated in her last interview with Van. After a long absence, he comes at her summons, and then with practised adroitness, he evades the unspoken appeal she makes for herself, so that she has to take the responsibility for smoothing over his refusal, allowing him to depart with his social tact unimpaired. He chatters her love to its death. She, having offered him her love, presents him with a graceful exit.

> what that she could ever do for him would really be so beautiful as this present chance to smooth his confusion and add as much as possible to that refined satisfaction with himself which would proceed from his having dealt with a difficult hour in a gallant and delicate way? (x 1)

She therefore turns the appeal for herself into an appeal for her mother, who has been even more desolated by the defection of Van.

This is Nanda's achievement of the 'beautiful', her moment of tragic intensity. And her acceptance is so complete that she is able, without irony, to apply the description to Van himself. 'He was beautiful all round,' she tells Mitchy. After her tragedy, this is her triumph, that she can ascribe her own quality of dedicated love to the man who has proved himself unworthy of it.

The Awkward Age is not weighty with pathos. Mrs Brookenham meets disaster with undiminished confidence, and Nanda's tragedy, a tragedy of sensitivity extended to its farthest limits, is played out in decorous understatement. The dispersal of Mrs Brookenham's salon is due to the failure of its intimates 'to fit propriety into a smooth general case which is really all the while bristling and crumbling into fierce particular ones', as James says in the Preface. But the 'moral, sharply pointed, of the fruits of compromise', does not only apply to Mrs Brookenham's vain though courageous endeavour. The arrival of a 'vague slip of a daughter', with 'an ingenuous mind and a pair of limpid searching eyes' (Preface), would be no more than the occasion

of her mother's embarrassment and the cause of her final despair.
Nanda is much more than a girl from the schoolroom, just as Hamlet
is much more than a student from Wittenberg. The precarious balance
of circumstances must be reflected in a mind and spirit caught in a trap
which precludes a saving decision. Nanda is the more aware of her
dilemma in that it is largely of her own creation. Had she not been
endowed with a sensitivity in excess of her status as an immature and
innocent girl, ways of escape would have been possible. She understands too much, and those surrounding her understand too little.
Mrs Brook does not realise the perilous implications of the modernity
she invokes, nor Mr Longdon the remoteness of the inflexible tradition
he depends upon. Nanda's awareness is the more poignant in that she is
condemned to silence, and in the crucial situation when she has to
decide whether to accept Mitchy or to wait for Van, the good-hearted
Mitchy cannot speak and the cold Van will not. Knowing Mitchy's
tender consideration, she cannot tell him why she prefers Van, and she
has silenced him by appealing to him to marry little Aggie. Van
cannot admit that Mr Longdon's secret settlement upon Nanda has
presented a problem which his social talents have not equipped him to
solve. Nanda cannot lean on her mother, her friend Tishy is too
dependent upon her, and Mr Longdon's unspoken advice is to accept
Mitchy. She faces her destiny without a confidant.

In this study of souls separated from each other by a torrent of talk,
James allows his actors to communicate in word gestures; 'beautiful',
like a gesture in a tragic mime, assumes symbolic significance. Since
art craves expression, however silent life may remain, the inner silence
of *The Awkward Age* is perhaps unnatural. Because Nanda combines a
vivid consciousness with a choked utterance, her election of silence in a
whirl of words has given James the opportunity of depicting a resigna-
tion which has a moral grandeur as stoical and as reticent as that of
Vigny's wolf, who inspires in the poet the apophthegm: 'Seul le
silence est grand'; and the command: 'Souffre et meurs sans parler'.

WALTER ISLE

The Romantic and the Real: Henry James's *The Sacred Fount* (1965)

I

No single work by Henry James is more strikingly experimental than *The Sacred Fount*. It may at times appear to be little more than the 'technical exercise' that Joseph Warren Beach first called it.[1] It does not attain the fullness of two other experiments, *What Maisie Knew* and *The Awkward Age*; the experimental, the even game-like aspects of the novel are never quite transformed, as they are in the two previous novels, to the successful, the proven. The degree of tenuousness and questioning, of hesitation and ambiguity in structure and meaning, suggests a new departure, but one made in the dark and toward an uncertain destination. *The Sacred Fount* is a trying-out, a final experiment before the achievements of the major phase. Since it was written, however, at the height of James's artistic powers, just after two successes and just before *The Ambassadors*, it has a strong claim on our attention. Much critical effort has been applied to the novel, particularly to its final meaning and to its literary value.[2] I believe that a clearer idea of that meaning and value can be attained by looking at the experimental aspects of the novel, especially in the light of this whole period of experiment from 1896 to 1901; technique, structure, and theme in the novel itself will then stand out more sharply.

An important fact in the history of *The Sacred Fount*, which has played a part in its evaluation, is that James did not include the novel in the New York Edition of 1907–9. His apparent rejection of the novel has led critics also to reject it. We must, however, form our judgment of the novel primarily on the novel itself. James was attempting in that collected edition to give a clear picture of his career as he saw it, and certain novels did not fit the plan. As Leon Edel notes: 'The exclusions were not merely matters of "taste" but related distinctly to the "architecture" of the Edition.'[3] That *The Sacred Fount* cannot be rejected simply because it did not fit into this edition is also apparent from a glance at the other novels excluded: *Watch and Ward, The Europeans, Confidence, Washington Square, The Bostonians,* and *The Other House,* at least three of which have central places in the James canon.

Since *The Sacred Fount* was not included, there is no preface in which James could provide us with information about his intentions and methods of composition; and there are only very brief notebook entries on the novel.[4] Nevertheless, certain features of its composition are similar to those of the other novels of the period and provide an initial insight. The notebooks are of some help here. James's first notebook entry on *The Sacred Fount* – 17 February, 1894 – comes in the middle of that dramatic period when he jotted down the subjects for most of his later novels. He mentions the novel again in February and May of 1899 and evidently began the novel some time after that. It is probable that he spent much of 1900 writing the novel. Never serialized, it was published in February 1901. As usual, James conceived the idea of *The Sacred Fount* as the subject of a short story, an 'anecdote' and a 'concetto' or conceit. And, again as usual, the novel expanded during composition, which will help account for certain structural features considered below. The short-story conception also helps somewhat to explain the use of a first person narrator, for the technique is common in James's short stories, particularly when that narrator is a detached observer, usually a critic or some kind of literary man, who objectively relates the story. The technique is often found in James's stories of artists and writers.[5]

In *The Sacred Fount* we find the same kind of observer, but James has transferred his attention to the subjective response of the man, rather in the manner of his use of the third person central consciousness in *The Spoils of Poynton* and *What Maisie Knew*. This transfer complicates story and theme, for the narrator's objectivity comes into doubt. *The Sacred Fount* is the only full-length novel in which James employs a first person narrator; only short novels like *The Aspern Papers* and *The Turn of the Screw* are comparable, and they have posed similar problems for the reader. The results of the use of this particular narrator and of James's focus on him are just those uncertain qualities which mark the novel as experimental, that mystification which the reader feels throughout. So our analysis must be concerned primarily with the peculiar problems of first-person narration, especially as that affects the style of the novel, and with the structure within which that narrator moves. Theme and meaning follow from these.

II

The Sacred Fount has a simplicity of outline which is somewhat like that of *The Other House*, the initial novel of this experimental period. There is none of the elaboration of character and society that can be found in *What Maisie Knew* or *The Awkward Age*. James again limits his characters to a handful. There are two perhaps symmetrically arranged couples: Mr and Mrs Brissenden, Gilbert Long and May Server; there is the narrator who observes the action and speculates on the arrangement; a painter, Ford Obert, with whom he discusses his ideas; and a subordinate figure, Lady John, who may or may not have some relation to one of the couples. None of the characters is developed at length, most have very little to say and are given only one or two individualizing traits. For the most part, they follow generally the Jamesian types found in the other novels of the period.[6] Gilbert Long, like Owen Gereth, is a hearty, robust gentleman, 'a fine piece of human furniture'; Guy Brissenden has all the helplessness of that type with none of its strength; Grace Brissenden combines traits of Mrs Gereth and Mrs Brookenham, intelligent, forceful, and somewhat suspect; and May Server is the charming, beautiful, red-haired *ingénue*, with some unaccountable tragic quality about her. May is like Jean Martle, Fleda Vetch, Nanda Brookenham, and all those heroines of Henry James who are reputed to be modeled on his cousin Minny Temple. In spite of the vagueness of outline, she clearly points ahead to Milly Theale. All of these characters, however, do very little; they exist as types. And this brings us to an essential difference between *The Sacred Fount* and a novel like *The Other House*.

In *The Sacred Fount* there is almost no external action; more even than *The Awkward Age* the novel is static, an exploration of a situation. The story itself is extremely simple. The narrator, taking a train to the country for a week-end at a house called Newmarch, meets two acquaintances, Mrs Brissenden and Gilbert Long. Mrs Brissenden seems younger than he remembers her, and Gilbert Long seems cleverer. When he arrives at Newmarch, the narrator meets Guy Brissenden,

who seems to have aged unnaturally, and he conceives the theory of the
sacred fount – that one partner to a couple will draw on the gifts of the
other, thus depleting the other's vitality. Mrs Brissenden draws on her
husband's youth and becomes younger while he ages too rapidly. To
prove the theory and to provide symmetry, there must also be some
woman who is giving Long his new intelligence. The remainder of the
novel is taken up with the narrator's thirty-six-hour search for the
woman and his effort to prove the theory. All of this search takes place
in conversations with the other characters and in the narrator's solitary
meditations. When Mrs Brissenden denies his theory late the second
night, the novel ends with the narrator's resolve to return to London
early the next day. That is the extent of the action. The novel moves
through a series of conversations which attempt to explore the central
situation, the relations among these people, in much the same manner
that conversation is the method of *The Awkward Age*.

This simplicity is merely on the surface, however, and considerable
complexity is introduced by James's narrative technique. All of the
details of character and all the elements of the story come to us through
the narrator, the 'I'. His theory of the sacred fount unifies the novel,
brings all the conversations into focus; and his meditations on his
theory, his sensitive response and endless intellectualizing upon that
response make up the major part of the subject matter. For the first-
person narrator in *The Sacred Fount* is not a detached observer, conveying to the reader as objectively as possible the details of what he
observes. His subjective experience of those objective details becomes
the focus of the novel, just as Fleda Vetch's responses become the subject, rather than merely the recording consciousness of *The Spoils of
Poynton*. In *The Sacred Fount* the mind of the narrator intrudes between
the reader and the experience. The first person narrator has, as James
says in the preface to *The Ambassadors*, 'the double privilege of subject
and object'.[7] The impressionism which results has a direct bearing on
both the difficulty and the meaning of the novel.

James also discusses in his preface to *The Ambassadors* his rejection of
the first-person technique for that novel, and his comments surely
reflect on *The Sacred Fount*, its immediate predecessor: 'Had I meanwhile made [the central figure – Strether] at once hero and historian,
endowed him with the romantic privilege of the "first person" – the
darkest abyss of romance this, inveterately, when enjoyed on the
grand scale – variety, and many other queer matters as well, might

have been smuggled in by a back door.'[8] He goes on to describe the 'looseness' of the technique and 'the terrible fluidity of self-revelation'.[9] Looseness, fluidity, and romance are directly related to James's distinctions between the romantic and the real in the preface to *The American*, distinctions which are of exceptional value in understanding *The Sacred Fount*, for they are central to perceiving the narrator's role in the novel:

> The real represents to my perception the things we cannot possibly *not* know, sooner or later, in one way or another; it being but one of the accidents of our hampered state, and one of the incidents of their quantity and number, that particular instances have not yet come our way. The romantic stands, on the other hand, for the things that, with all the facilities in the world, all the wealth and all the courage and all the wit and all the adventure, we can never directly know; the things that can reach us only through the beautiful circuit and subterfuge of our thought and our desire.[10]

James goes on to describe the kind of experience with which the romantic deals: 'Experience liberated, so to speak; experience disengaged, disembroiled, disencumbered, exempt from the conditions that we usually know to attach to it . . . and operating in a medium which relieves it . . . from the inconvenience of a *related*, a measurable state, a state subject to all our vulgar communities.'[11] The separation of the first-person narrator from his material, the subjective isolation of consciousness, is exactly the romantic nature of the form; the danger is that he will be cut off entirely from the real, that isolation will lead to 'the darkest abyss of romance'. The final meaning of the novel is directly involved in this dichotomy, and we can only get at that meaning through the narrator. The narrator of *The Sacred Fount* is one of James's most elaborate and disturbing characterizations, for he is a romantic confronting the materials of reality. James's innocents, Fleda Vetch especially, are in a similar situation; but in *The Sacred Fount* the technique places the reader in the narrator's mind, cut off from the 'vulgar community'. We see only his thought and his desire and share his inability to determine what is real.

The first-person narrative technique limits the reader to what the narrator tells him. Placed in this position, the reader is forced to concern himself with the characteristics of the mind within which he is confined. By understanding its nature we can better understand its special relation to the external world and the material it presents us. In this novel, James

focuses directly on the mind of the narrator, and that mind is so individualized, even eccentric, that it must have some effect on the
material that passes through it. James's primary interest is with that
effect, that subjective, romantic coloration and even transformation of
reality.

The narrator of *The Sacred Fount* is a highly idiosyncratic figure. We
learn early that he is an older man, that he is not attached to any of the
people at Newmarch; he is in much the same relation to his society as
Mr Longdon in *The Awkward Age*. He is a detached observer of those
around him. He is outwardly passive; we catch him at times lurking
outside windows, overhearing conversations, watching people from a
distance. He speaks of his 'general habit – of observation'.[12] Part of his
separateness is his sensitivity, his unusual response to nuance and detail,
to implication, he is almost hyper-observant. His shyness and careful
privacy are also part of the role of outsider or observer. He has a horror
of exposing his thoughts to the world. He does, however, have a great
curiosity about other people, and he is an inveterate theorizer about
their behavior. He speaks of his 'extraordinary interest in my fellow-
creatures. I have more than most men. I've never really seen anyone
with half so much. That breeds observation and observation breeds
ideas' (147). In addition to noting his habit of observation, two aspects
of this speech are remarkable: his extreme egotism and his commitment to 'ideas'. Half-way through the novel his exults in his theory,
describes it as 'an undiluted bliss, in the intensity of consciousness that I
had reached, *I* alone was magnificently and absurdly aware – everyone
else was benightedly out of it' (177). His egotism is grandiose; he thinks
of his theory and the other characters as his 'creations': 'to see all this
was at the time, I remember, to be as inhumanly amused as if one had
found one could create something' (104). Throughout he tends to see
himself as god or artist – Lady John at one point tells him to give up
'the attempt to be providence' (176).

His ideas are behind all his interests; he is drawn into the affairs of
others, 'though always but intellectually'. As his theory of the sacred
fount begins to form, he describes his feelings and thoughts as those of
the philosopher (and, interestingly, partly in the language of the
detective):

> I felt from the first that if I was on the scent of something ultimate I had
> better waste neither my wonder nor my wisdom. I was on the scent. . . .
> I was just conscious, vaguely, of being on the track of a law, a law that

would fit, that would strike me as governing the delicate phenomena – delicate though so marked – that my imagination found itself playing with. A part of the amusement they yielded came, I daresay, from my exaggerating them – grouping them into a larger mystery (and thereby a larger 'law') than the facts, as observed, yet warranted; but that is a common fault of minds for which the vision of life is an obsession. (22–3)

The result of this obsession is 'the joy of the intellectual mastery of things unamenable, that joy of determining, almost of creating results' (214). Two characteristics stand out in addition to his intellectual bent: his imagination and his obsession. The whole novel is a testament to the obsession; only an obsession could build so much on so slight a base. But to understand that obsession, his 'private madness', we must look further into his character.

His imagination combines with his intellect to give a compelling force to his vision. The artistic, creative nature of his hypothesis about the people around him is in part his imaginative coloration of the 'laws' of human behavior. The clearest indication of how his imagination enhances what he sees comes during a moment he spends alone in the gardens, away from people and the need to observe and theorize:

> There was a general shade in all the lower reaches – a fine clear dusk in garden and grove, a thin suffusion of twilight out of which the greater things, the high tree-tops and pinnacles, the long crests of motionless wood and chimnied roof, rose into golden air. The last calls of birds sounded extraordinarily loud; they were like the timed, serious splashes, in wide, still water, of divers not expecting to rise again. I scarce know what odd consciousness I had of roaming at close of day in the grounds of some castle of enchantment. I had positively encountered nothing to compare with this since the days of fairy-tales and of the childish imagination of the impossible. *Then* I used to circle round enchanted castles, for then I moved in a world in which the strange 'came true.' It was the coming true that was the proof of the enchantment, which, moreover, was naturally never so great as when such coming was, to such a degree and by the most romantic stroke of all, the fruit of one's own wizardry. I was positively – so had the wheel revolved – proud of my work. I had thought it all out, and to have thought it was, wonderfully, to have brought it. (128–9)

The passage touches on all his characteristics: intellect, egotism, sensitivity. But it is even more revealing of the narrator's romantic imagination, his painting of reality with strokes of beauty, strangeness, enchantment, wizardry. Characteristically, he has this romantic vision in solitude, just as, later in the novel, he moves out into the night alone and finds 'the breath of the outer air a sudden corrective to the grossness of our lustre and the thickness of our medium, our general heavy humanity' (199). The house then becomes 'our crystal cage'. The narrator's intellect and his imagination enable him to escape from this cage of reality into a romantic world which will accommodate his pure and elegant theory of the sacred fount.

At the same time, however, his imagination does not entirely free him from the 'grossness' and 'thickness' of 'heavy humanity'. Intellectually, it remains pure and light, but humanly it is often 'the imagination of atrocity' (173) or, as it is also for Fleda Vetch, 'the imagination of a disaster'. The odd and remarkable metaphor in the center of the passage quoted above is a brilliant example of that; the quiet notation of the 'divers not expecting to rise again' is an indication of this aspect of the narrator's imagination. The theory of the sacred fount, for all the symmetry and beauty it embodies for the narrator, is a theory of vampirism, the destruction of one human being by another, the drawing out of life. Although quieter and less explicit, it is much like Hawthorne's representation of evil in *The Scarlet Letter*.[13]

> The narrator, then, is a romantic egotist with an intellect of some power and an imagination of great force, capable of giving him joy but at the same time profoundly, though perhaps unconsciously, morbid. For him humanity offers little more than material for the pleasures of the mind, although a bleaker vision hides beneath joy. As he notes, 'Light or darkness, my imagination rides me.' (276)

The nature of the man is reflected in his language; we cannot escape his character for we must read his words. And one of the principal difficulties in reading this at times obtuse work is the style. As the narrator himself comments, when one of the characters accuses him of being crazy, of not being understandable: 'No, I daresay, to do you justice, the interpretation of my tropes and figures *isn't* "ever" perfectly simple' (284). The variety of his figures runs from those suicidal divers to the sacred fount itself, a horror under its sacredness, and to his conception of himself in the final scene with Mrs Brissenden as 'an exemplary Christian' watched by 'a Roman lady at a circus'.

'Tropes and figures' do provide one of the major vehicles of the narrator's thought, but even more prominent and finally more difficult in its sheer volume is his intellectual, abstract, elaborate prose style.

The whole of chapter 6 is an almost impenetrable example of his mental activity, an extreme form of the style found in the meditations of Fleda Vetch; but a few shorter passages must represent the quality of his mind and the nature of his expression. The narrator 'reflects' in the following manner: 'What was none of one's business might change its name should importunity take the form of utility. In resisted observation that was vivid thought, in inevitable thought that was vivid observation, through a succession, in short, of phases in which I shall not pretend to distinguish one of these elements from the other, I found myself cherishing the fruit of the seed dropped equally by Ford Obert and by Mrs Briss' (93-4). And again, later: 'If there had been, so to speak, a discernment, however feeble, of *my* discernment, it would have been irresistible to me to take this as the menace of some incalculable catastrophe or some public ugliness. It wasn't for me definitely to image the logical result of a verification by the sense of others of the matter of my vision' (174). This is James's prose at its densest and most abstract, and comprehending it takes some effort. Above all, the prose shows the density, the convolutions and intricate intellectual movements of the narrator's mind. The style mirrors the man in this first person narrative, and we finally agree with his own judgment: 'I daresay that . . . my cogitations – for I must have bristled with them – would have made me as stiff a puzzle to interpretative minds as I had suffered other phenomena to become to my own' (92). The intricate prose style presents the character and forms throughout the novel an abstract, almost unreal medium in which the drama of the novel takes place.

III

The drama and the style are present in the opening paragraph of the novel, a meditative passage in which the narrator reveals details of his character that will gain in significance as the 'action' progresses: 'It was an occasion, I felt – the prospect of a large party – to look out at the station for others, possible friends and even possible enemies, who might be going. Such premonitions, it was true, bred fears when they failed to breed hopes, though it was to be added that there were sometimes, in the case, rather happy ambiguities' (1). The narrator's logical turn of mind and his tendency to think in rather melodramatic blacks and whites is evident, although this is modified by the added third alternative, ambiguities – which he will not always find 'happy'.[14] A few lines below, the narrator mentions, only to disclaim, what will be his greatest weakness: 'the wish was father to the thought'. His sensitivity, even his fear of others, is noted as he chooses to avoid one of the other members of the party.

In that opening moment the character and mind of the narrator are hinted at, and we move on to be intensely present in each of his impressions and in his obsessions with the behavior of other people. *The Sacred Fount* is subtly dramatic, a further example of James's experimentation with the possibilities of the dramatic novel. Much of the novel is given over to conversations between the narrator and usually only one of the other characters, scenes in dialogue which are typically in the manner of *The Awkward Age* and the other novels of this period. Balancing this, however, is the dramatic immediacy of the meditations that go on in the mind of the narrator, and this is peculiar to *The Sacred Fount*. These passages can best be described as interior monologues which are controlled and intellectualized in a way that stream of consciousness usually is not. While they bear some similarity to passages of meditation involving centers of consciousness like Fleda Vetch or Maisie Farange, the analysis and abstraction are more extreme, as noted above, and at the same time the use of the first person strongly increases the sense of the dramatic present. Although he is recounting the story from a later time, the narrator seldom breaks the illusion of the present and tells more than he knows at a particular moment; James uses this to create drama and suspense and to keep the reader moving at the pace of the narrator, mystified and expectant.

The quality of suspense in the drama of the novel is partly that of the mystery story, and James from time to time, as noted in one of the passages above, uses imagery from the detective story. One of the other characters, Ford Obert, warns the narrator about prying and searching for 'material clues', but Obert assures the narrator that it can be an 'honorable' game – when it relies on 'psychologic signs alone, it's a high application of intelligence. What's ignoble is the detective and the keyhole' (66). The narrator takes this for assurance of his own purity of motive, although he still longs for a material clue. Moreover, scents, clues, false scents, covering one's tracks, and evidence of various sorts are all part of the narrator's vocabulary.

The suspense and immediacy of the drama are an integral part of the structure of the novel. James immerses us in the mind of the narrator as he wanders through his week-end at Newmarch. Each impression, each reflection is carefully recorded in its place, each conversation as it occurs. A good deal of the intensity of the drama is the result of this closeness to the present and the narrow limits of the duration of the action. James stays close to chronological time. The whole of the action takes about thirty-six hours; most of it occurs between morning and midnight of the second day. And James observes the other traditional dramatic unities of place and action.[15]

The drama of *The Sacred Fount* falls into phases typical of James's construction during this period. There are four or perhaps five 'acts' in the novel, and each serves a particular purpose in the development of the action and the narrator's thought. The first act or phase of the action, chapters 1 and 2, is a prelude which introduces the characters and gives an initial exposition of the narrator's theory and the themes of the novel. The act takes place the afternoon before the day of the main action. Act two begins the next morning, establishes the relationship between the narrator and Mrs Brissenden, and complicates the action and theme in a series of conversations and the scene before the picture of the man with the mask (chapters 3-5). Chapter 6 is partly transitional; it carries the action over a time interval until late afternoon and summarizes the narrator's mental and imaginative progress. It begins the third phase of the action, which continues through chapters 7 and 8. This third act concentrates on the two depleted figures in the formula of the sacred fount, Guy Brissenden and May Server. It also marks the narrator's closest approach to emotional involvement with the other characters. As the center of the novel, it illustrates the highest complication of his theory and his greatest confidence. After another time interval, the fourth act begins with the narrator's decision to give up his inquiry, partly because of his emotional identification with the depleted pair. The whole of the fourth phase, however (chapters 9-11), contains the narrator's gradual return to the theory, revealed mostly through his mental reactions to what he observes during an evening of wandering and watching. The section ends with a conversation with Ford Obert, who, through his own partial enthusiasm for the theory, is able to reinforce the narrator's obsession. The fifth phase (which might perhaps be considered part of the fourth, since there is no time interval) is the long scene with Mrs Brissenden and the narrator (chapters 12-14). Here the narrator's theory is apparently destroyed, and the focus of the action is on the irreconcilable split between his mind and reality, on his inability ever really to know the truth about the people he has been observing.[16]

The overall pattern in the action is simply a deepening of the narrator's consciousness and a more and more intense participation in the present. The first three phases take up the first half of the novel; the final two phases, the last evening, comprise the last half; and the final long scene with Mrs Brissenden, although it takes but one hour in the time of the action, occupies fully a quarter of the novel. This slowing of the pace actually marks a gradual increase in the drama, and the form is in this sense quite similar to that of *The Spoils of Poynton* or *What Maisie Knew*. It is as if James's further penetration into a subject means closer and closer attention to the present, to the immediate and dramatic. James gradually draws closer to the situation in order to explore every possible aspect; at the same time he moves slowly toward a complete recording of everything that transpires in a given moment. The effect of this movement in *The Sacred Fount* is progressively to heighten the intensity of the narrator's obsession and to emphasize in detail the final contrast between Mrs Brissenden and himself.

The dramatic structure of *The Sacred Fount* also parallels some of James's earlier experiments in the combination of scene and meditation. The scene presents the objective view and the meditation the subjective, with the qualification that the narrator's consciousness is to some extent present throughout most of the scenes; the continual alternation from scene to meditation keeps the structure of the novel balanced. The first two phases are made up of very short scenes followed by short meditations in which the narrator attempts to account for the objective details. This alternation continues through the third phase, although a predominance of meditation, especially in chapters 6 and 8, indicates the narrator's increasing subjective involvement. In the scene with the narrator and May Server, for example, in chapter 8, the woman says almost nothing; everything is given to the reader through the subjective filter of the narrator's speeches and thoughts. This subjective, meditative movement continues into the fourth section, broken only by the brief conversation with Lady John in chapter 9, until Ford Obert once more brings an objectivity into this almost stifling engrossment in the narrator's subjective speculations. The brilliant final scene with the narrator and Mrs Brissenden, one of the longest sustained scenes in the novels of this period, marks a balance between subjectivity and objectivity and reveals James's mastery of the scenic technique.

The narrator's thoughts are continually present, but they are repeatedly pierced by Mrs Brissenden's assertions. The subjective is presented in a balanced war with the objective, and the result is a stalemate. The pendulum swing from scene to meditation is finally balanced in a scene where both are fully present, as they were at times in *What Maisie Knew* and as they will be in *The Ambassadors*.

The dialogue of these scenes and the thought-patterns of the meditations follow forms common to the novels of this period, and they enhance the artistic construction of James's novel. The dramatic structure of acts divided into scenes and meditations is paralleled and reinforced by the balanced logic of the narrator's mind. One rather exaggerated example must serve to indicate his logical insistence: 'Lady John and Guy Brissenden, in the arbour, were thinking secludedly together; they were together, that is, because they were scarce a foot apart, and they were thinking, I inferred, because they were doing nothing else' (101). His mental patterns follow this deductive form; he invariably applies logic and reason to human behavior.[17] The theory of the sacred fount is an absolute, once the narrator has first propounded it, to which all evidence is submitted, then accepted if it fits or rejected if it does not. The conclusion of the novel results from this kind of thinking; the narrator's theory meets only with Mrs Brissenden's denial. The dichotomy remains unresolved, open. His theory is also formalized and balanced in a manner similar to the structure of the novel, although he can recognize, but not give up, the dangerous artificiality of his formula: 'These opposed couples balanced like bronze groups at the two ends of a chimney piece, and the most that I could say in lucid deprecation of my thought was that I mustn't take them equally for granted merely *because* they balanced. Things in the real had a way of not balancing; it was all an affair, this fine symmetry, of artificial proportion. Yet . . . it was vivid to me that, "composing" there beautifully, they could scarce help playing a part in my exhibition' (183). Opposition, balance, symmetry are opposed to 'things in the real', and they have all played a part in James's conceptions, as for example in the balanced form of *The Spoils of Poynton* or the intricate oppositions and symmetries of the couples in *What Maisie Knew* or *The Awkward Age*. In *The Sacred Fount* James uses the same kind of structure, yet the balance and symmetry, as we can see in the passage above, are also objectified by James and made a part of the mental bias of the narrator who insists on finding symmetries.

The dialogue in the novel also reinforces the form. When the narrator is not tracing out his syllogisms in his mind, he is trying them out on others. The question-and-answer technique in conversation, used in earlier novels in the period, is extremely valuable here in sustaining the mystery and heightening the quest for a solution. The conversations are much like the inquiries of a detective, in which the narrator attempts continually to gain information from the others, or in which they occasionally try to understand what he is getting at. The submerged effect, as usual in James's novels, is of a total failure of communication between, in this case, the narrator and every other person. In a similar fashion, James uses the technique of the debate in the last scene to point up elaborately the difference between Mrs Brissenden's and the narrator's visions of the world. The careful balance between assertion and admission of points only heightens the split between the two. The debate is a draw. The narrator is still unable to bridge the gap between himself and 'things in the real'.

IV

The balances, symmetries, and oppositions in the structure are paralleled by the thematic patterns which often exist as dialectical tensions. The final words of the novel, the narrator's statement that 'It wasn't really that I hadn't three times her method. What I too fatally lacked was her tone' (319) set up a dichotomy which in retrospect informs all the themes of the novel. The narrator attempts, using the methods of reason, to establish order, to find a theory which will account for the behavior of the observed characters. Mrs Brissenden finally contradicts this theory with a flat denial and a crude assertion of the realities of the social world.

The social situation is at the base of all this. In its way *The Sacred Fount* is as strong a criticism of James's society as *The Awkward Age* or *What Maisie Knew*. The narrator's theory is abstract, pure, and beautiful, as he maintains, but these qualities are a mask for the reality from which it derives. It raises to the level of apologue or parable, to metaphor, the corrupt conditions of life in the world of Newmarch. The masked assumption is of couples and coupling, of hidden liaisons and immoral arrangements. The sacred fount in itself is a euphemism for some sort of sexual depletion or vampirism; but the narrator sees in all these arrangements a purity and elegance. He sees them all as people 'deeply in love', with 'a great pressure of soul to soul' and 'the seal of passion' (16, 17). The one unquestionable example of a liaison, however, is 'that Mrs Froome and Lord Lutley were in the wondrous new fashion – and their servants too, like a single household – starting, travelling, arriving together' (4). Newmarch itself (as the name tells us) is in that 'wondrous new fashion', 'a funny house . . . I'm not sure that anyone *has* gone to bed. One does what one likes' (244-5). The new fashion here is the same modern morality that James found repellent in *What Maisie Knew* and *The Awkward Age;* it is a newness that James represents as 'moral squalor', to use F. R. Leavis's term for it. The narrator is reacting to the same situation that confronted Mr Longdon and endangered Maisie. His reaction is to try to enhance it, romanticize it, draw from it what beauty he can; but it remains squalid. He never judges the outside world morally in any direct way; all his moral judgments are usually turned on himself. But when he comes closest to being drawn in emotionally, he reveals the horror that has been masked by his intellectual joy. The atrocities he can imagine are then apparent. When he sees May Server, he sees the viciousness of the sacred fount: 'I saw as I had never seen before what consuming passion can make of the marked mortal on whom, with fixed beak and claws, it has settled as a prey. She reminded me of a sponge wrung dry and with fine pores agape. Voided and scraped of everything, her shell was merely crushable. So it was brought home to me that the victim could be abased' (136). The hollowness of the drained victim, the images of the scraped shell, the dry sponge, all this overwhelms any beauty; and the passion is one which consumes. Whether or not the narrator is right about May Server's place in his scheme, through his vision James gives us a profound comment on the effect of the fashionable love-game all these couples are engaged in. The society in *The Sacred Fount* is as corrupt as in *The Awkward Age*, but the narrator's romantic theory keeps him from seeing this very often.[18]

His theory also tends to cover up any difference between appearance and reality, a second major theme in the novel.[19] For the narrator, and to some extent even for the reader, there is finally no way of distinguishing between true and false, real and unreal. The narrator must, not knowing the truth, attempt to guess at it through the appearance of the other characters. When Mrs Brissenden asserts different relationships among the characters, the narrator has no way of knowing whether she is lying to protect herself or telling the truth. He has no way of knowing whether or not he is deceived by appearance, perhaps even crazy, as she says. Reality remains hidden to him.

This is nowhere better shown than in the symbolic portrait of the man with the mask in chapter 4. The narrator examines the portrait with May Server, Ford Obert, and Gilbert Long (a scene that is repeated in the same form and for some of the same purposes in *The Wings of the Dove*): 'The figure represented is a young man in black – a quaint, tight black dress, fashioned in years long past; with a pale, lean, livid face and a stare, from eyes without eyebrows, like that of some old-world clown. In his hand he holds an object that strikes the spectator at first simply as some obscure, some ambiguous work of art, but that on second view becomes a representation of a human face, modelled and coloured, in wax, in enamelled metal, in some substance not human' (55). May Server says that the object is 'the Mask of Death', but the narrator insists that it is 'much rather the Mask of Life', that it is the face of the man that is dead. Customary symbolism would indicate that May Server is right, that the mask is appearance, lifeless, while the face is reality, life. But the sort of reality that is hidden behind the narrator's theory of the sacred fount is death-in-life, as is evident from his description of May Server (quoted above), and this is the effect of the pale, livid man in black. The mask then has perhaps the quality of life that he attributes to it. It is, he says, 'blooming and beautiful', but it has a 'grimace' which the narrator cannot see. It is an 'obscure', 'ambiguous work of art', which is just what his theory is, for he can perceive only intermittently the grimace that is embodied in his theory, the horror that is transformed to art by his imagination. The portrait is consciously ambiguous itself. It represents both death and life, the reality of death-in-life of the face and the artifice of life-in-art of the mask, the appearance which masks reality. This central ambiguity is what keeps the narrator's romantic, artistic vision separate from the vision of all the others, as that is finally represented by Mrs Brissenden.[20]

In *The Sacred Fount*, as in *The Spoils of Poynton*, art and life are separate, and the artistic individual is divorced from life.[21] The narrator in this novel has some of the same innocence and inviolability of Fleda Vetch or Nanda Brookenham, and it keeps him apart from life. His essential sterility is the same as that which James objectified in other ways in all his tales of unlived life and half-dead, middle-aged men like John Marcher in 'The Beast in the Jungle'. The divorce between life and the individual in the novel is combined with the epistemological theme, the effort to detect the difference between appearance and reality. The effort here, however, ends in total failure. There is no way of distinguishing true and false. Out of these various themes and the narrator's speculations develops the final meaning of the novel, James's vision of truth in *The Sacred Fount*.

We have seen that the narrator has method, obsession, and an intense interest in his fellow-creatures. Out of this he spins a beautiful theory about the relationships among them. It is a theory with symmetry and balance, based on incessant observation and a belief in passionate love. At the heart, however, it is a theory of the destruction of one individual by another, for James as for Hawthorne the greatest of human sins. Based as it is on the appearances of people, there is no way of telling how accurate the theory is for the particular case. The narrator is so isolated from the rest of humanity that he has no way of verifying his hypothesis through experience or through getting the 'objective proof' for which he longs. His proof must remain subjective, based on his general knowledge of human nature. In this, the theory does point to a truth, reinforced as it is by the nature of the society and by the symbolic portrait of the man with the mask. But it remains a general, unparticularized truth. For all the narrator's observations and ratiocination, the truth remains intuitive and comes to him through his 'imagination of atrocity'. He had as much of it early in the novel as at the finish, perhaps more. What finally defeats him, refuses to accept him or his theory, calls him crazy, is the tone of the society which he observes, represented at the end by Mrs Brissenden, a tone of harsh, insolent reality. This is perhaps truly life, but it is disordered and meaningless. The narrator's vision, on the other hand, is art, ordered and beautiful. The two are separate worlds, united only by a general truth to human nature, the conditions of existence. James carefully introduces the allegory of the cave late in the novel to suggest that the narrator's theory is perhaps a way to reality. Obert, using the narrator's vision, has 'blown on my torch . . . till, flaming and smoking, it has guided me, through a magnificent chiaroscuro of colour and shadow, out into the light of day' (222). The narrator is 'dazzled' by the metaphor. It represents the possible triumph of his vision, the discovery of reality through art.[22]

But the narrator's paradoxically intuitive and logical approach, his artistic and intellectual vision comes up against Mrs Brissenden immediately after this. She denies, as we have seen, any truth to his theory of the sacred fount, and tells him that he may be insane. And so perhaps he finally is. *The Sacred Fount* may stand as a parable for Henry James's difficulties and beliefs as an artist, for his vision of the relationship between art and reality. But, if so, it is conceived in a moment of despair. For the whole structure of the novel points to the same meaning inherent in the themes. There is a final and total split between the vision of Mrs Brissenden and that of the narrator, between life and art.[23] We must, however, look further; there is a distinction to be made between the narrator's potential insanity and James's meaning.

The narrator's spirits have been high throughout the novel. His intellectual joy is marred only by fears of failure and, briefly, by his feelings for May Server. The last phase of the novel, however, is a movement farther and farther into doubt, until the narrator finally feels that he will never again 'quite hang together'. The effects on his intellectual egotism are even stronger, and he admits his alienation from life at the moment he most clearly recognizes the implications of his position: 'I could only say to myself that this was the price – the price of secret success, the lonely liberty and the intellectual joy. There were things that for so private and splendid a revel – that of the exclusive king with his Wagner opera – I could only let go, and the special torment of my case was that the condition of light, of the satisfaction of curiosity and of the attestation of triumph, was in this direct way the sacrifice of feeling. . . . I was there to save my priceless pearl of an inquiry and to harden, to that end, my heart' (296). The recognition of the price of art is complete. The divorce between art and life, even between the individual and the world, imposes sacrifices. Like Fleda Vetch and Nanda Brookenham, the narrator is left free, but it is a 'lonely liberty', a freedom provided by isolation. And the isolation means not only the death of the heart, but also never truly knowing the world, never being able to verify his intuitions. Any conception then is a dream, a vision, a madness.

But even if the narrator is left isolated, there is still some connection with the world through his theory. His egotism and his intellect contribute to his isolation, but his romantic imagination explains what kind of connection he has with the world he still lives in. The 'private and splendid revel', the Wagner opera, the 'priceless pearl of an inquiry' are all romantic visions of the real world. The ambiguous mask of life or death is separate from but contains some truth about the real world. The narrator at the end of the novel has come up against 'things in the real', 'the things we cannot possibly *not* know', the accidents of the world we live in – in this case the disordered, promiscuous relationships in the society which the narrator inhabits. These are, for James, the real. But the narrator cannot conceive or cannot admit promiscuity or chaos; he is obsessed with order. And so he discovers only the things 'we can never directly know; the things that reach us only through the beautiful circuit and subterfuge of our thought and our desire'.[24] He discovers the essence of the world through the romantic, which for James is 'experience disengaged', which is not 'a state subject to all our vulgar communities'.[25] *The Sacred Fount* points finally to the distinction between the romantic and the real. James's achievement is that he goes beyond the narrator and gives us, in the balanced structure of the novel, a vision of both states, of the romantic and the real, of the essence and accident of the world.

James achieves this, however, only with considerable sacrifice. *The Sacred Fount* is an obtuse, difficult novel, and the form is almost too limited a vehicle for James's vision. The confusions and limitations of the first-person narrator almost mask the success of the author. For the novel is one of despair; the final balanced vision means a loss of purity. The narrator disintegrates before us as a corrupt world imposes itself on his artistic vision, leaving doubt as the only possible attitude. *The Sacred Fount* has an undercurrent of despair that is not controlled by our final realization of the meaning of the narrator's experience. This kind of despair is controlled in a novel like *The Awkward Age*. The society may reject Nanda, but she remains intact; the narrator of *The Sacred Fount* does not.

The undertones of *The Sacred Fount* show a tragic vision of life which points forward to the twentieth century, to James's next novels and to other novelists who follow him. For what we are confronted with is a finely, complexly constructed novel in which the main sensations are of failure: the failure of perception, of communication, of belief. What remain most strongly with us are madness, alienation, the inability to feel, and the loneliness of freedom, central themes in many novels of this century. *The Sacred Fount* exhibits James's mastery of his dramatic techniques, his use of a kind of interior monologue, and his careful attention to structure, which almost results in that organic form so many novelists were consciously to work for. The form of the novel, with its

restriction to the subjective, individual consciousness, is one best understood in comparison to novels of a later period. At the same time James
is also close to offering one of the major, twentieth-century solutions to
the chaos of life – salvation through art. Proust, Joyce, and Virginia
Woolf all offered this as the only answer to the conditions James
presents in *The Sacred Fount*. The narrator's theory of the sacred fount is
an artistic vision for ordering experience similar in nature to Proust's
vision in the last volume of *A la Recherche du temps perdu*, when the
narrator of that novel decides that only by recreating his experience in a
work of art can he make it meaningful. James's narrator has not had and
never will have this final vision, for James in his synthesis of the
romantic and the real has ruled out the separate artistic vision which is
all the narrator can achieve; he rules out systems of the sort by which
his contemporary Henry Adams attempted to explain the same kind
of experience. Perhaps James's novel is closer in theme, in the delinea-
tion of the relationship between the romantic and the real, to a novel
by one of his contemporaries published only a year before his – Joseph
Conrad's *Lord Jim;* for James's art is always of the world he lives in, of
the individual alienated from but struggling with his world. It is the
true novelist's vision.

The close of *The Sacred Fount* marks the end of five years of experiments in the novel for Henry James, and he moves on to larger visions
of the individual struggling with the world in *The Ambassadors, The
Wings of the Dove*, and *The Golden Bowl*. The achievement of the period
of experiment in the form of the novel is best represented in *What
Maisie Knew* and *The Awkward Age;* but in the final novel of that period
James again demonstrates his mastery of form and the value of experiment in the novel. The complexity and vision in this experiment point
ahead. *The Sacred Fount* is of 1901.

NOTES

    1. *The Method of Henry James* (Philadelphia, 1954) pp. 250–4.
    2. The output begins to equal that dealing with *The Turn of the Screw*. The most
valuable essay remains Leon Edel's Introduction to his edition of *The Sacred Fount* (New
York, 1953). Other interesting general essays are Dorothea Krook, *The Ordeal of Consciousness in Henry James* (Cambridge, 1962) pp. 167–94; Laurence Holland, *The Expense
of Vision: Essays on the Craft of Henry James* (Princeton, 1964) pp. 183–226. Most of the
other essays of value will be cited in the notes below.
    3. Leon Edel and Dan H. Laurence, *A Bibliography of Henry James* (1957) p. 168.
    4. Henry James, *The Notebooks*, ed. F. O. Matthiessen and Kenneth B. Murdock (New
York, 1955) pp. 150–1, 275 and 292.

5. For an analysis of the background of the novel in the short story see Claire J. Raeth, 'Henry James's Rejection of *The Sacred Fount*', in *Journal of English Literary History*, XVI (Dec. 1949) 308–24.

6. For a discussion of character types in James's fiction of this period see J. A. Ward, *The Imagination of Disaster: Evil in the Fiction of Henry James* (Lincoln, 1961) pp. 86–7.

7. Henry James, *The Art of the Novel*, ed. R. P. Blackmur (New York, 1934) p. 321.

8. Ibid., p. 320.

9. Ibid., p. 321.

10. Ibid., pp. 31–2.

11. Ibid., p. 33.

12. Henry James, *The Sacred Fount*, ed. Leon Edel (New York, 1953) p. 89. All subsequent references are to this edition and will be included in the text.

13. Various comparisons with Hawthorne have been made. See also Leo B. Levy, 'What Does *The Sacred Fount* Mean?' in *College English*, XXIII 381; James K. Folsom, 'Archimago's Well: An Interpretation of *The Sacred Fount*', in *Modern Fiction Studies*, VII (Summer 1961) 141.

14. See also Robert J. Andreach, 'Henry James's *The Sacred Fount*: The Existential Predicament', in *Nineteenth-century Fiction*, XVII (Dec. 1962) 198–9.

15. See also R. P. Blackmur, 'The Sacred Fount', in *Kenyon Review*, IV (Autumn 1942) 347.

16. For a comparison of the structure of the novel with a double fugue, see Joseph Weisenfarth, F.S.C., *Henry James and the Dramatic Analogy* (New York, 1963) p. 104.

17. See Andreach, 'Henry James's *The Sacred Fount*', p. 203, for a discussion of the narrator's method of thought.

18. In *The Novels of Henry James* (New York, 1961) p. 287, Oscar Cargill argues that the narrator is corrupted by the society.

19. For a discussion of appearance and reality in the novel, see Edel's Introduction, pp. xvi–xx.

20. See also Edel's Introduction, pp. xviii–xx; Krook, *Ordeal of Consciousness*, p. 177n; Holland, *The Expense of Vision*, pp. 197–98; James Reaney, 'The Condition of Light: Henry James's *The Sacred Fount*', in *University of Toronto Quarterly*, XXXI (Jan. 1962) 143–4.

21. The classic identification of the narrator with James is in Wilson Follett, 'Henry James's Portrait of Henry James', in *New York Times Book Review* (23 Aug. 1936) 2, 16.

22. For a discussion of the epistemological theme, see the essays by Krook and Edel.

23. This recurrent theme in James's work finds its classic statements in the preface to *The Spoils of Poynton* in James, *The Art of the Novel*, p. 120: 'Life being all inclusion and confusion and art being all discrimination and selection'; life is 'nothing but splendid waste'; and in James's letters to H. G. Wells in *The Portable Henry James*, ed. Morton Dauwen Zabel (New York, 1951), pp. 482–9. See also Landon C. Burns, 'Henry James's Mysterious Fount', in *Texas Studies in Language and Literature* (Winter 1960–1), 524–6.

24. James, *The Art of the Novel*, p. 32.

25. Ibid., p. 33.

JEAN KIMBALL

The Abyss and *The Wings of the Dove*: the Image as a Revelation (1956)

> My heart is sore pained within me: and the
> terrors of death are fallen upon me.
> Fearfulness and trembling are come upon me,
> and horror hath overwhelmed me.
> And I said, Oh that I had wings like a dove!
> for then would I fly away and be at rest.
>
> Psalms lv 4–6

ONE of the early presentations of television's 'Studio One' was the touching story of a dying heiress who is tricked by a villainous English beauty and her reluctant fiancé. The girl's delicate hold on life is shattered by the realization of the plot against her, and she dies, but in dying wins her man after all. Now this was a dramatization of Henry James's *The Wings of the Dove*, and as such could be dismissed as a bald simplification of the plot of a very complex novel, except that this outline of the plot is the one accepted even by sympathetic James critics. With such an outline of the action, it is no wonder that Matthiessen himself questioned whether 'a character like Milly's is of sufficient emotional force to carry a great work' and concluded that 'her passive suffering is fitting for the deuteragonist rather than for the protagonist of a major tragedy'.[1]

It is high time to rescue Milly Theale from the martyr's grave to which she seems so conclusively to have been assigned and to restore her to her original luster as James's fictional portrait of his vivid young cousin, Minnie Temple, who died from tuberculosis at twenty-four. Minnie Temple remained a powerful symbol to James, not only because she was a beloved figure in life, but also because her early death fused in James's consciousness with his own 'private catastrophe', the 'obscure hurt' he suffered at eighteen, whose effects, as described in his autobiography, clearly seemed to him a kind of death.[2] Milly Theale is not only a memorial to Minnie Temple; she is also James's protagonist in a more personal sense. The central situation in *The Wings of the Dove* is not Milly's passive suffering in a world of uncomprehended evil, but rather her desperate effort, which is never passive, to 'achieve, however briefly and brokenly, the sense of having lived' (v),[3] and even further to live beyond death.

There are two sides to the story in *The Wings of the Dove*, and the confusion about what actually happens in the novel results from the fact that Milly Theale's side, her point of view, is obscured throughout the entire latter half of the novel, which, it should be noted, James has termed 'the false and deformed half' (xviii). Milly Theale is in focus only in a block of three books in the center of *The Wings of the Dove*. Surrounding this center is what James calls in his Preface the 'circumference', that is, the other half of her 'case', 'the state of others affected by her' (xi). James speaks of the two halves of the story as the two sides of a medal, 'its obverse and its reverse, its face and its back', which 'beautifully become optional for the spectator' (xi). In this discussion I should like to exercise the option in favor of Milly Theale, the 'regenerate young New Yorker' who is the center of the novel, and to look at the whole of the action from her point of view.

I

Milly Theale enters the novel in the third book, and with her enters the dominating, portentous image of the abyss. The first clear and striking picture of the heroine is Mrs Stringham's view of her seated on 'a slab of rock at the end of a short promontory' which 'merely pointed off to the right at gulfs of air' (I 123), and the portent implied in Milly's position is fully exploited. Milly's danger, 'her liability to slip, to slide, to leap, to be precipitated by a single false movement . . . into whatever was beneath' leaves Mrs Stringham 'intensely still and holding her breath' (I 123-4). The whole action of Milly's short life is consciously played out on the narrow edge of the abyss, the bottomless gulf that awaits her, and the awareness of her precarious foothold builds up in the novel until Merton Densher exactly duplicates Mrs Stringham's initial perception during the last days in Venice. He feels that 'action

itself, of any sort . . . had heard in it a vivid "Hush!" the injunction
to keep from that moment intensely still. . . . A single false motion
might . . . snap the coil' (II 252).

Mrs Stringham has earlier felt herself 'in presence of an explanation
[of Milly's reality] that . . . should it take on sharpness . . . would
become instantly the light in which Milly was to be read' (I 116). The
image which remains with her of Milly at 'the dizzy edge' of the abyss,
is this light; it has and keeps for Mrs Stringham 'the character of a
revelation' (I 125). It is Milly herself who later recognizes the image of
the dove as 'revealed truth' and feels that 'it lighted up the strange dusk
in which she lately had walked' (I 283). These two images are the two
revelations, the two symbolic lights on Milly Theale. If the abyss and
her position at the edge of the abyss define her 'practical problem of
life', the dove, with its wonderful wings, is the symbol for her final
solution. The images are introduced into the novel in their logical
order, so that the abyss comes first, and it recurs at critical points, in one
form or another, throughout the novel.

In the alpine scene Mrs Stringham withdraws, convinced that Milly,
'deeply and recklessly meditating' (I 124), is not meditating suicide,
that 'the future . . . would be a question of taking full in the face the
whole assault of life' (I 125) and Milly, returning from her climb,
confirms her companion's intuition. After wondering 'if I shall have
much of it' and 'for how long' (I 130–1), she announces, 'I want to go
straight to London' (I 133). Gaily she produces the ominous idea that
'if it wasn't for long – if nothing should happen to be so for *her* – why
[London] . . . would probably be less than anything else a waste of her
remainder' (I 134).

In London, during the whole of the fourth book, 'all the offered life
centres, to intensity, in the disclosure of Milly's single throbbing
consciousness' (xvii), but the abyss waits. Her introduction to Mrs
Lowder's circle Milly sees as a 'short parenthesis', which has begun in
Book·Fourth with Mrs Lowder's dinner party and is 'about to close'
with the 'admirable picture' (I 210) of the Matcham excursion at the
beginning of the fifth book. Enclosed in this parenthesis are all the ways
open to Milly to make the most of 'her remainder'.

During the dinner party she sees in Lord Mark the possible answer
to 'the very question she had suddenly put to Mrs Stringham on the
Brünig. Should she have it, whatever she did have . . . for long?
"Ah so possibly not," her neighbour appeared to reply; "therefore,

don't you see? *I'm* the way" ' (1 158–9). Kate Croy 'would perhaps be
the way as well', but the anomaly of Milly's having 'to recognise so
quickly in each of these glimpses of an instant the various signs of a
relation . . . might almost terribly have suggested to her that her doom
was to live fast' (1 159).

Milly quickly recognizes the 'sign of a relation' when Mrs Stringham
tells her of Mrs Lowder's concern about Kate's relationship with
Densher, a relationship which the English girl has not mentioned at all.
Milly says, 'Don't tell me that – in this for instance – there are not
abysses. I want abysses' (1 186), and she accepts Mrs Lowder's 'recom-
mendation that nothing should be said to Kate' as 'an interesting
complication', a 'new sort of fun'. The fun, however, involves a 'small
element of anxiety' (1 189), which quickly translates itself into a real
abyss, as Milly becomes 'conscious of being here on the edge of a great
darkness'. She will never really know how Kate Croy feels about her,
not because of Kate's 'ill will' or 'duplicity', but because of 'a sort of
failure of common terms' (1 190–1).

The parenthesis closes, and the 'great darkness' very nearly overwhelms Milly when Lord Mark confronts her with the Bronzino
portrait of the 'very great personage – only unaccompanied by a joy'
and 'dead, dead, dead' (1 221), which symbolizes for Milly not only a
premonition of her youthful death, but also the singular emptiness of
her life up to this juncture. As she has said to Susan Stringham earlier,
'Since I've lived all these years as if I were dead, I shall die, no doubt,
as if I were alive' (1 199).

Her tears during the moments before the portrait she later identifies
as 'the sign of her consciously rounding her protective promontory,
quitting the blue gulf of comparative ignorance and reaching her view
of the troubled sea' (II 144). Psychologically, this is a repetition of
Milly's alpine ramble, on a footpath which is 'always going up, up
. . . over a crest and to a place where the way would drop again'
(1 122). The 'descent of the path' comes to a 'sharp turn . . . masked
by rocks and shrubs', where it appears 'to fall precipitously and to
become a "view" ', and Milly goes 'straight down to it, not stopping
till it was all before her' (1 123). Her view is from the very end of the
short promontory; the 'protective promontory', which has masked the
sheer drop, the abyss.

During all of the fourth book of *The Wings of the Dove* Milly has
been engaged in an exploration which parallels the alpine exploration,

going up, up, tasting the 'success', however dubious, which Lord Mark and Mrs Lowder promise her, but coming to a precipitous drop, to an entirely conscious recognition of the great darkness, of the abyss, and Kate Croy is involved in her insight. She finds herself 'suddenly sunk in something quite intimate and humble', which 'had come up, in the form in which she had had to accept it, all suddenly'. Moreover, she knows that 'she had in a manner plunged into it to escape from something else' (1 225). What she is escaping from is her perception in Kate of the look which is 'perversely *there* . . . with every renewal of their meeting' (1 225), which Milly interprets as the way Kate looks to Mr Densher. To 'prove to herself that she didn't horribly blame her friend for any reserve' (1 229), she asks Kate to accompany her to Sir Luke Strett's office, for the time has come when she must have an authoritative answer to her reiterated question, 'How long?' After her first interview with Sir Luke, however, she again sees Kate 'in the light of her *other* identity' (1 232), and she refuses Kate's offer to accompany her on her second, and her decisive, visit to the doctor.

II

It is during the second interview that Milly feels that her life is being 'put into the scales', which represents 'her first approach to the taste of orderly living' (1 236). This scene with the doctor and the scene of her lonely meditation afterward in the streets of London and in the Regent's Park define in psychological, spiritual terms, her understanding of the abyss; and the scene with Kate Croy, which follows, introduces the dove, which symbolizes her hope for salvation. Together these three scenes comprise 'the whole actual centre' of *The Wings of the Dove*, which James says in his Preface is 'lodged in Book Fifth' (xxii). It is here that the parallel between Milly Theale's 'excluded disinherited state' and the 'extraordinarily intimate and quite awkwardly irrelevant'[4] relation to life which resulted for Henry James from his injury becomes clearly apparent.

James relates that he 'came to think of my injury as a *modus vivendi*, workable for the time',[5] and Milly Theale in the same spirit sees the possibility that 'learning . . . that she was in some way doomed' might very well 'for the time at least . . . give her something firm to stand on' (1 236). But if her life is being put in the scales, the scales must not be unfairly or unrealistically weighted, and when Sir Luke tries to people her world with friends, in order, as Milly sees it, 'to warm the air for her' (I 239), she feels she must persuade him to accept the fact that it is no use. 'The air, for Milly Theale, was, from the very nature of the case, destined never to rid itself of a considerable chill' (I 239). She assures him that her friends 'all together wouldn't make . . . the difference. I mean when one *is* – really alone'. 'One's situation', she reminds him, 'is what it is. It's *me* it concerns. . . . Nobody can really help' (I 239). Even though Sir Luke tells her she is all right, 'pity held up its telltale face like a head on a pike, in a French revolution. . . . He might say what he would now – she would always have seen the head at the window' (I 240–1). Milly has her answer.

The young Henry James also consulted a 'great surgeon' for an answer to the 'less and less bearable affliction with which I had been for three or four months seeking to strike some sort of bargain'.[6] Like Sir Luke, the Boston surgeon made 'quite unassistingly light of the bewilderment exposed to him', and Henry felt himself 'treated but to a comparative pooh-pooh'.[7] For James 'it was not simply small comfort, it was only a mystification the more, that the inconvenience of my state had to reckon with the strange fact of there being nothing to speak of the matter with me'.[8] Like Milly Theale, however, he concluded that 'the graceful course . . . was to behave . . . as if the assurance were true'.[9]

Milly may behave as if Sir Luke's assurance were true, but as she meditates alone in the streets of London, she recognizes that with 'beautiful beneficent dishonesty' Sir Luke has rejected her as a patient with 'some disguised intention of standing by her as a friend'. But this relationship she sees as analogous to the friendship of a woman with a man she has rejected. A friend is what women 'sincerely fancied they could make of men of whom they couldn't make husbands' (I 252). There is no basis for a doctor/patient relationship between Sir Luke and Milly Theale because there is nothing he can do for her. There is 'nothing to speak of the matter' with her, because there is no cure. This is 'a final and merciful wave, chilling rather, but washing clear' (I 252).

Still, Sir Luke's admonition to Milly to 'take the trouble' to live is a positive 'excitement', for although the question of 'living by option, by volition', as Sir Luke has put it to her, seems 'grey immensity' (I 247), she recognizes the mixture of gain and loss in her consciousness. 'The beauty of the bloom had gone from the small old sense of safety', but 'the beauty of the idea of a great adventure, a big dim experiment or struggle in which she might more responsibly than ever before take a hand, had been offered her instead' (1 248).

Right here Milly has stated the meaning of life on earth in the same terms which James later used in his essay, 'Is There a Life After Death?'[10] In that essay he speculates that 'the idea of an exclusively present world . . . may represent for us but a chance for experiment in the very interest of our better and freer being'. Life may indeed be 'but a chance for the practice and initial confidence of our faculties and our passions, of the precious personality at stake'.[11] In *The Wings of the Dove*, from the time that Milly realizes fully that she is soon to die, it is 'the precious personality at stake' which absorbs her and motivates her action. The assurance of the imminence of death forces her to recognize the possibility of the extinction of her personality and the correlative urgent necessity for 'experiment in the very interest of [her] better and freer being', on the off-chance that she is to have one after death.

The scene in the London streets and the Regent's Park recalls the portentous scene in the third book, when the image of the abyss was first introduced. Milly chose then to go 'straight to London' because 'it had rolled over her that what she wanted of Europe was "people" ' (1 134). It was 'the human, the English picture itself, as they might see it in their own way' (1 135) which Milly expected to find in London. Here in London, in the midst of 'the human, the English picture', Milly finds herself at the edge of a personal abyss, but her feeling of isolation melts away as she recognizes that there are 'hundreds of others just in the same box. Their box, their great common anxiety, what was it, in this grim breathing-space, but the practical question of life?' (1 250).

Henry James in his autobiography remembers that after his 'futile' consultation with the surgeon, he visited a gathering of convalescent troops,[12] a visit which served 'for my particular nearest approach to a "contact" with the active drama'.[13] This 'pilgrimage' and James's 'inward interpretation of it'[14] counterpoint the conditions of Milly's insight in the Regent's Park. It is particularly striking that Milly even thinks of herself as a 'soldier on the march', having shouldered 'some queer defensive weapon . . . demanding all the effort of the military posture' (1 248). For James the 'lasting value and high authority'[15] of his experience was his 'realisation . . . that, measuring wounds against wounds . . . one was no less exaltedly than wastefully engaged in the common fact of endurance'.[16]

James's recognition of the 'common fact of endurance' is then analogous to the 'great common anxiety' which Milly shares with the other 'wanderers anxious and tired like herself' (I 250) in the great public park. She sees finally that she, with the rest of the world, is faced with 'those two faces of the question [of life] between which there was so little to choose for inspiration. It was perhaps superficially more striking that one could live if one would; but it was more appealing, insinuating, irresistible in short, that one would live if one could' (I 254). The 'two faces' of the question are again delineated by James in his essay on immortality, with particular reference to life beyond death. Immortality, he says, 'isn't really a question of belief . . . it is on the other hand a question of desire, but of desire so confirmed . . . as to leave belief a comparatively irrelevant affair'.[17] The 'question of desire' corresponds to the 'more appealing, insinuating, irresistible' face of the question of life for Milly Theale, that 'one would live if one could'.

In *The Wings of the Dove*, after this statement about the two faces of life, 'life' and 'living' become thoroughly ambiguous terms, and the ambiguity should be recognized when in the 'deformed' half of the novel Milly tells Densher that she is 'capable of life', that 'I want so to live . . . that I know I *can*' (II 246). The ambiguity of this declaration for life is heightened by Milly's insistence to Densher that she does not see her way 'to peace and plenty', but only 'to keeping what one has'. When Densher says 'at random', 'Oh, that's success. If what one has is good . . . it's enough to try for', Milly says with finality, 'Well, it's my limit. I'm not trying for more' (II 248). James's view differs radically from the orthodox theology, which he admits it resembles, in its insistence that life after death is appealing only as it contains a promise of 'keeping what one has', only as it 'involves what . . . we have enjoyed and suffered, as our particular personal adventure'.[18] This states Milly Theale's 'limit'. She is 'not trying for more'. Her declaration, following as it does so many evidences of her clear recognition of the closeness of death, does not in fact make sense unless she means something quite different from what Densher understands. Certainly part of the 'falseness' of the latter half of the novel comes from an inevitable ambiguity in the basic term, 'life'.

When the scene in the Regent's Park ends with the picture of Milly as a 'poor girl – with her rent to pay . . . her rent for her future' (I 253-4), her future may be considered as a future beyond her physical doom, and the introduction of the concept of rent for the future marks for Milly the dawning of what James calls in his essay 'the splendid illusion of doing something myself for my prospect . . . of immortality'.[19] This is a very different concept from the one which the palace servant Eugenio suggests to her in Venice, the idea, that is, of 'some complete use of her wealth itself . . . as a counter-move to fate'. 'Prices of *his* kind were things she had never suffered to scare her', and she amuses herself 'with possibilities of meeting the bill' (II 142–3). Her legacy to Densher may very well be considered a 'counter-move to fate', 'meeting the bill', in Eugenio's prices, but her rent for her future requires 'a different sort of cash', involves 'amounts not to be named nor reckoned, and such moreover as she wasn't sure of having at her command' (II 142). In order to become 'capable of life' beyond death, Milly must, as she has earlier suspected, 'live fast', and yet live meaningfully, an assignment which is complicated for her by the fact that she is, as she has told Sir Luke, 'really alone' (I 254).

When Kate Croy comes to her for news of Sir Luke's verdict, she recognizes that, 'really alone' as she is, she is also 'enviably strong'. This 'truth' is 'oddly marked for her by her visitor's arrival' (I 261), when she sees Kate paying her cabman, waiting for her change, 'as the peculiar property of somebody else's vision'. The 'fine freedom' of Kate at that moment is 'the fine freedom she showed Mr Densher', and Milly accepts the implications of this perception, for 'it struck our young woman as absurd to say that a girl's looking so to a man could possibly be without connexions' (I 257). Here Milly quite positively recognizes and accepts the relation between Kate and Densher.

She evades Kate's question about her interview with Sir Luke, for to meet Kate 'with the note of the plaintive would amount somehow to a surrender, to a confession' (I 258), which Milly is not willing to make, then or ever. This 'principle of pride' is the 'treasure' which Milly later sees herself hiding from Kate, and 'not the treasure of a shy, an abject affection – concealment, on that head, belonging to quite another phase of such states' (II 139). Milly Theale is not pathetically involved in a sordid little triangle; she is holding fast to 'the truth about [her] own conception of her validity' (II 139).

Nevertheless, when she tells Kate that Sir Luke has advised her to 'go in for pleasure', she adds, 'You must help me' (I 260), for she knows that in order to 'achieve the sense of having lived', she must maintain some kind of relation to the ongoing action. James points out in his preface that 'she would found her struggle on particular human interests', and 'if her impulse to wrest from her shrinking hour still as much of the fruit of life as possible . . . can take effect only by the aid of others, their participation (appealed to, entangled and coerced as they find themselves) becomes their drama too' (vi–viii). This is the heart of the irony of *The Wings of the Dove*, for when Milly says to Kate, 'You must help me', she means it, and 'appealed to, entangled and coerced' as Kate actually is, she believes she is involving Milly in her life, using her, victimizing her.

It is Mrs Lowder who gives Milly the clue to a possible, though tenuous relation with a 'particular human interest' when she asks her to mention Densher to Kate, 'so that you may perhaps find out whether he's back' (I 264). 'Ever so many things, for Milly, fell into line at this' (I 264), and Kate, in the scene which follows, fills in the whole picture. She describes to Milly the situation at Lancaster Gate, and 'she gave away publicly, in this process . . . everything it contained . . . she gave herself away most of all' (I 277–8).

As Milly listens to Kate, she realizes that she is always 'in a current determined . . . by others', and that the 'keeper of the lock' is at present Kate, who has 'but to open the flood-gate: the current moved in its mass – the current . . . of her doing as Kate wanted' (I 274). This defines the nature of her relation to the action, and 'on this basis of being dealt with she would doubtless herself do her share of the conquering' (I 275). Her decision to go 'straight to London' had been, as she later recognizes, a 'plea . . . for life as opposed to learning',[20] and 'life' is now 'beautifully provided for' (I 287).

Milly's provision for life may seem tragically inadequate, but her problem is singular. The young Henry James, too, felt that he had a singular problem in 'getting somehow, and in spite of everything . . . at life'[21] during the year following his injury. He went to Cambridge to the Harvard Law School, which he 'thought of . . . under the head of "life"',[22] but 'life' was certainly not learning for him either. During this year at Cambridge, which James describes as 'the absurd little boxing-match within me between the ostensible and the real',[23] he regularly attended lectures, taking his seat on 'the rim of the circle, symbolising thereby all the detachment I had been foredoomed to',[24] listened to professors, 'not one ray of whose merely professed value so much as entered my mind'.[25] This was his preparation 'for an ordeal essentially intellectual', and it seemed to him 'at least a negative of combat, an organised, not a loose and empty one, something definitely and firmly parallel to action on the tented field. . . . The Cambridge campus was tented field enough for a conscript starting so compromised.'[26]

Milly Theale, also a compromised conscript, arrives in London and finds the scene dominated by Kate Croy; Henry James, arriving in Cambridge, 'was . . . to find my brother on the scene and already at a stage of possession of its contents that I was resigned in advance never to reach.[27] Peopled as [the scene] was with *his* people . . . it led me then to take the company . . . for whatever he all vividly and possessively pronounced it.'[28] It is important for an understanding of both Henry James and his heroine, Milly Theale, to note that he remarks that his acceptance of people entirely on William's terms 'was the truth at that season, if it wasn't always to remain the truth'.[29]

At Cambridge, however, he accepted William's domination much as Milly Theale accepts Kate's. 'I had only to like for my brother . . . his assured experience . . . to find the scene of action, or at least of passion . . . enriched.'[30] When he speaks of the scene of passion, James provides a name which may be applied to Milly's 'queer' relation to life, even as it may be applied to his own. 'Passion', as James uses it, is a way of life that is opposed to action, but it carries with it all the connotations of vehemence and strong emotion which are more commonly associated with passion. It is 'a negative of combat', but it always implies 'the high pitch of one's associated sensibility'.[31] Passion is an alternative to direct experience which should not be confused with passivity, first, because it is 'organised, not . . . loose and empty . . . definitely and firmly parallel to action', and second, because it is charged with intense, though 'associated' emotion and sympathy. Matthiessen may speak of the contrast between William and Henry James as 'active and passive',[32] but for Henry James himself it is a contrast between action and passion, and the difference for him is important.

The difference is important, too, for Milly Theale. Kate, after her magnificent monologue, gives Milly the cue which is to provide her with an inspired camouflage for 'being dealt with'. When Milly asks, 'Why do you say such things to me?' (I 282), Kate answers, 'Because you're a dove', and Milly immediately finds herself 'accepting as the right one . . . the name so given her' (I 283), for the dove image is one which can cover her role in whatever action there is. When Milly adopts the dove as a disguise, the action becomes for her, as the dove, a passion, 'a negative of combat', but her involvement is deliberate; her will is free; she is never simply passive. She studies 'the dovelike', it becomes her 'law' (I 284), and her actions from this point are to be deliberately 'pitched in the key of a merely iridescent drab' (I 285).

The dove, however, is a symbol with meanings on at least two levels. On the one level it is Milly's role in relation to her companions, and in this connection it is a disguise, consciously assumed, under which Milly's 'full-blown consciousness' is concealed for the remainder of the action. With the introduction of the dove disguise, the 'falseness' and 'deformity' of the novel begin in earnest.

On the intuitive level, however, the dove is the symbol for the struggle of Milly's soul or her personality to rise above annihilation, to strengthen itself for a life beyond death, and in this connection it is the wings which are vital. Milly's idea, expressed in her Venetian palace, of 'never going down' becomes for her 'an image . . . of remaining aloft in the divine dustless air, where she would hear but the plash of the water against stone' (II 147), an image which links in one picture the two integral images in this novel, the abyss and the wings of the dove. Whatever may be the protecting and even smothering effect of the wings upon those who surround her, this effect is at best incidental to Milly's own interest, which is, as James says Minnie Temple's was, 'the prospect of the soul and the question of interests on *its* part'.[33]

III

The real drama in *The Wings of the Dove* is the subjective drama, the entirely inward struggle for her own salvation which occupies Milly Theale during her time in London and in Venice, yet only in the center of the novel in Book Fifth do we see her directly engaged in this struggle. However, the center, as James promises in his preface, has 'a long reach' and contains 'the larger foreshortening' (xxii). The last pages of the fifth book, through a remarkable foreshortening, prefigure the action of the 'deformed' half of the novel, presenting this action from Milly's own point of view. If Milly's evening with Kate is a 'rough rehearsal of the possible big drama' (I 276), her visit to the National Gallery and the following scene at her hotel may be considered a full-dress rehearsal in miniature of the drama in Venice.

The National Gallery itself is like a prefiguring of the palace in Venice, 'the quiet chambers, nobly overwhelming' (I 288), and Milly recognizes in the 'benignant halls' that 'something within her was too weak for the Turners and Titians. . . . They were truly . . . not for the smaller life . . . of which the pitch . . . was an interest, the interest of compassion, in misguided efforts' (I 288–9). The 'interest of compassion in misguided efforts' may be considered an accurate description of her relationship with all those who see her through in Venice.

She sees Kate and Densher, and immediately Kate is 'literally in control of the scene' (I 294), even as she is at first in Venice. As in the Venice experience, 'the predicament of course wasn't definite nor phraseable', and the one thing Milly can 'think of to do . . . was to show him how she eased him off' (I 294). This is the beginning of Milly's 'easing them off'. Later Densher notes that she 'made of the air breathed a virtual non-conductor' (II 255–6), and she is toward the end of the time in Venice 'divine in her trust, or at any rate inscrutable in her mercy' (II 242).

Milly, reflecting on the scene at the National Gallery, wonders 'what in the world they had actually said, since they had made such a success of what they didn't say', and concludes that 'whatever the facts, their perfect manners, all round, saw them through' (I 295). This prefigures the experience in Venice, during which, as Densher finally realizes, everyone had 'actively fostered suppressions which were in the direct interest of every one's good manner' (II 298).

In the final scene in the foreshadowing drama, Milly assumes the identity of 'the American girl', becoming 'as spontaneous as possible and as American as it might conveniently appeal to Mr Densher . . . to find her' (I 296). This prefigures her relationship with Densher in the latter half of the novel, when he sees that 'there would scarce have been felicity . . . had not the national character so invoked been, not less inscrutably than entirely, in Milly's chords. It made up her unity and was the one thing he could unlimitedly take for granted' (II 255).

In this character, Milly takes over the immediate, superficial action, takes Kate and Densher to lunch at her hotel, gives Kate 'time', which 'the American girl could give . . . as nobody else could. What Milly thus gave she therefore made them take – even if, as they might surmise, it was rather more than they wanted' (I 296). She does the same thing in Venice, giving generously, not only of her substance, but of her belief, which amounts to the giving of time. She tells Lord Mark that she accepts the 'lovely account' they give of themselves, and 'I give you in return the fullest possible belief of what it would be – ' (II 160), and she stops short. But the time she gives by this 'fullest possible belief', what Densher sees as 'the queerest conscious compliance' (II 254), actually does become 'rather more than they wanted'. This is acutely true for Densher, and it is perhaps even more tragically the case for Kate, who has always recognized her 'danger of doing something base' (I 72), and who finds herself fulfilling her own prophecy under the pressure of Milly's 'fullest possible belief'.

The belief and conscious compliance operate even against odds in the final pages of Book Fifth, when Kate leaves Milly and Densher alone, foreshadowing the time when Kate leaves Densher in Venice to make what he can of the implied situation. Milly sees in the earlier scene in London exactly what the implied situation is: 'Merton Densher was in love and Kate couldn't help it . . . wouldn't that, without wild flurries, cover everything?' Milly tries it 'as a cover . . . drew it up to her chin with energy. If it didn't, so treated, do everything for her, it did so much that she could herself supply the rest' (I 298). She accepts the 'lovely account' which is presented to her, here in London as she does later in Venice, for she realizes that 'whatever he did or he didn't . . . she should still like [Densher]' (I 300).

She accepts him as a friend, and Densher recognizes and depends on 'their excellent, their pleasant, their permitted and proper and harmless American relation' (II 70). In Venice, too, it is 'settled . . . that they were indissoluble good friends, and settled as well that her being the American girl was . . . for the relation they found themselves concerned in, a boon inappreciable' (II 254).

The foreshadowing drama of Book Fifth ends, however, with the recurrence of the ominous image of the abyss, as Milly listens with a 'glassy lustre of attention' to Densher's 'pleasantness about the scenery in the Rockies'. Just beyond the wall is Susan Stringham 'full to the brim of Sir Luke Strett and of what she had had from him'. This knowledge looks 'stiff' to Milly, and it is because she is divided from it by 'so thin a partition' that she continues to cling to the Rockies (I 301–2).

IV

The abyss image is picked up again in the second volume when Kate sees that it is impossible for Milly to be explicit about her situation because 'to recognise was to bring down the avalanche – the avalanche Milly lived so in watch for and that might be started by the lightest of breaths' (II 141). It is significant that the avalanche implies a more generalized disaster than any of the other expressions of Milly's precarious position, for Kate always sees Milly's dying as involved with her own life, not as the intensely, peculiarly subjective experience it actually is. And it is Kate who is more nearly buried by the avalanche than anyone else.

Apparently it is Lord Mark who starts the avalanche; it is at least after his visit that Milly 'turns her face to the wall', but it is not an evil purpose which motivates his revelation to Milly; it is simply, as Milly herself told him at their first meeting, that he is 'familiar with everything, but conscious really of nothing', that he has 'no imagination' (I 162). It is Lord Mark, the man without imagination, the man who 'wasn't good for what she would have called her reality' (II 158), who reveals the 'truth' to Milly Theale. But it is at the same time obvious that he does not even understand Milly's truth, because he is incapable of facing 'the offensive real' (II 158). His behavior, like most civilized behavior, rests 'on the general assumption that nothing – nothing to make a deadly difference for him – ever *could* happen' (II 159). He 'recognizes' and thus destroys 'the logic of their common duplicity' (II 140), but Lord Mark does not kill Milly Theale.

The fact is that Milly Theale is dying, not from unrequited love, not from a lack of will, but from an incurable physical disease. Densher suddenly sees this as 'the truth that was truest about Milly.' (II 298) when Sir Luke appears in Venice after Lord Mark's visit. The 'great smudge of mortality across the picture' has never found any 'surface of spirit or of speech that consented to reflect it' because there is somehow an 'outrage to taste involved in one's having to *see*' (II 298–9). 'The facts of physical suffering, of incurable pain, of the chance grimly narrowed' (II 299) are intensely present to Milly Theale during the whole of this drama, even though, with a sublime courtesy, she has protected the others from having to 'see'.

The prefiguring drama in Book Fifth ends with Milly, clinging to Densher's 'pleasantness' and separated only by a 'thin partition' from the facts of her case. When she 'turns her face to the wall', in the ninth book, she turns away from Densher, who is her last hold on the world, to Sir Luke and 'incurable pain'. This is the last test of her being 'capable of life', the final stage in her struggle for 'wings like a dove', and, although the lonely ordeal continues for weeks, there is really not even an indirect vision of it included in the novel. The ninth book ends with Densher's seeing Sir Luke's face as the 'nearest approach to the utter reference they had hitherto so successfully avoided', and he asks himself 'into what abyss it pushed him' (II 309).

The view of Milly Theale begins with Mrs Stringham's perception of the abyss as the 'revelation' of Milly and ends with Merton Densher's understanding of the abyss as a revelation, not only of Milly, but also of himself. All men are mortal; Milly Theale differs from most men simply in her intense awareness that the old syllogism states a personal, as well as a universal fact. Only to the degree in which the other characters in *The Wings of the Dove* have been really aware of her consciousness of death and of the universal abyss do they benefit from her life. Still, her effect upon the others has no real bearing upon her own validity. Her life is justified, not by the use which others make of it, but by her own entirely subjective, entirely inward development of her self. There are indeed two sides to the story, but Milly Theale's side is the vital one; the rest is irony. As Milly herself says, 'It's *me* it concerns. The rest is delightful and useless.'

NOTES

1. F. O. Matthiessen, *Henry James, The Major Phase* (New York, 1944) pp. 78–9.

2. See Henry James, *Notes of a Son and Brother* (New York, 1914). All of chapter 9 (pp. 290–319) is concerned with the adjustment to the injury, but pp. 296–9 describe it specifically.

3. This page reference, as well as any subsequent reference within the text, is to *The Wings of the Dove* (New York, 1922), in the 'New York Edition'.

4. James, *Notes of a Son and Brother*, p. 297.

5. Ibid. p. 299.

6. Ibid.

7. Ibid. p. 300.

8. Ibid. pp. 300–1.

9. Ibid. p. 301.

10. This essay, James's contribution to a 1910 symposium on immortality, is printed in F. O. Matthiessen, *The James Family* (New York, 1948) pp. 602–14.

11. Ibid. p. 613.

12. Leon Edel, in *Henry James: The Untried Years* (New York, 1953) p. 169, points out that this visit actually occurred before James's accident, although James makes it a significant part of his adjustment to the injury. This rearrangement of chronology would seem to strengthen the probability of James's awareness of the analogy between his crisis and Milly Theale's.

13. James, *Notes of a Son and Brother*, p. 311.

14. Ibid. p. 318.

15. Ibid. p. 319.
16. Ibid. p. 318.
17. Matthiessen, *The James Family*, p. 614.
18. Ibid. p. 604.
19. Ibid. p. 614.
20. Note the Tauchnitz volume, discarded as 'an encumbrance', in the alpine scene (I 123).
21. James, *Notes of a Son and Brother*, p. 344.
22. Ibid. pp. 292–3.
23. Ibid. pp. 339–40.
24. Ibid. p. 346.
25. Ibid. p. 347.
26. Ibid. pp. 301–2.
27. Ibid. p. 302.
28. Ibid. p. 327.
29. Ibid. p. 323.
30. Ibid. p. 330.
31. Ibid. p. 361.
32. Matthiessen, *The James Family*, Preface, p. v.
33. James, *Notes of a Son and Brother*, p. 491.

IAN WATT

The First Paragraph of *The Ambassadors*: an explication (1960)

WHEN I was asked if I would do a piece of explication at this conference,* I was deep in Henry James, and beginning *The Ambassadors*:
so the passage chose itself; but just what was explication, and how did
one do it to prose? I take it that whereas explanation, from *explanare*,
suggests a mere making plain by spreading out, explication, from
explicare, implies a progressive unfolding of a series of literary implications, and thus partakes of our modern preference for multiplicity in
method and meaning: explanation assumes an ultimate simplicity,
explication assumes complexity.

Historically, the most systematic tradition of explication is presumably that which developed out of medieval textual exegesis and became
the chief method of literary instruction in French secondary and higher
education in the late nineteenth century. *Explication de texte* in France
reflects the rationalism of nineteenth-century Positivist scholarship. At
its worst the routine application of the method resembles a sort of
bayonet drill in which the exposed body of literature is riddled with
etymologies and dates before being despatched in a harrowingly
insensitive *résumé*. At its best, however, *explication de texte* can be
solidly illuminating, and it then serves to remind us that a piece of
literature is not necessarily violated if we give systematic attention to
such matters as its author, its historical setting, and the formal properties of its language.

Practical Criticism, on the other hand, as it was developed at
Cambridge by I. A. Richards, continues the tradition of the British
Empiricists. Inductive rather than deductive, it makes a point of
excluding linguistic and historical considerations, so as to derive – in
appearance at least – all the literary values of a work empirically from
the words on the page. In the last thirty years the emphasis of Practical
Criticism on the autonomy of the text has revolutionised the approach

* Ninth Annual Conference of Non-Professorial University Teachers at Oxford on
5 April 1959.

to literary studies, and has proved itself a technique of supreme value for teaching and examining students; I myself certainly believe that its use should be expanded rather than curtailed. Yet, at least in the form in which I picked it up as a student and have later attempted to pass it on as a teacher, both its pedagogical effects and its basic methodological assumptions seem to me to be open to serious question. For many reasons. Its air of objectivity confers a spurious authority on a process that is often only a rationalisation of an unexamined judgment, and that must always be to some extent subjective; its exclusion of historical factors seems to authorise a more general anti-historicism; and – though this objection is perhaps less generally accepted – it contains an inherent critical bias in the assumption that the part is a complete enough reflection of the literary whole to be profitably appreciated and discussed in isolation from its context. How far this is true, or how far it can be made to appear so by a well-primed practitioner, is a matter of opinion; but it is surely demonstrable that Practical Criticism tends to find the most merit in the kind of writing which has virtues that are in some way separable from their larger context; it favours kinds of writing that are richly concrete in themselves, stylistically brilliant, or composed in relatively small units. It is therefore better suited to verse than to prose; and better suited to certain kinds of either than to others where different and less concentrated merits are appropriate, as in the novel.

As for its pedagogical effects – and here again I have mainly my own past experience in mind – Practical Criticism surely tends to sensitise us towards objects only within a certain range of magnitude: below that threshold it becomes subjective and impressionist, paying very little attention to the humble facts of the grammar and syntax of the words on the page; while, at the other extreme, if often ignores the larger meaning, and the literary and historical contexts of that meaning.

As a practical matter these restrictions may all be necessary for the pupil and salutary for the teacher; and I mention them mainly to justify my present attempt to develop the empirical and inductive methods of Practical Criticism in such a way as to deal with those elements in a literary text whose vibrations are so high or so low that we Ricardian dogs have not yet been trained to bark at them.

It is mainly in these penumbral areas, of course, that the French *explication de texte* habitually operates; but its analysis of grammar and of the literary and historical background are usually a disconnected series of discrete demonstrations which stop short of the unifying critical synthesis that one hopes for. Until fairly recently the same could have been said, and perhaps with greater emphasis, about the German tradition of literary scholarship, with its almost entirely independent pursuit of philology and philosophy. More recent trends in *Stilforschung* however – of which Wolfgang Clemen's *The Development of Shakespeare's Imagery* (Bonn, 1936) was an early example – come closer to, and indeed partly reflect, the more empirical Anglo-American models of literary criticism; while, even more promising perhaps for the study of prose, though seemingly quite independent of the influence of Practical Criticism, is the development, mainly from Romance philology, of what has come to be called 'stylistics'.

For my purposes, however, it remains not so much a method as a small group of isolated, though spectacular, individual triumphs. I yield to no one in my admiration for Leo Spitzer's *Linguistics and Literary History* (Baltimore, 1948), or for the continual excitement and illumination offered in Erich Auerbach's *Mimesis* (1946: trans. Willard Trask, Princeton, N.J., 1953); their achievements, however, strike me mainly as tributes to the historical imagination and philosophical understanding of the German mind at its best; I find their brilliant commentaries on words or phrases or passages essentially subjective; and if I am tempted to emulate the *bravura* with which they take off from the word on the page to leap into the farthest empyreans of *Kulturgeschichte*, I soon discover that the Cambridge east winds have condemned me to less giddy modes of critical transport.

Yet what other models are there to help one to analyse a paragraph of Jamesian prose? Some of the historical studies of prose style could, conceivably, be applied; but I am fearful of ending up with the proposition that James was a Ciceronian – with Senecan elements, of course, like everyone else. As for the new linguistics, the promises as regards literary analysis seem greater than the present rewards: the most practical consequence of my exposure to Charles Fries's *The Structure of English: An Introduction to the Construction of English Sentences* (New York, 1952), for example, was to deprive me of the innocent pleasure that comes from imagining you know the names of things. Structural linguistics in general is mainly (and rightly) concerned with problems of definition and description at a considerably more basic level of linguistic usage than the analysis of the literary effect of Henry James's grammatical particularities seems to require.

Perhaps the most promising signs of the gaps being filled have come from what are – in that particular area – amateurs: from Francis Berry's *Poets' Grammar* (1958), or Donald Davie's *Articulate Energy* (1955). But they don't help much with prose, of course, and they aren't basically concerned with grammatical structure in the ordinary sense; although Davie's notion that the principle of continuity in poetry is, after all, primarily grammatical and rational, at least lessens the separation between the stylistic domains of poetry and prose, and suggests some ways of studying how syntax channels expressive force.

Virtually helpless,[1] then, I must face the James passage alone as far as any fully developed and acceptable technique for explicating prose is concerned; but there seem to be good reasons why practical criticism should be supplemented by some of the approaches of French and German scholarship, and by whatever else will lead one from the words on the page to matters as low as syntax and as high as ideas, or the total literary structure.

I

Strether's first question, when he reached the hotel, was about his friend; yet on his learning that Waymarsh was apparently not to arrive till evening he was not wholly disconcerted. A telegram from him bespeaking a room 'only if not noisy', reply paid, was produced for the
5 inquirer at the office, so that the understanding they should meet at Chester rather than at Liverpool remained to that extent sound. The same secret principle, however, that had prompted Strether not absolutely to desire Waymarsh's presence at the dock, that had led him thus to postpone for a few hours his enjoyment of it, now operated to
10 make him feel he could still wait without disappointment. They would dine together at the worst, and, with all respect to dear old Waymarsh – if not even, for that matter, to himself – there was little fear that in the sequel they shouldn't see enough of each other. The principle I have just mentioned as operating had been, with the most newly disembarked
15 of the two men, wholly instinctive – the fruit of a sharp sense that, delightful as it would be to find himself looking, after so much separation, into his comrade's face, his business would be a trifle bungled should he simply arrange for this countenance to present itself to the nearing steamer as the first 'note' of Europe. Mixed with everything
20 was the apprehension, already, on Strether's part, that it would, at best, throughout, prove the note of Europe in quite a sufficient degree.[2]

It seems a fairly ordinary sort of prose, but for its faint air of elaborate portent; and on second reading its general quality reminds one of what Strether is later to observe – approvingly – in Maria Gostrey: an effect of 'expensive, subdued suitability'. There's certainly nothing particularly striking in the diction or syntax; none of the immediate drama or rich description that we often get at the beginning of novels; and certainly none of the sensuous concreteness that, until recently, was regarded as a chief criterion of good prose in our long post-imagistic phase: if anything, the passage is conspicuously un-sensuous and un-concrete, a little dull perhaps, and certainly not easy reading.

The difficulty isn't one of particularly long or complicated sentences: actually they're of fairly usual length: I make it an average of 41 words; a little, but not very much, longer than James's average of 35.[3] The main cause of difficulty seems rather to come from what may be called the *delayed specification of referents:* 'Strether' and 'the hotel' and 'his friend' are mentioned before we are told who or where they are. But this difficulty is so intimately connected with James's general narrative technique that it may be better to begin with purely verbal idiosyncrasies, which are more easily isolated. The most distinctive ones in the passage seem to be these: a preference for non-transitive verbs; many abstract nouns; much use of 'that'; a certain amount of elegant variation to avoid piling up personal pronouns and adjectives such as 'he', 'his' and 'him'; and the presence of a great many negatives and near-negatives.

By the preference for non-transitive verbs I mean three related habits: a great reliance on copulatives – 'Strether's first question *was* about his friend', '*was* apparently not to arrive': a frequent use of the passive voice – '*was* not wholly *disconcerted*', 'a telegram . . . *was produced*', 'his business *would be* a trifle *bungled*': and the employment of many intransitive verbs – 'the understanding . . . remained . . . sound', 'the . . . principle . . . operated to'. My count of all the verbs in the indicative would give a total of 14 passive, copulative or intransitive uses as opposed to only 6 transitive ones: and there are in addition frequent infinitive, participial, or gerundial uses of transitive verbs, in all of which the active nature of the subject-verb-and-object sequence is considerably abated – 'on his learning', 'bespeaking a room', 'not absolutely to desire', 'led him thus to postpone'.

This relative infrequency of transitive verbal usages in the passage is associated with the even more pronounced tendency towards using abstract nouns as subjects of main or subordinate clauses: 'question',

'understanding', 'the same secret principle', 'the principle', 'his business'. If one takes only the main clauses, there are four such abstract
nouns as subjects, while only three main clauses have concrete and
particular subjects ('he', or 'they').*

I detail these features only to establish that in this passage, at least,
there is a clear quantitative basis for the common enough view that
James's late prose style is characteristically abstract; more explicitly,
that the main grammatical subjects are very often nouns for mental
ideas, 'question', 'principle', etc.; and that the verbs – because they are
mainly used either non-transitively, or in infinitive, participial and
gerundial forms – tend to express states of being rather than particular
finite actions affecting objects.

The main use of abstractions is to deal at the same time with many
objects or events rather than single and particular ones: and we use
verbs that denote states of being rather than actions for exactly the
same reason – their much more general applicability. But in this
passage, of course, James isn't in the ordinary sense making abstract or
general statements; it's narrative, not expository prose; what need
exploring, therefore, are the particular literary imperatives which
impose on his style so many of the verbal and syntactical qualities of
abstract and general discourse; of expository rather than narrative
prose.

Consider the first sentence. The obvious narrative way of making
things particular and concrete would presumably be 'When Strether
reached the hotel, he first asked "Has Mr Waymarsh arrived yet?" '
Why does James say it the way he does? One effect is surely that,
instead of a sheer stated event, we get a very special view of it; the
mere fact that actuality has been digested into reported speech – the
question 'was about his friend' – involves a narrator to do the job, to
interpret the action, and also a presumed audience that he does it for:
and by implication, the heat of the action itself must have cooled off
somewhat for the translation and analysis of the events into this form
of statement to have had time to occur. Lastly, making the subject of the
sentence 'question' rather than 'he' has the effect of subordinating the
particular actor, and therefore the particular act, to a much more
general perspective: mental rather than physical, and subjective rather

* Sentences one and four are compound or multiple, but in my count I haven't included
the second clause in the latter – 'there was little fear': though if we can talk of the clause
having a subject it's an abstract one – 'fear'.

than objective; 'question' is a word which involves analysis of a physical event into terms of meaning and intention: it involves, in fact, both Strether's mind and the narrator's. The narrator's, because he interprets Strether's act: if James had sought the most concrete method of taking us into Strether's mind – ' "Has Mr Waymarsh come yet?" I at once asked' – he would have obviated the need for the implied external categoriser of Strether's action. But James disliked the 'mere platitude of statement' involved in first-person narrative; partly, presumably, because it would merge Strether's consciousness into the narrative, and not isolate it for the reader's inspection. For such isolation, a more expository method is needed: no confusion of subject and object, as in first-person narration, but a narrator forcing the reader to pay attention to James's primary objective – Strether's mental and subjective state.

The 'multidimensional' quality of the narrative, with its continual implication of a community of three minds – Strether's, James's, and the reader's – isn't signalled very obviously until the fourth sentence – 'The principle I have just mentioned as operating . . .'; but it's already been established tacitly in every detail of diction and structure, and it remains pervasive. One reason for the special demand James's fictional prose makes on our attention is surely that there are always at least three levels of development – all of them subjective: the characters' awareness of events; the narrator's seeing of them; and our own trailing perception of the relation between these two.

The primary location of the narrative in a mental rather than a physical continuum gives the narrative a great freedom from the restrictions of particular time and place. Materially, we are, of course, in Chester, at the hotel – characteristically 'the hotel' because a fully particularised specification – 'The Pied Bull Inn' say – would be an irrelevant brute fact which would distract attention from the mental train of thought we are invited to partake in. But actually we don't have any pressing sense of time and place: we feel ourselves to be spectators, rather specifically, of Strether's thought processes, which easily and imperceptibly range forwards and backwards both in time and space. Sentence three, for example, begins in the past, at the Liverpool dock; sentence four looks forward to the reunion later that day, and to its many sequels: such transitions of time and place are much easier to effect when the main subjects of the sentences are abstract: a 'principle' exists independently of its context.

The multiplicity of relations – between narrator and object, and between the ideas in Strether's mind – held in even suspension throughout the narrative, is presumably the main explanation for the number of 'thats' in the passage, as well as of the several examples of elegant variation. There are 9 'thats' – only two of them demonstrative and the rest relative pronouns (or conjunctions or particles if you prefer those terms); actually there were no less than three more of them in the first edition, which James removed from the somewhat more colloquial and informal New York Edition; while there are several other 'thats' implied – in 'the principle [that] I have just mentioned', for instance.

The number of 'thats' follows from two habits already noted in the passage. 'That' characteristically introduces relative clauses dealing not with persons but with objects, including abstractions; and it is also used to introduce reported speech – 'on his learning that Waymarsh' – not 'Mr Waymarsh isn't here'. Both functions are combined in the third sentence where we get a triple definition of a timeless idea based on the report of three chronologically separate events: 'the same secret principle, however, that had prompted Strether not absolutely to desire Waymarsh's presence at the dock, that had led him thus to postpone for a few hours his enjoyment of it, now operated to make him feel that he could still wait without disappointment'.

Reported rather than direct speech also increases the pressure towards elegant variation: the use, for example, in sentence 1 of 'his friend', where in direct speech it would be 'Mr Waymarsh' (and the reply – 'He hasn't come yet'). In the second sentence – 'a telegram . . . was produced for the inquirer' – 'inquirer' is needed because 'him' has already been used for Waymarsh just above of course, 'the inquirer' is logical enough after the subject of the first sentence has been an abstract noun – 'question'; and the epithet also gives James an opportunity for underlining the ironic distance and detachment with which we are invited to view his dedicated 'inquirer', Strether. Later, when Strether is 'the most newly disembarked of the two men', we see how both elegant variation and the grammatical subordination of physical events are related to the general Jamesian tendency to present characters and actions on a plane of abstract categorisation; the mere statement, 'Mr Waymarsh had already been in England for [so many] months', would itself go far to destroy the primarily mental continuum in which the paragraph as a whole exists.

The last general stylistic feature of the passage to be listed above was the use of negative forms. There are 6 'noes' or 'nots' in the first four sentences; 4 implied negatives – 'postpone', 'without disappoint-ment', 'at the worst', 'there was little fear'; and 2 qualifications that modify positiveness of affirmation – 'not wholly' and 'to that extent'. This abundance of negatives has no doubt several functions: it enacts Strether's tendency to hesitation and qualification; it puts the reader into the right judicial frame of mind; and it has the further effect of subordinating concrete events to their mental reflection; 'Waymarsh was not to arrive', for example, is not a concrete statement of a physical event: it is subjective – because it implies an expectation in Strether's mind (which was not fulfilled); and it has an abstract quality – because while Waymarsh's arriving would be particular and physical, his *not* arriving is an idea, a non-action. More generally, James's great use of negatives or near-negatives may also, perhaps, be regarded as part of his subjective and abstractive tendency: there are no negatives in nature but only in the human consciousness.

II

The most obvious grammatical features of what Richard Chase has called Henry James's 'infinitely syntactical language'[4] can, then, be shown to reflect the essential imperatives of his narrative point of view; and they could therefore lead into a discussion of the philo-sophical qualities of his mind, as they are discussed, for example, by Dorothea Krook in her notable article 'The Method of the Later Works of Henry James',[5] our passage surely exemplifies James's power 'to generalise to the furthest limit the particulars of experience', and with it the characteristic way in which both his 'perceptions of the world itself and his perceptions of the logic of his perceptions of the world . . . happen simultaneously, are the parts of a single comprehensive experience'. Another aspect of the connection between James's meta-physic and his method as a novelist has inspired a stimulating stylistic study – Carlo Izzo's 'Henry James, Scrittore Sintattico'.[6] The connec-tion between thought and style finds its historical perspective in John Henry Raleigh's illuminating study 'Henry James: The Poetics of Empiricism',[7] which establishes connections between Lockian epistemo-logy and James's extreme, almost anarchic, individualism; while this epistemological preoccupation, which is central to Quentin Anderson's view of how James worked out his father's cosmology in fictional terms[8] also leads towards another large general question, the concern with 'point of view', which became a crucial problem in the history and criticism of fiction under the influence of the sceptical relativism of the late nineteenth century.

In James's case, the problem is fairly complicated. He may be classed as an 'Impressionist', concerned, that is, to show not so much the events themselves, but the impressions which they make on the characters. But James's continual need to generalise and place and order, combined with his absolute demand for a point of view that would be plastic enough to allow him freedom for the formal 'architectonics' of the novelist's craft, eventually involved him in a very idiosyncratic kind of multiple Impressionism: idiosyncratic because the dual presence of Strether's consciousness and of that of the narrator, who translates what he sees there into more general terms, makes the narrative point of view both intensely individual and yet ultimately social.

Another possible direction of investigation would be to show that the abstractness and indirection of James's style are essentially the result of this characteristic multiplicity of his vision. There is, for example, the story reported by Edith Wharton that after his first stroke James told Lady Prothero that 'in the very act of falling . . . he heard in the room a voice which was distinctly, it seemed, not his own, saying: "So here it is at last, the distinguished thing." ' James, apparently, could not but see even his own most fateful personal experience, except as evoked by some other observer's voice in terms of the long historical and literary tradition of death. Carlo Izzo regards this tendency as typical of the Alexandrian style, where there is a marked disparity between the rich inheritance of the means of literary expression, and the meaner creative world which it is used to express; but the defence of the Jamesian habit of mind must surely be that what the human vision shares with that of animals is presumably the perception of concrete images, not the power to conceive universals: such was Aristotle's notion of man's distinguishing capacity. The universals in the present context are presumably the awareness that behind every petty individual circumstance there ramifies an endless network of general moral, social and historical relations. Henry James's style can therefore be seen as a supremely civilised effort to relate every event and every moment of life to the full complexity of its circumambient conditions.

Obviously James's multiple awareness can go too far; and in the later novels it often poses the special problem that we do not quite know whether the awareness implied in a given passage is the narrator's or that of his character. Most simply, a pronoun referring to the subject of a preceding clause is always liable to give trouble if one hasn't been very much aware of what the grammatical subject of that preceding clause was; in the last sentence of the paragraph, for example, 'the apprehension, already, on Strether's part, that . . . it would, at best, . . . prove the note of Europe', 'it' refers to Waymarsh's countenance: but this isn't at first obvious; which is no doubt why, in his revision of the periodical version for the English edition James replaced 'it' by 'he' – simpler, grammatically, but losing some of the ironic visual precision of the original. More seriously, because the narrator's consciousness and Strether's are both present, we often don't know whose mental operations and evaluative judgments are involved in particular cases. We pass, for instance, from the objective analysis of sentence 3 where the analytic terminology of 'the same secret principle' must be the responsibility of the narrator, to what must be a verbatim quotation of Strether's mind in sentence 4: 'with all respect to dear old Waymarsh' is obviously Strether's licensed familiarity.

But although the various difficulties of tense, voice, and reference require a vigilance of attention in the reader which some have found too much to give, they are not in themselves very considerable: and what perhaps is much more in need of attention is how the difficulties arising from the multiplicity of points of view don't by any means prevent James from ordering all the elements of his narartive style into an amazingly precise means of expression: and it is this positive and, in the present case, as it seems to me, triumphant, mastery of the difficulties which I want next to consider.

Our passage is not, I think, James either at his most memorable or at his most idiosyncratic: *The Ambassadors* is written with considerable sobriety and has, for example, little of the vivid and direct style of the early part of *The Wings of the Dove*, or of the happy symbolic complexities of *The Golden Bowl*. Still, the passage is fairly typical of the later James; and I think it can be proved that all or at least nearly all the idiosyncrasies of diction or syntax in the present passage are fully justified by the particular emphases they create.

The most flagrant eccentricity of diction is presumably that where James writes 'the most newly disembarked of the two men' (lines

14–15). 'Most' may very well be a mere slip; and it must certainly seem indefensible to any one who takes it as an absolute rule that the comparative must always be used when only two items are involved.[9] But a defence is at least possible. 'Most newly disembarked' means something rather different from 'more newly disembarked'. James, it may be surmised, did not want to compare the recency of the two men's arrival, but to inform us that Strether's arrival was 'very' or as we might say, 'most' recent; the use of the superlative also had the advantage of suggesting the long and fateful tradition of transatlantic disembarcations in general.

The reasons for the other main syntactical idiosyncrasies in the passage are much clearer. In the first part of the opening sentence, for example, the separation of subject – 'question' – from verb – 'was' – by the longish temporal clause' when he reached the hotel', is no doubt a dislocation of normal sentence structure; but, of course, 'Strether' must be the first word of the novel: while, even more important, the delayed placing of the temporal clause, forces a pause after 'question' and thus gives it a very significant resonance. Similarly with the last sentence; it has several peculiarities, of which the placing of 'throughout' seems the most obvious. The sentence has three parts: the first and last are comparatively straightforward, but the middle is a massed block of portentous qualifications: 'Mixed with everything was the apprehension – already, on Strether's part, that he would, at best, throughout – prove the note of Europe in quite a sufficient degree.' The echoing doom started by the connotation of 'apprehension' – reverberates through 'already' ('much more to come later'), 'on Strether's part' ('even he knows'), and 'at best' ('the worst has been envisaged, too'); but it is the final collapse of the terse rhythm of the parenthesis that isolates the rather awkwardly placed 'throughout', and thus enables James to sound the fine full fatal note; there is no limit to the poignant eloquence of 'throughout'. It was this effect, of course, which dictated the preceding inversion which places 'apprehension' not at the start of the sentence, but in the middle where, largely freed from its syntactical nexus, it may be directly exposed to its salvos of qualification.

The mockingly fateful emphasis on 'throughout' tells us, if nothing had before, that James's tone is in the last analysis ironic, comic, or better, as I shall try to suggest, humorous. The general reasons for this have already been suggested. To use Maynard Mack's distinction,[10]

'the comic artist subordinates the presentation of life as experience,
where the relationship between ourselves and the characters experiencing it is a primary one, to the presentation of life as a spectacle,
where the primary relation is between himself and us as onlookers'.
In the James passage, the primacy of the relation between the narrator
and the reader has already been noted, as has its connection with the
abstraction of the diction, which brings home the distance between the
narrator and Strether. Of course, the application of abstract diction to
particular persons always tends towards irony,[11] because it imposes a
dual way of looking at them: few of us can survive being presented
as general representatives of humanity.

The paragraph, of course, is based on one of the classic contradictions
in psychological comedy – Strether's reluctance to admit to himself
that he has very mixed feelings about his friend: and James develops
this with the narrative equivalent of *commedia dell'arte* technique:
virtuoso feats of ironic balance, comic exaggeration, and deceptive
hesitation conduct us on a complicated progress towards the fore-
ordained illumination.

In structure, to begin with, the six sentences form three groups of
two: each pair of them gives one aspect of Strether's delay; and they
are arranged in an ascending order of complication so that the fifth
sentence – 72 words – is almost twice as long as any other, and is
succeeded by the final sentence, the punch line, which is noticeably
the shortest – 26 words. The development of the ideas is as controlled
as the sentence structure. Strether is obviously a man with an enormous
sense of responsibility about personal relationships; so his first question
is about his friend. That loyal *empressement*, however, is immediately
checked by the balanced twin negatives that follow: 'on his learning
that Waymarsh *was not* to arrive till evening, he *was not* wholly disconcerted': one of the diagnostic elements of irony, surely, is hyperbole
qualified with mock-scrupulousness, such as we get in 'not wholly
disconcerted'. Why there are limits to Lambert Strether's consternation
is to transpire in the next sentence; Waymarsh's telegram bespeaking
a room 'only if not noisy' is a laconic suggestion of that inarticulate
worthy's habitually gloomy expectations – from his past experiences
of the indignities of European hotel noise we adumbrate the notion
that the cost of their friendly *rencontre* may be his sleeping in the street.
In the second part of the sentence we have another similar, though
more muted, hint: 'the understanding that they should meet at

Chester rather than at Liverpool remained to that extent sound';
'to that extent', no doubt, but to *any other?* – echo seems to answer
'No'.

In the second group of sentences we are getting into Strether's mind,
and we have been prepared to relish the irony of its ambivalences. The
negatived hyperbole of 'not absolutely to desire', turns out to mean
'postpone'; and, of course, a voluntarily postponed 'enjoyment' itself
denotes a very modified rapture, although Strether's own consciousness
of the problem is apparently no further advanced than that 'he could
still wait without disappointment'. Comically loyal to what he would
like to feel, therefore, we have him putting in the consoling reflection
that 'they would dine together at the worst'; and the ambiguity of
'at the worst' is followed by the equally dubious thought: 'there was
little fear that in the sequel they shouldn't see enough of each other'.
That they should, in fact, see too much of each other; but social
decorum and Strether's own loyalties demand that the outrage of the
open statement be veiled in the obscurity of formal negation.

By the time we arrive at the climactic pair of sentences, we have
been told enough for more ambitious effects to be possible. The
twice-mentioned 'secret principle', it appears, is actually wholly
'instinctive' (line 15); but in other ways Strether is almost ludicrously
self-conscious. The qualified hyperbole of 'his business would be a
trifle bungled', underlined as it is by the alliteration, prepares us for a
half-realised image which amusingly defines Strether's sense of his role:
he sees himself, it appears, as the stage-manager of an enterprise in
which his solemn obligations as an implicated friend are counterbalanced by his equally ceremonious sense that due decorums must
also be attended to when he comes face to face with another friend of
long ago – no less a person than Europe. It is, of course, silly of him,
as James makes him acknowledge in the characteristic italicising of
'the "note" of Europe';[12] but still, he does have a comically ponderous
sense of protocol which leads him to feel that 'his business would be a
trifle bungled' should he simply arrange for this countenance to present
itself to the nearing steamer as the first 'note' of Europe. The steamer,
one imagines, would not have turned hard astern at the proximity
of Waymarsh's sacred rage; but Strether's fitness for ambassa-
dorial functions is defined by his thinking in terms of 'arranging' for a
certain countenance at the docks to give just the right symbolic
greeting.

Strether's notion of what Europe demands also shows us the force of his aesthetic sense. But in the last sentence the metaphor, though it remains equally self-conscious, changes its mode of operation from the dramatic, aesthetic, and diplomatic, to something more scientific: for, although ten years ago I should not have failed to point out, and my readers would not, I suppose, have failed to applaud, the ambiguity of 'prove', it now seems to me that we must chose between its two possible meanings. James may be using 'prove' to mean that Waymarsh's face will 'turn out to be' the 'note of Europe' for Strether. But 'prove' in this sense is intransitive, and 'to be' would have to be supplied; it therefore seems more likely that James is using 'prove' in the older sense of 'to test': Waymarsh is indeed suited to the role of being the sourly acid test of the siren songs of Europe 'in quite a sufficient degree', as Strether puts it with solemn but arch understatement.

The basic development structure of the passage, then, is one of progressive and yet artfully delayed clarification; and this pattern is also typical of James's general novelistic method. The reasons for this are suggested in the Preface to *The Princess Casamassima*, where James deals with the problem of maintaining a balance between the intelligence a character must have to be interesting, and the bewilderment which is nevertheless an essential condition of the novel's having surprise, development, and tension: 'It seems probable that if we were never bewildered there would never be a story to tell about us.'

In the first paragraph of *The Ambassadors* James apprises us both of his hero's supreme qualities and of his associated limitations. Strether's delicate critical intelligence is often blinkered by a highly vulnerable mixture of moral generosity towards others combined with an obsessive sense of personal inadequacy; we see the tension in relation to Waymarsh, as later we are to see it in relation to all his other friends; and we understand, long before Strether, how deeply it bewilders him; most poignantly about the true nature of Chad, Madame de Vionnet – and himself.

This counterpoint of intelligence and bewilderment is, of course, another reason for the split narrative point of view we've already noted; we and the narrator are inside Strether's mind, and yet we are also outside it, knowing more about Strether than he knows about himself. This is the classic posture of irony. Yet I think that to insist too exclusively on the ironic function of James's narrative point of view would be mistaken.

Irony has lately been enshrined as the supreme deity in the critical pantheon: but, I wonder, is there really anything so wonderful about being distant and objective? Who wants to see life only or mainly in intellectual terms? In art as in life we no doubt can have need of intellectual distance as well as of emotional commitment; but the uninvolvement of the artist surely doesn't go very far without the total involvement of the person; or, at least, without a deeper human involvement than irony customarily establishes. One could, I suppose, call the aesthetically perfect balance between distance and involvement, open or positive irony: but I'm not sure that humour isn't a better word, especially when the final balance is tipped in favour of involvement, of ultimate commitment to the characters; and I hope that our next critical movement will be the New Gelastics.

At all events, although the first paragraph alone doesn't allow the point to be established fully here, it seems to me that James's attitude to Strether is better described as humorous than ironical; we must learn like Maria Gostrey, to see him 'at last all comically, all tragically'. James's later novels in general are most intellectual; but they are also, surely, his most compassionate: and in this particular paragraph Strether's dilemma is developed in such a way that we feel for him even more than we smile at him. This balance of intention, I think, probably explains why James keeps his irony so quiet in tone: we must be aware of Strether's 'secret' ambivalence towards Waymarsh, but not to the point that his unawareness of it would verge on fatuity; and our controlling sympathy for the causes of Strether's ambivalence turns what might have been irony into something closer to what Constance Rourke characterises as James's typical 'low-keyed humor of defeat'.[13]

That James's final attitude is humorous rather than ironic is further suggested by the likeness of the basic structural technique of the paragraph to that of the funny story – the incremental involvement in an endemic human perplexity which can only be resolved by laughter's final acceptance of contradiction and absurdity. We don't, in the end, see Strether's probing hesitations mainly as an ironic indication by James of mankind's general muddlement; we find it, increasingly, a touching example of how, despite all their inevitable incongruities and shortcomings, human ties remain only, but still, human.

Here it is perhaps James's very slowness and deliberation throughout the narrative which gives us our best supporting evidence: greater love hath no man than hearing his friend out patiently.

III

The function of an introductory paragraph in a novel is presumably to introduce: and this paragraph surely has the distinction of being a supremely complex and inclusive introduction to a novel. It introduces the hero, of course, and one of his companions; also the time; the place; something of what's gone before. But James has carefully avoided giving up the usual retrospective beginning, that pile of details which he scornfully termed a 'mere seated mass of information'. All the details are scrupulously presented as reflections from the novel's essential centre – the narrator's patterning of the ideas going forwards and backwards in Strether's mind. Of course, this initially makes the novel more difficult, because what we probably think of as primary – event and its setting – is subordinated to what James thinks is – the mental drama of the hero's consciousness, which, of course, is not told but shown: scenically dramatised. At the same time, by selecting thoughts and events which are representative of the book as a whole, and narrating them with an abstractness which suggests their larger import, James introduces the most general themes of the novel.

James, we saw, carefully arranged to make 'Strether's first question', the first three words; and, of course, throughout the novel, Strether is to go on asking questions – and getting increasingly dusty answers. This, it may be added, is stressed by the apparent aposiopesis: for a 'first' question when no second is mentioned, is surely an intimation that more are – in a way unknown to us or to Strether – yet to come. The later dislocations of normal word order already noted above emphasise other major themes; the 'secret principle' in Strether's mind, and the antithesis Waymarsh–Europe, for instance.

The extent to which these processes were conscious on James's part cannot, of course, be resolved; but it is significant that the meeting with Maria Gostrey was interposed before the meeting with Waymarsh, which James had originally planned as his beginning in the long (20,000 word) scenario of the plot which he prepared for *Harper's*. The unexpected meeting had many advantages; not least that James could repeat the first paragraph's pattern of delayed clarification in the structure of the first chapter as a whole. On Strether's mind we get a momentously clear judgment at the end of the second paragraph: 'there was detachment in his zeal, and curiosity in his indifference'; but then the meeting with Maria Gostrey, and its gay opportunities for a much fuller presentation of Strether's mind, intervene before Waymarsh himself finally appears at the end of the chapter; only then is the joke behind Strether's uneasy hesitations in the first paragraph brought to its hilariously blunt climax: 'It was already upon him even at that distance – Mr Waymarsh was for *his* part joyless.'

One way of evaluating James's achievement in this paragraph, I suppose, would be to compare it with the opening of James's other novels, and with those of previous writers: but it would take too long to do more than sketch the possibilities of this approach. James's early openings certainly have some of the banality of the 'mere seated mass of information': in *Roderick Hudson* (1876), for example: 'Rowland Mallet had made his arrangements to sail for Europe on the 5th of September, and having in the interval a fortnight to spare, he determined to spend it with his cousin Cecilia, the widow of a nephew of his father.' Later, James showed a much more comprehensive notion of what the introductory paragraph should attempt: even in the relatively simple and concrete opening of *The Wings of the Dove* (1902): 'She waited, Kate Croy, for her father to come in, but he kept her unconscionably, and there were moments at which she showed herself, in the glass over the mantle, a face positively pale with irritation that had brought her to the point of going away without sight of him.' 'She waited, Kate Croy' – an odd parenthetic apposition artfully contrived to prefigure her role throughout the novel – to wait.

One could, I suppose, find this sort of symbolic prefiguring in the work of earlier novelists; but never, I imagine, in association with all the other levels of introductory function that James manages to combine in a single paragraph. Jane Austen has her famous thematic irony in the opening of *Pride and Prejudice* (1813): 'It is a truth universally acknowledged, that a single man in possession of a good fortune must be in want of a wife'; but pride and prejudice must come later. Dickens can hurl us overpoweringly into *Bleak House* (1852–3), into its time and place and general theme; but characters and opening action have to wait:

> London. Michaelmas Term lately over, and the Lord Chancellor sitting in Lincoln's Inn Hall. Implacable November weather. As much mud in the streets, as if the waters had but newly retired from the face of the earth, and it would not be wonderful to meet a Megalosaurus, forty feet long or so, waddling like an elephantine lizard up Holborn-Hill. Smoke lowering down from chimney-pots.

In Dickens, characteristically, we get a loud note that sets the tone, rather than a polyphonic series of chords that contain all the later melodic developments, as in James. And either the Dickens method, or the 'mere seated mass of information', seem to be commonest kinds of opening in nineteenth-century novels. For openings that suggest something of James's ambitious attempt to achieve a prologue that is a synchronic introduction of all the main aspects of the narrative, I think that Conrad is his closest rival. But Conrad, whether in expository or dramatic vein, tends to an arresting initial vigour that has dangers which James's more muted tones avoid. In *An Outcast of the Islands* (1896), for example:

> When he stepped off the straight and narrow path of his peculiar honesty, it was with an inward assertion of unflinching resolve to fall back again into the monotonous but safe stride of virtue as soon as his little excursion into the wayside quagmires had produced the desired effect. It was going to be a short episode – a sentence in brackets, so to speak, in the flowing tale of his life.

Conrad's sardonic force has enormous immediate impact; but it surely gives too much away: the character, Willems, has been dissected so vigorously that it takes great effort for Conrad – and the reader – to revivify him later. The danger lurks even in the masterly combination of physical notation and symbolic evaluation at the beginning of *Lord Jim* (1900): 'He was an inch, perhaps two, under six feet . . .': the heroic proportion is for ever missed, by an inch, perhaps two; which is perhaps too much, to begin with.

It is not for me to assess how far I have succeeded in carrying out the general intentions with which I began, or how far similar methods of analysis would be applicable to other kinds of prose. As regards the explication of the passage itself, the main argument must by now be sufficiently clear, although a full demonstration would require a much wider sampling both of other novels and of other passages in *The Ambassadors*.[14] The most obvious and demonstrable features of James's prose style, its vocabulary and syntax, are direct reflections of his attitude to life and his conception of the novel; and these features, like the relation of the paragraph to the rest of the novel, and to other novels, make clear that the notorious idiosyncrasies of Jamesian prose are directly related to the imperatives which led him to develop a narrative texture as richly complicated and as highly organised as that of poetry.

No wonder James scorned translation and rejoiced, as he so engagingly confessed to his French translator, Auguste Monod, that his later works were 'locked fast in the golden cage of the *intraduisible*'. Translation could hardly do justice to a paragraph in which so many levels of meaning and implication are kept in continuous operation; in which the usual introductory exposition of time, place, character, and previous action are rendered through an immediate immersion in the processes of the hero's mind as he's involved in preplexities which are characteristic of the novel as a whole and which are articulated in a mode of comic development which is essentially that, not only of the following chapter, but of the total structure. To have done all that is to have gone far towards demonstrating the contention which James announced at the end of the Preface to *The Ambassadors*, that 'the Novel remains still, under the right persuasion, the most independent, most elastic, most prodigious of literary forms'; and the variety and complexity of the functions carried out in the book's quite short first paragraph also suggest that, contrary to some notions, the demonstration is, as James claimed, made with 'a splendid particular economy'.

NOTES

1. This was before the appearance of the English Institute's symposium *Style in Prose Fiction* (New York, 1959), which offers, besides two general surveys and a valuable bibliography of the field, stylistic studies of six novelists, including one by Charles R. Crow, of 'The Style of Henry James: *The Wings of the Dove*'.

2. Henry James, *The Ambassadors* (Revised Collected Edition, Macmillan 1923). Since there are a few variants that have a bearing on the argument, it seems desirable to give a collation of the main editions; P is the periodical publication – *The North American Review*, CLXXVI (1903); IA the first American edition (Harper and Brothers, New York, 1903); IE the first English edition (Methuen, 1903); NY, the 'New York Edition', New York and London, 1907–9 (the London Macmillan edition used the sheets of the American edition); CR the 'Collected Revised Edition', London and New York, 1921–31 (which uses the text of the New York Edition). It should perhaps be explained that the most widely used editions in England and America make misleading claims about their text: the 'Everyman' edition claims to use the text 'of the revised Collected Edition', but actually follows the first English edition in the last variant; while the 'Anchor' edition, claiming to be 'a faithful copy of the text of the Methuen first edition', actually follows the first American edition, including the famous misplaced chapters.

l. 4.   *reply paid* NY, CR; *with the answer paid* P, IA, IE.

l. 5.   *inquirer* P, IA, IE, CR; *enquirer* NY.

l. 5.   *understanding they* NY, CR; *understanding that they* P, IA, IE.

l. 10.   *feel he* NY, CR; *feel that he* P, IA, IE.

l. 13.   *shouldn't* CR; *shouldn't* NY; *should not* P, IA, IE.

l. 14.   *newly disembarked*, all eds. except P: *newly-disembarked*.

l. 18.   *arrange for this countenance to present* NY, CR; *arrange that this countenance should present* P, IA, IE.

l. 19.   'note' of Europe CR; 'note', for him of Europe, P, 1A, 1E; 'note', of Europe, NY.

l. 20.   that it would P, 1A, NY, CR; that he would, 1E.

3. In book II, ch. 2. of *The Ambassadors*, according to R. W. Short's count, in his very useful article 'The Sentence Structure of Henry James', in *American Literature*, XVIII (March 1946) 71–88. I am also indebted to the same author's 'Henry James's World of Images', in *PMLA* LXVIII (Dec. 1953) 943–60.

4. *The American Novel and its Tradition* (New York, 1957).

5. In *London Magazine*, 1 (1954) 55–70.

6. In *Studi Americani*, II (1956) 127–42.

7. In *PMLA*, LXVI (1951) 107–23. Reprinted in this volume, pp. 52–70.

8. *The American Henry James* (New Brunswick, 1957).

9. Though consider *Rasselas*, ch. 28: 'Both conditions may be bad, but they cannot both be worst.'

10. In his Preface to *Joseph Andrews* (Rinehart Editions, New York, 1948).

11. As I have argued in 'The Ironic Tradition in Augustan Prose from Swift to Johnson', *Restoration and Augustan Prose* (Los Angeles, 1957).

12. See George Knox, 'James's Rhetoric of Quotes', in *College English*, XVII (1956) 293–7.

13. *American Humor* (1931).

14. A similar analysis of eight other paragraphs selected at fifty-page intervals revealed that, as would be expected, there is much variation: the tendency to use non-transitive verbs, and abstract nouns as subjects, for instance, seems to be strong throughout the novel, though especially so in analytic rather than narrative passages; but the frequent use of 'that' and of negative forms of statement does not recur significantly.

WILLIAM M. GIBSON

Metaphor in the Plot of
The Ambassadors (1951)

IN the course of elucidating the method and meaning of Henry James's fiction, such critics as F. O. Matthiessen, Austin Warren, and Adeline Tintner have thrown particular light on his use of works of art for compositional purposes, and have traced his developments from an early, almost unqualified worship of art for its own sake to a position in which possession of art objects without an understanding of their source and meaning in life becomes stultifying or even dangerous to the possessor.[1] From the Veronese marriage-feast of Cana of Galilee which Christopher Newman so admires to the Bronzino portrait in which Milly Theale sees herself reflected, or Strether's Lambinet, or the Chinese pagoda which Maggie Verver envisions as a symbol of her isolation from Charlotte and the Prince, it is abundantly clear that works of art, functioning metaphorically, are indispensable plot elements in James's fiction.

James's metaphors, however, include in their scope much more than art objects. They are pervasive and various. They are often sustained throughout a single novel, and when they are so linked, they contribute strongly to its structure and effect.[2] They may relate setting and character. They may define the character to which they are applied, and the consciousness which formulates them, and the relation of one character to another. They may give body to states of mind. They may dramatize discoveries, psychological tensions and conflicts. And in more complex and efficient fashion than has yet been suggested, they may aid in developing plot (both action and thought) within a single novel, particularly if it has been revised or is of the last period.

In *The Ambassadors*, here taken as representative of his later fiction, James employs metaphorical devices to two major ends: to dramatize and make vivid key stages in the developing action, and to make increasingly explicit the moral significance of Strether's experience to himself and to the reader. James was well aware of the nature of his problem in this serialized novel. His first task, and the simpler of the two posited, was to make Strether's 'fermentation', his almost total reversal of loyalty from Mrs Newsome to Madame de Vionnet, credible, and to enlist at every point the reader's sympathy for his change. The twelve long books, the carefully induced sense of time passing from March to mid-summer, the balance of 'the dramatic scene' and the 'indirect approach', the measured variations between comprehension and bewilderment all function toward this end. A number of images, occasional and sustained, function equally to dramatize the finely graduated change in Strether's allegiance.

A series of historical comparisons, for example, contributes to the continual redefinition of the essential conflict. At the beginning of Strether's adventure, he dines with Maria Gostrey and finds himself comparing her with Mrs Newsome. He had once told Mrs Newsome that she looked, with her black silk dress and her ruff, 'like Queen Elizabeth'. Now it comes over him that Maria Gostrey, bare-shouldered and with a red velvet ribbon around her throat, 'looked perhaps like Mary Stuart', and simultaneously that 'never before . . . had a lady dined with him at a public place' (I 50–2).[3] The contrast between the hot-blooded, French-born romantic and the successful, able, rather overwhelming virgin queen clarifies at once differences in the character and experience of Miss Gostrey and Mrs Newsome. Thus introduced, the historical comparisons take on added importance in the appearance of Marie de Vionnet. Early in his acquaintance with the French countess, Strether is struck by 'her rare unlikeness to the women he had known' (I 246), and is confirmed in his impression by Miss Barrace, who says, 'She's various. She's fifty women' (I 265). Late in his acquaintance, falling in love with her, he finds her still 'so odd a mixture of lucidity and mystery. . . . She spoke now as if her art were all an innocence, and then again as if her innocence were all an art' (II 115–16). He envisions her most fully as Cleopatra, in this manner:

Her head, extremely fair and exquisitely festal, was like a happy fancy, a notion of the antique, on an old precious medal, some silver coin of the Renaissance; while her slim lightness and brightness, her gaiety, her expression, her decision, contributed to an effect that might have been felt by a poet as half mythological and half conventional. He could have compared her to a goddess still partly engaged in a morning cloud, or to a sea-nymph waist-high in the summer surge. Above all she suggested to him that the *femme du monde* – in these highest developments of the type – was, like Cleopatra in the play, indeed various and multifold (I 270–1).

Strether's voyage will indeed end in shipwreck for his listening to this sea-nymph's singing. But the point is simply that for him 'age cannot stale, nor custom wither her infinite variety'. Finally Madame de Vionnet's tragic, ungovernable passion is embodied, again with an historical parallel, in Strether's last encounter with her: 'His hostess was dressed as for thunderous times . . . in simplest coolest white, of a character so old-fashioned, if he were not mistaken, that Madame Roland must on the scaffold have worn something like it' (II 275). Strether's perception of the beauty of his titled hostess is never sharper than at this moment, when he wonders how 'a creature so fine could be, by mysterious forces, a creature so exploited' (II 284) and discovers that she is 'afraid for her life'.

If Madame de Vionnet, then, is like Cleopatra various and multifold, Mrs Newsome and her ambassador daughter are, like Queen Elizabeth, relatively simple and, above all, cold. Upon the arrival of Sarah Pocock, we learn much from her manner, the 'dry glitter that recalled to [Strether] a fine Woollett winter morning' (II 96). Sarah's essential coldness thus links her strikingly to Strether's final vision of Mrs Newsome as 'all . . . fine cold thought' (II 222). This final vision is developed in conversation between Maria and Strether, for whom the 'whole moral and intellectual being or block' looms larger and larger until Strether absently echoes, 'I see it all', while, James adds, 'his eyes might have been fixing some particularly large iceberg in a cool blue northern sea' (II 223). The single developing metaphor here summarizes for the reader Strether's relationship to Mrs Newsome, for in it may be perceived her temperamental coldness, her resistance to change, her limited integrity, and her unmoving force. The meaning of the discovery for Strether is summed up in Miss Gostrey's eminently Jamesian comment, 'Well, intensity with ignorance – what do you want worse?' (II 225).

The reader, of course, is quite aware that Mrs Newsome and Mrs Pocock are not merely cold or passive. Jim Pocock has already warned Strether: 'Do you know what they are? They're about as intense as they can live. . . . They don't lash about and shake the cage . . . and it's at feeding-time that they're quietest. But they always get there' (II 86). This caged-beast figure, often evident in the late fiction and used to pronounced and sustained effect in *The Golden Bowl*, plainly warns Strether and the reader that a violent break with Sarah and her mother may be in the making.

A golden-nail image and a boat image recurrently serve to delineate Strether's movement from action and America to observation and Europe. On Strether's first committing himself to her cause, Marie de Vionnet thanks him, and, James notes, 'with her subtlety sensitive on the spot to an advantage, she had driven in by a single word a little golden nail'. Some weeks and thirty pages later, Strether obligates himself to see both Chad and Madame de Vionnet through. Again she thanks Strether, and, James adds, 'The golden nail she had then driven in pierced a good inch deeper' (1 276: 11 23). Similarly, Strether's progress in the interest of the countess is figured in a sustained boat image. In sequent scenes, Waymarsh deserts Strether's boat for Mrs Newsome's; Madame de Vionnet publicly draws Strether into her boat; Strether remaining in it is conscious of the vessel's movement; and Strether then becomes so bewildered that his remembered figure will no longer suffice for his sense of advance and change.[4] It is unlikely that these consciously linked and recalled boat images prefigure Strether's discovery of Chad and Marie de Vionnet on the river outside Paris: James, on the other hand, may well have intended a wry contrast of this crucial episode with Strether's innocuous hour on a *bateau-mouche* with Maria Gostrey, later in Paris.

The germ or *donnée* for *The Ambassadors* is impressive in its first notation by James in his notebook, in the 'scenario', and in the discussion of its development in the preface. But its full effect is not apparent until James gives it climactic statement near the center of the novel, in an evocative garden setting and with its own metaphorical development. Just as the like passage in Thoreau's *Walden* derives much of its force from the compressed metaphors of the savage's hunger, the Spartan's in-fighting, the New England farmer's scything skill, so James has Strether deliver his injunction to little Bilham by means of two homely metaphors wholly appropriate to the mild, self-conscious New Englander. Strether dramatizes for his young, compatriot his own sense of time and opportunity lost, thus:

It's not too late for *you*, on any side, and you don't strike me as in danger of missing the train; besides which people can in general be pretty well trusted, of course – with the clock of their freedom ticking as loud as

it seems to here – to keep an eye on the fleeting hour. All the same don't
forget that you're young . . . live up to it. Live all you can; it's a mistake
not to. . . . Oh, I *do* see, at least; and more than you could believe or I
can express. It's too late. And it's as if the train had fairly waited at the
station for me without my having had the gumption to know it was there.
Now I hear its faint receding whistle miles and miles down the line. What
one loses, one loses; make no mistake about that. (II 217–18)

The familiar idea of 'missing the train' expands to include the ticking
of the big station clock at Strether's back and the mournful 'faint
receding whistle miles and miles down the line' as he stands disappointed on the platform. The heightened sensibility of the older
man then produces a further image and warning:

The affair – I mean the affair of life – couldn't, no doubt, have been
different for me; for it's at the best a tin mould, either fluted and embossed,
with ornamental excrescences, or else smooth and dreadfully plain, into
which, a helpless jelly, one's consciousness is poured – so that one 'takes'
the form, as the great cook says, and is more or less compactly held by it:
one lives in fine as one can. Still, one has the illusion of freedom; therefore,
don't be, like me, without the memory of that illusion. (II 218)

Depressed and exalted both, yet still lucid, ironic, and imaginative,
Strether for the moment falls back on his Puritan forebears' idea of a
'dark necessity'.[5] But it is not on this note that he ends, as he says:
'Do what you like so long as you don't make *my* mistake. For it was
a mistake. Live!' Imperatives, short sentences, frequent pauses give the
passage colloquial directness. But much of its memorable force and the
conviction that Strether is wound-up to a high pitch are derived from
the developed, assimilated images of the train, the station clock, and the
cook's tin mould.

These are some of the major metaphors which James coined to
intensify internal conflict over personal allegiances. With the same
regard for organic fitness, James chooses his settings and elaborates
them metaphorically in order to reveal step by step the moral significance of Strether's whole experience.

Thus the recurrent balcony scenes, like certain of the images, mark
stages of Strether's learning 'to toddle alone', of his voyage from
innocence to experience. It is proper to Strether as fine central consciousness that James should create within him awareness of the related
meanings of these four scenes, with explicit avowals of their connection

and significance in the third and fourth. Each of these balcony episodes embodies a major discovery or decision for Strether and together they chart the rise and fall of his sense of freedom and of the value of youth, whether little Bilham's, Mamie's, his own, or Chad's.

Strether's first visit to Chad's third floor on the Boulevard Malesherbes, with its fine continuous balcony, ends with the simple action of his crossing the street and entering. But this action has been preceded by his lingering and looking, by a turmoil within his mind of wonder and discovery. For Strether it represents a real decision and a real step forward. He is choosing for the first time between Woollett and Paris; between returning to Waymarsh and the 'indoor chill, glass-roofed court and slippery staircase' of his secondary hotel, and meeting Chad's 'very young' friend who has been smoking on the balcony of Chad's admirable house, its fair gray stone 'warmed and polished a little by life' and its windows open to the 'violet air' of the early spring morning. James's tableau places Strether across the street and three floors down from the 'perched privacy' of little Bilham; separated, wondering, and even a little envious. So the balcony, 'the distinguished front testified suddenly, for Strether's fancy, to something that was up and up; they placed the whole case materially, and as by an admirable image, on a level he found himself at the end of another moment rejoicing to think he might reach' (1 98).

Strether takes another stride forward in his adventure, after the Pococks' arrival, when he discovers 'beautiful, brilliant, unconscious Mamie' alone and unaware of his presence one fine afternoon on the balcony of the Pococks' hotel suite. In the very attitude of little Bilham, 'with her arms on the balustrade and her attention dropped to the street, she allowed Strether to watch her . . . without her turning around' (1 146). Mamie, it becomes clear, has been waiting for Mr Bilham, and this perception for Strether brings 'a fresh flower of fancy . . . to bloom'. Talking with her, he discovers simply that Mamie has accomplished a change of base; unlike Sarah and Jim she knows perfectly what has become of Chad; she is now 'on the side and of the party of Mrs Newsome's original ambassador . . . in *his* interest, and not in Sarah's'. Prepared to save Chad by marrying him and reforming him, she has seen that Chad has already been reformed, and her unavowed desertion of the Woollett cause, her outspoken praise of Jeanne and Marie de Vionnet, render her behavior admirable and show her as young, generous and 'disinterestedly tender' (1 55).

Both these episodes prepare the reader for Strether's return to Chad's balcony three months later, on a hot night in June, immediately after Sarah Pocock's break with him. He sits in an easy chair with a lemon-colored French novel at hand, waiting for Chad to return, and finds himself 'in possession as he never yet had been'. He spends a long time on the balcony, hanging over it 'as he had seen little Bilham hang the day of his first approach, as he had seen Mamie hang over her own the day little Bilham himself might have seen her from below' (II 229). Strether's sense of freedom here reaches a high point, and this ease in turn recalls to him 'the youth of his own he had long ago missed' (II 230). By now, apparently, Strether *has* reached the level of the 'mystic troisième'. Here, if anywhere, Strether has freed himself from the New England 'failure to enjoy', and has acquired the 'common unattainable art of taking things as they came' (I 83). When Chad returns, the two men talk and smoke reflectively on the balcony 'as if their high place really represented some moral elevation from which they could look down on their recent past' (II 235). From the conversation three discoveries develop: that the Pococks came out to save Strether rather than Chad; that Strether may indeed be 'dished'; and that Chad and Strether have largely reversed their former positions as to Chad's return to Woollett. The total sense of the episode, then, is one of freedom and a renewal of youthful esthetic ambitions for Strether, premonitions of disaster troubling him scarcely at all. It is notable that his day in the country and the shattering of his belief in a 'virtuous attachment' follow immediately.

In the final balcony episode Strether must perform a last labor before he has done with his ambassadorship. As he approaches the house, he recalls the 'accident of little Bilham's appearance on the balcony . . . at the moment of his first visit' and feels 'as if his last day were oddly copying his first' (II 304–5), because Chad, in little Bilham's attitude, leans on the rail and looks down at him, his cigarette glowing in the darkness. Strether climbs the stairs, puffing a little and resting at the landings, to exact from Chad a promise that he will never forsake Marie de Vionnet. Chad's polite protestations, his new interest in the 'art' of advertisement, and his unmitigated youth lead Strether to the double realization that 'Chad is only Chad, for all his polish an uncertain moral quantity', and that he has missed his own life. He feels ancient and weary: 'Verily, verily, his labour had been lost' (II 266).

James places these four scenes in Parts Second, Ninth, Eleventh, and

Twelfth. If one adds to this series the related scene in the theater box of Part Third, it is apparent that the five balanced scenes serve James efficiently in making an almost complete reversal of loyalty for Strether credible, necessary, and moving. Each scene drives the action forward a notch and each is basically related to the germinal, centrally placed idea of the novel, 'Live all you can, it's a mistake not to.'

Quite as rich in meaning as these balcony scenes are the images and pictures which Madame de Vionnet's apartment and the city of Paris present to Strether's widening consciousness. On his second morning in the city, Paris hung before Strether, 'the vast bright Babylon, like some huge iridescent object, a jewel brilliant and hard, in which parts were not to be discriminated nor differences comfortably marked. It twinkled and trembled and melted together, and what seemed all surface one moment seemed all depth the next' (I 89). As we have seen, Madame de Vionnet was 'an obscure person, a muffled person one day, and a showy person, an uncovered person the next', a goddess, a sea-nymph, a *femme du monde*, Cleopatra (I 270-1). She is equally at home in the shadows of Notre Dame or the 'bright clean ordered water-side life' of a restaurant on the Seine. It is not by accident, certainly, that elements of mystery and complexity in Strether's perception of Paris reappear in the images used to describe the person of the Comtesse de Vionnet.

One notes, furthermore, that Marie de Vionnet's apartment appeals more and more strongly to Strether's esthetic and historic sense, as he commits himself to her cause and falls in love with her. On his first visit 'the house, to his restless sense, was in the high homely style of an elder day, and the ancient Paris he was always looking for' (I 243). The whole apartment reminds him of hereditary possession, of taste, of transmission. On a later occasion this first impression is strengthened as Strether is taking leave:

> Her noble old apartment offered a succession of three [rooms], the first two of which indeed, on entering, smaller than the last, but each with its faded and formal air, enlarged the office of the antechamber and enriched the sense of approach. Strether fancied them, liked them, and passing through them with her more slowly now, met a sharp renewal of his original impression. He stopped, he looked back; the whole thing made a vista, which he found high melancholy and sweet – full once more, of dim historic shades, of the faint far-away cannon-roar of the great Empire.
> (II 125)

The description of the three rooms clearly suggests a perspective into the past, into the history of Paris, itself an epitome of France. Madame de Vionnet's 'beautiful formal room' figures a third time in Strether's last encounter with her. He might have proposed for their meeting the 'cold hospitality of his own *salon de lecture*' (II 271), in which the chill of Sarah Pocock's last visit still seemed to linger, but he knows that half the value of meeting Madame de Vionnet again will be in 'seeing her where he had seen her best'. The candles glimmer over the chimney-piece 'like the tall tapers of an altar', Marie de Vionnet now seems less exempt from the touch of time, and indeed Strether comes to see that in the future he will look back 'as on the view of something old, old, old, the oldest thing he had ever personally touched' (II 274, 276).

James says in his 'Project' for the novel: 'Singularly, admirably, Mme de Vionnet comes after a little to stand, with Strether, for most of the things that make the charm of civilization as he now revises and imaginatively reconstructs, morally reconsiders, so to speak, civilization.'[6] The jewel image of Paris with the richly varied images applied to Marie de Vionnet, and the three scenes set in her ancient house, then, work contrapuntally. Strether's increasing passion for France and the past symbolizes the infinitely various countess. Strether's falling in love with Marie de Vionnet symbolizes his growing sense of Paris, France, and the past.

One further use of metaphorical setting remains for analysis. Because James was fond of the freshness and spaciousness of European parks and gardens and their mingling of art and nature, he made dominant use of them as settings in his fiction. Even in his criticism he may remark, as in the essay on Balzac, that 'the great garden of life presented itself to him absolutely and exactly in the guise of the great garden of France, a subject vast and comprehensive enough, yet with definite edges and corners',[7] or as in the Preface to *The Ambassadors* that 'Art deals with what we see, it must first contribute full-handed that ingredient; it plucks its material, otherwise expressed, in the garden of life – which material elsewhere is stale and uneatable'. William Troy has observed that the garden scenes in James's novels, notably *The Portrait of a Lady*, are intended to remind the reader of the garden of Eden.[8] This is strikingly true in *The Ambassadors*. The four major garden scenes of the novel (in Parts First, Second, Fifth, Eleventh) constitute crucial stages in Strether's eating of the fruit of the tree; and his enrichment in knowledge of the world, of good and evil, is certainly one of the 'values infinitely precious' sealed up with the 'old Paris garden' which James speaks of in his Preface when he is recalling his *donnée*.

In the opening pages, Strether enjoys the ordered English garden of his hotel at Chester, and strolling through it with Maria Gostrey 'feels such a consciousness of personal freedom as he hadn't known for years' (I 4). This scene serves as a prelude to Strether's sitting to rest in the Luxembourg gardens a few days later. Here the 'cup of his impressions seemed truly to overflow' and he feels free and young as he had never expected to again. Seen the day before in booksellers' windows, tempting 'lemon-colored volumes . . . fresh as fruit on the tree' have been reminding him of his youthful passion for letters and the 'temple of taste that he had dreamed of raising up' (I 80, 86, 87) on his return from Europe in the sixties. (They remind him as well of the drab green covers of the Woollett journal of economics, politics and ethics which he had been editing for Mrs Newsome as her 'tribute to the ideal'.) It here comes to him that 'Everything he wanted was comprised . . . in a single boon – the common unattainable art of taking things as they came' (I 83).

Then in the sculptor Gloriani's 'queer old garden' Strether fully realizes for the first time how far he has failed to live, and delivers himself of the eloquent injunction to little Bilham to 'live all you can'. In this earthly paradise, it is true, runs an undercurrent of insolence and lurks the possibility of a cold betrayal; Strether feels this as 'a waft from the jungle' (I 219) while he watches the Duchess and Gloriani and envies Chad's ease in the great world. But this bird-haunted garden full of the sense of art, of tradition, and of Old Paris is chiefly the place of Strether's meeting the Comtesse de Vionnet, the symbol of what he has *not* lived for, and in his final judgment, 'the finest and subtlest creature, the happiest apparition, it had been given to him, in all his years, to meet' (II 286).

Strether's most startling revelation, finally, comes to him while he is in a garden within a garden: that is, the garden of a village inn at the heart of rural France. In this richly pictorial, climactic book, Strether feels freer and younger than he ever will again. The softly colored French countryside he views all day as through the frame of a small painting by Lambinet which he wanted to buy, but could not afford, in the Boston of his youth. The Pococks have retreated, and his relationship to Marie de Vionnet trembles on the edge of courtship, with Chad almost forgotten. The mood of Strether's whole idle, restful, intensely pleasant day is the mood of Eden before the fall, and it has been firmly prepared for by the three garden scenes preceding it. Here in this fresh, idyllic setting Strether feels the conditions of his day as *the thing . . .* even to a greater degree than Madame de Vionnet's old high salon where the ghost of the Empire walked' (II 253). But here he also discovers the truth: that the attachment of Chad Newsome and Marie de Vionnet is not a virtuous one, that she has been and still is Chad's mistress. He 'kept making of it that there had been simply a *lie* in the charming affair – a lie on which one could now, detached and deliberate, perfectly place one's finger' (II 262-3).

The overtones of Eden in these four related garden scenes (with perhaps a faint echo in Maria Gostrey's 'scrap of old garden' in the epilog) would seem to accord wholly with the revealed moral significance of Strether's adventure. James is unable to praise 'a fugitive and cloister'd vertue', innocence which is untried. Strether is thus like James's post-Civil War American – the good American in his essay on Hawthorne: he 'has eaten of the tree of knowledge' and he attains stature only as he acquires, however painfully, knowledge of the world and of good and evil.

The apparently disparate images and scenes of *The Ambassadors* are scarcely hinted at in James's 'Project' for the novel. Exactly applied, metaphorically enriched, related, and often extended throughout the novel they nonetheless form an essential element of James's meaning when he explained at the end of his 'Project': 'Here again I have something that I can't fully trot out for you; here again I can only put in the picture with a single touch of the brush. It will be brushed in another fashion in its order and proper light . . . everything will in fact be in its place and of its kind.'[9]

NOTES

1. 'James and the Plastic Arts', in *Kenyon Review*, V (Autumn 1943) 544-50; 'Myth and Dialectic in the Later Novels', in *Kenyon Review*, V 551-68; 'The Spoils of Henry James', *PMLA* LXI (March 1946) 239-51.

I wish to thank my former honors student, Edwin N. Perrin, for several insights developed in this article and first formulated in his honors study of James's metaphor in the late novels.

2. Citing the art metaphors, Adeline Tintner demonstrates their organic function especially well in *The Portrait of a Lady* and *The Golden Bowl*.

3. *The Ambassadors* (New York, 1909); the 'New York Edition'. Hereafter referred to only by volume and page. Although two chapters are transposed in this edition (and all other American editions), it is cited because the correctly ordered text of the first edition published in England is not easily available and because the reversed chapters do not affect the conclusions drawn in this article. See Leon Edel, in *American Literature*, XXIII (March 1951) 128–30.

4. II 64–5, 94, 111, 130. Strether's figure for his state of mind just before seeing Chad for the last time is that he was 'well in port, the outer sea behind him, and it was only a matter of getting ashore' (II 294). These rather mechanical boat images anticipate the remarkable sustained marriage-boat imagery of *The Golden Bowl* and the closely related set of equilibrium figures.

5. Compare Strether's metaphor at the end of the novel: 'He found on the spot the image of his recent history; he was like one of the figures of the old clock at Berne. *They* came out, on one side, at their hour, jigged along their little course in the public eye, and went in on the other side' (II 322).

6. *Hound and Horn*, VII (April-June 1934) 556; *The Notebooks of Henry James*, ed. F. O. Matthiessen and Kenneth B. Murdock (New York, 1947) p. 396.

7. *Notes on Novelists* (New York, 1914) p. 112.

8. William Troy, 'The Altar of Henry James', reprinted in this volume, pp. 46–51.

9. *The Notebooks of Henry James*, pp. 414, 415.

WALTER WRIGHT

Maggie Verver: Neither Saint Nor Witch (1957)

REALITY and myth have always been restless in their literary wedlock. We need myth, of course, to find order in reality, but we are constantly tempted to use it to oversimplify the reality we are seeking. A remarkable example appears in the diverse interpretations of Henry James's *The Golden Bowl*. Critics of the novel have often been at war as to the appropriate myth, and they have contorted reality to make it conform.

James himself saw life under the shadow of myth, and he chose the names and the features of many of his characters in accord with established folk and literary associations. Because he needed perspectives, he accepted the basic concepts which came to him out of the past. It has always been men's habit to give their longings and their anxieties palpable form. Hence come witches, beasts in the jungle, lares and penates, perfect crystals, Adam and Eve, the symbolic discovery of new worlds, the transformation of souls into illuminated altars. James used these images and myths. As revealed in his letters and notebooks, he was sometimes willing to take them in their most stereotyped form. In fact, the myth of the antithesis of the old world, Europe, and the new, America, was for him at first hardly more than a shallow, arbitrary simplification. So, too, were the myth of Puritanism as spiritual fetters and the concept of estheticism as a parasitic growth.

But these hastily accepted analogies bear the same resemblance to the best of James's fiction as do some of the little anecdotal scenarios in his notebooks, anecdotes which suggest casual half-truths, with no hint of the wisdom into which they were to be transmuted. The pleasure which James took in artistic creation was in giving, as he once remarked, another 'turn of the screw'. His works are not to be interpreted merely in stereotyped symbols, and they cannot always be classified under the usual descriptions of tragedy or simple romance. For James, as for

Meredith, reality was not to be sacrificed for artistic simplicity; instead, art must show its validity by illuminating reality.

The Golden Bowl has remained one of the most controversial of James's major works because it deals with untraditional substances and, since the novelist was careful not to pronounce his meaning explicitly, a critic is easily led to assume James's tacit agreement with his own conventional, even stereotyped, interpretation. There have been two types of oversimplification of the novel, depending on the dominant myth or literary convention chosen by the interpreters. The extreme of one makes Maggie, the heroine, virtually a saint or even the personification of Divine Grace. She has never known evil before her marriage; she learns of it as she becomes more and more certain that her husband, Amerigo, is having an affair with her close friend, and now stepmother, Charlotte; and through her perfect love she leads her husband to repent and return to the ways of virtue.[1] There are two unsatisfactory aspects to this religious mythological interpretation. First of all, the evidence does not bear it out. Take, for example, Maggie's wish, in chapter 32: 'If Charlotte, while she was about it, could only have been *worse*! – that idea Maggie fell to invoking instead of the idea that she might desirably have been better.' The wish is very human and, under the circumstances, quite forgivable, but it is not an expression of love. Secondly, Maggie's story, so interpreted, does not make a novel. One could tolerate a short, essentially lyrical presentation of such a heroine as Maggie would need to be. But even the life of the sweet-natured Milly Theale, of *The Wings of the Dove*, is much more complex and hence interesting than such a Maggie, as the central character in the second half of *The Golden Bowl* could possibly be. Moreover, even in medieval allegory the moral transformation of a character, in this case Amerigo, demanded focus on him rather than on what went on in the mind of another mortal. There would be no justification of long passages on her own mental conflict if Maggie merely confronted evil in another person. Such an interpretation makes the novel a simple religious romance or even an allegory; it has no place for a psychological flaw in the heroine – a flaw that might bring tragedy.

A less extreme view, dependent on traditional literary motif rather than on religion, parallels the religious, though with no invoking of grace. It maintains that Maggie, a good wife, sees that she is about to lose her husband to a rival and so she sets out with all her skill to fight for her rights and the cause of virtue. She is justified in so doing, and her story ends with her success.[2] We thus have a simple, conventional love triangle and a simple victory of good over evil, with a conventional reward. Such an explication, based on the secular myth of poetic justice, the triumph of virtue in worldly affairs, likewise reduces the novel to a contest in which the heroine fights against *external* evil. Not only does this, like the religious view, make irrelevant all the turmoil inside Maggie by turning her into a static agent of ingenuity; it, too, poses ethical questions. There are rules even in championing virtue, and they do not accord with some of the thoughts that go through Maggie's mind. Again it is the potentially tragic aspect of Maggie's struggle which this view overlooks.

The evidence against both these related approaches has been pounced upon by Joseph Firebaugh, and to a lesser degree by others, to make of Maggie a creature not of virtue but of evil. In the most extreme interpretation her history is the ironic presentation of witchcraft or of the intrusion of Satan – represented by Maggie and her father – into the Garden of Eden.[3] If we put Maggie's case in the crudest possible form, by lifting incidents from context and giving an unfavorable résumé of the general pattern of her life, we may find that she is the spoiled daughter of a seemingly meek but actually ruthless agressor, who uses his money to buy whatever he wants. He purchases Maggie a prince for husband – for by any interpretation the Prince recognizes the financial considerations in his marrying Maggie; otherwise he might have married Charlotte. Maggie regards her husband as her possession – James considered the attempt to possess another soul as a supreme evil. Adam, with Maggie's encouragement, purchases Charlotte as a work of art and a protection against the marriage designs of other women. He controls Charlotte with faint tugs on a silken halter – several times mentioned in the novel – and Maggie delights with a witch's malice in the power she has over both Charlotte and Amerigo. She finally manages to force Charlotte into the presumably horrible exile of American City, while she herself overmasters Amerigo and has him as a helpless possession at the close. She represents evil destroying all attempts to live, to be free. And the justification of the novel is that James is being bitterly ironic on the evils of American materialism and Puritanism. The evidence can be quoted, provided that one ignores all else, and, above all, provided that one considers Maggie, as in each of the other two interpretations, as a static creature

and forgets the important fact that in a Jamesian story we are never
finished on any point until the last line. James would be most unhappy
to be quoted without regard to the progression of the action.

Moreover, James knew very well how to tell a good tale of witchcraft. In 'Europe' every sentence about Mrs Rimmle shows the horror
of her witchlike tyranny over her daughters and the sheer hell of her
own wretched existence. As a psychological writer he was interested
less in the harm that a sinister mind did to others, diabolical though
this might be, than in the mad anarchy, the abysmal isolation, within
that mind itself.

Let us return to Maggie. We have to learn a great deal about the
Prince and certain essential facts about Charlotte and Adam before
we can understand Maggie, because we see Maggie primarily in so far
as she is preoccupied with her relations with them. Mainly we want
to know what they represent to Maggie, and we find that before the
end of the novel they come to mean for her what all our objective
evidence should make them mean for us. And we find why she cannot
break spiritually from any of the three, why, in fact, she needs them,
imperfect though they are. She needs them because she also is imperfect,
because she lacks understanding and must come of age.

When both Adam and Mr Assingham say that Maggie has never
known evil,[4] and Adam that she must not learn of it, they place her
in the Garden of Eden, and the only direction open to a dramatic novel
requires that she eat of the fruit of the tree of knowledge.[5] She is no
more a saint than Eve, nor is she a witch. She is simply, so far as the
action of this novel is concerned, a wholesome, sensitive, ignorant girl.
She is sufficiently noble in personality to demand our sympathy. She
is highly perceptive, as are James's other protagonists, because James
wanted to determine all he could about life, and he could do so only
by imagining the thoughts and impressions of a sensitive mind. In his
Preface to *The Princess Casamassima* James later wrote, 'I should note
the extent to which these persons [Amerigo, Maggie, *et al.*] are so far
as their other passions permit, intense *perceivers*, all, of their respective
predicaments.' Maggie is capable of understanding. When, in the same
preface James insisted that a character not be too knowing, he meant –
as did Conrad in his use of a perplexed, truth-seeking Marlow – to
learn and assist the reader in learning by following a good human
mind through its experimental quest for knowledge. Maggie is in a
general way therefore comparable to Othello or to other tragic heroes

in that she has a flaw – the flaw of ignorance, with the concomitant tendency to substitute an inferior illusion of an ideal for the much better reality of actual life. The basic difference between her and Othello is that, like most people, she manages to avoid absolute disaster, and then, again like most of us, to find resilience to start up again.

Maggie is selfish, but her selfishness is normal. We have no right to ask whether down through the years, as a rich girl, she should have learned to think more of others. We do not imagine either Eve or Venus as a child; they appear before us suddenly without a past. But even if we were to have a biography of Maggie's childhood and it were to include many incidents in which in one respect or another she ate the fruit of knowledge, she could still be ignorantly selfish in respect to the action of the novel. What matters for us is that the evidence about the selfishness of both father and daughter comes early from Adam, later mainly from Maggie's own self-analysis, and it comes because they have wrestlings of conscience. The selfishness is unavoidable because they have had no experience in imagining what goes on in the consciousness of others. They know only their own little world of two planets revolving around each other.

They are not sinister in intent. They are also not, as they have been called, malevolent 'do-gooders'. They are, of course, capable of thoughtless cruelty. Even so, the silken halter with which Maggie sees Charlotte being led and the cage in which she imagines her confined are not objective evidence of Adam's callousness. The images show rather Maggie's awakening pity; and, viewed objectively, they characterize the pathetic circumstances into which Charlotte, because of her own nature, her willingness to subjugate her feelings for the sake of security has wandered. By the very act of marrying Adam she pledged herself to sacrifice, and we cannot imagine Adam's being able to to do anything to free her. She is destined to melancholy. Nor can Maggie by a mere voluntary act extricate the Prince from any cage. In marrying her he imposed restrictions upon himself. No matter what Maggie might do, he would still know that he married with concern for money and that he assumed obligations in return. Maggie may come to pity him as a possession, but he wrote the contract in his own conscience.

Maggie is ignorant, but she has a capacity for appreciation. She naturally thinks in terms of the one element of the past that is projected into the story, the quest for art. We are to suppose that she and Adam have fair, though not exquisite, taste in art. They want to possess beauty and to be beautiful in conduct. Christopher Newman, in *The American*, is drawn to Madame de Cintré because of the aura of refinement of a strange new world which surrounds her. Strether finds in Madame de Vionnet a beauty refined by sorrow, a civilization maintained by the utmost effort of the mind. Maggie similarly is drawn to Charlotte. She has known only enough to be aware that Charlotte has suffered and that she has studied to live a poised, graceful life. Her highest praise for her – and, for that matter, for Adam – is habitually in language she would use for a work of art.

Likewise, when she marries him, she is ignorant of nearly everything about the Prince. Yet he has an air of melancholy grace and seems to live in a strange world, very different from her own. Maggie is drawn toward him, too, in terms of what she can understand. Stransom, another imperfect but percipient Jamesian protagonist, at one time almost wishes that his friends will die. When he lights candles for the dead he can imagine them as he wants them. Maggie, too, would like to have Charlotte and the Prince as securely arranged as sculpture. Then she will be safe with them; they will retain their strange charm but never destroy her old, familiar world which she has known with her father. She is both fascinated and afraid. She would have her husband, yet refuse to abandon the habits of thinking which have no relation to the world he represents.

What gives Maggie significance is the struggle within her and the final resolution of that civil war. In fact, if Charlotte remained merely a quiet, patient friend and the Prince a patient, enduring husband, Maggie would never grow up. She would have both of them as static as works of art in her mind, and they would never cause her to use her imagination. It is only by internal upheaval that the old world can be reshaped into a new; and the upheaval must be induced by the very worst, the most shocking, experience that Maggie can suffer. James did not invent such a concept of plot; it is ancient in literature because it is true to life.

For Maggie the worst possible shock is knowledge of her husband's adultery, not necessarily in the legal sense, but in the realm of the affections. Her distress is not based on so-called puritan moral prudery or subservience to conventions. James uses the language of decorum to describe what others might put in a blunt, unreflecting way. Maggie sees the life of her father, Amerigo, Charlotte, and herself as 'arranged'.

All four are riding 'in a train' together. Both before and after her
suspicions are aroused she senses their relationships in images of groups.
All four are together, or the other three are and she is outside, or
Charlotte is the one outside, or her father or the Prince is alone. Put
crudely, her concern for herself is jealousy. Put more philosophically,
it represents man's desperate need to identify himself completely in
his universe, to feel that he is inseparable from it, essential to it. Maggie
suddenly feels shunted aside, an unnecessary object, a burden.

What follows is a battle that merits comparison with that undergone
by Othello. It is as violent as the most savage struggle of a barbarian.
In the midst of the tumult Maggie at times envies and at other times
gloats. She is stricken with panic and convulsed in self-pitying abjection.
But the more bitter the provocation to despair – which would mean
an open accusation, a crashing of two marriages, and a scattering of
wrecked souls, including her own – the more remarkable are the forces
which come to her rescue. If she hates Charlotte, she must cast away
the excellence she has represented; and Charlotte has never appeared
more excellent than in meeting all the forms demanded of her as
Adam's wife and Maggie's friend. So, too, has the Prince. Moreover,
Maggie's discipline in decorum makes her reject the image of ruthless
revenge:

> She might fairly . . . have yearned . . . for the straight vindictive view,
> the rights of resentment, the rages of jealousy, the protests of passion, as
> for something she had been cheated of not least: a range of feelings which
> for many women would have meant so much, but which for *her* husband's
> wife, for *her* father's daughter, figured nothing nearer to experience than a
> wild eastern caravan, looming into view with crude colours in the sun,
> fierce pipes in the air, high spears against the sky, all a thrill, a natural joy
> to mingle with, but turning off short, before it reached her and plunging
> into other defiles. (ch. 36)

In fighting her unhappy thoughts Maggie comes suddenly outside
herself. When she thinks intensely of Charlotte as having wronged
her – and she has justification for so doing – she cannot escape the
image of Charlotte as a pathetic creature in a cage or as a helpless
animal at bay; and she sees, too, how lonely and bored the Prince
must be. The struggle is not one short, simple battle, for in life itself
evil spirits are usually not exorcised from the mind in one brief contest.
Several times Maggie is on the verge of apparent victory, the admission
of dependence on the love of the husband whom she insists that she

loves, but each time she draws back from the admission and so remains alone.[6] On each occasion except the last of all there could really be no true victory because the Prince, too, is still lacking in understanding. Neither dares make an overture to the other, beyond timid, ambiguous gestures, as they are unsure both of themselves and of each other.

What saves Maggie? Charlotte and the Prince, as Maggie increasingly realizes, must have great self-discipline to adhere as they do to the 'forms'.[7] More important is the fact that in a crisis the forms do come to one's rescue; they help Maggie in the midst of her mental bewilderment. When she is in confusion, knowing that she has been badly sinned against yet wondering about her own selfishness, about her possible cruelty to Charlotte and the Prince, her habitual concern for decorum carries her through. In *Typhoon* Conrad stressed Captain MacWhirr's insistence upon proper order; matches, for example, must have a definite location. During the typhoon MacWhirr finds them in their proper place, and he is steadied by the familiar experience. Maggie, likewise, is steadied by the outer, familiar forms. There are certain things which a woman of Maggie's position and pretensions must do; the very world of art in which she shapes her own life and judges Charlotte and Amerigo as if they were works of art is a world in which tensions, however violent, are held in control so that the surface remains almost tranquil. However chaotic the battle within, Maggie will not take part in a vulgar clash, but will turn the 'caravan' aside. She will imitate the poise and artistic grace which she finds in Charlotte and the Prince and which she knows manifest self-sacrifice and self-control.

When she is at her lowest point of doubt, her admiration of the Prince and Charlotte helps her.[8] More and more she comes to imagine what life must be to them, and in so doing she ceases to be terrified by her own loneliness and to pity them for theirs. She senses poignantly Amerigo's compassion for Charlotte. She can see why he should want to get away 'from that constant strain of the perfunctory to which he was exposed at Fawns', and she can visualize, too, his desolation in his rooms in London. She is beginning to appreciate the depth which accounts for the outer Prince, the work of art she has admired and thought she possessed. Most wonderful of all, having previously been determined to believe in his duplicity, she discovers in him the very opposite: 'then it came over her that he had, after all, a simplicity, very considerable, on which she had never dared to presume' (ch. 12). She also becomes more sympathetically aware of Charlotte's invisible cage and of her obedience to the silken halter. Whilst she is still ambivalent in her feelings toward Charlotte, and while she is indulging in self-pity, she suddenly thinks of herself as the possible bearer of tidings that should lead Amerigo to show special kindness to Charlotte. More frequently by now she succeeds in escaping from her isolation as she thinks of the isolation of the others.

Early in the first part of the novel, where the focus is on the Prince, he tells Mrs Assingham that he has something that 'sufficiently passes' for a moral sense, though it lacks the strength of the Americans' moral code. His moral standard agrees with James's own in that he does not want to cause needless pain. Later, James speaks of the 'sovereign law' which is to guide Amerigo and Charlotte; it is 'never rashly to forget and never consciously to wound'. Amerigo would like independence and happiness, but he is willing to deny himself when he thinks of his debt to Maggie and Adam. The complex relation of his ethics, his culture, and his natural human longings Maggie at last perceives. The man with whom she is in love at the end is the true prince, not her earlier illusion. No longer can she insist on her freedom by drawing back from a confession of dependence on her husband; she accepts his standards with no reservations. She needs him and waits for proof of his needing her.

What of Amerigo? In the second half we see little of what goes on in his mind when he thinks of Maggie. But at the end he knows what she has gone through because of him. She has never had the Old World culture in which he has been reared; but she has shown herself a woman of imagination and sensibility. Her concern for right conduct has not hardened her into a stern, uncouth avenger; it has led her to consider the sensibility of others. Instead of inhibiting, it has expanded her life to include imaginative, sympathetic participation in Amerigo's own life and that of Charlotte. The converse of Maggie's discovering simplicity in her husband is his coming, with equal wonder, to discover a new 'majesty' in her. He is prepared finally to love his wife without reservation.

In 'The Altar of the Dead' Stransom's love for the woman and hers for him is for long incomplete because he can never forgive the dead man whom she has loved. At the end he does forgive and she in turn no longer demands the forgiveness. Love, says James, is not a compromise; it consists of absolute acceptance of the other person's faith, of his way of life, and it means spiritual exaltation. So here. In the last scene, as Maggie waits for the Prince to join her, she has a moment of fear that he may show less love than she has hoped; but when he appears, she begins 'to be paid in full'. We are not told that the Prince and Maggie will be forever happy. But we do know that with tragic anguish they have come out of the Garden of Eden of illusion and have found their way out of the wilderness of doubt. Because they accept the truth about each other they have a new adventure before them. It may be perilous, as they start afresh; and certainly Maggie is tremulous with awe because she has at last acknowledged unqualifiedly her dependence on her husband's love. But since the two have suffered for each other with tragic intensity, they have renewed hope. Their story is well knit, tightly unified. It is, however, neither a typical tragedy nor the usual sort of romance of adventure. Instead, it is the highest kind of romance of adventure precisely because it achieves the spiritual purification of tragedy.

NOTES

1. Quentin Anderson, 'Henry James and the New Jerusalem', in *Kenyon Review*, VIII (Autumn 1946) 557–8, goes so far as to call Maggie 'the selfless principle . . . prior and primary in God's nature'. She is 'Divine Love', Adam 'Divine Wisdom'. R. P. Blackmur, *The Golden Bowl* (New York, 1952) p. x, says Maggie 'is in intention rather like Beatrice in the *Divine Comedy*, the Lady of Theology, and suffers the pangs of the highest human love'. Jacques Barzun, 'James the Melodramatist', in *Kenyon Review*, V (Winter 1943) 511, sees the novel as one of 'two stage moralities . . . a story of supreme goodness overcoming surreptitious evil'. Dorothea Krook, 'The Golden Bowl', in *Cambridge Journal*, VII (Sept. 1954) 724 and 731, compares Maggie to 'other holy persons' – 'Maggie, the scapegoat and redeemer, is of course the principal sufferer'. Elizabeth Stevenson, *The Crooked Corridor* (New York, 1949) p. 89, writes, 'the injured one, the good one, pays and expiates, not for the wrong she has done, but for the wrong which has been done her'.

2. Like the first group, the following agree in stressing Maggie's victory over Amerigo and Charlotte rather than her own psychological reversal. Austin Warren, 'Myth and Dialectic in the Later Novels', in *Kenyon Review*, V (Winter 1943) 565, writes that Maggie 'learns how so to fight evil as to save what she prizes . . . the great theme of *The Bowl* is the discovery that evil exists in the forms most disruptive to civilization: in disloyalty and treason'. Pelham Edgar, *Henry James: Man and Author* (1927) p. 330, speaks of Maggie's 'conquest . . . of people, who . . . have lived scrupulously "in the forms" '. Philip Rahv, 'The Heiress of All the Ages', in *Partisan Review*, X (May–June 1943) 232, calls the marriage 'symbolic of the reconciliation of their competing cultures'. He adds: 'Observe, though, that this happy ending is postponed again and again until the American wife, in the person of Maggie Verver, has established herself as the ruling member of the alliance.' C. B. Cox, 'The Golden Bowl', in *Essays in Criticism*, V (April 1955) 193, makes the contest explicitly against external forces: Maggie is 'a woman battling for her rights as an individual'.

3. F. O. Matthiessen, *Henry James, the Major Phase* (1944) p. 100, thinks James meant

Maggie and Adam to be noble, but was unaware of their evil: 'But James' neglect of the cruelty in such a cord [as Maggie feels is around Charlotte's neck], silken though it be, is nothing short of obscene.' F. R. Leavis, *The Great Tradition* (1948) pp. 159–60, asserts that we cannot with James approve of Maggie and Adam 'without forgetting our finer moral sense. . . . That in our feelings about the Ververs there would be any element of distaste Henry James, in spite of the passages quoted, seems to have had no inkling.' Oliver Elton, 'The Novels of Mr Henry James', in *Modern Studies* (1907) pp. 274 and 283, writes, 'Our sympathy, at the last, turns away from the rightful avenger to one of the culprits' [Charlotte]. Adam is 'fundamentally hard and strong like his daughter'. Miriam Allott, 'Symbol and Image in the Later Work of Henry James', in *Essays in Criticism*, III (July 1953) 336, says that Adam's and Maggie's ' "power of purchase" and their possessions are revealed as the agents of a general corruption'. Ferner Nuhn, *The Wind Blew from the East* (New York, 1942) pp. 134 and 138, calls Maggie's spending her time with Adam while leaving Amerigo and Charlotte together 'a piece of contriving that opens up – as James himself might say – the more lurid reaches of the fiendish . . . but if the daughter-princess is a witch in disguise, the father-king may well be a wizard'. Finally, J. J. Firebaugh, 'The Ververs', in *Essays in Criticism*, IV (Oct. 1954) 401 and 404, insists that James knew fully what he was doing: 'Maggie is an all but unmitigated tyrant. . . . Life terrifies this Machiavellian creature not at all. She manipulates it to her purposes. . . . Marrying him [Adam] to Charlotte is a symbolic incest.'

4. Typical of James's turn of the screw and reminiscent of Meredith's Sir Willoughby, Austin Feverel, and husband in *Modern Love*, Mrs Assingham is an imperfect, yet shrewd commentator. Her *amour propre* colors some of her analyses, but otherwise she is absolutely accurate.

5. The title of his short story 'The Tree of Knowledge' is only one of several examples of James's use of that myth as a guiding perspective.

6. In chapter 27, for example: 'Touch by touch she thus dropped into her husband's silence the truth about his good nature and his good manners; and it was this demonstration of his virtue, precisely, that added to the strangeness, even for herself, of her failing as yet to yield to him.' In ch. 41, the next to last, she is almost ready to 'surrender': 'He has only to press, really, for her to yield inch by inch.'

7. For example, 'he stood out so wonderfully, to the end, against admitting, by a weak word at least, that any element of their existence *was*, or ever had been, an ordeal; no trap of circumstance, no lapse of "form", no accident of irritation, had landed him in that inconsequence' (ch. 40).

8. 'He had given her [Maggie] something to conform to, and she hadn't unintelligently turned on him, "gone back on" him, as he would have said, by not conforming' (ch. 36). The concept is re-emphasized in later chapters.

NAOMI LEBOWITZ

Magic and Metamorphosis in *The Golden Bowl* (1965)

Near the royal castle there was a great dark wood, and in the wood under
an old linden-tree was a well; and when the day was hot, the King's
daughter used to go forth into the wood and sit by the brink of the cool
well, and if the time seemed long, she would take out a golden ball and
throw it up and catch it again, and this was her favourite pastime. Now it
happened one day that the golden ball, instead of falling back into the
maiden's little hand which had sent it aloft, dropped to the ground near
the edge of the well and rolled in. The King's daughter followed it with
her eyes as it sank, but the well was deep, so deep that the bottom could
not be seen. Then she began to weep, and she wept and wept as if she
could never be comforted. And in the midst of her weeping she heard a
voice saying to her, 'What ails thee, King's daughter? Thy tears would
melt a heart of stone.' And when she looked up to see where the voice
came from, there was nothing but a frog stretching his thick ugly head
out of the water. 'Oh, is it you, old waddler?' she said. 'I weep because
my golden ball has fallen into the well.'

'The Frog Prince', *Grimm's Fairy Tales*

IT is an intriguing paradox that Henry James measured his most
essential realism by the world of magic. He meant his readers to see
behind the appealing pictures of the innocent rich American girl in
Europe the image of Cinderella and Miranda, but the image reflects
on the ease of fantasy. The metamorphosis is gradual, painful, and in
only one of James's major novels completed. Only in *The Golden Bowl*
is a princess allowed to live in the world of romance, but she does not
earn her palace and her prince until her mind and her heart have gone
beyond the powers of magic. James had always been fascinated with
the way in which the idea of magical manipulation of life could throw
into relief the anguish of moral responsibilities. When Henrietta
Stackpole, in *The Portrait of a Lady*, begins to worry about the tarnishing

image of her American princess, Isabel Archer, she playfully, but significantly, escapes to the world of magic in the hopes of recomposing her cherished portrait. In a conversation with Ralph Touchett she says of Isabel: 'She's not the same as she once so beautifully was.' Ralph asks: 'As she was in America?' 'Yes, in America,' answers Henrietta. 'Do you want to change her back again?' queries Ralph. 'Of course I do, and I want you to help me,' states Henrietta. 'Ah,' replies Ralph, 'I'm only Caliban; I'm not Prospero.' 'You were Prospero enough to make her what she has become,' returns Henrietta. 'You've acted on Isabel Archer since she came here, Mr Touchett.' But Isabel can never be restored, nor is she allowed any satisfying reformation of the world of romance. Henrietta is the first of the major 'false', though well-meaning, fairy godmothers that James attached to his most brilliant heroines.

In *The Wings of the Dove*, Susan Stringham, sensing the poignant emergence of Milly Theale from the beauties of romance to the terrors of the real, comes to Merton Densher and attempts to confine her tragic princess safely to the magic of portraiture: 'She's lodged for the first time as she ought, from her type, to be; and doing it – I mean bringing out all the glory of the place – makes her really happy. It's a Veronese picture, as near as can be – with me as the inevitable dwarf, the small blackamoor, put into a corner of the foreground for effect. If I only had a hawk or a hound or something of that sort I should do the scene more honour.' But Milly, in her tower, can only dream of never leaving it: 'Ah . . . never, never to go down.' Death claims James's second princess, and no magic could prevent disillusionment.

In *The Golden Bowl* at last we witness the complete and happy cycle of metamorphosis from dream princess, through disillusionment, to real princess. Fanny Assingham is, in her very ineffectiveness, the most significant of all the self-styled fairy godmothers. When she breaks the golden bowl and the Prince appears, we are not to suppose that her wand effected the romance. Rather, the impulsive smashing of the bowl vividly reveals how all the real controls of magic and metamorphosis are in the naked hand of the princess, Maggie Verver. James has finally entrusted full compositional powers of life and literature to a heroine, and she carries the day. Maggie is her own Prospero and returns confidently to her brave new world without a wand.

Critics have been persistently annoyed that James should select an atmosphere of palaces and carriages for the display of his most mature performance. F. O. Matthiessen emphatically articulates this annoyance when he terms *The Golden Bowl* 'a decadent book': 'With all its magnificence, it is almost as hollow of real life as châteaux that had risen along Fifth Avenue and that had also crowded out the old Newport world that James remembered.'[1] F. R. Leavis's preference for Charlotte Stant over Maggie Verver, ultimately on the grounds of Charlotte's apparently more vivid life,[2] is generally supported. But these opinions indicate, I believe, a misjudgment of the success of James's projection. The fairy façade, instead of undercutting the serious moral substance of the novel, forces it to the center of our vision by freeing us from the usual fixed social and historical attachments and concerns. It makes the rejection of easy magic all the more conspicuous.

James's realism needs no defense, for he is aiming at the realism he most cherished, one that featured the evolution of a character from innocence to full knowledge and love. The preference of Leavis is analogous to that of Dante's readers, of whom T. S. Eliot complains, who believe in the reality of hell more than that of the state of beatitude. Maggie's final victory only *seems* to be marked by the complacency of beatitude and magic. It is actually a victory that will have to be continually re-earned. While Maggie moves into the romantic possibilities of a real marriage, Charlotte is reduced to Adam Verver's puppet, bobbing at the end of an imaginary silk halter. Maggie, at the end of her metamorphic exposure, is finally as real as she is right. She is so real, in fact, that she is the only heroine that James ever permitted to share his task of composition.

The narrator in *The Sacred Fount* says to his 'helper', Mrs Briss: 'We're like the messengers and heralds in the tale of Cinderella, and I protest, I assure you, against any sacrifice of our dénouement. We've still the glass shoe to fit.' Let us turn to an examination of the processes by which Maggie Verver is allowed to fit her own glass shoe.

In both the Eden of Genesis, where marriage is a beginning, and the imaginary garden of the fairy tale, where marriage is an end, squats the real toad, who is the catalyst of metamorphosis; and the real princess, to recover her golden ball (her golden bowl), must be willing to expose herself to the risks and riches of the metamorphic state. The carriage which ultimately rolls away from the realm of the Father-King to the kingdom of the Frog Prince is formed out of the burdens and beauties of one of life's great metamorphoses: that of child to bride, the metamorphosis of marriage. In the domain of *The Golden Bowl*, Henry James lets marriage carry us into the world of romance, that 'beautiful circuit and subterfuge of our thought and our desire', but we ride heavily on real wheels, wheels that stand for 'the things we cannot possibly *not* know'. Whether we travel in the realm of the fairy godmother or in that of God it is the little child who leads us, but she leads us by outgrowing her first Eden and growing into her second. Though she is expelled from the garden, she has gained firm possession of her golden ball and her frog has become a prince.

With the advent of consciousness, and hence pain, the child-princess, Maggie Verver, assumes the risks of working in the metamorphic state, the risk of composition, and guides with her strengthening vision, not only souls, but scenes and images to marriage. While Fanny Assingham, in Part One, composes loudly, intelligently, making sure that Colonel Assingham (and the rest of us) can hear and understand, in Part Two, we are led, with the surging lift in image and conscience, into deeper chambers of involvement; and a conscious Maggie goes morally deeper than the socially thorough Fanny. Because Maggie plans, not for an audience but for her father, whose involved sensibility contrasts with the Colonel's 'non-amphibious' state, she must take care not to injure the quality of relationship. She must work quietly and without help. She must pay a price for her painful control, for her almost religious consistency. As the metaphoric priestess-princess she carries her hard-earned, and newly re-formed, golden bowl, just before her last great sacrificial scene with Charlotte: 'just now she was carrying in her weak, stiffened hand a glass filled to the brim, as to which she had recorded a vow that no drop should overflow. She feared the very breath of a better wisdom, the jostle of the higher light, of heavenly help itself.'

Maggie, of course, can know only part of the larger authorial reference which makes this pictured gesture a climax of metamorphic process. We understand, as she cannot, that her willingness to risk metamorphosis, a risk which includes the use of deliberate lies and of appearance for the sake of reality, at times even, 'not by a hair's breadth, deflecting into truth', contrasts with the uneasy bravado of the Prince and Charlotte, as we remember their words on the great Matcham afternoon. Charlotte, thinking of the golden bowl, remonstrates with the Prince: 'Don't you think too much of "cracks", and aren't you too afraid of them? I risk the cracks.' The Prince answers:

'risk them as much as you like for yourself, but don't risk them for me'. Before that, the Prince had felt the day 'like a great gold cup that we must somehow drain together'. Eventually, by attaining full consciousness, Maggie herself may guide the Prince, together with Charlotte and the golden bowl, to the climax of her metamorphic stand. With the changing bowl, she projects to the end her vivid cage imagery with which she has surrounded the doomed Charlotte. She carefully brings the two long tracings together as she imagines Charlotte plea from behind a confining glass:

> You don't know what it is to have been loved and broken with. You haven't been broken with, because in *your* relation what can there have been, worth speaking of, to break? Ours was everything a relation could be, filled to the brim with the wine of consciousness; and if it was to have no meaning, no better meaning than that such a creature as you could breathe upon it, at your hour, for blight, why was I myself dealt with all for deception? Why condemned after a couple of short years to find the golden flame – oh, the golden flame! – a mere handful of black ashes?

Of course, Charlotte cannot know how Maggie, using her metamorphic magic on character and image, has made her own golden fire rise like the phoenix from Charlotte's ashes. It is in the second part of *The Golden Bowl*, in which Maggie controls and guides with growing consciousness and courage the readjusted proportions of the enlarged family, that metamorphosis of major image is pressed into service for the larger moral ends of life, ends which must be nourished by the fairy, the religious, and the real. It is here that the fairy godmother, the priestess, and the woman are one.

Larger scene, as well as image, must submit to the metamorphic process for the sake of marriage. Scenically, gardens must be revisited and carriage rides retaken before the right human balance is established. Maggie must revisit gardens because she must see Eden changing, and she must project voyages because the magic carriage must hold the right relationship. The final projected voyage of Charlotte and Adam to the New World, with all its potential of art and science, is, in effect, a banishment from the second Eden of Maggie's marriage. Maggie's mind, flourishing in her great second part, plays with poetic and dramatic necessity upon scenes of garden and voyage. Her visions are rooted in a crucial garden interview between father and daughter, where Adam Verver pictures, in terms suggestive of godlike royalty, the danger of the original Edenic state of king and princess as a 'selfish prosperity': 'That's the only take-off, that it has made us perhaps lazy, a wee bit languid – lying like gods together, all careless of mankind. . . .' 'Well, I mean too . . . that we haven't, no doubt, enough, the sense of difficulty.' 'Enough? Enough for what?' asks Maggie, and her father answers, 'Enough not to be selfish.' Mr Verver goes on daringly to suggest that there might be even a kind of immorality in their happiness. Becoming, like Maggie, conscious of new problems of relationship, Mr Verver can ask his daughter: 'You think then you could now risk Fawns?' 'Risk it?' asks Maggie. 'Well, morally – from the point of view I was talking of; that of our sinking deeper into sloth,' replies Mr Verver. Maggie is face to face with the necessity of taking moral and aesthetic risk in the metamorphic state, and she is aware that only by passing through such a state, by ordering it, can she become the real princess. Later we see how Maggie has accepted this challenge as she submits to and controls a garden scene which, according to the aesthetic and ethic of metamorphosis, reflects and refines an earlier one:

> It was positively as if, in short, the inward felicity of their being once more, perhaps only for half an hour, simply daughter and father had glimmered out for them, and they had picked up the pretext that would make it easiest. They were husband and wife – oh, so immensely! – as regards other persons; but after they had dropped again on their old bench, conscious that the party on the terrace, augmented, as in the past, by neighbours, would do beautifully without them, it was wonderfully like their having got together into some boat and paddled off from the shore where husbands and wives, luxuriant complications, made the air too tropical.

She is tempted to sail off to that first, incest-tainted Byzantium. But, as so often in the major James (in *The Ambassadors* and 'The Beast in the Jungle' both literally and figuratively), the boat trip, the shoving off from shore, represents the deepest, most energetic and fruitful engagement, and Maggie will not be lured by her father's phantom sail. Once she recognizes the changes that have separated the two garden scenes, she is at most willing to accept the present moment only as a game, to play with the unmarried ease of her first paradise: 'Well, then, that other sweet evening was what the present sweet evening would resemble; with the quite calculable effect of an exquisite inward refreshment.' The climactic garden, containing Charlotte and Maggie, offers, like all magical gardens from a distance, the temptation of sloth, the easy avoidance of engagement. Maggie is, like Milly, and like

Isabel, tempted 'never to go down' when she sees the doomed Charlotte wandering in the garden at Fawns. She looks down from her 'perched position' as if from some 'castle-tower mounted on a rock'. The noon garden has changed from former Edens: 'The miles of shade looked hot, the banks of flowers looked dim; the peacocks on the balustrades let their tails hang limp and the smaller birds lurked among the leaves.' But she knows she must descend because 'the act of sitting still had become impossible'. The economical observer, involved in her own drama, who sees metamorphosis in scene, must also, of course, make the scene count for something in the metamorphosis of spirit. As she sees the scene then, Maggie meditates:

> The resemblance had not been present to her on first coming out into the hot, still brightness of the Sunday afternoon . . . but within sight of Charlotte, seated far away, very much where she had expected to find her, the Princess fell to wondering if her friend wouldn't be affected quite as she herself had been, that night on the terrace, under Mrs Verver's perceptive pursuit. The relation, to-day, had turned itself round; Charlotte was seeing her come, through patches of lingering noon, quite as she had watched Charlotte menace her through the starless dark; and there was a moment, that of her waiting a little as they thus met acrosss the distance, when the interval was bridged by a recognition not less soundless, and to all appearance not less charged with strange meanings, than that of the other occasion. The point, however, was that they had changed places.

This is our clearest perception of Maggie's assumption of the metamorphic process. Maggie's identifications are apt, of the doomed Charlotte with the doomed Ariadne 'roaming the lone sea-strand' or Io 'goaded by the gadfly', women who lived in a mythical world, where transmutation was the magic of easy punishment or capture. But Maggie sees herself as 'some far-off harassed heroine', and her role, because she is living it as well as observing it, has no precedent. Imagistically as well as morally the new dawning for Maggie comes in terms of Edenic light and flowers which emerge from the night. Maggie has had to accustom herself to the role of 'mistress of shades' before she can stand the glare of the garden at noon. After Maggie's crucial meditation following the Matcham affair, a meditation which exposed the already changing proportions of relationship, James writes with moving formality: 'and it was in the mitigated midnight of these approximations that she had made out the promise of her dawn'. Ultimately, she sees the Prince, emerging from his silent purgatory, full of something of the same promise, granted to *him* by one of Maggie's last visions. Maggie lends beauty to his obscure intentions: 'It was like hanging over a garden in the dark; nothing was to be made of the confusion of growing things, but one felt they were folded flowers, and their vague sweetness made the whole air their medium.' This obscurity is a fine counterpart to the obscure moral intention which the Prince originally felt behind the American Poe-curtain of white mist. In the end, the second Eden must always emerge from obscurity, but the obscurity will be friendly. The terrible loss of the first Eden does not necessarily, as some readers of *The Golden Bowl* have felt, make the second Eden false, empty, or impossible to face. In thinking of Maggie's future we must choose between a theory of fortunate fall and one of total cynicism. In this case, hope is deeper than despair.

The purgatory of metamorphosis, then, leads Maggie out of one garden and into another, and her sacred Sunday noon 'sacrifice' for the sake of Charlotte's soul (a sacrifice made more poignant by the babbling Father Mitchell in the background and by the remembrance of Charlotte's Judas kiss on the terrace) carries all the religious intensity that witnesses to expulsions from and openings into Eden might anticipate. But the vehicle in which she rides through her gardens is still the carriage of the fairy tale, and it too rides through metamorphic and metaphoric magic. Maggie's most persistently painful pictures of the family relationships come in visions of vehicles and voyages. She sees Charlotte's entrance into the family in an image burdened with the humiliation of ignorance:

> She might have been watching the family coach pass and noting that, somehow, Amerigo and Charlotte were pulling it while she and her father were not so much as pushing. They were seated inside together, dandling the Principino and holding him up to the windows, to see and be seen, like an infant positively royal; so that the exertion was *all* with the others.

So disturbing is this picture of royal sloth (paralleling that of Adam Verver's sprawling garden gods) that she sees herself 'suddenly jump from the coach; whereupon, frankly, with the wonder of the sight, her eyes opened wider and her heart stood still for a moment'. Her action is sure, but the form of the picture is still in doubt, and she must mold that with subsequent carriage trips, in which real life complements image, just as the climactic boat scene in *The Ambassadors* complements the many mental images of watery involvement in Strether's mind. A mere carriage ride from Eaton Square to Portland Place had grave import at the beginning of Part Two, and when Maggie begins to have the form of the picture as well as its substance clearly in mind, when she stays painfully in control of the consistency of her 'plan', she remembers a former ride when she was prey to the Prince's easy magic:

> and there were hours when it came to her that these days were a prolonged repetition of that night-drive, of weeks before, from the other house to their own, when he had tried to charm her, by his sovereign personal power, into some collapse that would commit her to a repudiation of consistency.

She must always resist easy magic, that of the Frog Prince, that of the Father-King (which eventually imitates the silent control of Maggie herself by means of a visionary halter around the neck of Charlotte). We know from our fairy tales how dangerous is the misuse of magic. The image of royal sloth returns to haunt Maggie when consciousness grows, and again the state of resistance to metamorphosis, to the 'lurches of the mystic train', carries with it the taste of humiliation:

> We're in the train . . . we've suddenly waked up in it and found ourselves rushing along, very much as if we had been put in during sleep – shoved like a pair of labelled boxes, into the van. . . . I'm moving without trouble – they're doing it all for us!

Maggie must eventually open the doors which will allow the right people in and the right people out. She must stand firm against the magic of surrender in her father and the magic of demonstrative love in the Prince. That the pain of knowledge accompanies, on this journey, the expulsion from the first Eden is emphasized by the proliferation of childhood imagery, which serves naturally as a bridge between the fairy and Edenic strands. Adam Verver is persistently pictured as childlike in his absorptions, and it is this image, especially established in Part One, which Maggie must break through. The metaphorical translation of a projected trip with her father into terms of child growth shows Maggie that the journey is a false one:

> There had been, from far back . . . a plan that the parent and the child should 'do something lovely' together, and they had recurred to it on occasion, nursed it and brought it up theoretically, though without as yet

quite allowing it to put its feet to the ground. The most it had done was to try a few steps on the drawing-room carpet, with much attendance, on either side, much holding up and guarding, much anticipation, in fine, of awkwardness or accident. Their companions, by the same token, had constantly assisted at the performance, following the experiment with sympathy and gaiety, and never so full of applause, Maggie now made out for herself, as when the infant project had kicked its little legs most wildly – kicked them, for all the world, across the channel and half the Continent, kicked them over the Pyrenees and innocently crowed out some rich Spanish name.

It is when Maggie sees the journey itself as childish, not only in her own eyes, but in the tolerantly amused eyes of the Prince and Charlotte, who are always willing to reduce Maggie and her father to the state of childhood, that she sees most clearly the need for terrible consistency in her plan.

Maggie's dual role of observer and actor once she has confronted the 'bad-faced stranger' of Evil, is most brilliantly assumed in the great terrace scene of Part Two, where, looking in on a card game from outside, she sees before her 'figures rehearsing some play of which herself was the author'. She tracks and hunts her victims with her silent spear, with her silent pen, for, having the added role of involvement, she does not have open to her, as does Fanny, 'the straight vindictive view, the rights of resentment, the pangs of jealousy, the protests of passion'. How far Maggie has travelled in Part Two from the first Eden can be seen best by contrast with Part One. Backing down from this rich second part, we slide into the plodding mind of Fanny Assingham, who must abandon composition when Maggie's deeper consciousness makes the imagery too rich for her blood. While Maggie worries about saving lives, Fanny bemoans the fact that her characters are 'making a mess of such charming material'. Maggie's emergence into the light of consciousness is witnessed by the outgoing composer, Fanny Assingham, at Maggie's party. Now, while Fanny stands 'like one of the assistants in the ring at the circus', Maggie herself emerges modestly skipping 'into the light' with 'a show of pink stocking and . . . an abbreviation of white petticoat', ready at last to become the real Princess, 'to fill out as a matter of course her appointed, her expected, her imposed character'. She now feels the pea through her mattress, but, unlike the real Princess of the fairy tale, she cannot complain about it. Fanny, on the other hand, could complain about what she didn't feel, and it is this complaint, as much inferior to the tone of Maggie's visions as is Colonel Assingham himself to Adam Verver as audience, which sets the tone of the first part of *The Golden Bowl*. Maggie herself senses Fanny's limitations once she herself 'could boast of touching bottom'. Fanny cannot touch bottom because her mind, unlike Maggie's, resists metamorphosis and flattens into pattern. Until we share the purgatory of metamorphosis with Maggie, until imagery becomes deep and varied and people are looked at, not romantically but realistically, we live in a world of Fanny's composition, of the picturesque, the static, a world which (despite Fanny's good intentions and because of her moral limitations) James condemns in all his great novels, in *The Portrait of a Lady*, *The Ambassadors*, *The Wings of the Dove*. The Prince is persistently, in the first part, seen by Maggie (her humoring of this vision does not soften its outline), by her father, by Fanny herself, as an item in Mr Verver's collection. Maggie is perfectly willing to share her father's vision: 'His relation to the things he cares for – and I think it beautiful – is absolutely romantic.' How completely this vision must be broken is Maggie's story, for here, as yet, she does not understand that the needs of a king, of a divinely permissive king, differ from those of a very human princess. The 'taste' which substitutes in the Prince for morality is adequate for Part One, where romance serves for reality and the picturesque for dynamism. But when Maggie sets in motion her purgative metamorphosis, the Prince's taste, by his own admission, can no longer guide. This world demonstrates just how far Maggie's metamorphosis has taken her. While in Part Two she is busily opening doors of locked chambers, trains, launching ships freely into James's beloved waters of relationship, how poorly her conception of marriage as voyage began: 'I've divided my faith into water-tight compartments. We must manage not to sink. . . . Why, it's the best cabin and the main deck and the engine-room and the steward's pantry! It's the ship itself – it's the whole line.' It is Maggie's romantic vision, of course, nourished ironically by her 'familiarity with "lines", a command of "own" cars, from an experience of continents and seas', which seals off her faith from the test of the real. Meanwhile, Fanny Assingham encourages the pernicious romanticism of static vision. The Prince identifies Fanny's penchant toward pattern with that of the Ververs: 'She had *made* his marriage, quite as truly as his papal ancestor had made his family – though he could scarce see what she had made

it for unless because she too was perversely romantic.' In his early
section, the Prince, with Charlotte, sees clearly through the romance
in the Verver vision, but it is for him to use it, not to change it. As
long as Maggie and her father see the Prince as art and architecture,
they remain, like the childlike Colonel Assingham, together in a
'non-amphibious' state. It is no accident that the first vision of Maggie's
section is that of the outlandish pagoda of her 'situation' in the center
of her garden, and her first desire that of breaking through, of finding
doors and windows. For Maggie does not abandon the romantic; she
learns to use it, just as she does not abandon Eden or the fairy garden,
but learns to open them to her greater needs. It is she who must
replace Fanny as her own fairy godmother, and she makes passions
of patterns, relationships of rituals. Fanny's constant clucking over
poor Maggie's innocent ignorance is turned to full irony when Maggie,
working in a higher ethic and aesthetic, leaves her behind. Maggie must
do her own acting, because, as in *The Wings of the Dove*, those who
surround innocence want, for their own comfort, to keep it isolated.
Just as Fanny's composition depends upon keeping Maggie ignorant,
so Charlotte can act only if she freezes Maggie's relationships to ritual:

> But it was all right – so Charlotte also .put it: there was nothing in the
> world they [Maggie and Mr Verver] liked better than these snatched
> felicities, little parties, long talks, with 'I'll come to you to-morrow,' and
> 'No, I'll come to *you*,' make-believe renewals of their old life. They were
> fairly, at times, the dear things, like children playing at paying visits, play-
> ing at 'Mr Thompson' and 'Mrs Fane,' each hoping that the other would
> really stay to tea.

We have seen before that it is just this recurrent image of childhood
which Maggie must learn to resist in her growth to greatness. Even
Fanny sees that the Prince and Charlotte were wrong to accept the
innocence of Maggie as closed, to accept their idea of the guilelessness
of the Ververs as something that could save them. It is not the isolated
innocence of the 'early' Ververs, nor the isolating knowledge of the
Prince and Charlotte, which saves, but the expansion of innocence
open to life, and knowledge, into wisdom and love.

Maggie's passage from victim to saviour is her emergence into
greatness. She has an opportunity to go beyond Milly, to break the
vision of herself as ritual. She breaks through the sentimentality of
Fanny's picture of her 'brave little piety' to its truth in relationship.
All of the irony which metamorphosis carries turns upon the reversal

of the cared for and the cared by, the victims and the saviours. It is contained in the vague perception of Fanny concerning Maggie: 'It will be *she* who'll see us through.' This irony, which in the richest state of consciousness repeats experience to which unconsciousness has already been exposed, is strongly rooted in the Jamesian definition of greatness. At an early stage in the book, Maggie and Adam are having one of their talks which reform so effectively in Part Two. The subject of the talk is greatness, Charlotte's greatness, and Maggie, who sees herself in comparison to Charlotte as 'a small creeping thing', is, while defining Charlotte, defining herself as she finally is, when she has, according to her prescription, acted upon her freedom and experienced the expense of greatness: 'I may be as good, but I'm not so great – and that's what we're talking about. She has a great imagination. She has, in every way a great attitude. She has above all a great conscience.' It is Maggie who restores Charlotte's dignity; it is she who has greatness of imagination, attitude, and conscience; it is she who has become James's most *real* princess.

NOTES

1. F. O. Matthiessen, *Henry James: The Major Phase* (New York, 1944) p. 104.
2. F. R. Leavis, *The Great Tradition* (New York, 1954) p. 195.

Select Bibliography

BIBLIOGRAPHY

Henry James (Soho Bibliographies 8) compiled by Leon Edel and
D. H. Laurence, 2nd ed. (Hart-Davis, 1961)

BIOGRAPHY

Leon Edel, *The Untried Years* (Lippincott, 1953; Hart-Davis, 1953)
The Conquest of London (Hart-Davis, 1962)
The Middle Years (Hart-Davis, 1963)
(The last two volumes were also published under the title *The
Middle Years*, 2 vols (Lippincott, 1962)
F. O. Matthiessen, *The James Family* (Knopf, 1947)
Clinton H. Grattan, *The Three Jameses* (New York U.P., 1962)

CRITICISM

Quentin Anderson, *The American Henry James* (Rutgers U.P., 1957;
Calder, 1958)
Osborn Andreas, *Henry James and the Expanding Horizon* (University of
Washington P., 1948)
Joseph Warren Beach, *The Method of Henry James* (Yale U.P., 1918)
Marius Bewley, *The Complex Fate* (Chatto, 1952; Grove P., 1954)
R. P. Blackmur, *The Lion and the Honeycomb* (Harcourt, Brace, 1955;
Methuen, 1956)
Theodora Bosanquet, *Henry James at Work* (Hogarth, 1924)
Edwin Turner Bowden, *The Themes of Henry James* (Yale U.P., 1956;
Oxford U.P., 1956)
Van Wyck Brooks, *The Pilgrimage of Henry James* (E. P. Dutton, 1925;
Cape, 1928)
Oscar Cargill, *The Novels of Henry James* (Collier-Macmillan, 1961)
C. B. Cox, *The Free Spirit* (Oxford U.P., 1963)

Frederick C. Crews, *The Tragedy of Manners* (Yale U.P., 1957; Oxford U.P., 1957)

F. W. Dupee, *Henry James* (Sloane, 1951; Methuen 1951)

The Question of Henry James, ed. F. W. Dupee (H. Holt, 1945)

Leon Edel and Gordon Ray, *Henry James and H. G. Wells* (Hart-Davis, 1958)

Pelham Edgar, *Henry James: Man and Author* (Grant Richards, 1927)

Robert Gale, *The Caught Image* (University of N. Carolina P., 1964)

Maxwell Geismar, *Henry James and His Cult* (Chatto, 1964)

Alexander Holder-Barell, *The development of Imagery and its Functional Significance in the Novels of Henry James* (Franke Verlag, 1964)

Laurence Holland, *The Expense of Vision* (Princeton U.P., 1964)

Irving Howe, *Politics and the Novel* (Horizon P., 1957; Stevens, 1961)

Ford Madox Hueffer, *Henry James: A Critical Study* (Secker, 1913)

Douglas Jefferson, *Henry James and the Modern Reader* (St. Martin's P., 1964; Oliver & Boyd, 1964)

Cornelia Pulsifer Kelley, *The Early Development of Henry James* (rev. ed., Illinois U.P., 1965)

Dorothea Krook, *The Ordeal of Consciousness in Henry James* (Cambridge U.P., 1962)

F. R. Leavis, *The Great Tradition* (Chatto, 1948; New York U.P., 1963)

Leo Levy, *Versions of Melodrama* (University of California P., 1957)

Bruce Lowery, *Marcel Proust et Henry James; une confrontation* (Paris, 1964)

Percy Lubbock, *The Craft of Fiction* (Cape, 1921; Viking, 1957)

F. O. Matthiessen, *Henry James: The Major Phase* (Oxford U.P., 1946)

H. T. McCarthy, *Henry James: The Creative Process* (Yoseloff, 1958)

Simon Nowell-Smith, *The Legend of the Master* (Constable, 1947; Scribners, 1948)

Richard Poirier, *The Comic Sense of Henry James* (Chatto, 1960; Oxford U.P., New York, 1960)

Georges Poulet, *Studies in Human Time* (John Hopkins P., 1956; H. Hamilton, 1959)
(see the important Appendix on 'Time and American Writers')

Elizabeth Stevenson, *The Crooked Corridor* (Macmillan Co., 1961)

Tony Tanner, *The Reign of Wonder* (Cambridge U.P., 1965)

Lionel Trilling, *The Liberal Imagination* (Viking, 1950; Secker & Warburg, 1951)

Krishna Vaid, *Technique in the Tales of Henry James* (Harvard U.P., 1964)

Austin Warren, *Rage for Order* (University of Michigan P., 1958)

Christof Wegelin, *The Image of Europe in Henry James* (Southern Methodist U.P., 1958)

Edmund Wilson, *The Triple Thinkers* (Oxford U.P., 1952)

Morton Dauwen Zabel, *Craft and Character* (Viking, 1957)

Notes on Contributors

Maurice Beebe is a Professor of English at Purdue University, Indiana. He is the author of *Literary Symbolism* and edited *Ernest Hemingway: configuration critique*.

Oscar Cargill is a Professor Emeritus of English at New York University. He is the author of *Intellectual America, Thomas Wolfe and Washington Square*, and *The Novels of Henry James*.

James W. Gargano is a Professor of English at Washington and Jefferson College, Washington.

William M. Gibson is a Professor of English at New York University. He is co-author of the *Bibliography of W. H. Howells* and co-editor of the *Mark Twain – Howells Letters*.

H. K. Girling is an Associate Professor of English at York University, Toronto.

Viola Hopkins teaches English at Hunter College, New York.

Walter Isle is an Assistant Professor of English at Rice University, Texas.

Naomi Lebowitz is an Assistant Professor of English at Washington University, Missouri. She edited the pamphlet on Henry James in D. C. Heath's Discussion of Literature series.

Robert C. McLean is an Associate Professor of English at Washington State University. He is the author of *George Tucker: Moral Philosopher and Man of Letters*.

William McMurray is an Associate Professor of English at Madison College, Virginia. He has written essays on Henry James and William Dean Howells in *Nineteenth Century Fiction*, *American Literature* and *New England Quarterly*.

WILLIAM MASEYCHIK is a graduate student at Harvard University.

LYALL H. POWERS is a Professor of English at the University of Ann Arbor, Michigan, where he teaches English, American and French literature from 1850 to 1950.

J. H. RALEIGH is a Professor of English at the University of California at Berkeley. He is the author of *Matthew Arnold and American Culture* and edited *History and the Individual*.

TONY TANNER is a Fellow of King's College, Cambridge, and a Lecturer on the English Faculty in the University of Cambridge. He is the author of *The Reign of Wonder: Naivety and Reality in American Literature* and *Saul Bellow*.

JOSEPH A. WARD is an Associate Professor of English at Rice University, Texas. He is the author of *The Imagination of Disaster: Evil in the Fiction of Henry James*.

IAN WATT is a Professor of English at the University of Stanford, California. He is the author of *The Rise of the Novel* and edited *Jane Austen: A Collection of Critical Essays*.

WALTER WRIGHT is a Professor of English at the University of Nebraska. He is the author of *Romance and Tragedy in Joseph Conrad*, *Art and Substance in George Meredith*, and *The Madness of Art: a Study of Henry James*.

Index